Message Formation

skill builders — ADAPT LANGUAGE TO LISTENERS

SKILL
Using vocabulary, jargon, and slang that listeners understand.

USE
To avoid words that listeners do not understand

PROCEDURE
1. Use simpler synonyms or familiar terms for words.
2. Explain jargon terms to listeners who may not understand them.
3. Use slang only with listeners who understand the words.

EXAMPLE
Instead of saying, "Jose is in his penultimate year of work," Larry can say, "Jose is in his next to last year of work."
Sally can say, "Your asset-to-liability ratio, which is a calculation of how much money you have compared to how much money you owe, is really quite good."
Judy can say a rock star is "hot" when talking with a friend, but describe the star as "cute" when talking with her aunt.

skill builders — DATING INFORMATION

SKILL
Including a specific time referent that indicates when a fact was true.

USE
To avoid the pitfalls of language that allow you to speak of a dynamic world in static terms.

PROCEDURE
1. Before you make a statement, consider or find out when the information was true.
2. If not based on present information, verbally acknowledge when the statement was true.

EXAMPLE
When Jake says, "How good a hitter is Steve?" Mark replies by dating his evaluation: "When I worked with him two years ago, he couldn't hit the curve."

skill builders — OWNING FEELINGS AND OPINIONS

SKILL
Making an "I" statement to identify yourself as the source of an idea or feeling.

USE
To help others understand that the feeling or opinion is yours.

PROCEDURE
When an idea, opinion, or feeling is yours, say so.

EXAMPLE
Instead of saying, "Maury's is the best restaurant in town," say, "I believe Maury's is the best restaurant in town."

Responding Supportively (continued)

skill builders   FRAMING

SKILL	USE	PROCEDURE	EXAMPLE
Offering information, observations, and opinions with the goal of helping the receiver to understand or reinterpret an event or circumstance.	To support others when you believe that people have made interpretations based on incomplete information or have not considered other viable explanations that would be less threatening to the individuals' self-esteem.	1. Listen to how your partner is interpreting events. 2. Notice information that your partner may be overlooking or overemphasizing in the interpretation. 3. Clearly present relevant, truthful information, observations, and opinions that enable your partner to develop a less ego-threatening explanation of what has happened.	Pam: "Katie must be really angry with me. Yesterday she walked right by me at the market and didn't even say 'Hi.'" Paula: "Are you sure she's angry? She hasn't said anything to me. And you know, when she's mad I usually hear about it. Maybe she just didn't see you."

skill builders   OTHER-CENTERED MESSAGES

SKILL	USE	PROCEDURE	EXAMPLE
Expressing compassion and understanding and encouraging partners to talk about what has happened and to explore their feelings about the situation.	To help partners in their efforts to cognitively reappraise an emotionally disturbing event.	1. Ask questions that prompt the person to tell and elaborate on what happened. 2. Emphasize your willingness to listen to an extended story. 3. Use vocalized encouragement and nonverbal behavior to communicate your continued interest without interrupting your partner as the account unfolds. 4. Affirm, legitimize, and encourage exploration of the feelings expressed by your partner. 5. Demonstrate that you understand and connect with what has happened but avoid changing the focus to you.	Angie begins to express what has happened to her. Allison says: "Really, what happened then?" As Angie utters one more sentence and then stops, Allison says: "You've simply got to tell me *all* about it, and don't worry about how long it takes. I want to hear the whole thing from start to finish." During Angie's discussion, Allison shows her encouragement: "Go on …," "Wow …," "Uh huh …," and she nods her head, leans forward, etc. To affirm, Allison says: "Yes, I can see that you're disappointed. Most people would be disappointed in this situation. Is this as difficult as when…?" Allison then continues: "I know that I felt angry when my sister did that to me. So what happened then?"

Responding Supportively (continued)

skill builders — GIVING ADVICE

SKILL
Presenting suggestions and proposals a partner could use to satisfactorily resolve an emotionally difficult situation.

USE
To comfort our partners when we have established a supportive climate and they are unable to find their own solutions.

PROCEDURE
1. Ask for permission to give advice.
2. Word the message as one suggestion in a way that the recipient can understand.
3. Present any potential risks or costs associated with the following the advice.
4. Indicate that you will not be offended, should your partner choose to ignore your recommendation or look for another choice.

EXAMPLE
After a friend has explained a difficult situation she faces, Felicia might say something like the following:
"I have a suggestion if you'd like to hear it. As I see it, one way you could handle this is to …."
"This is just one idea—you may come up with a different solution that's just as good. So think this one over, and do what you believe is best for you."

skill builders — CLARIFYING SUPPORTIVE INTENTIONS

SKILL
Openly stating that your goal in the conversation is to support and help your partner.

USE
To enable your partner to easily interpret messages without searching for a hidden agenda. To communicate that someone is "on their side" and to provide a context for understanding supportive comments.

PROCEDURE
1. Directly state your intentions, emphasizing your desire to help.
2. Remind your partner about your ongoing relationship.
3. Indicate that helping is your only motive.
4. Phrase your clarification in a way that reflects helpfulness.

EXAMPLE
After listening to Sonja complain about flunking her geology midterm, her friend Deepak replies:
"Sonja, you're a dear friend, and I'd like to help if you want me to. I did well enough on the midterm that I think I could be of help; maybe we could meet once a week to go over the readings and class notes together."

skill builders — POSITIVE FACEWORK

SKILL
Messages affirming a person or a person's actions in the face of a difficult situation.

USE
To protect the other's positive face needs (to be respected, liked, and valued) in situations where other messages are perceived to be FTAs.

PROCEDURE
1. Describe and convey positive feelings about what the other has said or done in the situation.
2. Express your admiration for the person's courage or effort in the situation.
3. Acknowledge how difficult the situation is.
4. Express your belief that the other has the qualities and skills to endure or succeed.

EXAMPLE
Jan has learned that Ken has suffered his brother's anger because of an intervention by which Ken had intended to help his sibling. Jan says: "I really respect you for the way you have acted during this. It takes a lot of guts to hang in there like you've been doing, especially when you've been attacked for doing so. I know that you've got the skills to help you get through this."

Message Formation (continued)

skill builders — INDEXING GENERALIZATIONS

SKILL	USE	PROCEDURE	EXAMPLE
Mentally or verbally accounting for individual differences.	To avoid "allness" in speaking.	1. Before you make a statement, consider whether it pertains to a specific object, person, or place. 2. If you use a generalization, inform the listener that it does not necessarily apply in the situation being discussed.	"He's a politician and I don't trust him, although he may be different from most politicians I know."

Listening for Understanding

skill builders — TURN-TAKING

SKILL	USE	PROCEDURE	EXAMPLE
Engaging in appropriate turn-taking.	Determining when a speaker is at a place where another person may talk if he or she wants to.	1. Take your share of turns. 2. Gear turn length to the behavior of partners. 3. Give and watch for turn-taking and turn-exchanging cues. Avoid giving inadvertent turn-taking cues. 4. Observe and use conversation-directing behavior. 5. Limit interruptions.	When John lowers his voice as he says, "I really thought they were going to go ahead during those last few seconds," Melissa, noticing that he appears to be finished, says, "I did, too. But did you notice …"

skill builders — PARAPHRASING

SKILL	USE	PROCEDURE	EXAMPLE
A response that conveys your understanding of another person's message.	To increase listening efficiency; to avoid message confusion; to discover the speaker's motivation.	1. Listen carefully to the message. 2. Notice what images and feelings you have experienced from the message. 3. Determine what the message means to you. 4. Create a message that conveys these images and/or feelings.	Grace says, "At two minutes to five, the boss gave me three letters that had to be in the mail that evening!" Bonita replies, "If I understand, you were really resentful that your boss dumped important work on you right before quitting time, when she knows that you have to pick up the baby at daycare."

Responding Supportively

skill builders — EMPATHIZING

SKILL
The cognitive process of identifying with or the vicarious experiencing of the feelings, thoughts, or attitudes of another.

USE
To prepare yourself for making an appropriate comforting response.

PROCEDURE
1. Show respect for the person by actively attending to what the person says.
2. Concentrate on observing and understanding both the verbal and nonverbal messages, using paraphrases and perception checking to aid you.
3. Experience an emotional response parallel to another person's actual or anticipated display of emotion. Imagine yourself in the place of the person, and feel concern, compassion, or sorrow for the person because of his or her situation or plight.

EXAMPLE
When Jerry says, "I was really hurt when Sarah returned the ring I had given her," Mary experiences an emotional response parallel to Jerry's, imagines herself in Jerry's situation, or feels concern, compassion, or sorrow for Jerry.

skill builders — NEGATIVE FACEWORK

SKILL
Using verbally indirect methods when offering information, opinions, or advice.

USE
To protect the other's negative face needs (for independence and autonomy) when presenting opinions or advice.

PROCEDURE
1. Ask for permission before making suggestions or giving advice.
2. After stating the advice verbally, defer to the opinions and preferences of the other person.
3. Use tentative language to hedge and qualify opinions and advice.
4. Offer suggestions indirectly by telling stories or describing hypothetical options.

EXAMPLE
Judy has learned that Gloria has really been hurt by rejection from a best friend. Judy says: "Would you like any advice on this?" Gloria says that she would, and Judy then offers suggestions:
"These are just a few suggestions, and I think you should go with what you think is best. Now, I'm not sure that these are the only way to go, but I think…."
After stating her opinions, Judy says, "Depending on what you want to accomplish, I can see a couple ways that you might proceed…."

Listening for Understanding (continued)

skill builders — PERCEPTION CHECKING

SKILL
A statement that expresses the meaning you get from the nonverbal behavior of another.

USE
To clarify the meaning of nonverbal behavior.

PROCEDURE
1. Watch the behavior of another.
2. Ask yourself: What does that behavior mean to me?
3. Describe the behavior (to yourself or aloud) and put your interpretation of the nonverbal behavior into words to verify your perception.

EXAMPLE
As Dale frowns while reading Paul's first draft of a memo, Paul says, "From the way you're frowning, I take it that you're not too pleased with the way I phrased the memo."

skill builders — QUESTIONING

SKILL
Phrasing a response designed to get further information, to clarify information already received, or to encourage another to continue speaking.

USE
To help get a more complete picture before making other comments; to help a shy person open up; to clarify meaning.

PROCEDURE
1. Note the kind of information you need to increase your understanding of the message.
2. Deliver questions in a sincere tone of voice.
3. Put the burden of ignorance on your own shoulders.

EXAMPLE
When Connie says, "Well, it would be better if she weren't so sedentary," Jeff replies, "I'm not sure I understand what you mean by 'sedentary'—would you explain?"

Disclosure

skill builders — ASKING FOR FEEDBACK

SKILL
Asking others for their reaction to you or to your behavior.

USE
To get information that will help you understand yourself and your effect on others.

PROCEDURE
1. Outline the kind of feedback you are seeking.
2. Avoid verbal or nonverbal negative reactions to criticism.
3. Paraphrase what you hear.
4. Give positive reinforcement to those who take your requests seriously.

EXAMPLE
Lucy asks, "Tim, when I talk with the boss, do I sound defensive?"
Tim replies, "I think so—your voice gets sharp and you lose eye contact, which makes you look nervous."
"So you think that the tone of my voice and my eye contact lead the boss to perceive me as defensive?"
"Yes."
"Thanks, Tim. I've really got to work on this."

Disclosure (continued)

skill builders — DESCRIBING FEELINGS

SKILL
Putting emotional state into words.

USE
For self-disclosure; to teach people how to treat you.

PROCEDURE
1. Indicate what has triggered the feeling.
2. Mentally identify what you are feeling—think specifically. Am I feeling hate? Anger? Joy?
3. Verbally own the feeling. For example, "I'm (name the emotion)."

EXAMPLE
"As a result of not getting the job, I feel depressed and discouraged."
"Because of the way you stood up for me when I was being put down by Leah, I'm feeling very warm and loving toward you."

skill builders — DESCRIBING BEHAVIOR, CONSEQUENCES, AND FEELINGS SEQUENCE

SKILL
Describing the basis of a conflict in terms of behavior, consequences, and feelings (b-c-f).

USE
To help the other person understand the problem completely.

PROCEDURE
1. Own the message.
2. Describe the behavior that you see or hear.
3. Describe the consequences that result.
4. Describe your feelings.

EXAMPLE
Jason says, "I have a problem that I need your help with. When I tell you what I'm thinking and you don't respond (b), I start to think you don't care about me or what I think (c), and this causes me to get very angry with you (f)."

skill builders — GIVING CONSTRUCTIVE CRITICISM

SKILL
Describing the specific negative behaviors or actions of another and the effects that these behaviors have on others.

USE
To help people see themselves as others see them.

PROCEDURE
1. Describe the person's behavior accurately.
2. Preface negative statements with positive ones if possible.
3. Be specific.
4. When appropriate, suggest how the person can change the behavior.

EXAMPLE
Carol says, "Bob, I've noticed something about your behavior with Jenny. Would you like to hear it?" After Bob assures her that he would, Carol continues, "Although you seem really supportive of Jenny, there are times when Jenny starts to relate an experience and you interrupt her and finish telling the story."

Disclosure (continued)

skill builders — ASSERTIVENESS

SKILL
Standing up for yourself and doing so in interpersonally effective ways that describe your feelings honestly and exercise your personal rights while respecting the rights of others.

USE
To show clearly what you think or feel.

PROCEDURE
1. Identify what you are thinking or feeling.
2. Analyze the cause of these feelings.
3. Choose the appropriate skills necessary to communicate these feelings, as well as any outcome you desire.
4. Communicate these feelings to the appropriate person. Remember to own your feelings.

EXAMPLE
When Gavin believes that he is being unjustly charged, he says, "I have never been charged for a refill on iced tea before—has there been a change in policy?"

skill builders — PRAISE

SKILL
Describing the specific positive behaviors or accomplishments of another and the effects that the behaviors have on others.

USE
To help people see themselves positively.

PROCEDURE
1. Make note of the specific behavior or accomplishment that you want to reinforce.
2. Describe the specific behavior and/or accomplishment.
3. Describe the positive feelings or outcomes that you or others experience as a result of the behavior or accomplishment.
4. Phrase the response so that the level of praise appropriately reflects the significance of the behavior or accomplishment.

EXAMPLE
"Marge, that was an excellent writing job on the Miller story. Your descriptions were particularly vivid."

Inter-Act

ELEVENTH EDITION

*interpersonal communication
concepts, skills, and contexts*

KATHLEEN S. VERDERBER
NORTHERN KENTUCKY UNIVERSITY

RUDOLPH F. VERDERBER
UNIVERSITY OF CINCINNATI

CYNTHIA BERRYMAN-FINK
UNIVERSITY OF CINCINNATI

NEW YORK   OXFORD
OXFORD UNIVERSITY PRESS
2007

Oxford University Press, Inc., publishes works that further Oxford University's
objective of excellence in research, scholarship, and education.

Oxford   New York
Auckland   Cape Town   Dar es Salaam   Hong Kong   Karachi
Kuala Lumpur   Madrid   Melbourne   Mexico City   Nairobi
New Delhi   Shanghai   Taipei   Toronto

With offices in
Argentina   Austria   Brazil   Chile   Czech Republic   France   Greece
Guatemala   Hungary   Italy   Japan   Poland   Portugal   Singapore
South Korea   Switzerland   Thailand   Turkey   Ukraine   Vietnam

Published by Oxford University Press, Inc.
198 Madison Avenue, New York, New York 10016
http://www.oup.com

Oxford is a registered trademark of Oxford University Press

ISBN-13: 978-0-19-530064-2
ISBN 0-19-530064-5

Printing number: 9 8 7 6 5 4 3 2 1

Printed in Peru on acid-free paper

Brief Contents

CONTENTS

PART II Developing Interpersonal Communication Skills

Chapter 7: Listening Effectively   173

PART III Using Communication Skills to Improve Relationships

PREFACE

We are delighted to welcome Cynthia Berryman-Fink, Ph.D., as a co author on this the 11th edition of *Inter-Act: Interpersonal Communication Concepts, Skills, and Contexts*. She is an accomplished teacher, scholar, administrator, and student of interpersonal communication. We think you will be pleased with how her extensive knowledge of interpersonal communication and her love of teaching have helped us to make the 11th edition of *Inter-Act* the best yet.

We began this revision as we always do. We carefully considered feedback from instructors across the country informing us about the changing needs of their students. We reviewed the latest scholarship. And we revised the book to reflect what we learned. In each edition our goal is to make *Inter-Act* a better tool for teaching the current generation of students about interpersonal communication and about how to ethically use interpersonal communication skills to establish, develop, maintain, and end their relationships.

Because interpersonal communication theorizing and research are dynamic and continue to evolve, in this revised edition we have incorporated new concepts, theories, and skills into most chapters (the major changes to this edition are detailed later in this Preface). In order to keep the text a reasonable length, we have also pruned from the text the material that instructors have told us is less central to their courses or less useful to their students. In the process we have retained the signature elements that have made *Inter-Act* a favorite teaching tool for many of our colleagues. We are very excited about the new edition and hope you will find that this text stimulates you to think about and to improve your interpersonal communication skills.

Philosophy of the Text

For most students the study of interpersonal communication is a practical study. You want to learn in order to understand and become more skilled in handling your relationships with others. This text both describes and prescribes. We describe interpersonal communication concepts, frameworks, and theories to help you understand how your communication behavior and that of your partner creates, develops, maintains, or ends your relationship. Then we identify and prescribe specific communication skills you can learn to use that will help you make interactions more effective and satisfying. Since there is cultural variation in what behaviors lead to effective relationships, the text describes variations and encourages you to learn to use a variety of skills so that you develop flexibility and can adapt your communication behavior to be appropriate within a variety of cultural contexts.

Student Learning Goals

There are six specific learning goals that guide this text: (1) to present you with important communication concepts, frameworks, and theories that have been consistently supported by careful research so that you can understand the conceptual foundations of interpersonal relationship competence; (2) to teach you specific communication skills that research has shown facilitate effective relationships; (3) to present you with ethical frameworks that can guide competent communication; (4) to encourage you to consider how communication needs, rules, and processes differ among diverse people; (5) to challenge you to think critically and creatively about the concepts and skills that you are learning; and (6) to provide you with features and activities that significantly enhance your learning.

Chapters and Key Features

For the convenience of those who are familiar with the previous edition of *Inter-Act*, the chapters, except the last one, remain in the same order. We have integrated information on electronically mediated interpersonal communication throughout the book rather than address such topics in a final chapter. With this change, you will find issues of electronic communication grounded in interpersonal communication theory and informing interpersonal communication practice. We have addressed a greater range of interpersonal topics affected by technology including meeting acquaintances and projecting impressions online, maintaining relationships electronically, language features of instant messages, emoticons as nonverbal communication, having conversations and listening in cyberspace, obtaining social support through the Internet, and using online job search options.

New Feature: The Gray Zone

This new feature is designed to show the contingencies and complexities of enacting some interpersonal communication skills. This feature addresses exceptions to prescriptive advice based on unique aspects of the situation, relationship, context, or culture. The Gray Zone offers a rich and realistic view of interpersonal communication. This edition of *Inter-Act* includes Gray Zone features on exchange versus communal relationships, strategic ambiguity, conversation as argument, and positive misunderstanding.

New Feature: Learn About Yourself

This new feature allows readers to take short surveys to examine aspects of their own interpersonal communication styles. Eight new instruments will measure ethnocentrism, orientation toward time, satisfaction with a conversation, listening effectiveness, empathic tendency, self-disclosure, assertiveness, conflict management style, and respect for a partner.

Chapters Strengthened in this Edition

- **Chapter 3, Communicating in Relationships: Basic Concepts,** now includes discussions of relational dialectics and turning points in relationships.
- **Chapter 4, Verbal Communication,** has been substantially revised to include more theoretical material, including the Sapir-Whorf hypothesis, Burkean concepts, the Coordinated Mangagement of Meaning, and Communication Accommodation. The practical application of such theory has been emphasized. This chapter also includes new sections on the language of humor and language use in cyberspace.
- **Chapter 5, Communicating Through Nonverbal Behaviors,** includes new information on the functions of nonverbal communication as well as material on the use of time and olfactory senses as types of nonverbal communication.
- **Chapter 6, Holding Effective Conversations,** introduces formality, turn-taking, topic change, talk time, scriptedness, and conversational audience as six characteristics of conversations. Additionally, we added a discussion of the balance between appropriateness and effectiveness in conversations as well as an examination of issues of privacy.
- **Chapter 12, Communicating in Intimate Relationships: Friends, Spouses, and Family,** has been revised to include new information on intergenerational family communication, loneliness, and relational uncertainty.
- **Chapter 13, Communicating in the Workplace,** retains information on the hiring process and communicating in managerial and coworker relationships, but now includes contemporary topics of communicating on a work team, and dealing with organizational romance, sexual harassment, multicultural work styles and inter-generational differences at work.

Features Strengthened in this Edition

- **Focus on Skills.** Previous users of *Inter-Act* will find that most of the skills presented in previous editions remain unchanged. However, in this edition we have added new skills that are based on recent scholarship. These skills are described and exemplified in the text and in Skill Builders boxes, which highlight each skill with a definition of the skill, brief description of its use, the steps for enacting the skill, and an example that illustrates the skill in use. A convenient tear-out chart at the beginning of the book also provides a summary of all Skill Builders. The skills in the chart have been grouped into categories for easy reference.
- **Skill Practice.** The Test Yourself feature that appeared in the last edition has been retitled "Skill Practice" and can now be found in the end-of-chapter material. Additional activities can be found on our companion website (www.oup.com/us/interact). These short self-tests challenge students to practice the material they have read in each chapter.
- **Student Activities** presented in the text have been streamlined. The Observe & Analyze features have been edited, and some now appear on our companion website (www.oup.com/us/interact). All can still be used as journal or short paper assignments.

- **Inter-Act with Technology** is a feature that helps students think about how things like cell phones, e-mail, and the Internet affect our ability to communicate. This feature has been thoroughly revised so that it now focuses more solidly on helping students examine on how modern forms of communication technology influence our interpersonal communication styles.
- **Diverse Voices,** excerpts of previously published selections, appear in most chapters of the text to give voice to the experiences of people from a wide range of backgrounds and cultural experiences. Five of the ten selections are new to this edition and address a greater range of diversity including Japanese, Native American, Middle Eastern, and lesbian communication practices.
- **What Would You Do? A Question of Ethics** is a feature that outlines ethical challenges and requires students to think critically in sorting through a variety of ethical dilemmas faced by communicators. Thirty percent of the cases in this edition are new and are designed to help students explore the ethical ramifications of some of the new material being presented to them.
- **Spotlight on Scholars** features continue to explore the work of eleven eminent communication scholars. Based on interviews with the scholars, this feature is designed to help undergraduates understand the research and theory building process and what motivates the people who do this work.
- **Chapter Resources** have been streamlined. Communication improvement plans and key terms lists are still included. Inter-Act with Media still includes suggestions for films and websites that can enhance a student's study of interpersonal communication; however, suggestions for theater, literature, and academic work have been moved to the companion website (www.oup.com/us/interact). Skill Practice activities are now found in the Chapter Resource section as well.
- **Examples and Dialogues** have been reviewed by a college student and revised for relevancy, contemporary tone, and authenticity of language.

Supplementary Materials

As a user of this text you also have access to supplementary materials developed at Oxford University Press. Materials prepared by Oxford are divided into those that are relevant for students and those for faculty.

Student Materials

CD. The student CD, which is packaged in each new copy of *Inter-Act, eleventh edition*, has been expanded to include the following items:

- **Complete Student Workbook:** A revised student workbook, written by Mary Hoeft and Sharon Rubin, both of the University of Wisconsin-Barron County, is now included free of charge on the in-text CD. The workbook includes a wealth of exercises that reinforce text content. For each chapter, students will find an interactive chapter outline, a key terms list, a variety of exercises, helpful URLs, and a chapter quiz (with an answer key for self-evaluation). This is an invaluable student resource.

- **Video Clips:** The CD also contains video footage of four of the Inter-Action Dialogues that appear in the textbook. Students can watch these videos and then use the CD to analyze the skills that are demonstrated in each conversation. A click of a button allows students to compare their analyses to those written by the authors.

Companion Website: For Students. The companion website for *Inter-Act, eleventh edition,* can be found at http://www.oup.com/us/interact. It contains additional resources for students wishing to reinforce their study of interpersonal communication. On the companion website, students will find: an online glossary with glossary flash cards, links to all websites mentioned in the text, and a variety of exercises designed to help students think further about material they encounter in the textbook. Additional Observe & Analyze and Skill Practice features, as well as a Communication Improvement Plan worksheet, can also be found on our website. Also provided is a link to an Oxford site called "Now Playing," which discusses interpersonal communication issues as seen in recent popular films.

Faculty Materials

Instructor's Manual/Test Bank. For the eleventh edition of *Inter-Act,* the *Instructor's Manual/Test Bank* has been revised by Leonard Assante of Volunteer State Community College. The *Instructor's Manual* contains new teaching resources, including class-tested exercises, surveys, role-playing exercises, experiential learning exercises, suggested journal topics, discussion questions, written assignments, possible course schedules, and an extensive test bank.

Computerized Test Bank. The text bank from the *Instructor's Manual* is also available on CD. The electronic format allows users to customize tests to suit any style of exam.

Companion Website: For Instructors. The companion website for *Inter-Act, eleventh edition,* can be found at: http://www.oup.com/us/interact. It contains additional helpful resources for instructors teaching classes in interpersonal communication. One such resource is the *Media Guide for Interpersonal Communication,* by Charles G. Apple, University of Michigan, Flint. The *Media Guide* is a wonderful resource, expanding on the Inter-Act with Media listings that accompany each chapter in the text. The *Media Guide* provides compelling examples of interpersonal communication in an engaging format that generates student interest and motivates learning through the use of films, books, plays, websites, and journal articles.

For additional information regarding these supplementary materials, please call your Oxford sales representative at 1-800-280-0280, or visit the Oxford Higher Education website at http://www.oup.com/us/highered.

Acknowledgments

Although the writing team is ultimately responsible for what appears in print, we would be unable to do our jobs without the help of many people who generously gave of their time and talents to help us birth this new edition. We acknowledge the following colleagues who reviewed the last edition and provided us with useful suggestions about what to keep, what to change, and what to trim: Rebecca Ann Lind, University of Illinois at Chicago; Ceilidh Charleson-Jennings, Collin County Community College; Phyllis Taylor, Skyline College; Leonard Assante, Volunteer State Community College; Lon Green, Ferris State University; Tanya Boone, California State University, Bakersfield; Anneliese Harper, Maricopa Community College; Beverly Kelley, California Lutheran University; David Majewski, Richard Bland College. We thank Charles Apple of University of Michigan, Flint for his assistance and creativity in updating several of the "A Question of Ethics" features, the Inter-Act with Technology features, and the Inter-Act with Media features (including the *Media Guide* which is found on our website). We are grateful for the work of Leonard Assante, of Volunteer State Community College, who revised the *Instructor's Manual*, as well as Mary Hoeft and Sharon Rubin, both of the University of Wisconsin-Barron County, who revised the *Student Workbook* material that is found on your in-text CD. We sincerely appreciate the help of our Oxford team: Peter Labella, Editor, along with the members of his group: Sean Mahoney, Shiwani Srivastava, and Erika Wise; Linda Harris, Development Editor, and her assistant Neil Abell; Karen Shapiro, Managing Editor; and others who helped to make this revision process a smooth and enjoyable one. Finally, we thank our families for putting up with us during this process. A special debt of gratitude belongs to Chuck Fink who patiently helped Cynthia cope with the frustrations of working with embedded text styles and other computer related anomalies that are inherent in preparing textbook revisions in the electronic age. We thank Drew Fink for revising sample dialogues and examples so they would sound real and hold the interest of readers in the 20-something age range.

Kathleen S. Verderber
Rudolph F. Verderber
Cynthia Berryman-Fink

Inter-Act

interpersonal communication
concepts, skills, and contexts

an orientation to interpersonal communication

After you have read this chapter, you should be able to answer these questions:

- What is interpersonal communication?

- Why is interpersonal communication important?

- How does the interpersonal communication process work?

- What principles provide the foundation for interpersonal communication?

- What is communication competence?

- What are major ethical issues facing communicators?

- Why should a communicator be concerned about diversity?

- How can you improve your interpersonal communication?

"Hello?"

"Hi—where are you? I've been waiting for twenty minutes for you."

"Where am I? Where are you? I thought we were going to meet at Denny's for breakfast."

"I am waiting at the restaurant but you're not here."

"Don't mess with me. You're not at Denny's right now."

"I'm sitting right in the front waiting for you to get here."

"Come on, you're not at Denny's on Montgomery Road near Cold Creek Park."

"No, I'm at the Denny's on the corner of Main and Sanford, where you said to meet."

"Oh, this is great. We're at two different restaurants!"

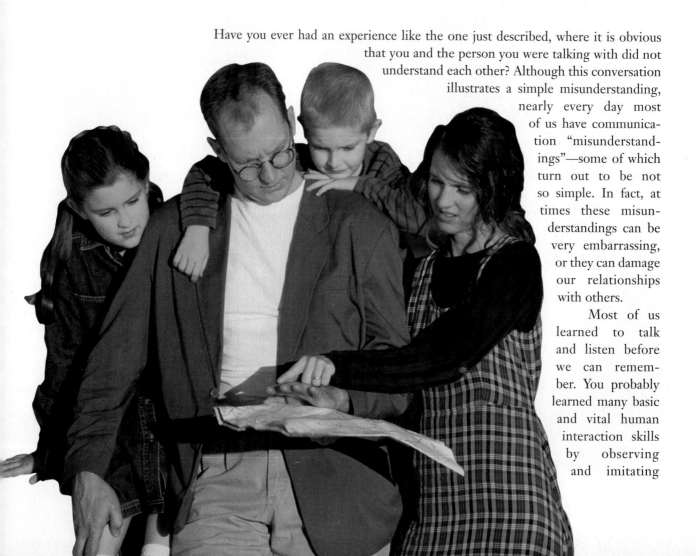

Have you ever had an experience like the one just described, where it is obvious that you and the person you were talking with did not understand each other? Although this conversation illustrates a simple misunderstanding, nearly every day most of us have communication "misunderstandings"—some of which turn out to be not so simple. In fact, at times these misunderstandings can be very embarrassing, or they can damage our relationships with others.

Most of us learned to talk and listen before we can remember. You probably learned many basic and vital human interaction skills by observing and imitating the communication behaviors of those around you. Through these observations you formed your own "theories of communication." You draw on these "implicit theories" to help you when you need to communicate with others. When your personal theories are correct, you are effective in your interactions with others, but when your theories are incorrect or incomplete, you may create misunderstanding and harm your relationships.

During this term you will begin a formal study of the theories of interpersonal communication that are based on the research of communication scholars—theories that are more valid, reliable, and complete than many of your personal theories. By understanding the concepts, relationships, and predictions of these theories, you will become better equipped to behave in ways that result in improved relationships. Moreover, you will learn and practice a variety of communication skills in a "safe" classroom setting before you try them out in your other relationships.

In this first chapter, we present introductory information for this study. We (1) define interpersonal communication, (2) discuss the functions that it serves, (3) present interpersonal communication components, (4) identify the basic principles that are fundamental to understanding interpersonal communication, (5) discuss the ethical principles that underlie interpersonal communication, (6) explain how human diversity complicates the interpersonal communication process, and (7) describe what it means to be competent in interpersonal communication.

Interpersonal Communication Defined

We define **interpersonal communication** as the process through which people create and manage their relationships, exercising mutual responsibility in creating meaning. Let's explore this definition to see its importance.

First, interpersonal communication is a process. A process is a systematic series of behaviors with a purpose that occurs over time. During a twenty-minute phone call with your mother to catch up on family news or during a five-minute impromptu meeting with a co-worker to solve a customer problem, a series of behaviors is occurring. These behaviors are purposeful. You ask your mom for your brother's new cell phone number so you can get in touch with him about sharing the cost of an anniversary present for your grandparents. You tell your co-worker the background of the customer complaint so that she can help you arrive at a solution that is fair to the customer and in keeping with company policy.

Second, interpersonal communication depends upon the meaning created by the people involved.

Imagine Tonika says to her roommate, "How about if we keep it a little cleaner around here?" Her roommate may think that means just keeping the kitchen clean. So the interpersonal communication that has taken place between the roommates does not depend on what one of them says or does, but rather depends on the meaning that is created between them.

> **Interpersonal communication**—the process through which people create and manage their relationships, exercising mutual responsibility in creating meaning.

observe & analyze

Communication Processes Define Relationships

Think about one relationship you have that is "easy" and very satisfying. Then think about one relationship you have that is "difficult" and not satisfying. *Briefly* describe the last conversation you had with each person. How do these conversations compare? Describe how they are similar; then describe how they differ. How does your communication pattern change? ■

Third, through communication, we create and manage our relationships. Without communication your relationships could not exist. A relationship begins when you first interact with someone. Over time, through your interactions with that person, you continue to define the nature of the relationship and what it will become. Is the relationship more personal or impersonal, closer or more distant, romantic or platonic, healthy or unhealthy, dependent or interdependent? The answer to these questions depends on how the people in the relationship talk and behave toward each other.

The Functions of Interpersonal Communication

You may have registered for this course because you were curious, because a friend or a teacher recommended it, because it fit your schedule, or because it is a requirement for your major. Whatever may have brought you to this class, we believe that before the term is over you'll be thankful that you have studied interpersonal communication. Why? Because interpersonal communication serves at least five functions that are important to your social and psychological health.

1. Through interpersonal communication we attempt to meet our social/psychological needs. Because we are by nature social animals, we need to interact with other people just as we need food, water, and shelter. Often what we talk about is unimportant. We may just "hang out," conversing happily for hours about relatively inconsequential matters, exchanging little real information, or we may have "heart to hearts," where we probe deep feelings that are central to our well-being. Regardless of how serious or important the conversation may be, we may carry away from it a pleasant, satisfied feeling that comes from having met the need to talk with someone.

2. Through interpersonal communication we attempt to achieve goals. Although we may not be consciously aware of any goals when communicating, we are always trying to achieve some purpose. The goal may be as simple as trying to be friendly or as complex as trying to influence a boss to authorize a raise.

3. Through interpersonal communication we develop a sense of self. Through our communication and relationships, we learn who we are, what we are good at, and how people react to how we behave. We explore this important function of interpersonal communication in detail in Chapter 2, "Forming and Using Social Perceptions."

4. Through interpersonal communication we acquire information. While we get some information through direct observation, some through reading, and some through the media, we receive a great deal of the information upon which we base our

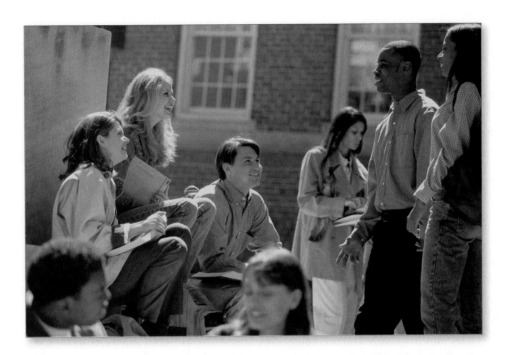

How are our social needs met in large gatherings?

decisions during our conversations with others. For example, Jeff runs out to get a bagel and coffee. When he returns, Tom asks, "What's it like out there this morning?" Jeff replies, "Wow, it's cold—it couldn't be more than twenty degrees." Tom reacts to this news by sighing and says, "I was just going to wear a sweatshirt, but I guess I'd better break out the old winter coat." From subjects as mundane as this one to others that are more important, we acquire a great deal of information on which we act from conversing with others.

5. Through interpersonal communication we influence and are influenced by others. In a typical day you engage in countless exchanges where the purpose is to influence. From convincing your roommate to loan you a sweater, to listening to a political candidate who is campaigning door-to-door, to persuading your children to do their homework, to trying to convince an instructor to change your course grade, you use interpersonal communication to try to change the beliefs and behaviors of others. And others use the same process to try to influence you.

Interpersonal Communication Components

Because you've been communicating for as long as you can remember, you really don't consciously think about what takes place. The thoughts and behaviors of communicating have become automatic. In reality, however, any interpersonal communication episode is the result of a complex series of both cognitions (thinking) and behaviors (doing). Let's begin by describing the components that make up the communication process (see Figure 1.1).

Participant Characteristics and Roles

Participants—the people who communicate by assuming the roles of senders and receivers during the communication.

The **participants** are the people who communicate, assuming the roles of senders and receivers during the communication. As senders, participants form messages and attempt to communicate them to others through verbal symbols and nonverbal behavior. As receivers, they interpret the messages and behaviors that they receive and react to them. Participating in interpersonal communication can be thought of as playing two roles, sender and receiver. In most interpersonal situations participants enact the two roles simultaneously.

In general, it is easier for participants to share meaning when they are similar and have a common base for understanding. According to Berger (2002), when people share similar knowledge, assumptions, or beliefs, they are said to have common ground, which makes communication more accurate and more efficient (p. 182). It would be easier, for instance, for two people who have worked in retail sales jobs to quickly and accurately understand a story about the stress of working on the day after Thanksgiving than it would for someone who has never held a retail sales job.

Context

Context—the setting in which communication occurs, including what precedes and follows what is said.

Physical context—where a communication takes place, the environmental conditions (temperature, lighting, noise level), the distance between communicators, seating arrangements, and time of day.

Social context—the nature of the relationship that exists between the participants.

Context is the setting in which a communication encounter occurs, including what precedes and follows what is said. The context affects the expectations of the participants, the meaning these participants derive, and their subsequent behavior. Context includes (1) physical, (2) social, (3) historical, (4) psychological, and (5) cultural circumstances that surround a communication episode.

Physical Context. The physical context includes location, environmental conditions (temperature, lighting, noise level), distance between communicators, seating arrangements, and time of day. Each of these factors can affect the communication. For instance, the meaning shared in a conversation may be affected by whether it is held in a crowded company cafeteria, an elegant candlelit restaurant, over the telephone, or on the Internet.

Social Context. The social context is the type of relationship that may already exist between the participants. Whether communication takes place

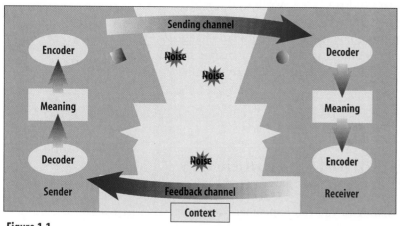

Figure 1.1

A model of communication between two individuals

among family members, friends, acquaintances, work associates, or strangers influences what and how messages are formed, shared, and understood. For instance, most people change how they interact when talking with their parents or siblings as compared to how they interact when talking with their friends.

Historical Context. The historical context is the background provided by previous communication episodes between the participants. It influences understandings in the current encounter. For instance, suppose one morning Chad tells Shelby that he will get the draft of the report that they had left for their boss to read. As Shelby enters the office that afternoon, she sees Chad and says, "Did you get it?" Another person listening to the conversation would have no idea what "it" is. Yet Chad may well reply, "It's on my desk." Shelby and Chad understood one another because of the contents of the earlier exchange.

> **Historical context**—the background provided by the previous communication episodes between the participants that influences understandings in the current encounter.

Psychological Context. The psychological context includes the moods and feelings each person brings to the interpersonal encounter. For instance, suppose Corinne is under a great deal of stress. While she is studying for an exam, a friend stops by and pleads with her to take a break and go to the gym with her. Corinne, who is normally good-natured, may explode with an angry tirade. Why? Because her stress level provides the psychological context within which she hears this message and it affects how she responds.

> **Psychological context**—the moods and feelings each person brings to an interpersonal encounter.

Cultural Context. The cultural context includes the beliefs, values, attitudes, meanings, social hierarchies, religion, notions of time, and roles of the participants (Samovar & Porter, 2000, p. 7). Culture penetrates into every aspect of our lives, affecting how we think, talk, and behave. Everyone is a part of one or more ethnic cultures, though we may differ in how much we identify with our ethnic cultures. When two people from different cultures interact, misunderstandings may occur because of cultural variation.

> **Cultural context**—the set of beliefs, values, attitudes, meanings, social hierarchies, religion, notions of time, and roles of the participants.

Message Formation

Interpersonal communication takes place through the exchange of **messages,** which are a person's verbal utterances and nonverbal behaviors. To appreciate the complex way in which messages work, you need to understand meaning, symbols, and encoding and decoding.

> **Messages**—a person's verbal utterances and nonverbal behaviors to which meaning is attributed during communication.

Meaning. Meanings include the thoughts in one person's mind as well as interpretations one makes of another's message. "Meanings" refers to the ways that communicators make sense of messages. It is important to realize that meanings are not transferred from one person to another, but are created together in an exchange. For instance, if Sarah says to Tiffany that her cat is old and fat, through the exchange of messages, they must together come to some degree of similarity of what "old" and "fat" mean.

> **Meaning**—thoughts in our minds and interpretations of other's messages.

Symbols. To express yourself, you form messages comprising verbal symbols and nonverbal behaviors. Symbols are words, sounds, and actions that seek to represent specific ideas and feelings. As you speak, you choose word symbols to express your meaning. At the same time, facial expressions, eye contact, gestures, and tone of voice—all symbolic nonverbal cues—accompany your words in an attempt to

> **Symbols**—words, sounds, and actions that are generally understood to represent meaning.

express your meaning. As a listener, you make interpretations or attribute meaning to the message you received.

Encoding—the process of putting our thoughts and feelings into words and nonverbal cues.

Decoding—the process of interpreting another's message.

Encoding and Decoding. Encoding is the process of putting our thoughts and feelings into words and nonverbal cues. Decoding is the process of interpreting another's message. Ordinarily you do not consciously think about either the encoding or the decoding process. Only when there is a difficulty, such as speaking in a second language or having to use an easier vocabulary with children, do you become aware of encoding. You may not think about decoding until someone seems to be speaking in circles or starts using unfamiliar technical words and you have difficult interpreting or understanding what is being said.

Channels

Channels—both the route traveled by the message and the means of transportation.

Channels are both the route traveled by the message and the means of transportation. Messages are transmitted through sensory channels. Face-to-face communication has two basic channels: verbal symbols and nonverbal cues. Online communication uses these same two channels, though some of the nonverbal cues like movements, touch, and gestures may be missing. Many aspects of the nonverbal channel, such as facial expressions, aspects of voice, and use of time, do occur online, however. We will explain more of these concepts in Chapter 5, "Communicating Through Nonverbal Behaviors."

Noise

Noise—any stimulus that gets in the way of sharing meaning.

External noises—the sights, sounds, and other stimuli that draw people's attention away from intended meaning.

Internal noises—the thoughts and feelings that interfere with meaning.

Semantic noises—unintended meanings aroused by a speaker's symbols.

Noise is any stimulus that interferes with the process of making sense of messages. Noise can be external, internal, or semantic.

External noises are sights, sounds, and other stimuli in the environment that draw people's attention away from what is being said or done. For instance, while a person is giving directions on how to work the new MP3 player, your attention may be drawn away by the external noise of a radio playing an old favorite song of yours. External noise does not have to be a sound, however. Perhaps, while the person gives the directions, your attention is drawn momentarily to an attractive man or woman. Such visual distractions are also external noise.

Internal noises are thoughts and feelings that compete for attention and interfere with the communication process. If you have tuned out the message of the person with whom you are communicating and tuned into a daydream or a past conversation, then you have experienced internal noise.

Semantic noises are distractions aroused by certain symbols that take our attention away from the main message. If a friend describes a forty-year-old secretary as "the girl in the office," and you think "girl" is an odd and condescending term for a forty-year-old woman, you might not even hear the rest of what your friend has to say. Whenever we react emotionally to a word or a behavior, we are experiencing semantic noise.

observe & analyze

The Communication Process

Describe two recent communication episodes that you participated in. One should be an episode that you thought went really well. The other should be one that you thought went poorly. Compare and contrast the episodes. Describe the context factors in the episode, the participant similarities and differences, the messages that were used to create the meaning, the channels used, any noise that interfered with the messages and meaning, and the feedback that was shared. ■

Feedback Messages

Feedback is the response to messages that indicates to the sender whether and how that message was heard, seen, and interpreted. We can express feedback verbally through words or nonverbally through body language. We continuously give feedback when we are listening to another, if only through paying attention, giving a confused look, or showing signs of boredom. Or we may provide very direct feedback by saying "I don't understand the point you are making," or "That's a great comment you just made." It is important that communicators pay attention to all the feedback from others during interaction so they may adjust their messages to enhance others' understanding.

Feedback—responses to messages.

Interpersonal Communication Principles

Now that we have described the interpersonal communication process, we will explain the five basic principles (or essential qualities) that describe interpersonal communication: (1) Interpersonal communication is purposeful. (2) Interpersonal communication is continuous. (3) Interpersonal communication is transactional. (4) Interpersonal communication is relational. (5) Interpersonal communication is irreversible.

Interpersonal Communication Has Purpose

When people communicate with one another, they have a purpose for doing so. Or, as Charles Berger (2002), a leading researcher on interpersonal contexts, puts it, —"Social interaction is a goal-directed activity" (p. 181). The purpose of a given interaction may be serious or trivial, but one way to evaluate the success of the communication is to ask whether it achieved its purpose. When Beth calls Leah to ask whether she'd like to join her for lunch to discuss a project they are working on, her purpose may be to resolve a misunderstanding, to encourage Leah to work more closely with her, or simply to establish a cordial atmosphere.

People may not always be aware of their purpose in a given communication. For instance, when Jamal passes Tony on the street and says lightly, "Tony, what's happening?" Jamal probably doesn't consciously think, "Tony's an acquaintance and I want him to understand that I see him and consider him worth recognizing." In this case the social obligation to recognize Tony is met spontaneously with the first acceptable expression that comes to Jamal's mind. Regardless of whether Jamal consciously thinks about the purpose, it still motivates his behavior. In this case, Jamal will have achieved his goal if Tony responds with an equally casual greeting.

Interpersonal Communication Is Continuous

Because interpersonal communication can be nonverbal as well as verbal, we are always sending and receiving messages. Whenever two people are in each other's presence and one is aware of the other, communication is occurring. Even if you are silent, another person may infer meaning from your silence. If you are cold, you may shiver; if you are hot or nervous, you may perspire; if you are bored, happy, or confused, your face may show it. Whether you like or dislike what you are hearing, your body will reflect it. As skilled communicators, we need to be aware of the messages, whether explicit or implicit, we are constantly sending to others.

Interpersonal Communication Is Transactional

In a transaction, each person gives and gets something. So too in an interpersonal communication episode, each person gives and receives messages, gives and receives feedback, gets needs met and helps others to satisfy needs, and gives and receives self-concept information. Each person is changed, if ever so slightly, with each interaction. It is impossible for only one of the parties to get something from an interpersonal communication episode. Because interpersonal communication is a transaction, both parties get something, even if there are differences in what each person gets or how much information, feedback, or need fulfillment each person gets.

Interpersonal Communication Is Relational

In many interpersonal communication settings people not only share messages about content, but also negotiate their relationship. For instance, when Laura says to Jenny, "I've remembered to bring the map," she is not only reporting information, but through the way she says it she may also be communicating "You can always depend on me" or "I am superior to you—if it weren't for me we'd be missing an important document for our trip."

Two aspects of relationships can be negotiated during an interaction. One aspect is the affect (love to hate) present in the relationships. For instance, when Jose says "Hal, good to see you," the nonverbal behavior that accompanies the words may show Hal whether Jose is genuinely happy to see him (positive affect) or not. For instance, if Jose smiles, sounds sincere, looks Hal in the eye, and perhaps pats him on the back or shakes hands firmly, then Hal will recognize the signs of affection. If, however, Jose speaks quickly with no vocal inflection and a deadpan facial expression, Hal will perceive the comment as solely meeting some social expectation.

Another aspect of the relational nature of interpersonal communication concerns the definition of who is in control (Watzlawick, Beavin, & Jackson, 1967, p. 51). Thus, when Tom says to Sue, "I know you're concerned about the budget, but I'll see to it that we have money to cover everything," he can, through his words and the sound of his voice, be saying that he is "in charge" of finances, that he is in control. It is how Sue responds to Tom, however, that determines the true nature of control in the relationship. She may respond by subtly showing that she accepts his control, or she may challenge him and assert her desire to control the financial aspects of the situation. The control aspect of the relationship can be viewed as complementary or symmetrical.

How do people communicate power differences in complementary relationships?

In a **complementary exchange** there are differences in power between the people involved. Thus, the communication messages of one person may assert dominance while the communication messages of the other person may acknowledge the dominance. For instance, if Joey says to Jason, "Pick me up at work at 4 o'clock," and Jason says, "OK, I'll be there," a complementary exchange has taken place.

In a **symmetrical exchange** there is similarity in power between the people involved. That may be because both desire to share control, or it may be because one person asserts control and the other person refuses to accept the assertion. The sharing of control through agreement may be illustrated by the following exchange. Elka: "How can we decide on a restaurant and a movie that we're both excited about?" Eileen: "Maybe we could make a list of restaurant choices and movie choices, with you picking the restaurant and me selecting the movie." Elka: "That's a great idea as long as we both agree on all the choices on the lists." An exchange with similar control achieved through disagreement would sound quite

Complementary exchanges—communications that reflect difference in power between people in an interaction.

Symmetrical exchanges—communications that reflect similarity in power between people in an interaction.

different. For example, Tom may say, "I think we need to cut back on credit card expenses for a couple of months," and Sue may respond "No way! I need a new suit for work, the car needs new tires, and you promised we could replace the couch." Here, both people are asserting similar levels of control.

The overall patterns of relational control are not negotiated in a single exchange. Relational control is determined through many message exchanges over time. There may or may not be one type of exchange that most characterizes a relationship. Two people could typically engage in complementary exchanges throughout their relationship, or they may have mostly complementary exchanges regarding social aspects of the relationship and symmetrical exchanges regarding child-rearing practices.

Interpersonal Communication Is Irreversible

Once an interpersonal exchange has taken place, we can never ignore it, take it back, or pretend that it did not occur. In other words, we can never go back in time and erase the communication. Both the individuals and the relationship are affected by each occurrence of communication.

Sometimes we may say something hurtful that we later regret. Or we may make a promise that we are not able to keep. At these times we may wish to undo the communication. We may even ask the other person to disregard what we have said, but people cannot totally strike from consciousness or from memory something they have heard.

Ethics—a set of moral principles that may be held by a society, a group, or an individual.

The Ethics of Interpersonal Communication

In any encounter we choose whether or not we will communicate ethically. **Ethics** is a set of moral principles that may be held by a society, a group, or an individual. Although in this book we are focusing on the word *ethics*, as Terkel and Duval (1999) point out in their *Encyclopedia of Ethics*, the words *ethics* and *morals* are often used interchangeably. These authors go on to say that even though some philosophers show shades of difference in the words by holding that ethics refers to "cultivation of character and practical decision making" and morals refers to "the set of practices that society holds to be right or just," a considerable overlap is clearly recognized (Terkel & Duval, 1999, p. 80).

In this text then, we are particularly interested in ethical issues, which, according to Richard Johannesen (2002), a noted communication scholar, "denotes general and systematic study of what ought to be the grounds and principles for right and wrong human behavior" (p. 2). Although what is considered ethical is to some extent a personal matter, we still expect society to uphold certain standards that can help us with our personal value judgments. Families, schools, and religion all share the responsibility of helping individuals develop ethical standards that can be applied to specific

inter-act with

Technology

How do various forms of technology impact the communication process in your relationships? List each form of technology that you use to communicate with others (such as land line telephones, cell phones, e-mail, answering machines). Now examine how each form of technology helps or hinders your overall communication. For example, what is the impact of being able to send off a print message when you will not have to actually face the recipient in the near future, or ever? When you communicate via technology, do you send messages that are more candid, use harsher language, or make claims that you would not make in person? ■

situations. Although an ethical theory does not tell us what to do in any given situation, it does tell us what to consider in making decisions. It directs our attention to the reasons that determine the rightness or wrongness of any act.

Although ethical theory tells us what is acceptable or unacceptable in general, each of us develops a personal ethic—one that guides our specific behavior. Your personal ethic is based on your belief and acceptance of what the communities or groups with which you most closely identify consider moral and ethical. When you behave ethically, you voluntarily act in a manner that conforms to expected behavior. Why do people internalize morals and develop a personal ethic? Because most of us regard ourselves as accountable for our conduct, and even to some extent for our attitudes and character, and blame ourselves when we fall short of these ideal principles (Pritchard, 1991, p. 39).

When we communicate, we make choices with ethical implications. So we should understand the general ethical principles that form a basis for ethical interpersonal communication.

1. Ethical communicators are truthful and honest. Truthfulness and honesty are standards that compel us to refrain from lying, cheating, stealing, or deception. "An honest person is widely regarded as a moral person, and honesty is a central concept to ethics as the foundation for a moral life" (Terkel & Duval, 1999, p. 122).

Truthfulness and honesty—refraining from lying, cheating, stealing, or deception.

Although most people accept truthfulness and honesty as a standard, they still confess to lying on occasion. But even when we face what appears to be a **moral dilemma,** a choice involving an unsatisfactory alternative, we should look for a response that doesn't require us to lie.

Moral dilemma—a choice involving unsatisfactory alternatives.

An operating moral rule is to tell the truth if you possibly can. The fundamental requirement of this rule is that we should not intentionally deceive, or try to deceive, others or even ourselves. Only when we are confronted with a true moral dilemma involving making a choice that most people would deem justified by the circumstances (such as lying to avoid warning an enemy about a planned attack) or selecting the lesser of two evils (lying to protect confidentiality) should we even consider lying. Usually we can avoid direct lies by simply refusing to discuss the issue.

2. Ethical communicators act with integrity. Integrity means maintaining a consistency of belief and action (keeping promises). Terkel and Duval (1999) say, "A person who has integrity is someone who has strong moral principles and will successfully resist the temptation to compromise those principles" (p. 135). Integrity then is the opposite of hypocrisy. A person who had promised to take a friend to the doctor would live up to this promise even if he or she had an opportunity to go out with another friend.

Integrity—having a consistency of belief and action (keeping promises).

3. Ethical communicators behave fairly. Fairness means achieving the right balance of interests without regard to one's own feelings and without showing favor to any side in a conflict. Fairness implies impartiality or lack of bias. To be fair to someone is to gather all the relevant facts, consider only circumstances relevant to the decision at hand, and not be swayed by prejudice or irrelevancies. For example, if two children are fighting, their mom is exercising fairness if she allows each one to "explain" before she decides who is at fault.

Fairness—achieving the right balance of interests without regard to one's own feelings and without showing favor to any side in a conflict.

Respect—showing regard or consideration for a person and for that person's rights.

4. Ethical communicators demonstrate respect for the ideas, opinion, and feelings of others. **Respect** means showing regard or consideration for a person and for that person's rights. Often we talk of respecting another as a fellow human being. For instance someone's affluence, job status, or ethnic background should not influence the amount of respect we show that person. We demonstrate respect through listening and understanding others' points of view, even when they are vastly different from our own.

Responsibility—accountability for one's actions.

5. Ethical communicators are responsible. Responsibility means being accountable for one's actions. A responsibility is a duty that one is bound to perform either through promise or obligation or because of one's role in a group or community. A responsibility may indicate a duty to the moral law or a duty to another human being. Some would argue that we have a responsibility not to harm or interfere with others. Others would argue that not only do we have a responsibility not to harm others, but that we also have a responsibility to help others.

At various places in this text we will confront situations where these issues come into play. We face ethical dilemmas where we must sort out what is more or less right or wrong. In making these choices, we usually reveal what values we hold most dear. So in this book, at the end of Chapters 2 through 13, you will be asked to think about and discuss an ethical dilemma that relates to the content of each chapter.

Interpersonal Communication and Diversity

Diversity—variations between and among people.

Diversity, variations between and among people, affects nearly every aspect of the communication process we have just discussed. Whether we understand each other depends as much on who we are as it does on the words we use. We in the United States are part of a multicultural nation.

Throughout the history of the United States, we've experienced huge migrations of people from different parts of the world. According to the *New York Times Almanac* (Wright, 2002), the latest census shows that the largest number of new immigrants is from Latin America and Asia. At the end of the twentieth century people of Latin and Asian decent constituted 12.5 and 3.8 percent, respectively, of the total U.S. population. About 2.4 percent of the population regards itself as multiracial. Combined with the approximately 13 percent of our population that is of African descent, these four groups account for nearly 32 percent of the total population. The U.S. Census Bureau predicts that within the next forty-five years, this figure will rise to nearly 50 percent.

Culture—systems of knowledge shared by a relatively large group of people.

Certainly the most widely discussed aspect of diversity is cultural. You'll recall from our discussion of the cultural context of communication that **culture** may be defined as systems of knowledge shared by a relatively large group of people. It includes a system of shared beliefs, values, symbols, and behaviors. Peter Andersen, a well-respected intercultural communication scholar, goes so far as to say that "culture is a critical concept to communication scholars because every communicator is a product of his or her culture" (Andersen, 2000, p. 260). Thus, as we become an increasingly diverse nation, the study of intercultural communication is more important than ever.

We need to look carefully at ourselves and our communication behavior because, as we interact with others with cultural backgrounds that differ from our own, we are vulnerable to unintentionally communicating in ways that are culturally inappropriate or insensitive and in so doing, we may be undermining our relationships.

Although the most widely discussed aspect of diversity is cultural, we must also be sensitive to how differences among people based on sex, age, class, physical characteristics, and sexual orientation affect communication. Failure to take those differences into account when we interact can also lead us to behave insensitively.

Within each chapter of this book we will discuss the diverse ways people act in communication situations. In addition, the feature "Diverse Voices" provides opportunities for us to empathize with the communication experiences of a variety of individuals whose voices are being heard. In this chapter we present the voice of Arturo Madrid. Although writing as a Latino, Madrid expresses sentiments that capture the feelings and experiences of a vast number of Americans. We who live in

How does diversity affect aspects of the communication process?

the United States of America hold to the ideal that this is the land of opportunity and a place of equal opportunity, while simultaneously knowing that it is also a land of hypocrisy, where people are afforded unequal treatment and opportunity based on their race, sex, religion, class, ability, country of origin, or sexual orientation.

Over the years as authors we have been increasingly aware of how the cultural diversity of our country makes simplistic prescriptions about interpersonal communication a problem and how our own cultural perspectives limit our viewpoints on these issues. When we write, no matter how sensitive we try to be, our writings will continue to be shaped by our own cultural perspectives. We hope that when you encounter implicit cultural assumptions, you will consider alternative perspectives critically and offer your thoughts to your classmates.

Increasing Interpersonal Communication Competence

Communication competence—the impression that communicative behavior is both appropriate and effective in a given relationship.

Communication competence is the impression that communicative behavior is both appropriate and effective in a given relationship (Spitzberg, 2000, p. 375). Communication is *effective* when it achieves its goals; it is *appropriate* when it conforms to what is expected in a given context. Specifically, when communication is appropriate, each person believes that the other person has abided by the social rules of behavior that apply to the type of relationship they have and the conversational situation they are in.

The definition of competent communication acknowledges that competence is an impression or judgment that one person makes about another. We try to project that we are competent communicators by the verbal messages we send and the nonverbal behaviors that accompany them. But the impression of our competence always rests with the other person.

Since communication is at the heart of how we relate to one another, one of your goals in this course will be to learn those things that will increase the likelihood that others will view you as competent. In the Spotlight on Scholars on pages 19 and 20, we review the development of Brian Spitzberg's thinking on interpersonal communication competence. Spitzberg believes that perceptions of competence depend in part on personal knowledge, skills and motivation (see also Spitzberg, 2000, p. 377). In other words, we have to know what to say and do, and how to say and do it; and we must have the desire to use our knowledge and skills.

First, as communicator knowledge increases, communicator competence increases. People need knowledge about communication to be effective. The more people understand how to behave in a given situation, the more likely they are to be perceived as competent. We gain knowledge about how to interact by

Social Perception *By Arturo Madrid*

Arturo Madrid is the Norine R. and T. Frank Murchison Distinguished Professor of Humanities at Trinity University. From 1984 to 1993 he served as the founding president of Tomas Rivera Center, the nation's first institute for policy studies on Latino issues. In 1996 he was awarded the Charles Frankel Prize in Humanities by the National Endowment for the Humanities. In this classic selection, Madrid describes the conflicting experiences of those who see themselves as different from what has stereotypically been described as "American." Experiencing oneself and being perceived as "other" and "invisible" are powerful determinants of one's self-concept and form a very special filter through which one communicates with others.

My name is Arturo Madrid.

I am a citizen of the United States, as are my parents and as were my grandparents, and my great-grandparents. My ancestors' presence in what is now the United States antedates Plymouth Rock, even without taking into account any American Indian heritage I might have.

I do not, however, fit those mental sets that define America and Americans. My physical appearance, my speech patterns, my name, my profession (a professor of Spanish) create a text that confuses the reader.

I am very clearly the *other,* if only your everyday, garden-variety, domestic *other.* I've always known that I was the *other,* even before I knew the vocabulary or understood the significance of otherness.

Despite the operating myth of the day, school did not erase my *otherness.* The true test was not our speech, but rather our names and our appearance, for we would always have an accent, however perfect our pronunciation, however excellent our enunciation, however divine our diction. That accent would be heard in our pigmentation, our physiognomy, and our names. We were, in short, the *other.*

Being the *other* involves a contradictory phenomenon. On the one hand, being the *other* frequently means being invisible. On the other hand, being the *other* sometimes involves sticking out like a sore thumb. What is she/he doing here?

If one is the *other,* one will inevitably be seen stereotypically; will be defined and limited by mental sets that may not bear much relation to existing realities.

There is sometimes a darker side to otherness as well. The *other* disturbs, disquiets, discomforts. It provokes distrust and suspicion. The *other* frightens, scares.

For some of us being the *other* is only annoying; for others it is debilitating; for still others it is damning. For the majority otherness is permanently sealed by physical appearance. For the rest otherness is betrayed by ways of being, speaking, or of doing.

The first half of my life I spent downplaying the significance and consequences of otherness. The second half has seen me wrestling to understand its complex and deeply ingrained realities; striving to fathom why otherness denies us a voice or visibility or validity in American society and its institutions; struggling to make otherness familiar, reasonable, even normal to my fellow Americans.

One of the principal strengths of our society is its ability to address on a continuing and substantive basis the real economic, political, and social problems that have faced and continue to face us. What makes the United States so attractive to immigrants are the protections and opportunities it offers; what keeps our society together is tolerance for cultural, religious, social, political, and even linguistic difference; what makes us a unique, dynamic, and extraordinary nation are the power and creativity of our diversity.

The true history of the U.S. is the one of struggle against intolerance, against oppression, against xenophobia, against those forces that have prohibited persons from participating in the larger life of the society on the basis of their race, their gender, their religion, their national origin, their linguistic and cultural background. These phenomena are not only consigned to the past. They remain with us and frequently take on virulent dimensions.

If you believe, as I do, that the well-being of a society is directly related to the degree and extent to which all of its citizens participate in its institutions, then you will have to agree that we have a challenge before us. In view of the extraordinary changes that are taking place in our society we need to take up the struggle again, unpleasant as it is. As educated and educator members of this society we have a special responsibility for assuring that all American institutions, not just our elementary and secondary schools, our juvenile halls, or jails, reflect the diversity of our society. Not to do so is to risk greater alienation on the part of a growing segment of our society; is to risk increased social tension in an already conflictive world; and, ultimately, is to risk the survival of a range of institutions that, for all their defects and deficiencies, provide us the opportunity and the freedom to improve our individual and collective lot.

Let me urge you, as you return to your professional responsibilities and to your personal spaces, to reflect on these two words—*quality* and *diversity*—and on the mental sets and behaviors that flow out of them. And let me urge you further to struggle against the notion that quality is finite in quantity, limited in its manifestations, or is restricted by considerations of class, gender, race, or national origin; or that quality manifests itself only in leaders and not in followers, in managers and not in workers; or that it has to be associated with verbal agility or elegance of personal style; or that it cannot be seeded, or nurtured, or developed. ■

Excerpted from Madrid, A. (1994). Diversity and its discontents. In *Intercultural Communication: A Reader* (7th ed., pp. 127–131). L. A. Samovar & R. E. Porter (Eds.), Belmont, Calif.: Wadsworth. Reprinted by permission of Black Issues in Higher Education.

observing what others do, by asking others how we should behave, by engaging in formal study, and by learning through trial and error. For instance, to be regarded as competent in talking with her boss about increasing her responsibilities, Annette must know about the various ways of presenting her request that her boss would find acceptable and persuasive. As our knowledge and understanding of how and when to ask questions, disclose information, or describe feelings increases, the likelihood that others will see us as competent is likely to increase as well.

Second, as communicator skill increases, communicator competence increases. **Skills** are goal-oriented actions or action sequences that we can master and repeat in appropriate situations. The more skills you have, the more likely you are to be able to structure your messages to be effective and appropriate. For instance, Annette must not only know how to influence her boss, she must also be able to do so during the actual conversation. The more practice she has had in using specific skills, the more likely it is that she will be able to draw on these skills in real situations.

Third, as communicator motivation increases, communicator competence increases. That is, perceived competence depends in part on how much a person wants to use the knowledge and skills to communicate effectively. People are likely to be more motivated if they are confident and if they see potential rewards. If Annette has confidence in her ability to persuade her boss and/or if she thinks it's likely that the conversation will result in more challenging job responsibilities,

Skills—goal-oriented actions or action sequences we can master and repeat in appropriate situations.

spotlight on scholars

Brian Spitzberg, Professor of Communication at San Diego State University, on
Interpersonal Communication Competence

Although Brian Spitzberg has made many contributions to our understanding of interpersonal communication, he is best known for his work in interpersonal communication competence. This interest in competence began at the University of Southern California. For an interpersonal communication seminar assignment he read the research that had been done on interpersonal competence and found that the researchers' conclusions went in different directions. Spitzberg believed the time was ripe for someone to synthesize these perspectives into a comprehensive theory of competence. His final paper for the seminar was his first effort into trying to construct a competence theory.

Today, the model of interpersonal communication competence that Spitzberg has formulated guides most of our thinking and research in this area. He views competence neither as a trait nor as a set of behaviors. Rather, Spitzberg says that interpersonal communication competence is a perception that people have about themselves or another person. Since competence is a perception, then it follows that your perception of your interpersonal communication competence or that of your relationship partner would affect how you feel about that relationship. So people are more

likely to be satisfied in a relationship when they perceive themselves and the other person as competent. According to Spitzberg, we make these competence judgments based on how each of us acts when we talk together. But what determines how we act in a particular conversation?

As Spitzberg was trying to organize his thinking about competence, he was taking another course in which he became acquainted with theories of dramatic acting. These theories held that an actor's performance depended on the actor's motivation, knowledge of the script, and acting skills. Spitzberg found that these same variables could be applied to communication competence, and he incorporated them into his theory. How we behave in a conversation depends first, on how personally motivated we are to have the conversation; second, on how personally knowledgeable we are about what behavior is appropriate in situations like this; and third, on how personally skilled we are at actually using the appropriate behaviors during the conversation. In addition, Spitzberg's theory suggests that context variables such as the ones discussed in this chapter also affect how we choose to act in a conversation and the perceptions of competence that they create.

While Spitzberg formed most of these ideas while he was still in graduate school, he and others have spent the last twenty years refining the theory, conducting programs of research based on his theory, and measuring the effectiveness of the theory. The research has fleshed out parts of the theory and provided some evidence of the theory's accuracy. Over the years Spitzberg has developed about a dozen specific instruments to measure parts of the theory. One of these measures, the Conversational Skills Rating Scale, has been adopted as the standard measure of interpersonal communication skills by the National Communication Association (a leading national organization of communication scholars, teachers, and practitioners). His most recent work involves translating the model and measures of competence into the computer-mediated context. To what extent are the skills we use in face-to-face communication similar to those we use in computer-based interaction? Several research projects are currently investigating this question.

Spitzberg's continuing interest in communication competency has led him to study abusive or dysfunctional relationships from a competence perspective. Recently he has studied obsessive relational intrusion (ORI) and stalking. In ORI and stalking situations, the intruder's motivation is at odds with the motivation of the victim. Specifically the intruder is wishing to begin, escalate, or continue a relationship with the victim, who does not agree with the relationship definition that the intruder is operating under. Their interactions, then, are really "arguments" over the very definition of the relationship. The intruders may perceive themselves to be "competent" within what they consider the relationship to be, while victims may respond in ways they believe to be "competent" within their definition. Spitzberg's research with his colleagues has begun to identify the profile of ORI, which may signal the development of stalking. Such a profile could assist relationship partners to see the stalking coming and remove themselves from a relationship before it becomes dangerous. Recently, Spitzberg has expanded his ORI work to examine the new phenomenon of "cyber-stalking."

Whether the situation is a first date or a job interview, a conflict with a roommate or an intimate discussion of your feelings, Spitzberg believes it is important that others perceive you to be competent. For some of Spitzberg's publications on competence, see Spitzberg & Duran (1995) and Spitzberg (2000). ∎

then she will be motivated to communicate in ways that are likely to be seen as competent.

The combination of our knowledge, skills, and motivation leads us to perform competently in our encounters with others. The rest of this book is aimed at helping you increase the likelihood that you will be perceived as competent. In the pages that follow you will learn about theories of interpersonal communication that can increase your knowledge and your motivation. You will also find how to perform specific skills, and you will be provided with opportunities to practice them. Through this practice you can increase the likelihood that you can actually perform these skills during conversations.

Understanding the Concepts and Developing Skills that Lead to Competence

Throughout this book we will describe skills that you can draw upon to help you become more competent as a communicator. These skills are based on interpersonal communication theories and research. Understanding this knowledge base is critical if you are to become more competent in interpersonal settings. So we will be introducing you to important concepts and theories that will lay a foundation for skill development. By understanding the concepts and theories, you will be better prepared to know when, where, and how to apply specific skills to the communication situations you encounter. Further, by understanding why certain behaviors and skills are effective, you will be better equipped to improvise and creatively use the skills in unfamiliar and ambiguous situations. We will also point out some of the more recent research findings that relate to the theories, concepts, and skills that we discuss. Communication scholars are continually studying interpersonal behavior, and we continue to learn more about how people interact and what specific behaviors, messages, and strategies help to develop and maintain relationships.

Although each skill can be used in a variety of settings and all skills contribute to perceptions of competence, we have grouped the skills into diagnostic categories so that you may review the skills more easily when you are searching for help with improving a particular aspect of your communication repertoire. These five categories are as follows:

1. **Message-formation skills** increase the accuracy and clarity of the messages you send.

2. **Conversational-climate skills** increase the likelihood that you and your partner will develop a supportive relationship in which you trust each other.

3. **Listening-for-understanding skills** increase the likelihood that you will be able to understand the meaning of another person.

4. **Empathic-response skills** increase the likelihood that you will be able to understand and respond to the emotional experiences of another person.

5. **Disclosure skills** increase the likelihood that you will share your ideas and feelings in an honest and sensitive manner.

Super Skill: Behavioral Flexibility

Even if you develop the ability to use all of the skills described in this textbook, there is a larger skill that encompasses use of all the others: **behavioral flexibility.** With behavioral flexibility you can effectively use a variety of communication skills during an interaction and appropriately modify your behavior in accordance with the feedback that is received. In other words, behavioral flexibility is based on an analysis of the situation; it means that you are capable of performing a wide range of interpersonal communication skills and that you are good at making decisions about what skills to use in what situations and able to modify your communication when things are not going well. We can break behavioral flexibility into several steps.

Behavioral flexibility—analyzing a communication situation and adapting your use of skills to fit the situation.

First, you must make a prediction about what type of communication would be appropriate for a particular situation. Second, you enact or use that type of communication. Third, you pay attention to how the other person is reacting. In other words, you use the feedback the other person is giving you. Fourth, you either change your communication based on the feedback or not. If the feedback tells you that your original communication is not working, then you should modify your communication somewhat or change to another type of communication. If the feedback tells you that your original communication is working well, then you can continue the same type of communication. Basically, you use these steps over and over to achieve behavioral flexibility. The rest of this book will teach you how to be capable of performing a wide range of interpersonal communication skills. It will also give you information to help you decide whether or not a skill is working effectively. But it is up to you to pay attention to feedback and to use it to influence your subsequent communication.

Let's look at a concrete example of behavioral flexibility. Imagine that Mary Lou starts sharing many of her problems with Grace, just as Grace is about to leave to go to the library. Based on many of the factors we have already discussed, Grace must make many decisions about her communication in this situation. She should analyze whether this location is the best physical context for such a sensitive inter-action, whether her relationship with Mary Lou is more important than a visit to the library at this time, whether past history with Mary Lou indicates that this is a serious or routine situation for Mary Lou, and whether Grace herself is in the best psychological state to help Mary Lou right now.

If Grace decides to stay and interact with Mary Lou, she has many choices about what to say and how to behave. Should she merely listen and be a sounding board? Should she offer messages of comfort? Should she disclose her own feelings and experiences with related problems? Should she offer advice? Should she offer Mary Lou a temporary escape from her problems by suggesting a fun activity the two could do together? As part of behavioral flexibility, Grace must decide what communication strategies and skills she thinks are best for this situation. Suppose she starts to offer comforting, supportive messages, but she receives feedback that Mary Lou wants her advice about a problem. In that case, Grace should be adaptable, moving to a different communication strategy or skill. With each new interpersonal skill she tries, Grace must analyze whether that skill is effective or not while adapting to what the situation requires, within the bounds of appropriateness and her own needs.

Some of the skills presented in this book are universal. Others, which are grounded in the dominant cultural system of the United States, may seem odd to you if you are from a different cultural background. Throughout the text you will notice that we try to point out how cultural differences may affect skill usage. We invite you to be active in this process and to think about and discuss in class any observations, insights, and concerns that you have about the appropriateness and effectiveness of these skills for communicating in other cultures with which you are familiar.

Learning to use new skills is difficult. You must not only understand the skills but also become comfortable using them in real-life situations. Improving commu-nication skills is like learning a new hobby or sport. If you are learning to play golf, for instance, you will know lots of techniques that feel uncomfortable at first. You will find it difficult to know what skill to use when or how to use the techniques smoothly and effortlessly. The more you practice, the easier it becomes to use a skill smoothly and with little conscious effort. Because some of the communication skills may not be in your repertoire now, as you work on them you are likely to feel awkward and to see the skills as creating messages that are unrealistic or "phony" sounding. Communication skills must be practiced until they feel comfortable and automatic.

Writing Communication Improvement Goal Statements

You are unlikely to master all of these skills during a single course. Becoming competent in our communication is a lifelong journey. This course will be one opportunity to focus your energy on learning about communication and working to improve your skillfulness. If you want to get the most from this course, we suggest that you set personal goals to improve specific skills in your own interpersonal communication repertoire. One way we recommend that you do this is to commit to specific goals by writing formal communication improvement plans.

Before you can set goals or write communication improvement goal statements, you must analyze your current communication skills repertoire and determine where you can make improvement. We recommend that after you have studied and practiced using the skills in each chapter of the book, you choose the one or two that you think would help you the most. Once you have identified these, you should write a communication improvement goal statement.

1. State the problem. Start by stating a communication problem that you have. For example: "Problem: Even though my boss consistently gives all the interesting tasks to co-workers, I haven't spoken up because I'm not very good at describing my feelings."

2. State the specific goal. A goal is *specific* if it is measurable and you know when you have achieved it. For example, to deal with the problem just stated, you might write, "Goal: To describe to my boss my feelings about task assignments."

3. Outline a specific procedure for reaching the goal. To develop a plan for reaching your goal, first consult the chapter that covers the skill you wish to hone. Then translate the general steps recommended in the chapter to your specific situation. This step is critical because successful behavioral change requires that you state your objective in terms of specific behaviors you can adopt or modify. For example: "Procedure: I will practice the steps of describing feelings. (1) I will identify the specific feeling I am experiencing. (2) I will encode accurately the emotion I am feeling. (3) I will include what has triggered the feeling. (4) I will own the feeling as mine. (5) I will then put that procedure into operation when I am talking with my boss."

4. Devise a method of determining when the goal has been reached. A good goal is measurable, and the fourth part of your goal-setting effort is to determine your minimum requirements for knowing when you have achieved a given goal. For example: "Test of Achieving Goal: This goal will be considered achieved when I have described my feelings to my boss on the next occasion when he bypasses me for an interesting assignment."

At the end of each chapter you will be challenged to develop a goal statement related to the material presented. Figure 1.2 provides another example of a communication improvement plan, this one relating to a public-speaking problem.

Once you have written a communication improvement goal statement, you may want to present it to someone who will witness your commitment and serve as a consultant, coach, and support person. This gives you someone to talk with about your progress. You might choose to form a partnership with a classmate from this course, with each one serving as witness and consultant for the other. When one of your goals relates to a particular relationship you have with another person, you should also consider telling that person about your goal. If that person knows what you are trying to do, he or she may be willing to help. If you have a consultant, you might meet with this person periodically to assess your progress, troubleshoot problems, and develop additional procedures for reaching your goal.

Figure 1.2 Communication Improvement Plan

GOAL STATEMENT

Problem: I have developed the bad habit of ending sentences with "you know." This has become noticeable and results in others perceiving me as less self-assured. I tend to use this language when the person with whom I am speaking is not providing enough verbal feedback. I need to become aware of when I am using this phrase and consciously choose to avoid saying it.

Goal: To improve my message formation skills by avioding the overuse of "you know" by specifically requesting feedback.

Procedure: I will monitor my messages for excessive use of "you know." When I detect a problem I will use the skill of questioning to get direct feedback from the receiver.

Test of Acheiving Goal: This goal will be considered achieved when I am aware of excessive "you knows" and able to reduce my usage by directly requesting feedback.

Summary

We have defined interpersonal communication as the process through which people create and manage their relationships, exercising mutual responsibility in creating meaning.

Interpersonal communication is important because it helps us to meet five basic functions: to meet our social/psychological needs, achieve goals, develop our sense of self, acquire information, and influence others.

Interpersonal communication is based on five components: participants assume roles of senders and receivers, who function in a variety of contexts, to form and exchange messages, that are transmitted through sensory channels, the meaning of which can be affected by external, internal, and semantic noise, and are responded to through receiver feedback. Five principles underlie our interpersonal communication. (1) Interpersonal communication is purposeful. (2) Interpersonal communication is continuous. (3) Interpersonal communication is relational, negotiating the power and affection between people. Relational definitions can be complementary or symmetrical. (5) Interpersonal communication is irreversible.

Ethics is a set of moral principles that may be held by a society, a group, or an individual. When we communicate, we make choices with ethical implications involving truthfulness and honesty, integrity, fairness, respect, and responsibility. These and other issues are dramatized in Ethical Interaction boxes at the end of each chapter.

Diversity, the variations between and among people, affects nearly every aspect of the communication process we have just discussed. Certainly the most widely discussed aspect of diversity is culture, but diversity also encompasses differences among people based on sex, age, class, physical characteristics, and sexual orientation. The "Diverse Voices" feature in various chapters provides a different sort of learning about diversity and interpersonal communication processes.

A primary goal of this course is to become a more competent interpersonal communicator. Competence is the impression that our communication behavior is both appropriate and effective in a given relationship. It involves increasing knowledge, skills, and motivation. Five categories of skills are message-formation, conversational-climate, listening-for-understanding, empathic-response, and disclosure skills. Behavioral flexibility is a super-skill needed in the enactment of all other skills.

These skills can be learned, developed, and improved. You can enhance your learning this term by writing goal statements to systematically improve your skills repertoire.

Chapter Resources

Key Words

Interpersonal communication, *p. 3*	**Semantic noise,** *p. 8*
Participants, *p. 6*	**Feedback,** *p. 9*
Context, *p. 6*	**Complementary exchanges,** *p. 11*
Physical context, *p. 6*	**Symmetrical exchanges,** *p. 11*
Social context, *p. 6*	**Ethics,** *p. 11*
Historical context, *p. 7*	**Truthfulness and honesty,** *p. 13*
Psychological context, *p. 7*	**Moral dilemma,** *p. 13*
Cultural context, *p. 7*	**Integrity,** *p. 13*
Messages, *p. 7*	**Fairness,** *p. 13*
Meaning, *p. 7*	**Respect,** *p. 14*
Symbols, *p. 7*	**Responsibility,** *p. 14*
Encoding, *p. 8*	**Diversity,** *p. 14*
Decoding, *p. 8*	**Culture,** *p. 14*
Channels, *p. 8*	**Communication competence,** *p. 16*
Noise, *p. 8*	**Skills,** *p. 18*
External noise, *p. 8*	**Behavioral flexibility,** *p. 21*
Internal noise, *p. 8*	

Skill Practice

Skill Practice exercises challenge you to master the material you have read in this chapter. For additional Skill Practice activities, visit our website at http://www.oup.com/us/interact

IDENTIFYING COMMUNICATION ELEMENTS

For the following episode identify the contextual factors, participant differences, channels, messages, noise, and feedback.

Jessica and her daughter Rita are shopping. As they walk through an elegant boutique, Rita, who is feeling particularly happy, sees a blouse she wants. With a look of great anticipation and excitement, Rita says, "Look at this, Mom—it's beautiful. Can I try it on?" Jessica, who is worried about the cost, frowns, shrugs her shoulders, and says hesitantly, "Well—yes—I guess so." Rita, noticing her mother's hesitation, continues, "And it's marked down to twenty-seven dollars!" Jessica relaxes, smiles, and says, "Yes, it is attractive—try it on. If it fits, let's buy it."

Inter-Act with Media

C I N E M A

Alexander Payne (Director). (2004). *Sideways.* Paul Giamatti, Thomas Haden Church, Virginia Madsen, Sandra Oh.

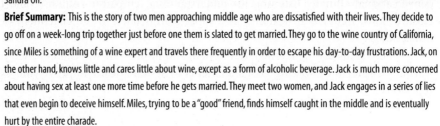

> **Brief Summary:** This is the story of two men approaching middle age who are dissatisfied with their lives. They decide to go off on a week-long trip together just before one them is slated to get married. They go to the wine country of California, since Miles is something of a wine expert and travels there frequently in order to escape his day-to-day frustrations. Jack, on the other hand, knows little and cares little about wine, except as a form of alcoholic beverage. Jack is much more concerned about having sex at least one more time before he gets married. They meet two women, and Jack engages in a series of lies that even begin to deceive himself. Miles, trying to be a "good" friend, finds himself caught in the middle and is eventually hurt by the entire charade.

> **IPC Concepts:** This is an excellent case study of the communication process. It illustrates the ways in which communicators can deceive others in order to serve a wide variety of psychological needs. The film also demonstrates how context can alter how we behave, our perceptions of self and others, and the effect our messages can have on other people.

WHAT'S ON THE WEB

Donald Clark, Leadership Communication.

http://www.nwlink.com/~donclark/leader/leadcom.html

Brief Summary: This site offers an excellent overview of the entire communication process. There are tips aimed at interpersonal applications as well as other forms of communication.

IPC Concepts: The site illustrates every aspect of the process, with special details on barriers, listening, feedback, and nonverbal communication.

Peter K. Gerlach, *Map Your Communication Sequences: Learn What You're Doing Now, and Your Options for Improving It.*

http://sfhelp.org/02/evc-maps.htm

Brief Summary: The site offers a series of exchanges between Jack and Jill and between Jack and Marsha. The exchanges provide opportunities to learn about mapping communication cycles.

IPC Concepts: The site offers concrete examples of a number of concepts in the communication process, such as feelings, needs, thoughts, attitudes, and inner conflict as they function in the process of message creation and in relation to our response to messages.

forming and using social perceptions

After you have read this chapter, you should be able to answer these questions:

- What is perception?

- How does the mind select, organize, and interpret information?

- What is the self-concept, and how is it formed?

- What is social construction of the self?

- What is self-monitoring?

- What is self-esteem, and how is it developed?

- How do our self-concept and self-esteem affect our communication with others?

- What affects how accurately we perceive others?

- What methods can we use to improve the accuracy of social perception?

> As Dwayne and Miguel are leaving work one day, Dwayne comments: "This job is getting to me. There are so many pointless rules. They watch our every move and treat us like we are dumb. I'm going to start looking for a better job."
>
> "Really?" replies Miguel. "I like the job. It pays well, the hours aren't bad, it's close to home, and I like the work. I think this is a fine job."

Have you and a friend ever seen the same situation in two totally different ways? How can two people come to have such different takes on the same situation? Why are the views of Dwayne and Miguel so different? They work in the same job, but carry away different perceptions. Because much of the meaning we share with others is based on our perceptions, a careful study of interpersonal communications begins with understanding the perceptual process and social perceptions.

In this chapter we describe the basic process of perception. Then we examine how the perceptions we have about ourselves are formed and changed. Next we explain how we perceive others. Finally, we discuss how you can increase the accuracy of your self-perception as well as your perceptions of others. As you will see, perception is a foundation piece in both our own communication and our interpretation of the communication of others.

The Perception Process

Perception—the process of selectively attending to information and assigning meaning to it.

Perception is the process of selectively attending to information and assigning meaning to it. At times our perceptions of the world, other people, and ourselves agree with the perceptions of others. At other times our perceptions are significantly different from the perceptions of other people. For each person, perception becomes reality. In other words, what one person sees, hears, and interprets is real and considered true by that person. Another person who may see, hear, and interpret something entirely different from the same situation will regard that different perception as real and true. So when our perceptions are different from those with whom we interact, sharing meaning becomes more challenging.

Your brain selects the information it receives from your senses, organizes the information, and then interprets it.

Attention and Selection

Although we are subject to a constant barrage of sensory stimuli, we focus attention on relatively little of it. How we choose depends in part on our needs, interests, and expectations.

Needs. We are likely to pay attention to information that meets our biological and psychological needs. When you go to class, how well in tune you are to what is being discussed is likely to depend on whether you believe the information is important to you—that is, does it meet a personal need?

Interests. We are likely to pay attention to information that pertains to our interests. For instance, you may not even recognize that music is playing in the background until you find yourself suddenly listening to some "old favorite." Similarly, when we are really interested in a person, we are more likely to pay attention to what that person is saying.

Expectations. Finally, we are likely to see what we expect to see and to ignore information that violates our expectations. Take a quick look at the phrases in the triangles in Figure 2.1.

If you have never seen these triangles, you probably read "Paris in the springtime," "Once in a lifetime," and "Bird in the hand." But if you reexamine the words, you will see that what you perceived was not exactly what is written. Do you now see the repeated words? It is easy to miss the repeated word because we don't *expect* to see the word repeated.

Organization of Stimuli

Even though our attention and selection process limits the stimuli our brain must process, the absolute number of discrete stimuli we attend to at any one moment is still substantial. Our brains use certain principles to arrange these stimuli to make sense out of them. Two of the most common principles we use are simplicity and pattern.

Simplicity. If the stimuli we attend to are very complex, the brain simplifies the stimuli into some commonly recognized form. Based on a glance of what someone is wearing, how she is standing, and the expression on her face, we may perceive her as "a successful businesswoman," "a flight attendant," or "a soccer mom." Similarly, we simplify the verbal messages we receive. So, for example, Tony might walk out of his hour-long performance review meeting with his boss in which the boss described four of Tony's strengths and three areas for improvement and say to Jerry, his co-worker, "Well, I better shape up or I'm going to get fired!"

Figure 2.1

A sensory test of expectation

Patterns—sets of characteristics that differentiate some things from others used to group items having the same characteristics.

Pattern. A second principle the brain uses when organizing information is to find **patterns,** sets of characteristics that differentiate some things from others used to group items having the same characteristics. A pattern helps us to interpret stimuli. For example, when you see a crowd of people, instead of perceiving each individual human being, you may focus on the characteristic of sex and "see" men and women, or you may focus on age and "see" children, teens, adults, and seniors.

In our interactions with others we try to find patterns that will enable us to interpret and respond to their behavior. For example, each time Jason and Bill encounter Sara, she hurries over and begins an animated conversation. Yet when Jason is alone and runs into Sara, she barely says "Hi." After a while Jason may detect a pattern to Sara's behavior. She is warm and friendly when Bill is around and not so friendly when Bill is absent.

Interpretation of Stimuli

As the brain selects and organizes the information it receives from the senses, it also interprets the information by assigning meaning to it. Look at these three sets of numbers. What do you make of them?

A. 631 7348

B. 285 37 5632

C. 4632 7364 2596 2174

In each of these sets, your mind looked for clues to give meaning to the numbers. Because you use similar patterns of numbers every day, you probably interpret A as an in-area telephone number. How about B? A likely interpretation is a Social Security number. And C? People who use credit cards may interpret this set as a credit card number.

Because two people are unlikely to select the same stimuli, or to organize stimuli in the same way, they are also not likely to arrive at the same interpretation of events or other people. Yet the unique portrait we derive from a situation directly affects our communication and our behavior. For instance, suppose Sal and Daniel pass Tito on the way to eat lunch. Even though they both greet him, Tito walks past without saying a word. Sal notices that Tito looks troubled, is walking quickly, and is carrying a load of books. Daniel notices that Tito glanced at them quickly, grimaced, and then averted his eyes. "Boy," says Sal, "I guess Tito must really be worried about the paper that is due in history." "You think so?" Daniel replies. "I'd say that he's still angry at me for hitting on Carmen."

Social perception—a set of processes by which people perceive themselves and others (also known as **social cognition**).

While general perception processes are used to make sense of both physical and social phenomena, the study of **social perception,** or **social cognition,** has focused on the specific processes by which people perceive themselves and others. In the study of social perception, particular emphasis is placed on how people interpret their own and others' behavior, how people categorize themselves and others, and how people form impressions of themselves and others. Since social perceptions form the basis of our interpersonal communication, understanding them is critical to interpersonal competence.

In the remainder of this chapter we will apply this basic information about perception to the study of perceptions of self and others in our communication.

Self-concept—self-identity; the idea or mental image that we have about our skills, our abilities, our knowledge, our competencies, and our personality.

Self-esteem—our overall evaluation of our competence and personal worthiness.

Perceptions of Self: Self-Concept and Self-Esteem

Self-concept and self-esteem are the two self-perceptions that have the greatest impact on how we communicate. **Self-concept** is one's self-identity (Baron & Byrne, 2000, p. 160). It is the idea or mental image that you have about your skills, your abilities, your knowledge, your competencies, and your personality. **Self-esteem** is your overall evaluation of your competence and personal worthiness (based on Mruk, 1999, p. 26). In this section we explain how we form our self concept and how we develop our self-esteem to understand who we are and how we determine whether what we are is good. Then we describe what determines how well our self-perceptions match others' perceptions of us and the role these self-perceptions play when we communicate with others.

Forming and Maintaining a Self-Concept

How do we learn what our skills, abilities, knowledge, competencies, and personality are? Our self-concept comes from the unique interpretations about ourselves that we make based on our experience and from others' reactions and responses to us.

If we form impressions about ourselves based on our own perceptions gained through our experiences, how does practice affect our perceptions about how well we will perform?

Self-Perception. We form impressions about ourselves based on our own perceptions. Through our experiences, we develop our own sense of our skills, our abilities, our knowledge, our competencies, and our personality. For example, if you perceive that it is easy for you to strike up conversations with strangers and that you enjoy chatting with them, you may conclude that you are outgoing or friendly (Kenny, 1994, p. 220).

We place great emphasis on the first experience we have with a particular phenomenon (Centi, 1981). For instance, someone who is rejected in his first try at dating may perceive himself to be unattractive to the opposite sex.

If additional experiences produce results similar to the first experience, the initial perception will be strengthened. But even when the first experience is not repeated, it is likely to take more than one contradictory additional experience to change the original perception.

When we have positive experiences, we are likely to believe we possess the personal characteristics that we associate with that experience, and these characteristics become part of our picture of who we are. So if Sonya quickly debugs a computer program that Jackie has struggled with, Sonya is more likely to incorporate "competent problem solver" into her self-concept. Her positive experience confirms that she has that skill, so it is reinforced as part of her self-concept. Likewise, if our experiences have been negative, we are likely to describe ourselves differently. For example, when David began school, he found that he disliked arithmetic and could not understand math concepts as quickly as other children. As time went on, he continued to struggle in mathematics. If asked to describe his strengths, David would be unlikely to say that he is good at math.

Reactions and Responses of Others. In addition to our self-perceptions, our self-concept is formed and maintained by how significant others react and respond to us (Rayner, 2001, p. 43). For example, if during a brainstorming session at work, one of your co-workers tells you "You're really a creative thinker," you may decide that this comment fits your image of who you are. And as Rayner suggests, such comments are especially powerful in affecting your self-perception if you respect the person making the comment. Moreover, the power of such comments is increased when the praise is immediate rather than delayed (Hattie, 1992, p. 251).

We use other people's comments as a check on our own self-descriptions. They serve to validate, reinforce, or alter our perception of who and what we are. Some people have very rich or strong self-concepts; they can describe numerous skills, abilities, types of knowledge, competencies, and personality characteristics that they possess. Others have weak self-concepts; they cannot describe their own skills, abilities, knowledge, competencies, or personality characteristics. The stronger our self-concept, the better we know and understand who we are and the better we are able to cope with the challenges we will face as we interact with others.

Our self-concept begins to form early in life, and information we receive from our families shapes our self-concept (Demo, 1987). One of the major responsibilities that family members have is to talk and act in ways that will help develop accurate and strong self-concepts in other family members. For example, the mother who says "Roberto, your room looks very neat; you are very organized," or the brother who comments "Kisha, lending Tomika five dollars really helped her out; you are very generous," is helping a family member to recognize an important part of the individual's personality.

Unfortunately, in some families members do not fulfill these responsibilities. Sometimes family members actually do real damage to each other's self-image, especially to the developing self-images of children. Communicating blame, calling names, and repeatedly pointing out another's shortcomings are particularly damaging behaviors.

Self-Monitoring

In order to decide what aspects of oneself to use in a certain situation, a person needs to make predictions about and to analyze the actual situation to determine the appropriate roles to play. **Self- monitoring** is an internal process of being aware of yourself and how you are coming across to others. It involves being sensitive to other people's expressions and reactions (feedback) and using this information in deciding how to behave. In other words, it is a process of observing and regulating your own behavior in relation to the response of others. Self-monitoring goes on inside your head, so others will not observe you monitoring your communication.

Have you ever interacted with others who do little self-monitoring? They tend to say and do the wrong things because they are not paying attention to how they are coming across. The inability to self-monitor leads to inappropriate behavior in a situation. It is important to monitor one's thoughts, emotions, and behaviors.

Think of the times when we consciously monitor the role we are playing in a situation. This may occur in an unfamiliar situation such as a first date or a job interview. Because we are not sure of how to act in an unfamiliar situation, there is more uncertainty and more analysis about how to present ourselves. When we are communicating in an unfamiliar situation, we may be saying to ourselves things like "Why did I make that silly remark?" or "I'm not coming across well here," or "I think he liked that comment I just made." We've all had these silent conversations with ourselves. When we find ourselves engaging in this kind of mental self-talk, then we are practicing the skill of self-monitoring. Even in familiar and comfortable situations, skilled communicators should engage in some degree of self-monitoring. Being self-aware and attentive to others' feedback is part of the important skill of behavioral flexibility, which we described in Chapter 1 as necessary to all communication interactions.

Self-monitoring—an internal process of observing and regulating your own behavior based on others' responses.

observe & analyze

Who Am I?

Write a short essay on the subject "Who am I?" To begin this task, list all the skills, abilities, knowledges, competencies, and personality characteristics that you believe describe you. To generate this list, think of the skills, abilities, types of knowledge, competencies, and personality characteristics that describe how you see yourself. To begin, try completing the sentences "I am skilled at …," "I have the ability to …," "I know things about …," "I am competent at doing …," and "One part of my personality is that I am…." Do this over and over again. List as many characteristics in each category as you can think of.

Then develop a second list, only this time, complete the following statements: "Other people believe that I am skilled at …," "Other people believe that I have the ability to …," "Other people believe that I know things about…," "Other people believe that I am competent at doing …," and "One part of my personality is that other people believe that I am…." Again, complete these statements over and over, as many times as you can.

Compare your two lists of self-perceptions and others' perceptions. How are they similar? Where are they different? Do you understand why they differ? Are your lists long or short? Why do you suppose that is? Reflect on how your own interpretations of your experiences and what others have told you about you have influenced your self-concept. Now organize the lists you have created, perhaps finding a way to group characteristics. Use this information to write an essay titled "Who I Am, and How I Know This." ■

Developing and Maintaining Self-Esteem

You'll recall that our *self-esteem* is our overall evaluation of our competence and personal worthiness—it is our positive or negative evaluation of our self-concept. Our evaluation of our personal worthiness is rooted in our values and develops over time as a result of our experiences. As Mruk (1999, p. 27) points out, self-esteem is not just how well or poorly we do things (self-concept), but the importance or value we place on what we do well or poorly. For instance, as part of Chad's self-concept, he believes he is physically strong. But if he doesn't believe that physical strength or other characteristics he possesses are worthwhile or valuable characteristics to have, then he will not have high self-esteem. Mruk explains that it takes both the perception of having a characteristic and a personal belief that the characteristic is of positive value to produce high self-esteem.

When we successfully use our skills, abilities, or knowledge in worthwhile endeavors, we raise our self-esteem. When we are unsuccessful in using our skills, abilities, and/or when we use them in unworthy endeavors, we lower our self-esteem.

It is important to notice that self-esteem depends on what each individual views as worthwhile. Yet we know that what we believe to be valuable is based both on our personal ideas and on the ideas, morals, and values of the society or group with which we identify. In the dominant culture of the United States, as elsewhere, some skills, abilities, knowledge, competencies, and personality characteristics are valued more than others. People who perceive that they have these characteristics are likely to have higher self-esteem than those who have other characteristics that are less valued. For example, since education is valued, people who finish high school and graduate from college raise their self-esteem. Likewise, if people who accept the dominant culture's valuing of education drop out of school, they will lower their self-esteem. In fact, research consistently finds high correlation between academic achievement and self-concept (Rayner, 2001, p. 42).

Social Construction of Self

We create multiple selves in an ongoing manner through our relationships with many different people. All people progressively modify and reinvent their public personas. We create different characters to respond to different situations, and we change ourselves in the process. We socially construct ourselves through the roles we enact. A **role** is a pattern of learned behaviors that people use to meet the per-

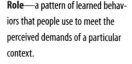

Role—a pattern of learned behaviors that people use to meet the perceived demands of a particular context.

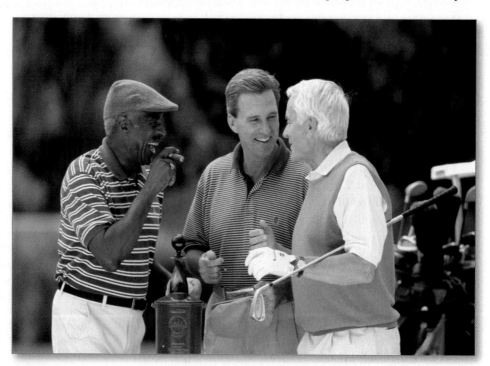

We present our self-image and self-esteem to others through the roles we enact.

Michael L. Hecht, Professor of Communication Arts and Sciences in the College of the Liberal Arts, Pennsylvania State University, on
Interethnic Communication and Ethnic Identity

Michael L. Hecht's passion

is people. His native curiosity has led him to devote his life to scholarly endeavors that help us understand how people from different ethnic backgrounds interact in ways that they perceive are satisfying and effective. When he was in graduate school many scholars were interested in studying ineffective communication. But Hecht, an optimist, was more interested in understanding what led people to feel satisfied with a conversation. For his Ph.D. dissertation at the University of Illinois, Hecht developed a theory to help us understand and to measure communication satisfaction. His theory and measures are widely used today. But Hecht's contribution to our understanding of communication satisfaction and effectiveness did not end when he received his degree. Instead, it provided the foundation from which he continues to explore what leads people to be effective and satisfied with their conversations.

As a Jewish American, Hecht has always been interested in intergroup communication. His earliest work in this area examined perceptions of conversational satisfaction in conversations between African Americans and European Americans. After graduate school, Hecht teamed up with a grad school contemporary and friend, Sidney Ribeau (who is now president of Bowling Green State University), to study communication satisfaction between African Americans and European Americans. At that time, communication satisfaction had been studied only from a European American perspective.

Hecht and Ribeau discovered that African Americans and European Americans abide by different communication rules. Thus when African Americans and European Americans interact, one party is likely to violate the communication rules expected by the other. These rule violations make conversations between people from these two groups less likely to be perceived as satisfying.

Hecht is also fascinated with how people form and communicate their personal identities. Recently, he formulated the communication theory of identity. The basic premise of this theory is that identity is a communicative process. Hecht and his co-authors believe that there are four different "frames" or perspectives from which we can understand identity.

First, we can view identity through a personal frame. This would suggest that identity is based on your self-concept or self-image derived from your own feelings, self-knowledge, or spiritual sense of self. A second way to view identity is to see that identity is enactment; that is, you act out who you are as you talk. During interaction with others, we consciously and unconsciously communicate our identity to others. Third, you can view identity from a relational perspective. In this light, you negotiate your identity within a particular relationship. You may interact differently in a relationship where you are a parent than in a relationship where you are a child. In addition, while talking with a parent, a child works out what it means to her to be a "child." The relational perspective also allows us to notice how relationships take on identities themselves. When people get married they often find that others see them as a couple or that they perceive themselves to be a couple. As a couple, their identity is different from what it was when they were not "being a couple." Finally, according to this theory, we can think of identities from a communal frame. Groups of people have identities that bond them to one another. These communities develop certain behaviors, which they teach to new members and expect members to enact. Hecht and his colleagues suggest that if we want to understand identities, we must look at all four levels in combination. I work out who I am (personal identity) by trying out certain behaviors as I interact (enactment) with others in my relationships (relational). In part, how I act is based on the behavior that is expected of members of those groups to which I see myself belonging (communal).

Recently Hecht's research has combined his interest in understanding identity theory with a desire to use his research to help others. So Hecht has worked with an interdisciplinary team to identify strategies (refuse, explain, avoid, and leave) that teens use to resist invitations to use drugs. An educational program using these strategies was developed for groups of ethnically diverse junior high students. Early results suggest that this approach is slowing the rate at which students begin using drugs. In addition, the study has provided evidence that Latino and African American teens who are proud of their ethnic identity are less prone to drug use. This finding is in keeping with the communication theory of identity.

Although it is common for faculty to invite graduate students to work with them on projects, Hecht finds doing research with undergraduate students to be especially rewarding. Hecht has created undergraduate research apprenticeship programs. In the program, undergraduates receive classroom credit for becoming part of research teams. Some students make substantial contributions to projects and are invited to co-author scholarly articles.

Since his drug resistance studies are financed by large grants from outside agencies to whom he must account and report, Hecht finds himself doing more administrative work these days. Nonetheless, Professor Hecht still finds time for his first love, teaching courses in interpersonal and nonverbal communication at the undergraduate level and courses in identity and intergroup communication at the graduate level.

Hecht and his colleagues created a multicultural prevention program for seventh graders in Phoenix, and it was credited with reducing alcohol, marijuana, and tobacco use. This program is one of the few that are effective and targeted to Mexican American youth. ∎

ceived demands of a particular context. For instance, during the day you may enact the roles of "student," "brother/sister," and "sales associate."

Let's look at all the different personas or selves that one person may create and present across a few days. Ashley presents certain aspects of herself at work as a restaurant server, where she is very polite, helpful, agreeable, and attentive to others. She does not talk about herself much or use cusswords. She is confident, moves quickly, and cares about being efficient and productive. When Ashley goes out with her friends after work, she is more casual and less concerned about time. Perhaps she is louder and more boisterous. She may talk about herself more, cuss occasionally, and get into heated debate of issues and ideas. When Ashley visits her grandmother, she may act more childlike; she is cautious not to mention topics that may offend her grandmother, and she may listen more than she talks. Ashley will enact other selves at school, as a babysitter of young children, on a date, or with her siblings. Which is Ashley's real self? They all are. We are not unitary beings. Our sense of self is the total of all the selves we play and how others react to those selves. Ashley and society will create and recreate her sense of self continuously throughout her life.

Michael Hecht and his colleagues believe that our identity is developed and manifested through our communication. This communication theory of identity suggests that there are four different aspects of identity, which we work out in our transactions and relationships with others. In the "Spotlight on Scholars" feature that appeared on pages 37 and 38, you read about Michael Hecht and the communication theory of identity.

Accuracy of Self-Concept and Self-Esteem

The accuracy of our self-concept and self-esteem depends on the accuracy of our own perceptions and how we process others' perceptions of us. All of us experience success and failure, and all of us hear praise and criticism. If we are overly attentive to successful experiences and positive responses, our self-concept may become overdeveloped and our self-esteem inflated. If, however, we perceive and dwell on failures and give little value to our successes, or if we remember only the criticism we receive, our self-image may be negative and our self-esteem low. In neither case does our self-concept or self-esteem accurately reflect who we are.

Incongruence, the gap between our inaccurate self-perceptions and reality, is a problem because our perceptions of self are more likely to affect our behavior than our true abilities (Weiten, 1998, p. 491). For example, Sean may actually possess all the skills, abilities, knowledge, competencies, and personality characteristics for effective leadership, but if he doesn't perceive that he has these characteristics, he won't step forward when leadership is needed. Unfortunately, individuals tend to reinforce their self-perceptions by adjusting their behavior to conform to perceived self-conceptions. That is, people with high self-esteem tend to behave in ways that lead to more affirmation, whereas people with low self-esteem tend to act in ways that confirm the low esteem in which they hold themselves. The inaccuracy of a distorted picture of oneself is magnified through self-fulfilling prophecies and by filtering messages.

> **Incongruence**—the gap between inaccurate self-perceptions and reality.

Self-Fulfilling Prophecies. Self-fulfilling prophecies are events that happen as the result of being foretold, expected, or talked about. They may be self-created or other-imposed.

> **Self-fulfilling prophecies**—events that happen as the result of being foretold, expected, or talked about.

Self-created prophecies are those predictions you make about yourself. We often "talk ourselves into" success or failure. Researchers have found that when people expect rejection, they are more likely to behave in ways that lead others to reject them (Downey, Freitas, Michaelis, & Khouri, 2004, p. 437). For example, Stefan sees himself as quite social and able to get to know people easily; he says, "I'm going to have fun at the party tonight." As a result of his positive self-concept, Stefan looks forward to encountering strangers and, just as he predicted, makes several new acquaintances and enjoys himself. In contrast, Aaron sees himself as unskilled in establishing new relationships; he says, "I bet I'll know hardly anyone there—I'm going to have a miserable time." Because Aaron fears encountering strangers, he feels awkward about introducing himself and, just as he predicted, spends much of his time standing around alone thinking about when he can leave.

Self-esteem has an important effect on the prophecies people make. For instance, people with positive self-esteem view success positively and confidently prophesy that they can repeat successes; people with low self-esteem attribute their successes to luck and so prophesy that they will not repeat them (Hattie, 1992, p. 253).

The prophecies others make about you also affect your performance. For example, if the soccer coach tells Javier, "I can see that you have good judgment on the field. I expect you will be a field leader during games," Javier is likely to believe this and will come to act in ways that are consistent with the prophecy.

Other-created prophecies have a powerful way of changing our self-concepts. For instance, doctors report that when they tell their patients they will recover, a much higher percentage improve than when doctors are noncommittal or show doubt about recovery. In other words, a doctor's statement about a person's health seems to invoke the self-perception "healthy," which leads to real health. Similarly, there have been countless cases of teachers imposing prophecies on students that the students then lived up—or down—to. When teachers believe that their students are able, students "buy into" the expectation and succeed. A lesson to be learned from this is that we should take care what we say to others lest we place unnecessary limitations on people. For instance, in the family, a parent should avoid predicting failure for a child.

Filtering Messages. A second way that our self-perceptions can become distorted is through filtering what others say to us. We are prone to pay attention to messages that reinforce our current self-image, while messages that contradict this image may not "register" or may be downplayed. For example, suppose you prepared a fund-raising plan for your service organization. Someone comments that you're a good organizer. You may not really hear the remark, ignore it, or reply, "Anyone could have done that—it was nothing special." If, however, you think you are a good organizer, you will pay attention to the compliment and may even reinforce it by responding, "Thanks, I've had a lot of experience with organizing fund-raising campaigns and really like being able to contribute."

Changing Self-Concepts and Self-Esteem

Self-concept and self-esteem are enduring characteristics, but they can be changed. At times, comments that contradict self-prophecies will get past the filter and can begin to change the self-image. Then, the newly changed self-perceptions begin to filter other comments and are used as the basis of new self-created, self-fulfilling prophecies. So over the course of your life, your self-concept and self-esteem may change.

Certain situations seem to lend themselves to expediting this process. When people experience profound changes in their social environments, they are likely to drop their filters and absorb information that in other circumstances they would have filtered out. Life transitions can be times when we become more susceptible to dropping our filters. So, when children begin school, when teens begin the independence process, when young adults leave home, when people start new jobs or begin college, fall in love, commit to or dissolve relationships, become parents, retire, and grieve the death of someone they love, they are more likely to attend to messages that are at odds with their current self-conceptions. As a result of these new experiences, people change their picture of who they are and begin to predict new things for themselves.

The use of therapy and self-help techniques can assist in the goal of changing one's self-concept and improving self-esteem. In his analysis of numerous other research studies, Christopher Mruk (1999) found that self-esteem is increased through "hard work and practice, practice, practice—there is simply no escaping this basic existential fact" (p. 112). So why is this important? Because our self-esteem affects with whom we choose to form relationships. Researchers have found that "people with high self-esteem are more committed to partners who perceive them very favorably, while people with low self-esteem are more committed to partners who perceive them less favorably" (Leary, 2002, p. 130).

Self-Concept, Self-Esteem and Communication

Just as our self-concept and self-esteem affect how accurately we perceive ourselves, so too do they influence our communication by moderating competing internal messages in our self-talk and influencing our personal communication style.

Self-Perception Influences How We Talk to Ourselves

If we feel good about ourselves, then our self-talk is likely to be more accurate. If we have negative self-perceptions, then our self-talk is likely to be distorted and negative. People with positive self-esteem generally are better able to accurately monitor how they come across in a situation. They can be more realistic about what they are doing well and about what they are not doing well. People with negative self-esteem often overemphasize negative self-talk or, ironically, they may inflate their sense of self. To compensate for a sense of insecurity, they may tell themselves they are good at everything they do, thus showing an inability to accurately self-monitor.

Self-Perception Influences How We Talk about Ourselves with Others. If we feel good about ourselves, we are likely to communicate positively. For instance, people with a strong self-concept and higher self-esteem usually take credit for their successes. Likewise, people with healthy self-perceptions are inclined to defend their views even in the face of opposing arguments. If we feel bad about ourselves, we are likely to communicate negatively by downplaying our accomplishments.

Why do some people put themselves down regardless of what they have done? People who have low self-esteem are likely to be unsure of the value of their contributions and to expect others to view them negatively. As a result, perhaps, people with a poor self-concept or low self-esteem find it less painful to put themselves down than to hear the criticism of others. Thus, to preempt the likelihood that others will comment on their unworthiness, they do it first.

Self-Perception Affects Our Perceptions of Others. Self-image and self-esteem are important not only because of the way they moderate our self-talk, but also because they affect how we perceive others. First, the more accurate our self-image, the more accurately we are likely to perceive others. Both self-perception and perception of others start with our ability to process data accurately. Second, the higher our self-esteem, the more likely we are to see others favorably. Studies have shown that people who accept themselves as they are tend to be more accepting of others; similarly, those with low self-esteem are more likely to find fault in others. Third, our own personal characteristics influence the types of characteristics we are likely to perceive in others. For example, people who are secure tend to see others positively rather than negatively. If you recall that we respond to the world as we perceive it to be (and not necessarily as it is), you can readily see how low self-esteem can account for misunderstandings and communication breakdowns.

Self-Perception Influences How We Communicate with Others. Research demonstrates that we communicate our self-concept and our self-esteem when we interact with others (Campbell, 1990, p. 538). For instance, Jan, who has low self-esteem, may comment to her friend David, "What I did probably wasn't that important to the company, so I don't deserve a raise and won't get one." Or Troy, who is unclear about his abilities, may say, "Please go ahead and take that book. I probably wouldn't be able to understand it anyway." In contrast, people with richer self-concepts and higher self-esteem usually present themselves positively and make statements that show an expectation of acceptance. They are likely to take credit for their successes: "My suggestions helped Kappa Xi Phi recruit new members, so I think I'm likely to be asked to run for president next year." Likewise, people with healthy self-perceptions are likely to defend their views even in the face of opposing arguments. For instance, Amber might say to a critic, "You may not like my position, but I've thought this through carefully and believe that I have good reasons to support my position."

observe & analyze

Monitor Your Enacted Roles

For three days, record the various situations you experience. Describe the images you chose to enact in each. At the conclusion of this three-day observation period, write an analysis of your self-monitoring. To what extent does your communication behavior differ and remain the same across situations? What factors in a situation seem to trigger certain roles? How satisfied are you with the images or "selves" that you displayed in each role? Where were you most pleased? Least pleased? ▪

Cultural and Gender Influences

A person's culture has a strong influence on the perception process (Chen & Starosta, 1998, p. 35). In some cultures, described as individualistic, people stress the self and personal achievement. In these cultures, the individual is treated as the most important element in a social setting. In individualistic cultures, people care about self-concept, self-esteem, and self-image. The United States is considered an individualistic culture. In fact, all the information thus far in this chapter reflects an individualistic cultural perspective on perception and the self-concept. On the other hand, cultures that are considered collectivist tend to downplay the individual. Groups and social norms are more important in collectivist cultures. People are expected to be interdependent and to see themselves in terms of the group. Notions of self-concept and self-esteem have little meaning in collectivist cultures.

Similarly, men and women are socialized to view themselves differently and to value who they are based on whether their behavior corresponds to or challenges the behavior expected of their sex in their culture. There are norms of what it means to be feminine and what it means to be masculine in our society. Gender expectations in a society inevitably influence our perceptions, sense of self, social construction of self, and self-monitoring behavior. Thus, it is difficult to generalize about social perception without taking into consideration the influences of culture and gender.

Perception of Others

As you encounter others, you are faced with a number of questions: Do you have anything in common? Will they accept you? Will you be able to get along? Because this uncertainty is uncomfortable, you will try to alleviate it by finding answers to questions. Charles Berger and James Bradac (1982) suggested that **uncertainty reduction theory** explains the ways individuals monitor their social environments in order to know more about themselves and others (Littlejohn, 2002, p. 243).

Uncertainty reduction theory—explains the ways individuals monitor their social environments and come to know more about themselves and others.

We seek information about others because if we are uncertain about what they are like, we will have a difficult time predicting their behavior and the outcome of our interaction, and this uncertainty will make us uncomfortable. Many years ago, two interpersonal communication researchers, Gerald Miller and Mark Steinberg, proposed a theory about the levels of predictions we make in order to reduce uncertainty during initial interactions. Their work is still widely used today. They claimed that when we first meet someone, we don't have much information to use to make predictions. So we tend to make so-called cultural-level predictions about the person based on what we can see. We make such predictions based on stereotypes of race, sex, age, and appearance. Because these predictions are broad generalizations based on very abstract and general information, they frequently tend to be inaccurate.

As we get to know people initially, we often ask questions about the groups with which they affiliate. Getting-to-know-you conversations often involve a series of questions about each other's occupations, schools attended, neighborhoods of past and present residence, hobbies and interests. This questioning allows us to make sociological-level predictions based on others' membership groups and the roles they may play because of those memberships. These questions allow us to discover common ground between us and other people, which eases discomfort and makes our predictions more accurate.

As we come to know another person even better over time, we then can make predictions based on the unique experiences and qualities of that person. We no longer have to make predictions based on someone's appearance or group memberships. Instead, we come to know with much accuracy, though never total accuracy, how this unique person may respond in a situation. This last level of prediction is called the psychological level; and because it is based on individual differences among people rather than generalizations across large groups of people, it is the most accurate level of prediction. When we reach this level, our perceptions are most accurate, and we feel closer to and more comfortable with the other person.

First Impressions

When two people meet, both are trying to shape the first impression that they project about themselves as well as to form impressions (predictions) of the other person. **Impression management** is the process by which people consciously try to influence others' impressions of them.

Think of all the times you have carefully selected certain clothes, rehearsed in your mind what you were going to say in an upcoming encounter, and purposefully acted a certain way in order to make a good first impression on someone. People often practice impression management during a job interview, on a first date, during the first day on a new job, when appearing in court, or when making a presentation to a new audience. In trying to present a good first impression, we are paying close attention to the role we are playing and the image we are projecting. First impressions are based on how we appear and what we say, as well as the perceptions the other person forms about us. So it is not a one-way process. Neither party has total control over first impressions; instead, the parties interact as sender and receiver to jointly construct first impressions.

Researchers have found that first impressions are very powerful because they

Impression management—
the process of trying to influence others' impressions of them.

What are the individuals in this group communicating through their physical appearance, dress, and behavior?

often form the basis of whether two people will ever interact again (Hazen & Shaver, 2004). Let's assume that two people meet for the first time and there is no reason why they necessarily would have to interact again. In that case, any possible future relationship depends heavily on the first impressions and whether the pair discovered any common ground or developed any feelings of liking each other. You never get a second chance to make a good first impression. Evaluations formed during initial conversations have been found to influence long-term impressions of close relationships (Sunnafrank & Ramirez, 2004, p. 49). This means that even if you have known someone for years, the first impressions that you had of each other still influence the current relationship.

First impressions are formed not only in face-to-face communication, but in online interaction as well. People care about creating the right impression online through the timeliness of their responses, the use of chat room nicknames, and their use of appropriate vocabulary, grammar, and manners (sometimes called netiquette). Initial interaction online often begins with the question A/S/L? which asks for someone's age, sex, and location. This is a getting-to-know-you question, which allows for cultural-level predictions and the forming of first impressions. Creating personal home pages also relates to self-identity and first impressions. Creating a personal home page is an opportunity to reflect upon yourself and to think about how you want to represent yourself to the world. It is an attempt to influence others' first impressions (Thurlow, Lengel, & Tomic, 2004).

Perceptual Problems

There are many factors influencing our perceptions of others, which lead to distortions or inaccurate perceptions. Because perception is a complex process, we use shortcuts to help us focus attention, interpret information, and make predictions about others. Understanding some of the common problems involved in perceiving others is the first step toward improving our social perceptions.

Implicit Personality Theory. People develop assumptions about which physical characteristics and personality traits or behaviors are associated with another (Michener & DeLamater, 1999, p. 106). We expect certain characteristics of a person to be associated with other characteristics. Let's imagine that you have already perceived Francesca to be kind and caring. Once you have made those assumptions, you will be likely to associate other positive qualities, such as warmth and friendliness, with her. If you have perceived someone to be kind and caring, you will be unlikely to then perceive that person as cold or unfriendly. As you perceive various traits or behaviors of Francesca, initial positive perceptions will lead to more positive perceptions. The opposite is true also, since initial negative perceptions lead to more negative perceptions.

Halo Effect. Because your own implicit personality theory says that certain traits go together, you are likely to perceive that a person has a whole set of characteristics when you have actually observed only one characteristic, trait, or behavior. When you do this, your perception is exhibiting the **halo effect.** For instance, Heather sees Martina personally greeting and welcoming every person who arrives at the meeting. Heather's implicit personality theory views this behavior as a sign of the characteristic of warmth. She further associates warmth with goodness and goodness with honesty. As a result, she perceives that Martina is good and honest as well as warm. In reality, Martina may be a con artist who uses her warmth to lure people into a false sense of trust. This example demonstrates a "positive halo" (Heather assigned Martina positive characteristics). We also, however, use implicit personality theory to inaccurately impute bad characteristics. In fact, Hollman (1972) found that negative information more strongly influences our impressions of others than does positive information. So we are more likely to give others negative halos than positive halos.

Halo effects seem to occur most frequently under one or more of three conditions: (1) when the perceiver is judging traits with which he or she has limited experience, (2) when the traits have strong moral overtones, and (3) when the perception is of a person that the perceiver knows well.

Selective Perception. Selective perception is the tendency to pay attention only to what we expect to see or hear and to ignore what we don't expect to see or hear. Recall Figure 2.1 at the beginning of this chapter. Because we do not expect to read a line like "Paris in the the springtime," we do not pay attention to the repeated word. If you ask people "How many animals of each species did Moses take aboard the ark?" they are likely to say two. They expect to hear "Noah" in a question about animals in the ark, and so they may not pay attention to the trick word, "Moses."

Have you ever had the experience of buying a new type of car and then seeing that brand of car quite frequently on the road? Those cars were on the road before your purchase, but you were not noticing them. This is a classic example of selective perception. Sometimes we engage in selective perception regarding other people. For instance, if Donna sees Nick as a man with whom she would like to develop a strong relationship, she will tend to see the positive side of Nick's personality and overlook or ignore the negative side that is apparent to others. Similarly, if Dean thinks that his landlord is mean and unfair, he will ignore or disregard any acts of kindness or generosity by the landlord.

Attributions. Attributions are reasons we give for our own and others' behavior. In addition to making judgments about people, we attempt to construct reasons for why people behave as they do. According to attribution theory, what we determine—rightly or wrongly—to be the causes of others' behavior has a direct impact on our perceptions of them. For instance, suppose a co-worker with whom you had a noon luncheon date has not arrived by 12:20. If you like and respect your co-worker, you are likely to attribute his lateness to something external: an important phone call at the last minute, the need to finish a job before lunch,

Halo effect—perceiving that a person has a whole set of characteristics when you have actually observed only one characteristic, trait, or behavior.

Selective Perception—the tendency to pay attention only to what we expect to see or hear.

Attributions—reasons we give for others' behavior.

or an accident that may have occurred. If you are not particularly fond of your co-worker, you are likely to attribute his lateness to something internal: forgetfulness, inconsiderateness, or malicious intent. In either case, your causal attribution further affects your perception of the person. Causal attributions may be so strong that they resist contrary evidence. If you do not particularly care for the person, when he does arrive and explains that he had an emergency long-distance phone call, you are likely to disbelieve the reason or discount the urgency of the call.

Researchers have found a general tendency to make different kinds of attributions based on whether we are trying to explain our own or another person's behavior. When making judgments about our own positive behavior, we tend to make **dispositional attributions** or attribute causes related to the person. When judging someone else's behavior, we tend to make **situational attributions,** or attribute causes based on aspects of the situation (Hendrick, 2004). For instance, we may explain a co-worker's promotion in terms of the being in the right place at the right time, luck, or the supervisor's positive view of the co-worker. We would tend to explain our own promotion, on the other hand, in terms of our own intelligence, dedication, experience, or productivity.

Dispositional attributions— attributing causes related to a person.

Situational attributions— attributing causes based on aspects of a situation.

Consistency. People have a need to eliminate contradictions in their perceptions of a phenomenon. Sometimes we force consistency to make sure that several of our perceptions are in agreement with each other. Imagine that Leah does not like Jill, the office assistant at the car dealership where they both work. If Jill supplies some missing information on a form that Leah has given her to process, Leah is likely to perceive Jill's behavior as interference. If Leah likes Jill, however, she would likely perceive the very same behavior as positive—Jill has been helpful. In each case, the perception of "supplying missing information" is shaped by the need to have consistency. It is consistent to regard someone we like as doing favors for us. It is inconsistent to regard people we don't like as doing favors for us. So we impose consistency on our perceptions by interpreting a helpful act as interference.

Prejudice. According to Jones (2002), when we hold positive or negative attitudes or judgments directed toward people simply because they happen to be members of a specific group, we are exhibiting **prejudice** (p. 4). Negative prejudices can lead to **discrimination**, which is negative action toward a social group or its members on account of group membership (Jones, 2002, p. 8). Prejudice deals with attitudes, while discrimination involves negative action. For instance, when Laura discovers that Wasif, a man she has just met, is a Muslim, she may hold a negative attitude, a prejudice, perhaps assuming that he is a chauvinist who will not treat a woman as an equal. If she acts on her prejudice, she may discriminate against Wasif by refusing to partner with him on a class project. So her prejudice distorts her perception and affects her behavior. In this case, Wasif may never get the chance to be known for the person he really is, and Laura may have lost an opportunity to work with the best student in class.

Prejudice—a positive or negative attitude or judgment directed toward people simply because they happen to be members of a specific group.

Discrimination—a negative action toward a social group or its members on account of group membership.

There are certain common prejudices that are based on people's tendencies to view their own behaviors based on race, culture, sex, age, or physical ability are superior to others' behaviors. **Racism, ethnocentrism, sexism, ageism, able-ism,** and other "-isms" occur when a powerful group believes its members

Racism, ethnocentrism, sexism, ageism, able-ism—beliefs that the behaviors or characteristics of one group are inherently superior to those of another group and that this gives the "superior" group the right to dominate or discriminate against the "inferior" group.

are superior to those of another group and that this superiority gives the powerful group the right to dominate or discriminate against the "inferior" group. All people can be prejudiced and can discriminate. Nevertheless, "prejudices of groups with power are farther reaching in their consequences than others" (Sampson, 1999, p. 131). Because such attitudes can be deeply ingrained and are often subtle, it is easy to overlook behaviors we engage in that in some way meet this definition. A behavior may seem insignificant, such as gratuitously directing an African American student to the financial aid line. It may appear innocuous, such as leaving a lot of space between you and a blind person on a bus. Telling jokes, laughing at jokes, or encouraging repetition of jokes that demean women is sexist behavior. So is assuming that the women in the office should plan the holiday party because, well, you know, they're just better at that. It is ethnocentric behavior to assume that punctuality and multitasking, valued in one culture, also should be valued by other cultures and to label as lazy and inefficient people from a culture that does

learn about yourself

Take this short survey, adapted from Neuliep and McCroskey (1997), to learn something about yourself. Answer the questions based on your first response. There are no right or wrong answers. Just be honest in reporting your true attitudes. For each question, select one of the following numbers that best corresponds to your opinion.

1 = Strongly Agree	2 = Agree Somewhat	3 = Neutral	4 = Disagree Somewhat	5 = Strongly Disagree

_____ **1.** My country should be the role model for the world.

_____ **2.** Most other countries are backward compared to mine.

_____ **3.** People in my country have the best customs of anywhere.

_____ **4.** People in other cultures could learn a lot from my culture.

_____ **5.** Other cultures should try to be more like my culture.

_____ **6.** I respect the customs and values of other cultures.

_____ **7.** I am interested in the customs and values of other cultures.

_____ **8.** Each culture should preserve its uniqueness.

_____ **9.** People from my culture act strange when they go to other cultures.

_____ **10.** Although different, the values of other countries are as valid as ours.

SCORING THE SURVEY:

Add scores for questions 1, 2, 3, 4, and 5   Total 1: _____

Add scores for questions 6, 7, 8, 9, and 10   Total 2: _____

This is a test of ethnocentrism, the tendency to use your own cultural standards when perceiving people from different cultures. Each score for Total 1 and Total 2 separately can range from 5 to 25. The lower (closer to 5) your score on Total 1, the more you are exhibiting ethnocentrism. The higher (closer to 25) your score on Total 2, the more you are exhibiting ethnocentrism.

not share these values. Ageism might take the form of assuming that only people under age forty are proficient with computers, so someone over forty is not hired for a computer-programming job.

Improving Accuracy of Social Perception

Because inaccuracies in perception are common and because they influence how we communicate, improving perceptual accuracy is an important first step in becoming a competent communicator. The following guidelines can aid you in constructing a more realistic impression of others, as well as in assessing the validity of your own perceptions.

1. Question the accuracy of your perceptions. Questioning accuracy begins by saying, "I know what I think I saw, heard, tasted, smelled, or felt, but I could be wrong. What other information should I be aware of?" By accepting the possibility that you have overlooked something, you will become interested in increasing your accuracy. In situations where the accuracy of perception is important, take a few seconds to double-check. It will be worth the effort.

2. Seek more information to verify perceptions. If your perception has been based on only one or two pieces of information, try to collect further information so that your perceptions are better grounded. Note that your perception is tentative—that is, subject to change. The best way to get additional information about people is to talk with them. It's OK to be unsure about how to treat someone from another group. But rather than letting your uncertainty cause you to make mistakes, talk with the person and ask for the information you need to become more comfortable.

3. Try to get to the psychological level of predictions. Remember that the cultural and sociological levels of predictions lead to the least accurate perceptions. By getting to know each person as a unique individual, you will increase the accuracy of your perceptions and predictions.

4. Realize that your perceptions of a person will change over time. People often base their behavior on perceptions that are old or based on incomplete information. So when you encounter someone you haven't seen for a while, you will want to become reacquainted and let the person's current behavior rather than past actions or reputation inform your perceptions. A former classmate who was "wild" in high school may well have changed and become a mature, responsible adult.

5. Use the skill of perception checking to verify your impressions. A **perception check** is sharing your perception of another's behavior to see if your interpretation is accurate. It is a process of describing what you have seen and heard and asking for feedback from the other person. It is a way to verify or adjust the predictions we make about others. Perception checking calls for you to watch the behavior of the other person and ask yourself "What does that behavior mean to me?" Then you are ready to describe the behavior and put your interpretation into words to verify your perception.

Perception check—a message that reflects your understanding of the meaning of another person's nonverbal behavior.

The following examples illustrate the use of perception checking. In each of the examples, the final sentence is a perception check. Notice that body language sometimes provides the perceptual information that needs to be checked out, whereas at other times the tone of voice does. Also notice that the perception-checking statements do not express approval or disapproval of what is being received—they are purely descriptive statements of the perceptions.

> Valerie walks into the room with a completely blank expression. She neither speaks to Ann nor does she acknowledge that Ann is even in the room. Valerie sits down on the edge of the bed and stares into space. Ann says, "Valerie, did something happen? You look like you're in a state of shock. Am I right? Is there something I can do?"
>
> While Marsha is telling Jenny about the difficulty of her midterm exam in chemistry class, she notices Jenny smiling. She says to Jenny, "You're smiling. I'm not sure how to interpret it. What's up?" Jenny may respond that she's smiling because the story reminded her of something funny or because she had the same chemistry teacher last year and he purposely gave an extremely difficult midterm to motivate students, but then he graded them on a really favorable curve.
>
> Cesar, speaking in short, precise sentences with a sharp tone of voice, gives Bill his day's assignment. Bill says, "From the sound of your voice, Cesar, I get the impression that you're upset with me. Are you?"

So when we use the skill of perception checking we encode the meaning that we have perceived from someone's behavior and feed it back so that it can be verified or corrected. For instance, when Bill says, "I get the impression that you're upset with me. Are you?" Cesar may say (1) "No. Whatever gave you that impression?" in which case Bill can further describe the cues that he received; (2)

"What's up? You look bothered by something. Do you want to talk?"

"Yes, I am," in which case Bill can get Cesar to specify what has caused the feelings; or (3) "No, it's not you; it's just that three of my team members didn't show up for this shift." If Cesar is not upset with him, Bill can examine what caused him to misinterpret Cesar's feelings; if Cesar is upset with him, Bill has the opportunity to change the behavior that caused Cesar to be upset.

To see what might happen when we respond without checking the accuracy of our perceptions, suppose that in place of the descriptive perception check, Bill had said to Cesar, "Why are you so upset with me?" Rather than describing his perception, Bill has made a judgment based on the perception. Replying as if his perception were "obviously" accurate would have amounted to mind reading.

You will want to check your perceptions whenever the accuracy of your understanding is important (1) to your current communication, (2) to the relationship you have with the other person, or (3) to the conclusions you draw about that person. Perception checking is especially important in new relationships or when you haven't talked with someone for a long time.

Summary

Perception is the process of selectively attending to information and assigning meaning to it. Our perceptions are a result of our selection, organization, and interpretation of sensory information. Self-concept is the idea or mental image that we have about our skills, our abilities, our knowledge, our competencies, and our personality. Self-esteem is our overall evaluation of our competence and personal worthiness. Self-concepts come from interpretations of self, based on our experience and reactions and responses of others. We create multiple selves based on the different roles we play in various situations. By self-monitoring, we can observe

skill builders   PERCEPTION CHECKING

SKILL	USE	PROCEDURE	EXAMPLE
A statement that expresses the meaning you get from the nonverbal behavior of another.	To clarify the meaning of nonverbal behavior.	1. Watch the behavior of another. 2. Ask yourself: What does that behavior mean to me? 3. Describe the behavior (to yourself or aloud) and put your interpretation of the nonverbal behavior into words to verify your perception.	As Dale frowns while reading Paul's first draft of a memo, Paul says, "From the way you're frowning, I take it that you're not too pleased with the way I phrased the memo."

A Question of Ethics

Rustown was a small midwestern factory town. Over the years the white, middle-class citizens had grown together to form a close-knit community that prided itself on its unity. Corpex, a large out-of-town corporation, which had just bought out the town's major factory, decided to move its headquarters there and to expand the current plant, creating hundreds of new jobs. This expansion meant that the new people coming into the town to manage and work in the factory would spend money and build homes, but also it meant that the composition of the small community would change.

Rustown inhabitants had mixed reactions to this takeover. The owners of land and shops were excited by the increased business that was expected; but many in the community recognized that since most people in town had been born and raised there, the inhabitants of Rustown were pretty much alike—and they liked it that way. They knew that many of the new factory managers as well as some of the new employees were African and Latin Americans. Rustown had never had a black or Latino family, and some of the townspeople openly worried about the effects the newcomers would have on their community.

Otis Carr was one of the Corpex managers who had agreed to move to Rustown because of the opportunities that appeared to await him and his family, even though he recognized that as a black man he might experience resentment. At work on the first day, Otis noticed that the workers seemed very leery of him. By the end of the first week, however, the plant was running smoothly and Otis was feeling the first signs of acceptance. On Monday morning of the next week, Otis accidentally overheard a group of workers talking on their break, trading stereotypes about African Americans and Latinos and using vulgarities and racist slurs in discussing specific new co-workers.

A bit shaken, Otis returned to his office. He had faced racism before, but this time it was different. This time he had power and the responsibility to make a difference. He wanted to reach his workers for the sake of the company, the town, and other minority group members who would be coming to Rustown. Although he knew he had to do something, he realized that just using his power would get him nowhere. In a sick way he understood the prejudices, but not how to change them. How could he reach his workers?

Devise a plan for Otis. How could he use his own social perceptions of Rustown to address this problem in a way that is within ethical interpersonal communication guidelines?

others' reactions to us and adjust our behavior to fit the situation. The inaccuracy of a distorted picture of oneself becomes magnified through self-fulfilling prophecies and filtering messages. Our self-concept and self-esteem moderate competing internal messages in our self-talk, influence our perception of others, and influence our personal communication style. Cultural and gender expectations influence our perceptions.

Perception also plays an important role in forming impressions of others. People engage in impression management when they consciously try to influence the impressions that others have of them. Sometimes the shortcuts we take in perception, such as relying on implicit personality theory, the halo effect, selective perception, faulty attributions, and the need for consistency and prejudices lead to distortions or inaccuracies in perceiving others. You can learn to improve perception if you actively question the accuracy of your perceptions, seek more information to verify perceptions, try to get to the psychological level of predictions based on a person's uniqueness, talk with the people about whom you are forming perceptions, realize that perceptions of people need to change over time, and check perceptions verbally before you react.

Chapter Resources

Communication Improvement Plan: Perception

Would you like to improve your use of the following aspects of forming and using social perception discussed in this chapter?

Forming self-concepts

Developing and maintaining self-esteem

Presenting self

Perception checking

Pick one of these categories and write a communication improvement plan. You can find a communication improvement plan worksheet on our website at www.oup.com/us/interact

Key Words

Perception, *p. 30*	**Impression management,** *p. 44*
Patterns, *p. 32*	**Halo effect,** *p. 46*
Social perception, *p. 32*	**Selective perception,** *p. 46*
Self-concept, *p. 33*	**Attributions,** *p. 46*
Self-esteem, *p. 33*	**Dispositional attributions,** *p. 47*
Self-monitoring, *p. 35*	**Situational attributions,** *p. 47*
Role, *p. 36*	**Prejudice,** *p. 47*
Incongruence, *p. 39*	**Discrimination,** *p. 47*
Self-fulfilling prophecies, *p. 39*	**Racism, ethnocentrism, sexism, ageism, able-ism,** *p. 48*
Uncertainty reduction theory, *p. 43*	**Perception check,** *p. 49*

Skill Practice

Skill Practice exercises challenge you to master the material you have read in this chapter. For additional Skill Practice activities, visit our website at www.oup.com/us/interact

PERCEPTION CHECKING

Write well-phrased perception checks for each of the following situations:

Franco comes home from the doctor's office with pale face and slumped shoulders. Glancing at you with a forlorn look, he shrugs his shoulders.

You say:

As you return the tennis racket you borrowed from Liam, you smile and say, "Here's your racket." Liam stiffens, grabs the racket, and starts to walk away.

You say:

Natalie dances into the room with a huge grin on her face.

You say:

In the past, your advisor has told you that almost any time would be all right for working out your next term's schedule. When you tell her you'll be in on Wednesday at 4 P.M., she pauses, frowns, sighs, and says "Uh-huh" and nods.

You say:

Compare your written responses to the guidelines for effective perception checking discussed earlier. Edit your responses where necessary in order to improve them. Now say them aloud. Do they sound "natural"? If not, revise them until they do.

Inter-Act with Media

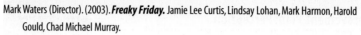

FIND MORE
on the web
Additional media entries @
www.oup.com/us/interact

CINEMA

Mark Waters (Director). (2003). *Freaky Friday.* Jamie Lee Curtis, Lindsay Lohan, Mark Harmon, Harold
Gould, Chad Michael Murray.

Brief Summary: The movie is about a contentious mother-and-daughter relationship. Mom is overworked and very uptight.
She does not take the time to understand her daughter or the problems that the teenager is experiencing in high school. Both
members of the pair act out one time too many, and as a result they are forced to switch bodies until they get it right.

IPC Concepts: The film is a very solid look at the need to see life through the eyes of the other person. It does an excellent job
of depicting the value of such empathy efforts and the long-term potential for relationship growth.

Sharon Maguire (Director). (2001). *Bridget Jones's Diary.* Renée Zellweger, Gemma Jones, Celia Imrie, James Faulkner, Jim
Broadbent, Colin Firth, Hugh Grant.

Brief Summary: This is the story of a young Englishwoman who wants to improve herself and have a successful romantic
relationship. She struggles with her weight, smoking, and other perceived imperfections. She goes through the fireworks of
a relationship with a manipulative, exploitive boss. She also comes into constant contact with a childhood friend who just
doesn't seem right until it is apparently too late.

IPC Concepts: The movie is presented as a running stream of Bridget's self-talk. We get a glimpse into her thoughts (happy,
sad, encouraged, discouraged, etc.).

WHAT'S ON THE WEB

Visual Cognition Lab

http://viscog.beckman.uiuc.edu/djs_lab/demos.html

Brief Summary: This Web site offers a range of short video files that give you a chance to test your ability to note subtle changes in people, setting, behavior, etc. It is an outstanding Web site for perception checking on ourselves.

IPC Concepts: Perception checking.

The Message

http://lynn_meade.tripod.com/id38.htm

Brief Summary: This site is rich in opportunities to gain more understanding of several aspects of the self as a communicator. The site offers links to four personality tests—Kiersey Temperament Personality Test, Learning Styles Test, Multiple Intelligence Inventory, and Personality Plus Test—as well as several very useful applications and examples of self-concept, schema, self-fulfilling prophecy, scripts, social comparison, and perception.

IPC Concepts: Perception, self-image, self-concept, self-talk, and scripts.

communicating *in* relationships:
BASIC CONCEPTS

After you have read this chapter, you
should be able to answer these questions:

- What are the major types of relationships?

- What is a "Johari window"?

- What are the stages of relationships?

- What strategies will maintain a relationship?

- What are relationship dialectics, and how do
  we manage them?

- What are relational turning points?

- What is interpersonal needs theory?

- What is exchange theory?

"Yvonne, wasn't that Pauli that I saw you with again? I thought you've been dating Lonnie."

"Yeah, I was with Pauli, but we're just friends."

"Just friends! Come on, girl, I see you with him a lot. Are you sure he doesn't think it's serious between the two of you?"

"I see him a lot because I am really able to talk with him. We're just comfortable with each other. But before you get too worried about his feelings, he and Leona are getting pretty close."

"And she doesn't mind you spending time with him? Are you sure you're not just kidding yourself?"

"Hey, I don't know whether she minds, but Pauli and I just aren't together—there's no chemistry. Actually, he's more like a brother to me. I tell him my problems as well as what's going right with me. And he talks with me about his problems, too. It's great to have a close guy friend to confide in. If something happened between us, I'd really miss him."

Relationship—a set of expectations two people have for their behavior based on the pattern of interaction between them.

Interpersonal relationship—a series of interactions between two individuals known to each other.

Good relationship—one in which the interactions are satisfying to and healthy for those involved.

Yvonne is lucky because she has someone she can really talk with—she has a good relationship. The interpersonal skills we will study can help you start, build, and maintain healthy relationships with others. "A **relationship** is a set of expectations two people have for their behavior based on the pattern of interaction between them" (Littlejohn, 2002, p. 234). An **interpersonal relationship** may be defined as "a series of interactions between two individuals known to each other" (Duck & Gilmour, 1981, p. 2). A **good relationship** is one in which the interactions are satisfying to and healthy for those involved.

Good relationships do not just happen, nor do they grow and maintain themselves automatically. In fact, as Canary and Dainton (2002, p. xiii) state, "Most sane people know that relationships require work. That is, partners need to spend time and effort to maintain functional, satisfying relationships. Without such efforts, relationships tend to deteriorate." In this chapter we will explain the types of relationships, discuss the stages that typically comprise the life cycle of a relationship, describe relational dialectics and how to manage them, discuss turning points in relationships, and consider two theories that help to explain relationships.

Types of Relationships

Our relationships vary in their intensity from impersonal to personal (LaFollette, 1996, p. 4). An **impersonal relationship** is one in which a person relates to the other merely because the other fills a role or satisfies an immediate need. In these circumstances, neither party is likely to care who occupies the role or fulfills the need, so long as it is done well. At a restaurant, for instance, Elaine may prefer a particular server, but she will be satisfied if whoever waits on her does it competently. A **personal relationship** is one in which people disclose information to each other and work to meet each other's interpersonal needs. So if Elaine and Juanita enjoy talking with each other and helping each other out, they have a personal relationship.

We also classify the people with whom we have relationships as acquaintances, friends, and close friends or intimates.

Acquaintances

Acquaintances are people we know by name and talk with when the opportunity arises, but with whom our interactions are limited. Many acquaintance relationships grow out of a particular context. We become acquainted with those who live in our apartment building or dorm or in the house next door, who sit next to us in class, who go to our church, or belong to our club. Thus Melinda and Paige, who meet in biology class, may talk with each other about class-related issues, but they make no effort to share personal ideas or to see each other outside of class.

Friends

Over time some acquaintances become our friends. **Friends** are people with whom we have negotiated more personal relationships voluntarily (Patterson, Bettini, & Nussbaum, 1993, p. 145). As friendships develop, people move toward interactions that are less role bound. For example, Melinda and Paige, who are acquaintances in biology class and have talked only about class-related subjects, may decide to get together after school to go to the gym. If they find that they enjoy each other's company, they may continue to meet outside of class and eventually become friends.

Some of our friendships are context bound. Thus, people often refer to their tennis friends, office friends, or neighborhood friends. These context friendships may fade if the context changes. For instance, your friendship with a person at the office may fade if you or your friend takes a job with a different company.

Impersonal relationship—one in which a person relates to the other merely because the other fills a role or satisfies an immediate need.

Personal relationship—one in which people share large amounts of information with each other and meet each other's interpersonal needs.

Acquaintances—people we know by name and talk with when the opportunity arises, but with whom our interactions are limited.

Friends—people with whom we have negotiated more personal relationships voluntarily.

Friendship Competencies. In order for friendships to develop and continue, some key behaviors must occur. Samter (2003) explains five important competencies necessary to friendship relationships.

- **Initiation.** One person must get in touch with the other, and the interaction must be smooth, relaxed, and enjoyable. A friendship is not likely to form between people who rarely interact or who have unsatisfying interactions.
- **Responsiveness.** Each person must listen to the other, focus on the partner, and respond to the other person. It is difficult to form friendships with people who focus only on themselves or their issues.
- **Self-disclosure.** Friends share personal feelings with each other. A friendship is unlikely to form if people discuss only abstract ideas or surface issues.
- **Emotional support.** People expect to be comforted and supported by their friends. We look to our friends for this type of confirmation.
- **Conflict management.** It is inevitable that friends will disagree about ideas or behaviors. Friendship depends on successfully handling these disagreements. In fact, by competently managing conflict, people can strengthen their friendships.

inter-act with

Technology

Record a portion of a movie or TV program where friends are having a conversation. Analyze it on the basis of expectations of friendship, including enjoyment of talking with each other, trust, sharing of personal feelings, high level of commitment, and enduring nature of friendship. Which of these seem evident in the conversation? What other elements were shown in the conversation? Did these seem to contribute to or detract from the relationship? Explain. ■

Close Friends or Intimates

Close friends or intimates—those with whom we share our deepest feelings.

Close friends or intimates are those few people with whom a person shares a high degree of commitment, trust, interdependence, disclosure, and enjoyment in the relationship. People may have countless acquaintances and many friends, but they are likely to have only a few truly intimate friends. With close friends, we show commitment by pledging ourselves and our time to each other. We show trust by having positive expectations of the other person and believing that he or she will behave fairly and honestly. With our close friends, our lives are interdependent or intertwined. We rely upon each other. We are more likely to share personal, private information about ourselves with close friends. While acquaintance relationships can be enjoyable, most people experience the greatest pleasure and enjoyment from relationships with close friends and intimates.

Research shows that women and men tend to differ on the factors that lead to close friendships. This may be because society teaches women and men to behave differently in order to follow norms of femininity and masculinity. Women tend to develop close relationships with others based on talking, opening up with the other, and sharing personal feelings. By gaining knowledge of the innermost being of their partner, women develop a sense of "we-ness" with others. Men tend to develop close friendships through joint activities, doing favors for each other, and being able to depend on one another. Men are less likely to define a close friend as someone with whom you can share feelings. For men, close friends are the people you can depend on to help you out of a jam and the people you regularly choose for pursuing enjoyable activities together (Wood & Inman, 1993). It is important to note that these differences are more pronounced in same-sex friendships. When men and women develop close friendships or intimate relationships with each other, these distinctions do not apply. We will elaborate on characteristics of intimate mixed-sex relationships in Chapter 12.

In close relationships, each person's self-concept tends to be somewhat related to the partner. There is some fusion of the self and the other in close relationships. The partner is perceived as part of oneself. In other words, you define who you are in part through your close relationships (Aron, Aron, Tudor, & Nelson, 2004). We discuss additional characteristics of close relationships in Chapter 12.

Disclosure and Feedback in Relationships

As people interact in a relationship, they will engage in some degree of disclosure with each other, and they will also give some amount of feedback to each other.

A healthy interpersonal relationship is marked by an appropriate balance of **self-disclosure** (sharing biographical data, personal ideas, and feelings that are unknown to the other person) and **feedback** (the verbal and physical responses to people and/or their messages) within the relationship. The **Johari window,** named after its two originators, Jo Luft and Harry Ingham, is a tool for examining the extent of and connection between disclosure and feedback in a relationship (Luft, 1970). The window represents all of the information about you that can be known. You and your partner each know some (but not all) of this information.

The window has four "panes" or quadrants, as shown in Figure 3.1. The first quadrant is called the "open" pane of the window because it represents the information about you that both you and your partner know. It includes information that you have disclosed and the observations about you that your partner has shared with you. It might include mundane information that you share with most people, such as your college major, but it also may include information that you disclose to relatively few people. Similarly it could include simple observations that your partner has made, such as how cute you look when you wrinkle your nose, or more serious feedback you have received from your partner about your interpersonal style.

The second quadrant is called the "secret" pane. It contains all those things that you know about yourself but your partner does not yet know about you. Secret information is made known through the process of self-disclosure. When you choose to share the information with your partner, the information moves into the open pane of the window. For example, suppose that you had been engaged to be married but on the day of the wedding your fiancé had backed out. You may not want to share this part of your history with casual acquaintances, so it will be in the secret pane of your window in many of your relationships. But when you disclose this fact to a friend, it moves into the open part of your Johari window with this person. As

Self-disclosure—sharing biographical data, personal ideas, and feelings that were unknown to the other person.

Feedback—verbal and physical responses to people and/or their messages.

Johari window—a tool for examining the relationship between disclosure and feedback.

	Known to self	Not known to self
Known to others	Open	Blind
Not known to others	Secret	Unknown

Figure 3.1

The Johari Window

you disclose information, the secret pane of the window becomes smaller and the open pane is enlarged.

The third quadrant is called the "blind" pane. This is the place for information that the other person knows about you, but about which you are unaware. Most people have blind spots—parts of their behavior or the effects of their behavior of which they are unaware. Information moves from the blind area of the window to the open area through feedback from others. When someone gives you an insight about yourself and you accept the feedback, then the information will move into the open pane of the Johari window you have with this person. Thus, like disclosure, feedback enlarges the open pane of the Johari window, but in this case it is the blind pane that becomes smaller.

The fourth quadrant is called the "unknown" pane. It contains information about you that you don't know and neither does your partner. Obviously, you cannot develop a list of this information. So how do we know that it exists? Well, because periodically we "discover" it. If, for instance, you have never tried hang gliding, then neither you nor anyone else can really know how you will react at the point of takeoff. You might chicken out or follow through, do well or crash, love every minute of it or be paralyzed with fear. But until you try it, all of this information is unknown. Once you try it, you gain information about yourself that becomes part of the secret pane, which you can move to the open pane through disclosure. Also once you have tried it, others who observe your flight will have information about your performance that you may not know unless they give you feedback.

As you disclose and receive feedback, the sizes of the various windowpanes change. These changes reflect the relationships. So the panes of the Johari window you have with different people will vary in size.

In Figure 3.2A we see an example of a relationship where there is little disclosure or feedback occurring. This person has not shared much information and has received little feedback from the partner. We would expect to see this pattern in a new relationship or one between casual acquaintances.

Figure 3.2B shows a relationship in which a person is disclosing to a partner, but the partner is providing little feedback. As you can see, the secret pane is smaller, but the hidden pane is unchanged. A window like this indicates that the individual is able to disclose information but the partner is unable or unwilling

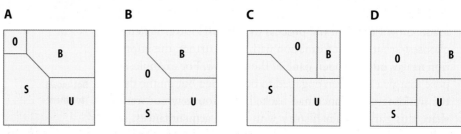

Figure 3.2

Sample Johari windows: (A) low disclosure, low feedback; (B) high disclosure, low feedback; (C) low disclosure, high feedback; (D) high disclosure, high feedback

to give feedback (or, perhaps, that the individual refuses to accept the feedback that is being given). Since part of the way that we learn about who we are comes from the feedback we receive from others, relationships in which one partner does not provide feedback can become very unsatisfying to the other individual.

Figure 3.2C shows a relationship where a partner is good at providing feedback, but the other individual is not disclosing. Since most of us disclose only when we trust our partners, this pattern may be an indication that the nondisclosing individual does not have confidence in the relational partner.

Figure 3.2D shows a relationship in which the individual has disclosed information and received feedback. So the open pane of the window has enlarged as a result of both processes. Windows that look like this indicate that there is sufficient trust and interest in the relationship that both partners are willing to risk by disclosing and giving feedback.

Obviously, to get a complete "picture" of a relationship each partner's Johari window would need to be examined. A healthy interpersonal relationship is marked by a balance of disclosure and feedback, so that both people are participating.

observe & analyze

Johari Windows

Working with a friend, let each one draw a window that represents his or her perception of the relationship with the other. Then each of you should draw a window that represents what you perceive to be the other's relationship with you. Share the windows. How do they compare? If there are differences in the representations, talk with your friend about them. ■

Communication Patterns During Stages of Relationships

Even though no two relationships develop in exactly the same manner, they tend to move through identifiable stages that follow a "life cycle" that includes a beginning and developing, a maintaining, and perhaps a deteriorating stage (Baxter; 1982, Duck, 1987; Knapp and Vangelisti, 2000; Taylor & Altman, 1987). How quickly a relationship moves through these stages depends on the interpersonal communication between relational partners. "Talking is fundamental to relationships—whether they are starting, getting better, getting worse, or just carrying on" (Duck, 1998, p. 7). In fact, as our Spotlight on Scholars: Steven Duck on Personal Relationships shows, how we talk with one another may be the most important variable in starting and building relationships.

Beginning and Developing a Relationship

The early stages of relationships depend on increasing knowledge of the other person, developing feelings of relaxation and confirmation, enhancing physical contact and psychological closeness, and increasing disclosure and support (Duck, 1999).

The communication during the first stage, beginning and building relationships, is initially focused on getting information about the other person.

Fundamental to beginning and developing a relationship is the need to reduce uncertainty (Berger & Bradac, 1982; Littlejohn, 2002, pp. 243–244). As we have explained, all initial interaction and prospective relationships begin with uncertainty. If we don't know anything about another person, we don't know how to treat that person because we don't know how to predict his or her behavior. As we gather information, we can make decisions about how to act with the other person.

Let's look at an example of two college roommates, Whitney and Madeline, who are beginning and developing a relationship. During their first few conversations, they will want to get to know each other so they can reduce uncertainty and better predict each other's behavior. So they may talk about where each one went to high school, what major each is pursuing, what hobbies they like, and their preferences for eating, studying, and sleeping schedules. This chitchat serves a real purpose in reducing uncertainty and gaining knowledge about another person.

In the beginning stages of relationship formation, we also look for feelings of relaxation and confirmation. It should be more comfortable conversing with someone over time. Conversational topics flow smoothly and we feel enjoyment during the interaction. We want the other person to listen and to confirm our sense of self as well as our ideas. When relaxation and confirmation happen, we consider that we are connecting with the other person. Only when both parties experience relaxation and confirmation is the relationship likely to proceed to a deeper level. Learning about another and developing a sense of relaxation and confirmation during interaction can occur in face-to-face conversations or in online exchanges.

Increasingly the initial stage of relationship development may occur electronically. Online communication may present a potentially less difficult way to meet and interact with others than traditional interactions. The initial interaction can occur in the comfort of your own home and at your own pace. You need not be concerned about physical aspects of the self or the other, and you can more precisely select what you are going to say (Ward & Tracy, 2004). Perhaps Whitney and Madeline e-mailed each other or spoke on the telephone once they were assigned as college roommates. The more connections they can make, the more relaxed and comfortable they can become with each other.

If a relationship is growing deeper, then people perceive it to have psychological closeness. They perceive that the relationship is developing to more interpersonally intimate levels. This also can happen via online relationships. Some people report that they achieve more closeness in online relationships than in equivalent, off-line relationships (Walther, 1996). Indeed, rapid and exaggerated intimacy can be part of the fun of online relationships (Rabby & Walther, 2003). Let's say the relationship between Whitney and Madeline is working out well. They spend time together, get to know each other well, and consider themselves to be close friends.

As the relationship escalates, it deepens and grows closer, and partners tend to share greater physical contact. Physical contact may involve sitting closer together, leaning toward each other, more eye contact, and more touch. Such physical behaviors may or may not involve romantic feelings. Even friends increase physical contact with each other as the relationship develops, though females and

spotlight on scholars

Steven Duck, Daniel and Amy Starch Research Chair at the Communication Studies Department at the University of Iowa, on
Personal Relationships

What began as a personal curiosity about the friendships he developed as a college student has turned out to be the focus of Steve Duck's lifelong work. He was curious about why some people become close friends, while others remain acquaintances, so he selected this topic for a research term paper assigned in one of his classes. At that time, Duck's hypothesis was that people who have similar attitudes are likely to become attracted to each other and to become friends. Over the years his understanding of how relationships are formed, developed, and maintained has changed considerably. In fact, in Duck's work you can see how scholars develop and test theories, only to replace them with more meaningful theories.

Many of Duck's breakthroughs in relationship theory came from his interdisciplinary study in psychology, sociology, family studies, and communication. Duck saw the need to integrate research findings across disciplines as so important that he founded the International Network on Personal Relationships and two international conferences on the subject to promote interdisciplinary scholarship.

While many disciplines have contributed to how he views relationships, Duck believes that his

move to the University of Iowa, where he encountered colleagues whose backgrounds were in rhetoric, caused a fundamental shift in his thinking. Based on discussions with these colleagues, who assume that people are connected to one another through language, Duck began to see that conversations and talk were more than the instrument through which relationships were developed.

Duck's early theories were based on the premise that what makes a relationship work is the degree of similarity between the personalities, backgrounds, etc. of the participants. He saw "talk" as simply the channel through which these similarities are uncovered. This model can be seen in the operation of most dating services. Clients with similar profiles are "matched" and come together to talk to each other in order to learn about their similarities. Then presto, the relationship develops. Although people with many similarities often don't develop lasting relationships, this premise dominated the thinking on personal relationships for many years.

In a chapter he coauthored in *Handbook of Interpersonal Communication* (Duck & Pittman, 1994), Duck first proposed a revision to his original premise. He

argued that we "do" our relationships in the everyday talk that happens as we interact. "I just don't enjoy talking with him," "I really feel like she listens to me and understands," "We seem to have a lot in common, but we just can't seem to connect," and "We've gotten good at talking things out so that we work through our differences and both feel good about it" are not simple statements about the communication in the relationship—they are statements about the relationship itself.

Thus, according to Duck's new model, when two people begin to date, the way their relationship develops most directly depends on how they talk to each other, not simply whether they have similar personalities. If this is so, then from a practical standpoint, it is important to pay attention to how we say things and to how we respond to what others say. So while a dating service may be a convenient way to meet new people with similar interests, whether a relationship develops, and what kind, depends on how the two people manage the relationship as they talk.

Duck thinks that it is time for scholars to focus more of their analysis on people's everyday talk in their ordinary conversations, rather than on what he calls the "peaks and valleys," since it is at the heart of understanding how relationships grow, stabilize, and change. For example, while we have studied how people deal with significant conflict, we have paid scant attention to studying how people manage minor conversational annoyances, such as unwanted swearing behavior. In addition, Professor Duck admires recent work on "the dark side of relationships," and has recently published an article on understanding "enemyship."

Duck, who received his Ph.D. from the University of Sheffield, U.K., in 1971, has taught in the United States for nineteen years. He has authored or edited over thirty-five books and hundreds of articles and papers on personal relationships. A prolific scholar, Duck still recognizes the need to refresh his own ideas by engaging in intense study of the work of other scholars. Periodically, professors take a break from the rigors of the classroom, administrative responsibilities, and discovery research and go back into a "learning model" on what is called a sabbatical. In the spring of 2000, Professor Duck spent his sabbatical in the library, reading and thinking about the recent work of other scholars of personal relationships. Refreshed by this intense study period, Duck returned to his classes and his scholarship prepared to continue making contributions to our knowledge of personal relationships. For some of Duck's major publications, see the reference list for this chapter at the end of the book.

Duck's work highlights the importance of integrating insights from a variety of disciplines as we seek to understand and manage our relationships. ∎

males may differ in how they show physical contact in same- and opposite-sex friendships. Females may hold hands or hug other female friends, while males may slap hands in a high-five gesture or punch each other's arms as examples of physical contact in a developing relationship. Of course, cultural norms and age also affect how people engage in physical contact in relationships. Perhaps Whitney and Madeline hug each other when they greet and depart, share their clothes, and do each other's hair, makeup, or nail polish. This physical contact would be a natural outgrowth of their relationship development.

The need for physical contact seems to be an important aspect of relationship development even for relationships that begin online. Two researchers of online relationships, James Katz and Philip Aspden (2004), have found that Internet relationships frequently lead to face-to-face meetings.

Many people who are escalating their relationship begin to share feelings and disclose more personal information, and to depend upon each other for favors and support. At this stage they are likely to seek each other out for help with a problem or to talk for hours, sharing both the joys and the sorrows of their lives. Over time, Whitney and Madeline may share their innermost feelings with each other, cry on each other's shoulder during hard times, or lend each other money. In Chapter 9, "Sharing Personal Information," we will discuss in some detail self-disclosure, describing feelings, and giving personal feedback both in face-to-face and online relationships.

Although the "getting-to-know-you" stage may go quite smoothly with people who are similar to you, the process may become more difficult when you try to move a relationship with someone different from you to a deeper level. In the "Diverse Voices" selection that appears on pages 69 and 70, Brenda J. Allen describes the process that resulted in her developing a deep intimate friendship with a person who differed from her in many ways. Perhaps as a result of reading this selection you will feel more comfortable in making the effort to get to know people from whom you differ.

Maintaining A Relationship

Maintaining a relationship means that both parties participate in keeping the relationship at a particular level of closeness or intimacy. Generally, the maintenance stage involves keeping the status quo so that the relationship is not escalating to greater closeness, nor is it moving to less closeness. Relationships can go in and out of maintenance and development (greater closeness) in almost imperceptible ways, so it may be difficult to accurately label a stage of the relationship. At times relationship stages may merge, and other times they may be quite distinct.

Researchers have cataloged many strategies that people use to maintain relationships (Rusbult, Olsen, Davis, & Hannon, 2004). You probably unconsciously use many of these techniques to maintain your relationships. If you desire to maintain a relationship, you choose to spend time with the other person, whether that is in face-to-face or online interactions. A relationship in which the parties rarely interact will likely move to lesser levels of closeness. Another technique that serves to maintain relationships is the merging of social networks. When some your partner's friends are your friends and vice versa, then relationships become easier to maintain. When two people have the essentially the same friendship networks, then time spent with friends becomes time spent together as well. Mutual friends tend to reinforce a relationship, while having no mutual friends tends to threaten a relationship. Sharing friendship networks does not preclude each person from having some separate friends as well. People maintain relationships by yet another strategy—thinking in "we" terms. Part of maintaining a relationship is thinking of yourselves as a unit. That does not mean that you sacrifice your individuality. But without some sense of "we-ness," the relationship will not continue.

Let's see how our roommates, Whitney and Madeline, use these strategies to maintain their relationship. Maybe they decide to take a few classes together, join some of the same clubs, and get to know each other's friends. Maybe they visit each other's hometowns and meet each other's families and high school friends.

Another relationship maintenance strategy involves a willingness to sacrifice. Since all relationships involve give and take, being willing at times to do what is best for the other person or the overall relationship can help maintain the relationship. Sacrifice means sometimes putting your own needs or desires on hold in order to maintain relationships. In order to maintain relationships people sometimes practice "positive illusion." This means emphasizing others' virtues and downplaying their faults. When we are realistic in relationships, we will always find some behaviors which we consider faults of the other person. But how we choose to perceive those faults is key. We can choose to see those faults in the foreground, overshadowing the person's strengths. Or, for the sake of maintaining the relationship, we can choose to downplay another's faults and move our negative perception to the background. Relationships can also be maintained by forgiveness. Since conflict is inevitable in close relationships, we may do or say things that hurt our partner. If not handled properly, such transgressions can harm the relationship and move it to a level of less intimacy. By forgiving minor transgressions, we can keep a relationship at the desired level of closeness.

Whitney and Madeline may each have little habits that annoy the other, but

Maintaining a relationship— keeping a relationship at a particular level of closeness or intimacy.

they choose not to let these annoyances get in the way of a good friendship. When Whitney gets ill, perhaps Madeline sacrifices a date in order to stay home and take care of her sick roommate. Other ways that people maintain their relationships include continuing mutually acceptable levels of affection, self-disclosure, favors, and support.

De-escalating and Dissolving a Relationship

Over time a relationship may become less satisfying to one or both relational partners. When this happens the partner or partners will change the relationship so that it is less intimate. They may maintain the relationship at the new level, or it may continue to deteriorate until the partners end it. The communication in deteriorating relationships is marked by three stages: the recognition of dissatisfaction, the process of disengaging, and ending.

Recognition of Dissatisfaction. The first sign that a relationship is de-escalating is a subtle indication of dissatisfaction. When one person begins to lose interest in the opinions and feelings of the other, the orientation of that person changes from we to I. The partners may begin to emphasize each other's faults and downplay virtues. Subjects that once yielded free and open discussion become off-limits or sources of conflict. As the relationship begins to be characterized by an increase in "touchy" subjects and more unresolved conflicts, partners become more defensive and less willing to foster a positive communication climate.

Disengaging. If the relationship continues to be dissatisfying, people begin to drift apart. They become less willing to sacrifice for each other, and they show less forgiveness. Their communication changes from deep sharing of ideas and feelings to small talk and other "safe" communication to no significant communication at all. It may seem strange that people who had so much to share can find themselves with nothing to talk about. Not only are they no longer interested in exchanging significant ideas, they may begin to avoid each other altogether, seeking out other people with whom to share interests and activities. They depend less on each other and more upon other people for favors and support. Hostility need not be present; rather, this stage is likely to be marked by indifference. Even though Whitney and Madeline have been very close during their first year at college, they may drift apart over time. Maybe one of them betrayed the trust of the other and the tension led to their becoming more annoyed with each other's faults. If this has happened, they will spend less time together and talk about less important topics.

Ending. If the relationship can't be maintained at a less intimate level, it will end. A relationship has ended when the people no longer interact with each other. As Cupach and Metts (1986) show, people give many reasons for terminating relationships, including poor communication, lack of fulfillment, differing lifestyles and interests, rejection, outside interference, absence of rewards, and boredom.

"If you really cared about me, you would dump me."
© The New Yorker Collection from CartoonBank.com/ Corbis.

Friendships that Bridge Differences *By Brenda J. Allen*

How do we come to develop relationships with people of different backgrounds? Brenda J. Allen, University of Colorado, describes her interracial friendship with a lesbian woman. As you read, try to identify the different stages of their relationship to determine how their windows of self-disclosure and feedback changed as the relationship developed.

I expected to like Anna

even before I met her.... Since that time over six years ago, Anna and I have evolved from colleagues to best friends. From the beginning, Anna seemed to exchange cordial greetings as we passed in the halls. Students liked and respected her and I heard many comments about her excellence in teaching. Because I enjoyed a similar reputation as a teacher, I felt a sort of kinship with Anna. In addition, she dressed with a certain flair that I appreciated because in the public housing development (a.k.a "the projects") where I grew up, we black people took a special pride in how we looked. I admired how Anna, a white woman, knew how to coordinate her clothes and jewelry.

As luck would have it, Anna and I were assigned adjacent desks. As a result of such proximity, I couldn't help but hear how she interacted with her students. I often teased her about her den-mother approach to their problems. She began to do the same with me and we would laugh at ourselves but feel good about our mutual concerns for the students' welfare. Anna and I also found that we had similar ideas about issues, activities, and improvements on our own critical thinking skills in the classroom.

We soon discovered that we had much more in common than our teaching philosophies. We were both baby boomers from the Midwest, only months apart in age. We also came from lower-class families, and religion played a strong role in our childhoods. We were both spiritually grounded and sometimes prayed together. We were both raised to be caring and nurturing. Early in our relationship I began to appreciate the strong sense of reciprocity that I felt with Anna.

About a year into our friendship, a major turning point occurred in our relationship. Anna invited me to lunch off campus, and when I met her at the restaurant, she seemed somber. "I have something that I must tell you because our friendship is important to me." She took at deep breath and told me that she was a lesbian. After my initial surprise I thanked her for sharing something so personal and assured her that it would never negatively affect our friendship.

To the contrary, we have grown closer. As a heterosexual I had never before given much thought to sexual orientation of gays, "coming out of the closet." Thanks to Anna, I have become far more sensitive and enlightened. When she first invited me to her home, she showed me the room that had become her bedroom when family members visited because only a few people know that she and her "roommate" were partners. I was amazed by the extent of the masquerade that she felt compelled to perform to maintain a façade of being straight. Anna has since related many stories about the effort that she and gays make to maintain a heterosexual image.

I tend to be a private person with a clear demarcation between my work and my personal life. Nonetheless, after Anna opened up to me about her personal life I began to reciprocate. We now discuss every aspect of our relationships with family, friends, significant others, colleagues, and students. Whenever I find a prospective mate, Anna is usually the first and often only person I will tell. Once the relationship fizzles, she is always there to help me to get back out there in my quest for a significant other. I have often been pleasantly surprised by the similarities of issues that confront us both as we try to develop and maintain positive, intimate relationships.

I have grown comfortable enough with Anna to let her in on the "black" ways of communicating. I find myself calling her "Girl," an affectionate appellation that I normally reserve for African American sisters.

When I moved from a predominately white neighborhood to a racially mixed neighborhood, Anna understood why I felt more at home in my new surroundings. She had felt the same way in settings with a majority of gays and lesbians. We both seem to enjoy a similar sense of validation and contentment that differs from how we feel at work, where I am the only African American and she is the only lesbian on the faculty.

Anna and I laugh a great deal, often at each other, as well as cry together about personal trials and tribulations and the plight of our world.

Despite our similarities in personal style and background, Anna and I would probably not have become such good friends if she were straight. Because of her sexual orientation she can be empathetic with me in ways that my other white straight friends cannot. Thus, I believe that our marginalized positions in society and academia have been a major factor in forming the center of our friendship.

In regard to the title of this essay, Sapphire was a black female character in the old radio and television series Amos 'n' Andy. She was sassy, verbose, and intensely expressive. Sappho was a Greek poet (circa 600 b.c.) from the isle of Lesbos who wrote about romantic love between women. Each of these characters personifies one aspect of the multifaceted identities that Anna and I rarely allow others to see. Because we trust and respect one another, we are comfortable being our authentic selves—in all their complexities—with one another. ■

Excerpted from Allen, B. J. (2001). Sapphire and Sappho: Allies in authenticity. In A. Gonzalez, M. Houston, & V. Chen (Eds.), *Our Voices—Essays in Cultural Ethnicity and Communication*, (3rd ed., pp. 179–183). Los Angeles: Roxbury Publishing Company.

Unfortunately, when people decide to end a relationship, they sometimes look for reasons to blame each other rather than to finding equitable ways of bringing the relationship to an acceptable conclusion. When this happens, other relationships are usually affected. According to Leslie Baxter (1982), in the termination stage people are likely to use strategies of manipulation, withdrawal, and avoidance. Though misguided and inappropriate, manipulation involves being indirect and failing to take any responsibility for ending the relationship. Manipulators may purposely sabotage the relationship in hopes that the other person will break it off. Withdrawal and avoidance, also less than competent ways of communicating desires to terminate a relationship, take a passive approach, which leads to a slow and often painful death of a relationship.

The most competent way to end a relationship is to be direct, open, and honest. It is important to clearly state your wish to end the relationship while being respectful of the other person and sensitive to the resulting emotions. If two people have had a satisfying and close relationship, they owe it to themselves and to each other to be forthright and fair about communicating during the final stage of the relationship.

Perhaps Whitney and Madeline decide, separately, that they want to room with someone different next year. As effective communicators, they would discuss the sensitive topic without blame or manipulation, acknowledge that their relationship is less close than it once was, and move in with new roommates for the second year of college.

Relational Dialectics

Relational dialectics refers to the opposite pulls or tensions that both people in any relationship feel individually and together. Three common types of opposites or tensions are the tugs between autonomy and connection, openness and closedness, and novelty and predictability (Baxter & Montgomery, 1996; Baxter & West, 2003).

These oppositional forces go on within one person and between two people in a relationship at the same time. In other words, the tensions occur within an individual and within a relationship. Such contradictions are inherent in all relationships. There is no way to escape relational dialectics. Let's look at how these three opposite forces (dialectical tensions) may affect a relationship.

Autonomy–Connection. Let's imagine that Joel and Shelly have been dating for about a year. Shelly wants to spend most of her free time with Joel, but Joel has a greater need than she does for time alone or time with people other than Shelly. Shelly has a greater need for connection, while Joel has a greater need for autonomy or freedom. Here we can see the tendency for each person to want something different from the relationship. But Shelly doesn't want total connection and Joel does not want total autonomy either. Shelly wants a lot of connection, but she still wants some autonomy or some freedom in her relationship with Joel. And Joel, while wanting autonomy, still wants some connection with Shelly. Here we see that each person desires opposite forces simultaneously. They both want autonomy and connection in the relationship at the same time. But notice how each person wants different amounts of autonomy and connection in the relationship. Shelly and Joel do not have the option of selecting just one of these forces in their relationship. Rather, they need to achieve both autonomy and connection at the same time in the relationship. This sounds like quite a dilemma.

Openness–Closedness. Let's say that Shelly discloses quite a bit to Joel. She believes that it is important to divulge her feelings and reactions to Joel, and she expects him to do the same. In other words, the open quadrant of Shelly's Johari window in her relationship with Joel is quite large. Joel,

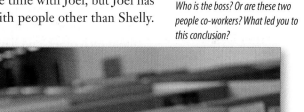

Relational dialectics—contradictory pulls in relationships.

Who is the boss? Or are these two people co-workers? What led you to this conclusion?

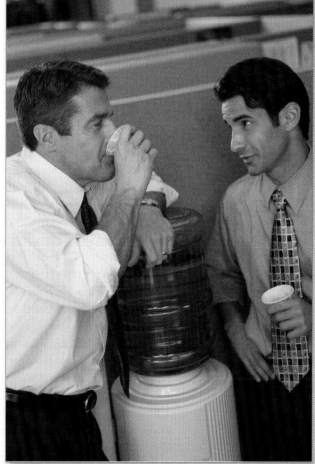

however, is a more private person. He does disclose to Shelly, but not as much as she would like. His secret quadrant of the Johari window is larger than Shelly would like it to be. The fact that Shelly and Joel differ in their preferred levels of self-disclosure is one source of tension in their relationship. But Shelly does not want complete openness all the time. She realizes that it is appropriate to be closed, or to refrain from self-disclosure with Joel, at times. So she seeks both openness and closedness in this relationship. Likewise Joel, while wanting more closedness than Shelly does, still wants some openness. So, like Shelly, he wants both opposite forces to occur simultaneously in this relationship.

Novelty–Predictability. A third common dialectical tension involves novelty and predictability. People want some degree of novelty as well as some degree of predictability in relationships. Because Shelly and Joel have been dating for a year, much of the uncertainty is gone from their relationship. We have already explained that people desire to reduce uncertainty because this measure makes communication more comfortable. But they do not want to eliminate uncertainty altogether. With no uncertainty at all, a relationship becomes so predictable and so routine that it is boring. While Shelly and Joel know each other well, can predict much about each other, and have quite a few routines in their relationship, there need to be surprises and newness in their relationship as well. Perhaps each one wants different amounts of novelty and predictability. Maybe Shelly wants Joel to surprise her with a novel date or wants them to make last-minute spontaneous decisions. Maybe Joel is a more cautious person and likes to operate by routines and with longer-range plans. Here is another contradiction between the two that must be managed in their relationship. But they must also cope with the fact that they each need some amounts of both novelty and predictability in the relationship.

Now let's consider two realities of dialectical tensions: They bring about change, and they occur in all interpersonal relationships.

Dialectical tensions bring about change in relationships. Dialectical tensions always exist in relationships, and they are ongoing and changing. Think of dialectical tensions as a pendulum making a wide swing. When a relationship moves toward too much autonomy, too much openness, or too much predictability, it will naturally swing to the opposite ends of these poles: connection, closedness, and novelty. Whenever a relationship involves too much of one side of the dialectic, the partners will move it toward the other side. So the relationship is always in flux. It is always changing as it moves between the opposite poles of the relational dialectics. No matter what stage a relationship is in, dialectical tensions exist. They might be in the foreground or in the background, but they keep the relationship in flux and evolving (Wood, 2000).

Dialectical tensions occur in all ongoing interpersonal relationships. Such tensions occur not just in romantic relationships, but also in friendships, family relationships, and work relationships. Think of the times that a parent wants more self-disclosure (openness) from a teenager than the teen wants to provide. Think of workplace situations where you want some rules (predictability) so you know how to behave, but you do not want too many rules so that you feel stifled. Perhaps you have disagreed with a friend about how much time you spend together or apart. These are all examples of dialectical tensions in relationships. If you have an interpersonal, rather than an impersonal relationship, with another person, then you are likely to experience the three dialectical tensions of autonomy–connection, openness–closedness, and novelty–predictability.

Managing Dialectical Tensions

You may be asking the question, "How do people cope with dialectical tensions in relationships?" How do people satisfy opposite needs at the same time in relationships? Several researchers (Baxter & Montgomery, 1996; Wood, 2000) have studied how people actually manage the dialectical tensions in relationships. People report using four types of strategies to manage dialectical tensions in relationships. Researchers have called these strategies temporal selection, topical segmentation, neutralization and reframing. In order to manage dialectical tensions, we may use any or all of these strategies. We may use a strategy without consciously realizing that we are doing so. It is important to understand these management strategies and to be able to employ these techniques so that we can reach agreement with a partner when a dialectical tension is jeopardizing our satisfaction in a relationship.

Temporal selection. Temporal selection involves selecting one side of the contradiction and ignoring the other side for a certain amount of time. Perhaps you and a friend realize that you have spent too much time apart lately (autonomy), so you make a conscious decision to pursue connection. That is, you agree that over the next few months, you will make a point of spending more time together. You schedule lots of plans together so you can be more connected. Remember, however, that over time, it will seem like you are spending too much time together, and so you will then move to the other end of the pole—autonomy. The selection of one side of a contradiction can never be permanent; it will last only for a certain period of time.

Temporal selection— selecting one side of a dialectical contradiction for a period of time.

Topical segmentation. You may satisfy contradictory needs in a relationship by separating situations or spheres of life. If a parent wants a teenager to be more open, perhaps the teen chooses to be open about certain topics or aspects of life such as feelings about school, work, or the future. The teen may opt to be closed about topics related to dating. This segmentation satisfies both parties' needs for balance in the openness–closedness dialectic. It is common for parents to disclose many things to their teens, but perhaps to be closed about the sexual or financial spheres of their lives.

Topical segmentation—separating situations or spheres of life as a way to manage dialectical tension in a relationship.

Neutralization. Neutralization is a compromise that partially meets the needs of both people in the relationship but does not fully meet the needs of either. A couple might pursue a moderate level of novelty and spontaneity in their lives, which satisfies both of them. The amount of novelty in the relationship may be less than what one person would ideally want and more than what the other would normally desire, but they have reached a middle point comfortable to both.

Neutralization—compromising in order to partially satisfy needs related to relationship contradictions.

Reframing. Reframing involves putting less emphasis on the dialectical contradiction. It means looking at our needs differently so they no longer seem quite so contradictory. Reframing is a type of change in one's perceptions. Maybe you are troubled by what seems like a large difference in openness between you

Reframing—putting less emphasis on a dialectical contradiction in a relationship.

and a partner. You think about how much you disclose to him and how little he discloses to you. You might even discuss this issue with your partner. Perhaps during the conversation you begin to realize the times that you refrain from disclosure (closedness), as well as the instances where he is open. After the conversation, you no longer see as strong a contradiction. You see yourselves as more similar than different on this dialectic. You have reframed your perception of the tension.

Turning Points in Relationships

Turning point—an event or occurrence associated with relationship change.

How do turning points in a family affect communication?

Not only do relationships go through stages and experience dialectical tensions, but they also have episodes of major change. A **turning point** is any event or occurrence associated with relationship change. Studies of romantic relationships (Baxter & Bullis, 1993; Baxter & Erbert, 1999) reveal some common turning points in the development of these types of relationships. Romantic couples often describe turning points such as the first date, first kiss, meeting the family, dealing with an old or new rival, sexual activity, going on vacation together, decision to date exclusively, a big fight, making up, a physical separation, living together, or getting engaged. A study of online romantic relationships (McDowell, 2001) revealed that the first phone call and first face-to-face meeting were turning points unique to developing relationships in cyberspace.

Turning points are marked occurrences that shape the direction and intimacy of the relationship. They are crucial junctures in the relationship that will affect the nature of the relationship and its future. This change can be positive or negative in the relationship. In many ways, a turning point moves a relationship forward on the path of development to greater intimacy, or it moves the relationship toward de-escalation to less intimacy, even dissolution.

Like progression through stages and managing dialectical tensions, turning points are elements of change in relationships. By examining turning points we can see how a relationship changes over time. When people are asked to think about the history of a relationship, they often refer to events that changed the relationship positively or negatively.

All relationships that have any history to them will have such turning points. Perhaps a certain episode of self-disclosure, a particular activity done together, or an important favor done for a partner characterize turning points in friendship relationships. Families often mark turning points in parent–child relationships with rituals, photographs, or memories. We commemorate the changing levels of dependence in the parent–child relationship marked by such turning points as the child's first day of school, religious coming-of-age ceremonies, obtaining a driver's license, going to college, and permanently moving out of the family home. All ongoing relationships have turning points.

We do not merely recollect turning points over the history of a relationship. It is important to recognize potential turning points as we experience them in our relationships. Oftentimes, it is necessary to talk about the relationship turning points that are emerging. In romantic relationships, clearly it is necessary to communicate directly about such turning points as dating exclusively, living together, or getting engaged. But it also may be productive to discuss relationship change associated with a first vacation together or a big fight. By talking about turning points, we can better understand their effects on our relationships.

> ### observe & analyze
>
> **Turning Points in Relationships**
>
> Select one long-term relationship in which you are involved. Identify what you consider to be the turning points in that relationship. For each turning point, indicate whether, in your opinion, the turning point was positive in deepening the relationship or negative in lessening relationship intimacy. For each turning point, indicate whether you discussed the turning point with the other person or not. ■

Theoretical Perspectives on Relationships

What determines whether or not we will try to build a lasting relationship with another person? Why do some relationships never move beyond a certain level or begin to deteriorate? Two theories, interpersonal needs theory and exchange theory, offer insights that help us to answer these questions.

Interpersonal Needs Theory

Relationships, like communication itself, exist in part because they satisfy basic human needs. **Interpersonal needs theory** proposes that whether or not a relationship is started, maintained, or developed depends on how well each person meets the interpersonal needs of the other. Psychologist William Schutz (1966, pp. 18–20) has identified three basic interpersonal needs that all of us have: affection, inclusion, and control.

Interpersonal needs theory— whether or not a relationship is started, built, or maintained depends on how well each person meets the interpersonal needs of the other.

The need for **affection** reflects a desire to express and to receive love. The people you know probably run the gamut of showing and expressing affection both verbally and nonverbally. At one end of the spectrum are the "underpersonal" individuals—those who avoid close ties, seldom show strong feelings toward others, and shy away from people who show or want to show affection. At the other end of the spectrum are the "overpersonal" individuals—those who thrive on establishing

Affection need—a desire to express and to receive love.

"close" relationships with everyone. They think of all others as intimates, confide in persons they have just met, and want everyone to consider them close friends. Somewhere in between these two extremes are "personal" people—those who can express and receive affection easily and who derive pleasure from many kinds of relationships with others.

Inclusion need—a desire to be in the company of other people.

The need for **inclusion** reflects a desire to be in the company of other people. According to Schutz, everyone has a need to be social. Yet people differ in the amount of interaction with others that will satisfy this need. At one extreme are "undersocial" persons—those who usually want to be left alone. Occasionally, they seek company or enjoy being included with others if specifically invited, but they do not require a great deal of social interaction to feel satisfied. At the other extreme are "oversocial" persons—those who need constant companionship and feel tense when they must be alone. If a party is happening, they must be there; if there is no party, they start one. Their doors are always open—everyone is welcome, and they expect others to welcome them. Of course, most of us do not belong to either of these extreme types. Rather, we are sometimes comfortable being alone and at other times need and enjoy interactions with others. The inclusion factor relates closely to the autonomy–connection dialectic discussed earlier. People with strong needs for inclusion are likely to want more connection with the relationship partner, while people with weaker needs for inclusion probably would want more freedom or autonomy.

Control need—a desire to influence the events and people around us.

The need for **control** reflects a desire to influence the events and people around us. As with the other two interpersonal needs, people vary in how much control they require. At one extreme are persons who need no control, who seem to shun responsibility and do not want to be in charge of anything. The "abdicrats," as Schutz calls them, are extremely submissive and are unlikely to make decisions or accept responsibility. At the other extreme are persons who like to be—indeed, who feel they must be—in charge. Such "autocrats" need to dominate others at all times and become anxious if they cannot. They may usurp responsibility from those who actually have the authority to control a situation, and they try to determine every decision. Again, most people fall somewhere between these two extremes. These "democrats" need to lead at certain times, but at other times they are content to follow the lead of others. Democrats can stand behind their ideas, but they also can be comfortable submitting to others, at least some of the time.

How can this analysis help us understand communication in relationships? Relationships develop and are sustained in part because the partners choose to meet each other's interpersonal needs. This can be difficult in relationships where individuals have different levels of needs. Through verbal and nonverbal communication behavior, we display cues that reveal the level of our immediate interpersonal needs. As you interact with others, you can detect whether their needs for affection, inclusion, and control seem different from yours. We also can talk to each other about relationship needs and negotiate ways to satisfy partners' different levels of needs.

Suppose that Emily and Dan have been seeing each other regularly and both see their relationship as close. If in response to Dan's attempt to put his arm around Emily while they are watching television, Emily slightly stiffens, it might suggest that Emily doesn't have quite the same need for affection as Dan. It should be emphasized that people's needs do differ; moreover, people's needs change over time. Differences in these and other needs may reflect the dialectical tensions in relationships. When other people's needs at any given time differ significantly from ours and we fail to understand that, we can misunderstand what's going wrong in our relationships and experience relationship dissatisfaction.

Exchange Theory

Another way of analyzing our relationships is on the basis of exchange ratios. **Exchange theory,** originated by John W. Thibaut and Harold H. Kelley, explains that relationships can be understood in terms of the exchange of rewards and costs that takes place during the individuals' interactions (Thibaut & Kelley, 1986, pp. 9–30). **Rewards** are outcomes that are valued by a person. Some common rewards are good feelings, prestige, economic gain, and fulfillment of emotional needs. **Costs** are outcomes that a person does not wish to incur and include time, energy, and anxiety. For instance, Sharon may be eager to spend time talking with Jan if she anticipates feeling good as a result; she may be reluctant to spend that time if she expects to be depressed at the end of the conversation.

According to Thibaut and Kelley, people seek interaction situations in which their behaviors will yield an outcome of high reward and low cost. For example, when Hunter and Jack spend the afternoon together, Jack talks mainly about himself and does not listen to Hunter. Hunter has a choice about whether to continue spending time with Jack or to leave. What Hunter does will depend in part on his cost/reward analysis of the interaction. While he perceives costs in spending time with Jack, he also enjoys being out of the house and spending time with a friend. Perhaps he would enjoy watching the ballgame together, even though he finds Jack's communication behavior today to be annoying. If Hunter sees more rewards in spending the afternoon with Jack than he sees costs, he will continue the interaction. If Hunter believes that the costs of being with Jack today exceed the rewards, then he is likely to leave.

This analysis can be extended from single interactions to relationships. If, over an extended period, a person's net rewards (reward minus cost) in a relationship fall below a certain level, that person will come to view the relationship itself as unsatisfactory or unpleasant. But if the net rewards are higher than the level viewed as minimally satisfactory, the person will regard the relationship or interaction as pleasant and satisfying.

Thibaut and Kelley suggest that the most desirable ratio between cost and reward varies from person to person and within one person from time to time. One reason people differ in their assessments of costs and rewards is that they have different definitions of what is satisfying. If people have a number of relationships they perceive as giving them a good cost/reward ratio, they will set a high satisfaction level and will probably not be satisfied with low-outcome relationships. By contrast, people who have few positive interactions will be satisfied with relationships and interactions that people who enjoy high-outcome relationships would

Exchange theory—relationships can be understood in terms of the exchange of rewards and costs that takes place during the interactions of individuals.

Rewards—outcomes that are valued by a person.

Costs—outcomes that a person does not wish to incur.

find unattractive. For instance, Calvin may continue to go out with Erica even if she treats him very poorly because based on his experiences in other relationships, the rewards he gets from being with Erica are on par.

The ratio of costs to rewards determines how attractive or unattractive a relationship or an interaction is to the individuals involved, but it does not indicate how long the relationship or interaction will last. Although it seems logical that people will terminate a relationship or an interaction in which costs exceed rewards, circumstances sometimes dictate that people stay in a relationship that is plainly unsatisfactory.

Comparison level of alternatives—other choices a person perceives as being available that affect the decision of whether to continue in a relationship.

Thibaut and Kelley's explanation for such a situation involves what they call the **comparison level of alternatives,** other choices a person perceives as being available that affect the decision of whether to continue in a relationship. A person who feels dissatisfied will tend to leave a relationship or interaction if there is a realistic alternative that seems to promise a higher level of satisfaction. But if there are no such alternatives, the person may choose to stay in the situation because, unsatisfactory though it is, it is the best the person believes can be attained at that time. Thus, if Joan has four or five men she gets along well with, she is less likely to put up with Charley, who irritates her. If, however, Joan believes that Charley is the only man who can provide the companionship she is seeking, she will be more inclined to tolerate his irritating habits.

Like Schutz's interpersonal needs theory, Thibaut and Kelley's exchange theory helps illuminate important aspects of relationship development. Yet critics of this theory point out an important limitation. Exchange theory suggests that people consciously and deliberately weigh the costs and rewards associated with any relationship or interaction. That is, people rationally choose to continue or ter-

What costs or rewards may be accruing to each person in this photo?

Communal Relationships

While exchange theory generally applies to our relationships, there can be relationships where we allow the costs to exceed the rewards yet still consider the relationships to be satisfactory. Communal relationships tend to be our very closest relationships with others, where we are less likely to regularly keep count of costs and rewards. We may consider these relationships so important that we will endure a situation of costs far exceeding rewards.

We are more concerned about the welfare of the other or about maintaining the relationship despite the uneven cost/reward ratio. You may maintain a relationship with a close friend, for example, if that friend has had a number of crises in her life and is unable to meet your emotional needs in the relationship. Maybe you give more to this person than you get in return, but your genuine concern for your friend's welfare keeps you in the relationship despite the costs to you.

Relationships between parents and adult children or between adult siblings may be described as communal in that they may persist even if one person bears more of the costs and other person reaps more of the rewards. For many people, maintaining nuclear family relationships takes precedence over an exchange theory analysis. ■

minate relationships. Thus, the theory assumes that people behave rationally from an economic standpoint: They seek out relationships that benefit them and avoid those that are costly (Trenholm, 1991, p. 72). In fact, although people may behave rationally in most situations, rational models such as Thibaut and Kelley's cannot always explain complex human behavior. Nevertheless, it can be useful to examine your relationships from a cost/reward perspective. Especially if a relationship is stagnating, you may recognize areas where costs are greater than rewards, either for you or for the other person. If so, you may be able to change some aspects of the relationship before it deteriorates completely.

You may discover that it is fruitful to use both the interpersonal needs theory and the exchange theory. What you (or your partner) count as "costs" and "rewards" may depend significantly on what your particular needs are. If your needs differ, you may misunderstand the other person's perceptions of rewards and costs. Looking at relationships in this way might help resolve misunderstandings and make you less defensive. That is, if you understand the other person's needs and can take his or her perceived costs and rewards into account, you may understand the situation better and in a way that is less destructive to your own self-esteem.

Communal relationships—
relationships where we allow the
costs to exceed the rewards.

Summary

One of the main purposes of interpersonal communication is developing and maintaining relationships. A good relationship is one in which the interactions are satisfying to and healthy for those involved.

People have three types of relationships. Acquaintances are people we know by name and talk with, but with whom our interactions are limited in quality and

A Question of Ethics

Madison has been dating Ron for about six months, and she is beginning to think that she might marry him in the next year or so because they seem to get along in every way. They have similar interests and values, and whenever they get together, their conversation flows freely. They can talk for a couple of hours without even trying. They are supportive of each other. In short, they just enjoy being with each other.

Yet Madison fears a potential problem: she was married for a short time to Chuck and has a three-year-old son named Sean who lives with her ex-husband and his parents. She has not seen her son for over a year. Madison didn't initially disclose any of this to Ron because he had mentioned that he wasn't really "kid oriented." Time passed and there never seemed to be a good time to tell him. Madison fears that if she tells Ron about her previous marriage, child, and divorce, the relationship

might break up. She does not want to continue to withhold this information, and yet she does not want to endanger the relationship.

As a good friend of Madison's, how would you advise her?

1. What are the ethical issues?
2. What should Madison do now?

---

quantity. Friends are people we spend time with voluntarily. We expect responsiveness, self-disclosure, emotional support, and conflict management from our friends. Close or intimate friendships are those in which we may share our deepest feelings, spend great amounts of time together, share activities and favors, and feel interdependence. People can examine the balance of disclosure and feedback in their relationships by drawing a Johari window to see whether both parties are sharing information in ways that help the relationship to grow.

Relationships go through a life cycle of building and developing, maintaining, and perhaps de-escalating and dissolving. Ways to maintain a relationship include spending time together, merging social networks, thinking of yourselves as a unit, sacrificing, emphasizing the positive, and forgiving.

Relationship dialectics are the inevitable tensions that occur in trying to meet our needs. Common relationship dialectics involve tensions between autonomy and connection, openness and closedness, and novelty and predictability. We manage contradictory needs through temporal selection, topical segmentation, neutralization, and reframing. Relationships experience turning points or events associated with relationship change.

Two theories are especially useful for explaining the dynamics of relationships. Schutz sees relationships in terms of their ability to meet the interpersonal needs of affection, inclusion, and control. Thibaut and Kelley see relationships as exchanges: People evaluate relationships through a cost/reward analysis, weighing the energy, time, and money invested against the satisfaction gained.

Chapter Resources

Communication Improvement Plan: Relationships

Do you have a relationship that you would like to change? Do you want to build, stabilize, or end the relationship? Using information in this chapter, write a communication plan to accomplish your goal. You can find a communication improvement plan worksheet on our website at www.oup.com/us/interact

Key Words

Relationship, *p. 58*	**Feedback,** *p. 61*	**Interpersonal needs theory,** *p. 75*
Interpersonal relationship, *p. 58*	**Johari window,** *p. 61*	**Affection need,** *p. 75*
Good relationship, *p. 58*	**Maintaining a relationship,** *p. 67*	**Inclusion need,** *p. 76*
Impersonal relationship, *p. 59*	**Relational dialectics,** *p. 71*	**Control need,** *p. 76*
Personal relationship, *p. 59*	**Temporal selection,** *p. 73*	**Exchange theory,** *p. 77*
Acquaintances, *p. 59*	**Topical segmentation,** *p. 73*	**Rewards,** *p. 77*
Friends, *p. 59*	**Neutralization,** *p. 73*	**Costs,** *p. 77*
Close friends or intimates, *p. 60*	**Reframing,** *p. 73*	**Comparison level of alternatives,** *p. 78*
Self-disclosure, *p. 61*	**Turning point,** *p. 74*	**Communal relationships,** *p. 79*

Inter-Act with Media

CINEMA

Tim Story (Director). (2002). ***Barbershop.*** Ice Cube, Cedric the Entertainer, Anthony Anderson, Sean Patrick Thomas, Eve, Troy Garity.

> **Brief Summary:** Barbershop is the story of how a young barber with dreams of a career as a famous musician learns to value the barbershop that he inherited from his father. Along the way, he learns about the value of relationships and contributing to his community.
>
> **IPC Concepts:** The movie is rich in all of the basics of relationships: types, communication patterns, exchange theory, need theory, and the ethical implications of how we treat those around us.

Chris Weitz and Paul Weitz (Directors). (2002). ***About a Boy.*** Hugh Grant, Nicholas Hoult, Toni Collette, Rachel Weisz.

> **Brief Summary:** The movie is based on a best-selling novel of the same title by Nick Hornby, a popular British novelist. In the story, Will Lightman is seen as a very hip Londoner who must come to terms with the importance of relational importance, responsibility, and morality. He initially prides himself on not needing anyone else until he meets a 12-year-old boy named Marcus. This young man is looking for what he calls "backup" for his relationship with him "mum." As he tries to engage Will in a backup role, two find themselves drawn into something greater than either individual.
>
> **IPC Concepts:** Close friends, intimates, disclosure, needs theory, exchange theory

WHAT'S ON THE WEB

Novaonline

> http://novaonline.nv.cc.va.us/eli/spd110td/interper/process/process.html
>
> **Brief Summary:** A wonderful Web site on various models of the communication process including relational models
>
> **IPC Concepts:** Relational model of communication, the role of the self

Love Test

> http://www.lovetest.com/
>
> **Brief Summary:** A fun and somewhat silly exercise that can put students in the mood or mind-set to discuss various attraction variables in relationships.
>
> **IPC Concepts:** Intimate relationships, needs theory, exchange theory

verbal communication

After you have read this chapter, you should be able to answer these questions:

- What is the relationship between language and perception?

- How do people assign meaning to words?

- How does culture affect language use?

- What is the difference between denotative and connotative meaning?

- What is the theory of muted groups?

- How can you improve your language usage so that it is more specific?

- How can you use the skills of dating information, indexing generalizations, and communication accommodation?

- How can you phrase messages so that they demonstrate sensitivity?

"Madge, Ed and I are having a really tough time."

"I'm sorry to hear that, Donna. What's happening?"

"Well, you know, it's just the way he acts."

"Is he being abusive?"

"Uh, no—it's not that. I just can't seem to figure him out."

"Well, is it the way he says things?"

"No, it's more what he doesn't say."

"What do you mean 'what he doesn't say'?"

"You know, he comes home and I ask him where he's been."

"And..."

"He says he was working overtime."

"And you don't believe him?"

"No, I believe him, it's just that he's working so much I'm just lonely."

"Have you talked with him about this?"

"No, I don't know how to say it and I don't think he'd understand me."

Given what Donna has said and the way she has said it, would you understand? Sometimes, for a variety of reasons, the way we form our messages makes it difficult for others to understand. Sometimes the problem is what we say—other times it's how we say it. In this chapter we will explain how the language we use to form our messages affects how accurately and easily we are understood.

The Nature of Language

As Thomas Holtgraves (2002) reminds us, "Language is one of those things that we often take for granted. It's almost like breathing—necessary for life but not something we pay much attention to unless problems develop. But unlike breathing, language has profound implications for our social existence. It plays a role in virtually every aspect of our dealings with others . . . . Understanding what we are doing when we use language can aid our understanding of what it means to be a social being" (p. 8).

First, we begin this chapter by explaining how language affects what we see and shapes what we think. Second, we describe the complex process by which people assign meaning to language. Third, we show how culture can affect language use. Fourth, we present many characteristics of language that affect our interpersonal exchanges. Fifth, we offer several skills for more effectively using language within interpersonal communication. In this section, we consider six skills that we can use to improve our use of language: using specific language, adapting language to listeners, dating information, indexing generalizations, practicing communication accommodation, and demonstrating linguistic sensitivity. Finally, we examine the unique use of language in two contexts: humor and cyberspace.

Language—the body of words and the systems for their use in messages that are common to a group of people.

How do we come to know what words mean?

Language and Perception

Language is both the body of words and the systems for their use in messages that are common to a group of people. A prominent language theorist, Kenneth Burke, describes the power of language when he explains that our use of symbols to name things is what makes us human. A symbol is something that refers arbitrarily to something else. For instance, the three letters, c a r, when combined into a word, form an arbitrary symbol for the machine that transports us from one place to another. Burke (1968) explains that for animals, reality just is. In other words, when an animal sees something, the animal perceives the object just as it appears in nature. The animal does not link a word or a term to the object. When your dog sees your car, the animal experiences the object directly, perhaps conjuring memories of going to the veterinarian or to the park. The dog does not link the letters "car" to the object. But for humans, reality is always filtered through symbols. For everything we see, there is a word that we cannot help but associate with the thing. This point may seem trivial, but you will see its relevance for shaping our behavior when we get to the subsequent part of this chapter on characteristics of language.

You may not have thought about it, but language allows us to perceive things. What we see in the world and the way we see it are shaped by language. Language allows us to perceive certain aspects of the world by naming them and allows us to ignore other parts of the world by not naming them. For instance, if you work in a job such as fashion or interior design that deals with many different words for color distinctions, you will be able to perceive finer differences in color. Knowing various words for shades of white, such as ecru, eggshell, cream, ivory, pearl, bone china white, and antique white, actually helps you see differences in shades of white. The same could be said for all the words for shades in the entire color spectrum. Similarly, there are concepts that people and society did not fully perceive until a word was coined to describe that concept. Think of the relatively new terms added to American English vocabulary in the last few decades such as date rape and male bashing. The behaviors to which those terms refer certainly existed before the expressions were coined. But as a society, we did not collectively perceive these behaviors until language allowed us to name them. A common example of how language shapes perception involves the multitude of words that Eskimos have for snow. Without an extensive vocabulary for snow, the average person can perceive only a few distinctions in snow. Sometimes, new words get created so that we perceive something differently. Employee layoffs have been renamed "downsizing," and that term is being replaced by "rightsizing." Notice how the first word leads us to see the job loss in terms of the employees, while the second and third terms shape our perception in terms of the organization's needs.

Sapir–Whorf hypothesis—a theory stating that a culture's language shapes how people think and perceive.

The concept that language affects perceptions is called the **Sapir–Whorf hypothesis**, named after two theorists, Edward Sapir and Benjamin Lee Whorf (Littlejohn, 2002). They expanded this concept a little further to say that the structure of a culture's language determines how people think in that culture. For instance, in English there are three verb tenses of past, present, and future. This language structure leads English-speaking people to think of life in terms of past, present, and future. The structure of the language shapes our view of reality. Another common cultural variation in language shaping people's ways of thinking concerns polarized language. **Polarized language** uses words that are opposites or extremes, like good/bad, right/wrong, love/hate, and beautiful/ugly. In Western societies like the United States, there are so many polar opposite words that people begin to perceive or think in terms of extremes. Try a free-association test with a friend to see how automatic polarized thinking is. For each word you state, your partner, in a Western society, is likely to state a word that conveys the opposite. This either/or thinking is not so common in Asian–Pacific cultures. The languages of many Eastern counties do not have as many pairs of polarized words, and so people are not as likely to perceive opposites, polarities, or dichotomies. (So the Sapir–Whorf hypothesis says that speakers of different languages will experience

Polarized language—words based on opposites or extremes.

the world differently.) These concepts show the enormous power of language. Though we may take language for granted, it is vitally important in shaping our reality.

Language and Meaning

On the surface, the relationship between language and meaning seems perfectly clear: We select the words, structure them using standard rules of syntax and grammar, and people will interpret our meanings correctly. In fact, the relationship between language and meaning is not nearly so simple. Instead, there is much complexity affecting how people derive meaning from words.

There are two theories that explain how people decide on the meaning of words: symbolic interactionism and coordinated management of meaning.

Symbolic interactionism is a theory that seeks to explain the relationship between language and meaning (Leeds-Hurwitz, 1995). This theory claims that the meaning of words is a product of social life. Whatever meaning a person has for a thing is a result of interactions with others about the thing. Again, you may not have thought about this concept, but none of your understanding of words or interpretation of concepts could have happened in a vacuum. As a child first developing language, you depended upon others to show you or model their interpretations of things. As an adult, even something as simple as looking up the standard meaning or definition of a word in a dictionary depends upon a type of interaction between you and the author of the dictionary. When we take something more complex, like a person's meaning of words like love, freedom, or responsibility, any understanding of those words can only have come through social interaction—through social experience with these abstract concepts or social interaction about our own and others' interpretations of these words.

> **Symbolic interactionism**—a theory stating that the meaning of words results from social interaction.

Coordinated management of meaning is a theory that elaborates on how people come to any agreement on the meaning of language and behavior (Philipsen, 1995). This theory explains that when people enter an interaction, they do not know exactly what to expect from that interaction. They do not know what rules of meaning the other person will be using. So in each exchange, people need to coordinate the rules of meaning for that interaction. The theory of coordinated management of meaning says that one individual may subtly propose enacting a certain type of communication (episode), but only when the other person accepts that proposal has the meaning of the symbols in that exchange been coordinated.

> **Coordinated management of meaning**—a theory explaining how people come to agree on the rules of meaning in an interaction.

Imagine for instance that Kacie subtly proposes a "flirting" episode of communication with Josh. There are certain behaviors, language, and nonverbal symbols that people generally associate with flirting. When Kacie enacts those behaviors, which she defines as flirting, Josh can accept or reject the type of communication she has offered. If he responds with flirting messages, then he has tacitly agreed with Kacie to enact a certain episode and they have together coordinated the meaning of their verbal and nonverbal symbols. In other words, they have agreed to similar rules and a similar interpretation of this exchange. It is important to note that only the communicators can coordinate the meaning of a communication episode. This explains why observers may misinterpret or get the wrong meaning from a situation of which they are not a part. Have you ever interpreted a couple's judgmental language and angry behavior as their "having an argument," while the participants themselves would describe the same exchange as "playful banter"?

The meaning of language is further complicated by the fact that words have two levels of meaning: denotation and connotation.

Denotation—the direct, explicit meaning a speech community formally gives a word.

Denotation. The direct, explicit meaning of a word is its **denotation,** the meaning found in a dictionary. In some situations, the denotative meaning of a word may not be clear. Why? First, dictionary definitions reflect current and past practice in the speech community; and second, the dictionaries use words to define words. The end result is that in addition to words being defined differently in various dictionaries, they may also have multiple meanings that change over time.

In addition, meaning may vary depending on the syntactic context (the position of a word in a sentence and the other words around it) in which the word is used. For instance, in the same comment a person might say, "I love vacationing in mountain areas. Mornings are really cool. Moreover, by getting out early you can see some really cool animals." Most listeners would understand that "mornings are really cool" refers to temperature and "see some really cool animals" refers to animals that are uncommon or special.

Connotation—the feelings or evaluations we personally associate with a word.

Connotation. The feelings or evaluations we personally associate with a word represent the **connotation** and may be even more important to our understanding of meaning. C. K. Ogden and I. A. Richards (1923) were among the first scholars to consider the misunderstandings resulting from the failure of communicators to realize that people's subjective reactions to words will be a product of their life experiences. For instance, when Tina says, "We bought an SUV. I think it's the biggest one Chevy makes," Kim might think, "Why in the world would anyone want one of those gas-guzzlers that take up so much space to park?" and Lexia might say, "Oh, I envy you. I'd love to afford a vehicle that has so much power and sits so high on the road." Word denotation and connotation are important because the only message that counts is the message that is understood, regardless of whether it is the one you intended.

Language and Culture

Cultures differ not only in the languages spoken but also in how messages should be worded. An important aspect of culture, which directly affects verbal communication, is the concept of low-context and high-context cultures. First, language use differs in low- and high-context cultures. In **low-context cultures**, messages are direct and language is very specific. Speakers are expected to say exactly what they mean. In low-context cultures, verbal messages are very explicit, with lots of details provided. There is a strong reliance on verbal means of communicating, and people can be forceful in persuading others. Generally, the United States, Germany, and Scandinavia are low-context cultures, using direct, specific, and detailed messages. In these cultures, you are expected to say exactly what you mean and get to the point. **High-context cultures**, on the other hand, prefer indirect messages with general, ambiguous language. People are more likely to talk around an issue rather

Low-context culture—a culture in which messages are direct, specific, and detailed.

High-context culture—a culture in which messages are indirect, general, and ambiguous.

than to be direct. There is more emphasis on nonverbal communication, and speakers more often use silence. Speakers are expected to be cautious and tentative in language used. Generally, Native American, Latin American, and Asian countries are high-context cultures using indirect, general, and simple messages (Chen & Starosta, 1998).

Such cultural variations in language can have a large effect on interactions between people of different cultural backgrounds. Imagine Isaac and Zhao, who have low- and high-context cultural expectations, respectively, trying to conduct business together.

> Isaac: *Let's get right down to business here. We're hoping that you can provide 100,000 parts per month according to our six manufacturing specifications spelled out in the engineering contract I sent you. If quality control finds more than 2 percent error, we will have to terminate the contract. Can you agree to these terms?*
>
> Zhao: *We are very pleased to be doing business with you. We produce the highest quality products and will be honored to meet your needs.*
>
> Isaac: *But can you supply that exact quantity? Can you meet all of our engineering specifications? Will you consistently have less than 2 percent error?*
>
> Zhao: *We are an excellent, trustworthy company that will send you the highest quality parts.*

Isaac is probably frustrated with what he perceives as general, evasive language used by Zhao, while Zhao may be offended by the direct questions, specific language, and perceived threat in the message. As global business and travel become more commonplace, we must understand the effect of culture on our communication.

How might culture affect the conversation between the people in this picture?

Power distance—the amount of difference in power between people, institutions, and organizations.

High power-distance culture—a culture in which power is distributed unequally.

Low power-distance culture—a culture in which power is distributed equally.

Second, language use differs based on the power distance of a culture. **Power distance** is the amount of difference in power between people institutions, and organizations. In **high power-distance cultures**, power is distributed unequally. Some people are perceived as having a great deal of power while others have very little. Thus a person with a title, rank, or status would be treated with much formality and respect. Formal terms of address like Mr. or Mrs., proper and polite forms of language, as well as nonverbal signals of status differences, would be evident in the exchange. The high-status person would control the interaction and others would listen without question. In **low-power distance cultures**, power is distributed equally. There is little perceived difference in power between people, regardless of actual titles, ranks, or status. People would address each other by first names rather than as Mr. or Mrs. The communication would be informal and casual. Neither person would control the exchange, and each person could question or confront the other.

Characteristics of Language

There are many characteristics of language that must be understood if we are to see how words affect our interpersonal communication. In this section, we will explain how language is arbitrary, ambiguous, abstract, self-reflexive, and changing, as well as how it reveals attitudes and emphasizes hierarchy and control.

Language is arbitrary. We have already explained that a word used to represent a thing is just an arbitrary selection. The machine that transports us from one place to another via the road would not be changed at all if we named it a "rul" rather than a "car." There is no physical connection between the word and its referent. Words are arbitrary symbols used by a speech community to represent objects, ideas, and feelings. While what word is used to represent the object or idea is arbitrary, for a word to be a symbol it must be recognized by members of the speech community as standing for a particular object, idea, or feeling. So different speech communities use different word symbols for the same phenomenon. The season for planting is called "spring" in English-speaking communities, but "printemps" in French-speaking communities. Speech communities not only vary in the words that they use, they also vary in how words are put together to form messages. The structure a message takes depends on the rules of grammar and syntax that have evolved in a particular speech community.

Language is ambiguous. No matter how specific you try to be with your words, there can always be multiple interpretations. We have already acknowledged that dictionary definitions of words can vary. Then there are the varying connotations or emotional meanings that people bring to words. Because the meaning of words is not in the words themselves but in the people, there cannot be total agreement between the sender and receiver. Even the notion of clarity in language can be misleading, because what is clear to you cannot be transferred to the mind of the other. To speak about clarity of communication implies a transfer of meaning. In other words, some speakers think that if they can just be clear enough in their language, then others will get their meaning. Interpersonal communication does not involve the transfer of meaning from one person's brain to the other person's brain. Instead, we should think of interpersonal communication as people working together to achieve similarity of meaning and consensus of interpretation.

Language varies in abstraction. A great number of the words we use really describe a category of similar items. Suppose you told your friend that you were about to buy a new car. "Car" is a category. At this point your friend might say, "What kind of car are you thinking about?" Now you're being asked to be more specific. What could you say? Let's look at the potential continuum from its most general to most specific. Figure 4.1 provides an illustration of this continuum.

The more abstract a word is, the more room for ambiguity of meaning between the communicators. If Rema refers to her pet, her co-worker Margi may think of a dog, cat, snake, bird, or hamster. Even if Rema specifically mentions her dog, Margi still has many possibilities for interpretation, including dogs of various breeds, sizes, colors, and temperaments. If words that refer to tangible objects like cars and pets vary in abstraction, imagine all the possibilities of meaning for non-tangible concepts such as honesty, patriotism, or justice.

Language allows for self-reflection. As symbol-using beings, we can talk about ourselves, discuss things outside our immediate experience, and discuss how well we are communicating. Reflexivity as an aspect of language has great impact on our lives. Because of language, humans have the capacity to think and talk about themselves. Thus, the notion of self-concept is an inherently linguistic and an inherently human invention. Language enables us to speak hypothetically, to talk about past and future events, and to communicate about people and things that are not present. Through language, we can discuss where we hope to be in five years, analyze a conversation two acquaintances had last week, or learn about the history that shapes the world we live in. Language enables us to learn from others' experiences, to share a common heritage, and to develop a shared vision for the future.

Language, coupled with the ability to reflect upon ourselves, allows for a higher-order communication, or communication about communication. Think of the possibility for improving interpersonal communication when people can comment on the very process of communicating.

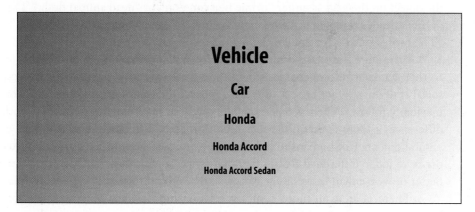

Figure 4.1

Level of Specificity

Language changes over time. Language changes in many ways, including the creation of new words, the abandonment of old words, changed word meanings developed by segments of society, and the influx of words from the mixing of cultures. For instance, the eleventh edition of *Merriam-Webster's Collegiate Dictionary* (2004) contains thousands of new words and usages. Younger generations will invent new words or assign different meanings to the words they learn. Terms such as *bling bling* (flashy jewelry and decorations) have come into common usage and may not be understood by your grandparents. In addition to new words created by young people, new inventions spur new words. Think of words related to technology that have entered our vocabulary: google, laptop, e-mail, DVD, and text message, to name a few. Terms used by older generation such as cellophane for plastic wrap, or piazza for porch, may fade from use over time. In addition, members of the speech community will invent new meanings for old words in order to differentiate themselves from other subgroups of the language community. For instance, in some parts of the country to teenagers *stupid* means *cool*, as in "That's a really stupid shirt," and *played* means *tiresome* or *boring*, as in "This party is played, let's split." As our society increases in multiculturalism, the English language gradually adopts what were once foreign words such as petite, taco, gelt, kindergarten, and lasagna, among thousands of others.

Language reveals attitudes. Language is not neutral. Most people do not realize the extent to which our word choice reveals our attitudes, judgments, or feelings.

Imagine that Shana routinely saves 60 percent of all money she earns. She lives in a very modest apartment, drives an old car, makes her own clothes, and rarely buys material possessions. What word comes to your mind to describe Shana's approach to money? Do you call her thrifty, budget-conscious, or frugal? Or do you select words such as tightwad, penny-pincher, or stingy? Notice how the first set of words tends to have a more positive connotation, while the second set of words conveys a negative connotation. By the word you use, a listener may infer your attitude toward the habit of saving versus spending one's income. If you see Hallie taking more time than others to make a decision, you could describe Hallie as either "thoughtful" or "dawdling." Likewise, someone may choose to refer to the object on the grill as either "prime filet mignon" or "dead animal flesh." Think of the attitudes revealed in such language as "She's just a housewife," "He's fat," or "The professor's a hard grader, but a good teacher."

Language can emphasize hierarchy and control. Kenneth Burke tells us that language allows comparisons and judgments and with comparisons come social orderings. Once we are able to compare, then notions of better and worse inevitably follow. When people compare anything with anything else and notice difference, seldom is that difference seen as merely difference. Instead, there is a natural tendency of humans to judge or evaluate difference in some way. This tendency to judge difference creates hierarchy, with some things (and people) seen as better or worse than others. Our words allow us to emphasize social hierarchies.

There is an even more complex relationship between language and social hierarchies, however, which can be explained by the **theory of muted groups** (Griffin, 1997). This theory claims that whoever is dominant in a social hierarchy has the power to shape everyone's perceptions via language. Thus the views of the

Theory of muted groups—a theory stating that whoever is dominant in a social hierarchy has the power to shape perceptions via language.

world of those who are subordinate will be repressed, and these people are effectively silenced; that is, their voices are muted. The novel *1984* by George Orwell illustrates the theory of muted groups well by showing that when those in power control the language, they also control thought and action. In this book, those in power created Newspeak, an official language in which war meant peace, freedom meant slavery, and ignorance was associated with strength. By changing the traditional meanings of words, those in power were able to prevent an entire population from rebelling against an oppressive totalitarian state.

You may be wondering how the theory of muted groups extends beyond Orwell's classic to affect your life today. All around you there are examples of powerful groups (the government, the media, your parents, your teachers) using language to impose their views of the world, thereby making it difficult or impossible for your view of the world to be heard. Imagine a teenager whose parents define her purchasing behavior as "wasteful spending." Once those words are invoked, all discussion between the teen and her parents centers around the issue of whether her spending is wasteful. It is difficult for the teen to speak positively about her spending because the conversation inevitably focuses on the concept of wastefulness. In essence her voice is muted. If she had initially defined her behavior as "wise spending," then the parents would have been more likely to let the conversation be framed by this term. When a government labels financial assistance to the poor as "wasteful spending," any further conversation on this issue is shaped by that term. A corporation may use the term "frivolous lawsuit," which makes it difficult for the plaintiffs in the case to move public perceptions toward the idea that the complaint has merit. Likewise, those in power can define war as a "peace-keeping effort," a reformer as an "agitator," or a less industrialized nation as "underdeveloped."

Improving Language Skills

There are many concrete skills that can improve our use of language in interpersonal situations. These include choosing specific language, adapting language to listeners, dating information, indexing generalizations, practicing speech accommodation, and demonstrating linguistic sensitivity.

Choosing Specific Language

When we speak in specific language, we reduce ambiguity and abstractness. This often helps speakers and listeners to assign similar meaning to words. Compare these two descriptions of a near miss in a car: "Some nut almost got me a while ago" versus "An hour ago, an older man in a banged-up Honda Civic ran the light at Calhoun and Clifton and almost hit me broadside while I was in the intersection waiting to turn left." In the second example, the message used language that was much more specific, so both parties are likely to have more similar perceptions of the situation than would be possible with the first description.

Specific words—words that clear up ambiguity caused by general words.

Often, as we try to express our thoughts, the first words that come to mind are general in nature. **Specific words** clear up ambiguity caused by general words by narrowing what is understood from a general category to a particular group within that category. Specific words are more concrete and precise than are general words. What can we do to speak more specifically?

We speak more clearly when we select a word that most accurately or correctly captures the sense of what we are saying. At first I might say, "Waylon was angry at the meeting today." Then I might think, "Was he really showing anger?" So I say, "To be more accurate, he wasn't really angry. Perhaps he was more frustrated or impatient with what he sees as lack of progress by our group." What is the difference between the two statements in terms of words? By carefully choosing words, you can show shades of meaning. Others may respond quite differently to your description of a group member according to whether they think the person is showing anger, frustration, or impatience. The interpretation others get of Waylon's behavior is very much dependent on the word or words you select. Specificity in language is achieved when words are concrete or precise or when details or examples are used.

Concrete words—words that appeal to our senses.

Use Concrete Words. Concrete words are words that appeal to our senses. Instead of saying that Jill "speaks in a peculiar way," we might be more specific by saying that Jill *mumbles*, *whispers*, *blusters*, or *drones*. Each of these words creates a clearer sense of the sound of her voice. Peculiar is an abstract word which should be replaced with a concrete verb to provide a clearer description.

Precise words—words that narrow a larger category to a smaller group within that category.

Use Precise Words. We speak more specifically when we are precise, narrowing a larger category to a smaller group within that category. For instance, if Nevah says that Ruben is a "blue-collar worker," she has named a general category; you might picture an unlimited number of occupations that fall within this broad category. If, instead, she is more precise and says he's a "construction worker," the number of possible images you can picture is reduced; now you can select your image only from a specific subcategory, construction worker. So your meaning is likely to be closer to the one Nevah intended. To be even more precise, she may identify Ruben as "a bulldozer operator"; this further limits your choice of images and is likely to align with the one she intended you to have.

In the examples that follow, notice how the use of concrete and precise language in the right-hand column improves the clarity of the messages in the left-hand column.

observe & analyze

Precision

Revise each of the following sentences to include words that are more precise.

The food was great.

Mary's stuff is really nice.

The new building is awful.

She's like, you know, really cool.

Stay away from Don—he's a real jerk.

He was really on me for being late.

Jones assigns a lot of outside reading for the course.

I like sweet potatoes, they're neat.

At the PGA, lots of players had trouble with the weather. ■

The senator brought *several things* with her to the meeting.	The senator brought *recent letters from her constituency* to the meeting.
He lives in a *really big house*.	He lives in a *fourteen-room Tudor mansion*.
The backyard has *several different kinds of trees*.	The backyard has *two large maples, an oak, and four small evergreens*.

Morgan is a *fair grader*.	Morgan *uses the same standards for grading all students*.
Many students *aren't honest* in class.	Many students *cheat on tests* in class.
Judy *hits* the podium when she wants to emphasize her point.	Judy *pounds on* the podium when she wants emphasize her point.

Provide Details and Examples. While choosing concrete and precise wordings enables us to improve clarity, there are times when a word may not have a more specific or concrete synonym. So another way to achieve specificity is to use a detail or an example to clarify. Suppose Linda says, "Rashad is very loyal." Since the meaning of loyal (faithful to an idea, person, company, and so on) is abstract, to avoid ambiguity and confusion Linda might add, "I mean he never criticizes a friend behind her back." By following up her use of the abstract concept of loyalty with a concrete example, Linda makes it easier for her listeners to "ground" their idea of this personal quality in a concrete or "real" experience.

Adapt Language to Listener

There are times when we use words that our listeners do not understand. Sometimes these words are so familiar to us that we forget that others are unaware of their meaning. When we adapt our language to our listeners we (1) use vocabulary the listener understands, (2) use jargon sparingly, and (3) use slang when speaking with others who know that vocabulary.

Use Vocabulary the Listener Understands. People vary in the extent to which they know and use a large variety of words. If you have made a conscious effort to expand your vocabulary, are an avid reader, or have spent time conversing with others who use a large and varied selection of words, then you probably have a large vocabulary. The larger your vocabulary, the more choices you, as a speaker, have from which to select the words you want. Having a larger vocabulary, however,

Strategic ambiguity—purposeful vagueness in interactions.

the gray zone

Strategic Ambiguity

In most situations, an effective communicator attempts to use clear, specific, and precise words in order to reduce ambiguity and misunderstanding. But in some situations a speaker may choose to use vague language when interacting with another person. Being purposefully vague when communicating is called using strategic ambiguity. There are many specific reasons a person may choose to be ambiguous, but most have to do with protecting either himself or herself or another person or the relationship.

For example, if a new co-worker asked your opinion about your manager, with whom you have a difficult working relationship, you might be cautious and vague in replying, "Most people feel that she's a hardworking person." By couching your answer as a group opinion, you have provided accurate information and have not actually been deceptive; however, by withholding your personal opinion, you have protected yourself.

Research shows that there can be positive benefits of strategically ambiguous messages in relationships. Teenagers, for instance, frequently choose to be more clear, specific, and definite when revealing information to peers than to parents. Being somewhat vague in communicating with parents serves to preserve family harmony and advances teens' natural drive toward independence (Sillars, 1998). ■

can present challenges when you are communicating with people whose vocabulary is more limited. For example, if Carl, an interior designer, phones his client Jim and says he has chosen an "ecru brocade fabric" for the couch in Jim's office, Jim might not picture the beige-toned cloth with a raised design. As a speaker, therefore, you must try to adapt your vocabulary to the level of your partner so that your words will be understood. One strategy for assessing another's vocabulary level is to listen to the types and complexity of words the other person uses—that is, to take your signal from your communication partner. So if Carl noticed Jim describing colors in very basic terms, Carl might want to explain the meaning of the more precise words he uses to describe colors. Adjusting your vocabulary to your partner is part of the concept of behavioral flexibility, which we discussed in Chapter 1. When you have determined that your vocabulary exceeds that of your partner, you can use simpler synonyms for your words or use word phrases composed of more familiar terms. Adjusting your vocabulary to others does not mean talking down to them. It is merely polite behavior and effective communication to try to select words that others understand. Think of your frustration in situations when speakers repeatedly used words that you could not comprehend.

Jargon—technical terminology whose meaning is idiosyncratic to a special activity or interest group.

How does jargon improve or hinder communication?

As a listener, there are other strategies we can use to better understand others' words. First, we can develop our own vocabulary. By learning new words, we will be in a better position to understand others, and we will have more choices of words to specifically and precisely express our thoughts. Second, we can question the speaker so that we come to understand any unfamiliar words the speaker has used. So when Carl tells Jim that the fabric is ecru, Jim might ask, "Is ecru an earth-toned color?" By asking for specifics, he can get clarification of the unfamiliar word.

Use Jargon Sparingly. Jargon refers to technical terms whose meaning is understood only by a select group of people based on their shared activity or interests. We may form a special speech community, which develops a common language (jargon) based on a hobby or occupation. Medical practitioners speak a language of their own, which people in the medical field understand and those outside the medical field do not. The same is true of lawyers, engineers, educators, and people in virtually all occupations. If you are an avid computer user, you may know lots of terms that non–computer users do not. Likewise, there are lingoes associated with sports, theater, wine tasting, and science fiction, to name just a few interest

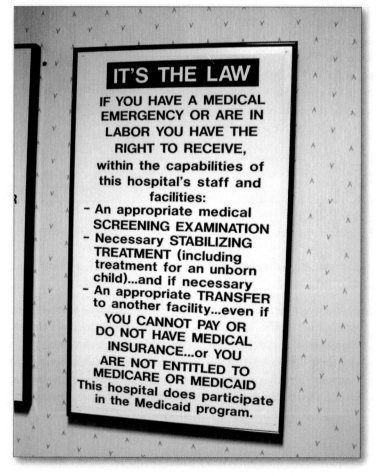

groups. Imagine a person interested in environmental concerns speaking about "PCBs" "brownfields," and "eco-terrorism" with someone who does not understand this jargon. The key to effective use of such specialized terms is to employ them only with people who speak the same jargon. When people understand the same jargon, then its use facilitates communication. Jargon becomes a shorthand way of expressing yourself within the jargon-based community. If you must use jargon with people outside that occupation or special interest group, remember to explain the terms you are using. Without explanation to outsiders, jargon becomes a type of foreign language.

Use Slang Appropriately. Slang refers to informal vocabulary developed and used by particular groups in society. It is casual and playful language deliberately used in place of standard terms. Slang is a type of alternative vocabulary that performs an important social function. Slang bonds those in an inner circle who use the same words to emphasize a shared experience. But slang simultaneously excludes others who don't share the terminology. The simultaneous inclusion of some and exclusion of others is what makes slang so popular with youth in all cultures. Young people often invent words (slang), which other youth understand but adults do not. Slang words do not last a long time because they either get adopted into standard language or they are dropped from usage because too many outsiders come to understand them, calling for the development of new slang words to again bond some people and exclude others.

Slang may emerge from teenagers, urban life, college life, gangs, or other contexts. A teenager might say, "I'm a beast" to mean "I performed very well." "My bad" is slang for "I made a mistake." "That's tight" could be translated as "That's great, fine, or excellent." Using slang appropriately means using it with people

Slang—informal, nonstandard use of vocabulary.

skill builders   ADAPT LANGUAGE TO LISTENERS

SKILL	USE	PROCEDURE	EXAMPLE
Using vocabulary, jargon, and slang that listeners understand.	To avoid words that listeners do not understand	1. Use simpler synonyms or familiar terms for words. 2. Explain jargon terms to listeners who may not understand them. 3. Use slang only with listeners who understand the words.	Instead of saying, "Jose is in his penultimate year of work," Larry can say, "Jose is in his next to last year of work." Sally can say, "Your asset-to-liability ratio, which is a calculation of how much money you have compared to how much money you owe, is really quite good." Judy can say a rock star is "hot" when talking with a friend, but describe the star as "cute" when talking with her aunt.

who understand the slang but avoiding it with people who do not share the slang terminology. If your communication purpose is to be understood, then you must give careful consideration to the words you use. If others are likely to understand your words, then feel free to use them. If listeners may not understand your words, then it is probably not wise to use those words with those people.

Date Information

Dating information means specifying the time or time period that a statement was true or known to be true. Why is this important? We draw conclusions based on information. If the information is inaccurate, the conclusions drawn from that information are likely to be inaccurate as well. A common source of inaccuracy is giving the impression that information is current when in fact it is not. For instance, Parker says, "I'm going to be transferred to Henderson City. As I remember, you are familiar with it." Laura replies, "Yes I am. Let me just say that they've had some real trouble with their schools." On the basis of Laura's statement, Parker may worry about the effect the move will have on his children. What he doesn't know is that Laura's information about this problem in Henderson City is five years old! Henderson City may still have problems, but then again, it may not. Had Laura replied, "Five years ago, I know they had some real trouble with their schools. I'm not sure what the situation is now, but you may want to check," Parker would have looked at the information differently.

Nearly everything changes with time. Some changes are imperceptible; others are so extensive that old information becomes inaccurate, obsolete, and even dangerous. We can make our messages clearer by using the skill of dating to indicate when the information we are conveying was accurate. To date information, we (1) consider or find out when the information was true, and (2) verbally acknowledge this time frame. This seems like a simple skill to put into practice—and it is. But often, we just don't think about the implication of evaluating a situation using old data. Consider each of the examples that follow. The statements on the left are undated generalizations; those on the right are carefully dated generalizations.

Cancún is really popular with the college crowd.	When we were in Cancún *two years ago*, it was really popular with the college crowd.
Professor Powell brings great enthusiasm to her teaching.	Professor Powell brings great enthusiasm to her teaching—at least she did *last quarter* in communication theory.
The Beast is considered the most exciting roller coaster in the country.	*Years ago*, the Beast was considered the most exciting roller coaster in the country.
You think Mary's depressed? I'm surprised. She seemed her regular high-spirited self when I talked with her.	You think Mary's depressed? I'm surprised. She seemed her regular high-spirited self when I talked with her *the day before* yesterday.

We have no power to prevent change. But we can increase the effectiveness of our messages if we verbally acknowledge the reality of change by dating the statements we make.

skill builders   DATING INFORMATION

SKILL	USE	PROCEDURE	EXAMPLE
Including a specific time referent that indicates when a fact was true.	To avoid the pitfalls of language that allow you to speak of a dynamic world in static terms.	1. Before you make a statement, consider or find out when the information was true. 2. If not based on present information, verbally acknowledge when the statement was true.	When Jake says, "How good a hitter is Steve?" Mark replies by dating his evaluation: "When I worked with him two years ago, he couldn't hit the curve."

Index Generalizations

Indexing generalizations is the mental and verbal practice of acknowledging the presence of individual differences when voicing generalizations. Generalizations allow people to use what they have learned from their experiences and apply them to others. For instance, when Glenda, a third grade teacher, learns that three of her students who have been absent frequently are at or near the bottom of her class in reading, she generalizes that students who fail to attend school regularly are likely to do poorly in reading.

Although the capacity to generalize carefully is important to all of us in our decision making, the misuse of generalization contributes to perceptual inaccuracies because it ignores individual differences. Thus, just because Alex and Manuel are better at math than Alicia does not mean that boys (or men) in general are better at math than girls (or women) or are better than Alicia in any other respect.

To avoid making misleading statements or even stating generalizations that may be true, we need to practice indexing, a skill that is borrowed from mathematics, where it is used to acknowledge individual elements within a group (X1, X2, X3, etc.). We mentally index by acknowledging that whether we have observed one, five, or ten or more, we can't always be sure that a generalization based on those examples or cases is valid. Thus just because we learn that Brent has bought a top-of-the-line Mercedes (a very expensive car), it does not mean that Brent is rich. So, if we were to say, "Brent bought a Mercedes, he must be rich," we should add, "of course not all people who buy Mercedes are rich."

Here are two steps to help you use the skill of indexing. (1) Consider whether what you want to say is about a specific object, person, or place, or whether it is a generalization about a class to which the object, person, or place belongs. (2) If what you want to say is based on a generalization about the class, qualify your statement appropriately so that your assertion does not go beyond the evidence that supports it.

In the examples that follow, the statements on the left are overgeneralizations, whereas those on the right have been carefully indexed.

Indexing generalizations—the mental and verbal practice of acknowledging the presence of individual differences when voicing generalizations.

Because men are stronger than women, Max is stronger than Barbara.	*In general*, men are stronger than women, so Max is probably stronger than Barbara.
State's got to have a good economics department; the university is ranked among the top twenty in the nation.	Because State's among the top twenty schools in the nation, the economics program should be a good one, *although it may be an exception.*
Jack is sure to be outgoing; Don is, and they're both Joneses.	Jack is likely to be outgoing because his brother Don is (they're both Joneses), *but Jack could be different.*
Your Chevrolet should go fifty thousand miles before you need a brake job; Jerry's did.	Your Chevrolet may well go fifty thousand miles before you need a brake job; Jerry's did, *but, of course, all Chevrolets aren't the same.*

All people generalize at one time or another, but by using indexing, we can avoid the misunderstandings that generalized statements can create.

Practice Communication Accommodation

Communication accommodation theory—describes the practice of changing language patterns to adjust to a speaker.

Convergence—making language similar to another's language.

Divergence—making language different from another's language.

Communication accommodation theory explains that people may change their language patterns to accommodate their partner (Giles & Coupland, 1991). These researchers observed that when we talk with someone we will adapt our language in one of two ways. We may try to match the style of our partner, which is called **convergence**, or we may try to speak differently from the other person, which is called **divergence**. When we want to signal that we are part of a group or show closeness to another person, we use language and language patterns that are more like those of the other. When we want to distance ourselves from a group or another person, we use language and language patterns that are different. The features we alter when practicing communication accommodation can include our verbal vocabulary (grammar, slang, jargon, and profanity). We might also modify nonverbal communication features, including volume, tone of voice, use of accents, pronunciation, and rate of speaking. We explore this option in the next chapter.

skill builders   INDEXING GENERALIZATIONS

SKILL	USE	PROCEDURE	EXAMPLE
Mentally or verbally accounting for individual differences.	To avoid "allness" in speaking.	1. Before you make a statement, consider whether it pertains to a specific object, person, or place. 2. If you use a generalization, inform the listener that it does not necessarily apply in the situation being discussed.	"He's a politician and I don't trust him, although he may be different from most politicians I know."

An elementary school teacher who also uses simple words with a lot of voice variety and a slow rate of speech when talking with her young students is using convergence to make her communication more like theirs. A college professor reprimanding her class, however, may accentuate the differences between them by using complex vocabulary, completely correct grammar, no slang, and a formal tone of voice.

Research has shown an interesting connection between culture and communication accommodation (Larkey, 1996). Perceptions of status, authority, and cultural identity affect how communication accommodation occurs. Those considered lower in status in a society are expected to adjust their communication to be more similar to higher-status speakers, not vice versa. For instance, Euro-American males are less likely to practice communication convergence. They typically maintain their language style as standard and others, such as women and minorities, accommodate to that style. Indeed, the unwillingness of a lower-status communicator to adjust to the higher-status speaker can be seen as a sign of disrespect because it seems to signal a desire to remain separate or distant.

Demonstrate Linguistic Sensitivity

It is important to be aware of potential language differences between people and to remember how our language reveals our attitudes and creates and reinforces notions of power. By realizing that people differ in the language they use and the ways they interpret words, we can try to be more sensitive in our use of language. You demonstrate linguistic sensitivity when you choose language that respects others and avoid usages that others perceive as offensive. Some of the mistakes in language that we make result from using expressions that are perceived by others as sexist, racist, or otherwise biased—that is, any language that is perceived as belittling any person or group of people. The most prevalent linguistic styles that are insensitive are those that use generic, nonparallel, or racist language.

Generic Language. In generic language speakers use words that may also apply only to one sex, race, or other group as though they represent everyone. This usage is a problem because it linguistically excludes a portion of the population it ostensibly includes. The following paragraphs contain some examples of generic language.

Generic language—words that may apply only to one sex, race, or other group used as though they represent everyone.

Traditionally, English grammar called for the use of the masculine pronoun *he* to stand for the entire class of humans regardless of gender. Under this rule, standard English called for such usage as "When a person shops, *he* should have a clear idea of what *he* wants to buy." Even though these statements are grammatically correct, they are sexist because the language (he) inherently excludes females. Despite traditional usage, it is hard to picture people of both sexes when we hear the masculine pronoun *he*.

So sensitive language avoids sentences that use only male pronouns when no specific gender reference is intended. You can avoid this in one of two ways. First, use plurals. For instance, instead of saying "Because a doctor has high status, his views may be believed regardless of topic," you could say, "Because doctors have

"S.P. — I suppose you realize that around here you're becoming like a son to me."

high status, their views may be believed regardless of topic." Alternatively, you can use both male and female pronouns: "Since a doctor has high status, his or her views may be believed regardless of topic." Stewart, Cooper, Stewart, and Friedley (1998, p. 63) cite research to show that using "he and she," and to a lesser extent "they," gives rise to listeners including women in their mental images, thus increasing gender balance in their perceptions. These changes are small, but the resulting language is more accurate than the generic option and demonstrates sensitivity.

A second problem results from the traditional use of the generic word *man*. "Generic man" refers to the use of *man* as part of a word when the referent is to all humans. Many words have become a common part of our language that are inherently sexist in that they apply to only one gender. Consider the term *man-made*. What this really means is "produced by human beings," but its underlying connotation is "made by a male human being." Some people try to argue that just because a word has "man" within it does not really affect people's understanding of meaning. But research has demonstrated that people usually visualize men (not women) when they read or hear these words. Moreover, when job titles end in "man," their occupants are assumed to have stereotypically masculine personality traits (Gmelch, 1998, p. 51).

In past generations this masculine generalization may have been appropriate, but that is no longer the case. Using generic terms when speaking about all human beings is troubling, but using them to describe the behavior or accomplishments of women (as in "Sally creates and arranges man-made flowers") is humorous.

For most sexist expressions, you can use or create suitable alternatives. For instance, use *police officer* instead of *policeman*, and substitute *synthetic* for *man-made*. Instead of saying *mankind*, change the construction—for example, go from "All of *mankind* benefits" to "All the *people in the world* benefit."

Nonparallel Language. Nonparallel language is language in which terms are changed because of the sex, race, or other characteristics of the individual. Because it treats groups of people differently, nonparallel language is also belittling. Two common forms of nonparallelism are marking and unnecessary association.

Marking means the unnecessary addition of sex, race, age, or other designations to a general word. For instance, "doctor" is a word representing a person with a medical degree. To describe Sam Jones as a doctor is to treat Jones linguistically as a member of the class of doctors. For example, you might say "Jones, a doctor, contributed a great deal to the campaign." If, however, you said, "Jones, a woman doctor" (or a black doctor, or an old doctor, or a handicapped doctor), you would be marking. Marking is offensive to some people because you may appear to be trivializing the person's role by laying emphasis on an irrelevant characteristic. For instance, if you say, "Jones is a really good female doctor" (or black doctor, or old doctor, or handicapped doctor), you may be intending to praise Jones. But your listeners may interpret the sentence as saying that Jones is a good doctor for

Nonparallel language—language in which terms are changed because of the sex, race, or other characteristic of the individual.

Marking—the unnecessary use of sex, race, age, or other designations in addition to a general word.

diverse voices

I Am ... *By Dolores V. Tanno*

How do you behave when you are asked to talk about yourself, especially when you are perceived as "different," whether that difference is by sex, religion, or ethnicity? Delores V. Tanno, University of Nevada, Las Vegas, describes how each ethnic self-reference communicates a story, and multiple stories provide significance to determining who "I am."

Over the course of my life

one question has been consistently asked of me: *"What are you?"* I used to reply that I was American, but it quickly became clear this was unacceptable because what came next was, "No, really what are you?" In my more perverse moments I responded, "I am human." I stopped when I realized that people's feelings were hurt. Ironic? Yes, but the motive behind the question often justified hurt feelings. I became aware of this only after asking a question of my own: "Why do you ask?"

Confronting the motives of people has forced me to examine who I am. In the process I have had to critically examine my own choices, in different times and contexts, of the names by which I am placed in society. The names are "Spanish," "Mexican American," "Latina," and "Chicana."

"I am Spanish." Behind this label is the story of my childhood in northern New Mexico. New Mexico was the first permanent Spanish settlement in the Southwest, and New Mexicans have characterized themselves as Spanish for centuries. My parents, grandparents, and great-grandparents consider themselves Spanish; wrongly or rightly they attribute their customs, habits, and language to their Spanish heritage, and I followed suit. In my young mind, the story of being Spanish did not include concepts of racial purity or assimilation; what it did do was allow me to begin my life with a clearly defined identity and a place in the world. For me, the story of being Spanish incorporates into its plot the innocence of youth, before the reality of discrimination became an inherent part of the knowledge of who I am.

"I am Mexican American." When I left New Mexico, my sense of belonging did not follow me across the state border. When I responded to the question, "What are you?" by saying, "I am Spanish," people corrected me: "You mean Mexican, don't you?" My initial reaction was anger; how could they know better than I who I was? But soon my reaction was one of puzzlement, and I wondered just why there was such insistence that I be Mexican. Reading and studying led me to understand that the difference between Spanish and Mexican could be found in the legacy of colonization. Thus behind the name "Mexican American" is the story of classic colonization that allows for prior existence and that also communicates duality. As Richard A. Garica argues: "Mexican in culture and social activity, American in philosophy and politics." As native-born Mexican Americans we also have dual visions: the achievement of the American Dream and the preservation of cultural identity.

"I am Latina." If the story behind the name Mexican American is grounded in duality, the story behind the name "Latina" is grounded in cultural connectedness. The Spaniards proclaimed vast territories of North and South America as their own. They intermarried in all the regions in which they settled. These marriages yielded offspring who named themselves variously as Cubans, Puerto Ricans, Colombians, Mexicans, and so forth, but they connect culturally with one another when they name each other Latinas. To use the name *Latina* is to communicate acceptance and belonging in a broad cultural community.

"I am Chicana." This name suggests a smaller community, a special kind of Mexican American awareness that does not involve others (Cubans, Puerto Ricans, etc.). The name was the primary political as well as rhetorical strategy of the Chicano movement of the 1960s. Mirande and Enriquez argue that the dominant characteristic of the name "Chicana" is that it admits a "sense of marginality." There is a political tone and character to

"Chicana" that signifies a story of self-determination and empowerment. As such, the name denotes a kind of political becoming. As the same time, however, the name communicates the idea of being American, not in a "melting pot" sense that presupposes assimilation, but rather in a pluralistic sense that acknowledges the inalienable right of existence for different peoples.

What, then, am I? The truth is I am all of these. Each name reveals a different facet of identity that allows symbolic, historical, cultural, and political connectedness. These names are no different than other multiple labels we take on. For example, to be mother, wife, sister, and daughter is to admit to the complexity of being female. Each name implies a narrative of experiences gained in responding to circumstances, time, and place and motivated by a need to belong.

In my case, I resort to being Spanish and all it implies whenever I return to my birthplace, in much the same way that we often resort to being children again in the presence of our parents. But I am also Mexican American when I balance the two important cultures that define me; Latina when I wish to emphasize cultural and historical connectedness with others; and Chicana whenever opportunities arise to promote political empowerment and assert political pride.

It is sometimes difficult for people to understand the "both/and" mentality that results from this simultaneity of existence. We are indeed enriched by belonging to two cultures. We are made richer still by having at our disposal several names by which to identify ourselves. Singly the names Spanish, Mexican American, Latina, and Chicana communicate a part of a life story. Together they weave a rhetorically powerful narrative of ethnic identity that combines biographical, historical, cultural, and political experiences. ∎

Excerpted from Tanno, D. V. (2001). Names, narratives, and the evolution of ethnic identity. In A. Gonzalez, M. Houston, & V. Chen (Eds.), *Our Voices—Essays in Cultural Ethnicity and Communication* (3rd ed., pp. 25–28). Los Angeles: Roxbury Publishing Company.

---

a woman (or a black or old or handicapped person) but not necessarily as good as a male doctor (or a white or young or able-bodied doctor).

If it is relevant to identify a person by sex, race, age, or other characteristic, do so, but leave markers out of your labeling when they are irrelevant. One test of whether a characteristic is a relevant marker and appropriate is whether you would mention the person's sex, race, or age regardless of what sex, race, or age the person happened to be. It is relevant to specify "female doctor," for example, only if in that context it would be equally relevant to specify "male doctor."

Unnecessary association— emphasizing one person's association with another when you are not talking about the second person.

Unnecessary association is putting emphasis on one person's association with another when you are not talking about the second person. You hear a speaker say something like "Gladys Thompson, whose husband is CEO of Acme Inc., is the chairperson for this year's United Way campaign." In response to this sentence, you might say that the association of Gladys Thompson with her husband gives further credentials to Gladys Thompson. But using the association may be seen to imply that Gladys Thompson is important not because of her own accomplishment but because of her husband's. The following illustrates a more flagrant example of unnecessary association: "Don Jones, the award-winning principal at Central High School and husband of Brenda Jones, local state senator, is chairperson for

spotlight on scholars

Molefi Kete Asante, Professor of Africology, Temple University, on
The Language of Prejudice and Racism

Molefi Kete Asante is an activist scholar who believes it is not enough to know, one must act to humanize the world. Throughout his career Asante has sought not only to understand what he studied, but also to use that knowledge to help people learn to exert their power.

In 1968, at the age of twenty-six, Asante completed his Ph.D. in communication at UCLA. As a graduate student, Asante studied language and the rhetoric of agitation. For his dissertation he analyzed the speeches of one of the most zealous agitators of the American Revolution, Samuel Adams. During the late 1960s, however, Asante focused his attention on another revolution occurring in the United States. While he was working on his dissertation he also wrote *The Rhetoric of Black Revolution,* published in 1969.

Grounded in communication and the rhetoric of agitation, Asante noticed how racism and communication were intertwined, and he began to formulate the theory that racism in our culture is embedded in our language system. According to Asante, racism stems from a thought system that values one particular race over another. As a phenomenon of language, racism is demonstrated by what

people say about others and how they justify their personal attitudes and beliefs. What Asante discovered is that our language reflects the "knowledge system" we are taught. In the United States, this knowledge system has reflected a European rather than a multicultural view of human events and achievements. For instance, in most schools the study of the arts, or philosophy, or science focuses only on the contributions made by Europeans or European Americans. As a result of this focus, we "learn" that nothing really important originated anywhere else. We come to value the music, literature, rituals, and values of Europeans over those of other cultural groups. Since racism comes from valuing one particular race above another, Asante reasons, it was inevitable that monoethnic, Eurocentric approaches to education would result in our developing racist thoughts and a racist language structure that reifies these thoughts. To combat racism and racist language, Asante believes we must first accurately learn the contributions that have been made by other racial and cultural groups. History needs to reflect the substantial contributions that people from Africa, China, and other non-European regions have made to

the development of humankind; literature and art need to include the work of various racial and ethnic groups. When people learn that all racial and cultural groups have made significant contributions, they will be less prone to view themselves as superior or inferior to others.

Seeking to reorient social science thinking regarding Africans and African Americans, Asante wrote three books that discussed the idea of Africans as agents rather than as victims; these works are *Afrocentricity, The Afrocentric Idea,* and *Kemet, Afrocentricity and Knowledge* (see citations in References at the end of the book). Asante has focused his own learning and his scholarship on discovering, reclaiming, and sharing the contributions of African culture and philosophy.

Asante's influence has been widespread. He served as the first director of Afro-American Studies at UCLA, department head of Speech Communication at SUNY Buffalo, and chair of the Department of African American Studies at Temple University, where he established the first Ph.D. program in African American studies. Asante has directed more than seventy-five doctoral dissertations. He is internationally known for his work on Afrocentricity and African culture. He has published fifty-two books and authored more than three hundred book chapters and journal articles. In the process, he has led an intellectual revolution among scholars working in numerous disciplines. Although he is noted for his scholarship, Asante says, "Working with students is the centerpiece of what I do." He currently teaches undergraduate courses on the African American church and modern mass media in black communities, and graduate courses in ancient Egyptian language and culture and Egyptian origins of rhetoric.

Personal interest in an African heritage has led Asante to trace his family ancestry back to Ghana. Recently, in Ghana, he was "enstooled," in a ceremony that formally acknowledges a person as a member of Ghanaian royalty. At that ceremony he was given the name Nana Okru Asante Peasah, Kyidomhene of Tafo. ■

this year's minority scholarship campaign." Here Brenda Jones's occupation and relationship to Don Jones is clearly irrelevant. In either case, the pairing takes away from the person who is supposed to be the focus. So, avoid noting the association one person has with others when the association is irrelevant.

Very few people can escape all insensitive language. By monitoring your usage, however, you can guard against saying or doing things that offend others because they perpetuate outdated sex roles, racial stereotypes, and other biases.

Racist Language. You've heard children shout, "Sticks and stones may break my bones, but words will never hurt me." This rhyme may be popular among children because even though they know it is untrue, it gives them a defense against cruel name-calling. Whether we admit it or not, words do hurt, sometimes permanently. Racist language refers to words designed to denigrate, stigmatize, or marginalize a person or group of people. It is always a sign of prejudice.

Where does offensive racist language come from? According to Molefi Asante, an internationally known scholar, racist language has its roots in our personal beliefs and attitudes. To a great extent these have been conditioned by the knowledge system to which we have been exposed. Until recently, the knowledge system prevalent in the United States has had a Eurocentric bias. Thus the contributions to the development of humankind by cultures other than European have been ignored or minimized. To get a more complete understanding of Asante's scholarship, read the Spotlight on Scholars selection devoted to him (pages 105-6).

Great personal damage has been done to individuals throughout history as a result of racist labeling. Of course, we all know that it is not the words alone that are so powerful; it is the context of the words—the situation, the feelings of the participants, the time, the place, or the tone of voice. You may recall circumstances in which a friend called you a racist name and you did not even flinch; yet you can probably recall other circumstances in which someone made you furious by using the same term. It may be permissible for members of a subculture to use

Cornered by Baldwin

1-10 © 2002 Mike Baldwin / Dist. by Universal Press Syndicate www.cornered.com
cornered@comic.com BALDWIN

I JUST FEEL SOOOO MUCH BETTER KNOWING I'M NOT ALONE...

Sarcasm support group

a racial slur when referring to a friend who is also a member of that subculture. But it is inappropriate for a nonmember to use that racial slur, and some members may be offended even if the speaker is from the same group. So in general you will want to avoid racist terms. One way to do this is to describe groups of people by using the words they prefer to have used. These may change with time and may even vary between members of a group. So if you are in doubt, it's a good thing to ask or not use the term at all.

We should always be aware that our language has repercussions. When we do not understand or are not sensitive to a listener's frame of reference, we may state our ideas in language that distorts the intended communication. Many times a single inappropriate sentence is enough to ruin an entire interaction. To use the skill of linguistic sensitivity: (1) choose to use inclusive rather than generic language; (2) avoid making unnecessary associations when describing; (3) use words to name a group that are preferred by that group rather than racist labels.

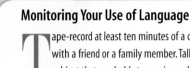

observe & analyze

Monitoring Your Use of Language

Tape-record at least ten minutes of a conversation with a friend or a family member. Talk about a subject that you hold strong views about: perhaps affirmative action, welfare, school levies, or candidates for office. Be sure to get the permission of the other person before you tape. At first you may feel self-conscious about having a recorder going. But as you get into discussion, it's quite likely that you'll be able to converse normally.

Play back the tape and take notes of sections where your language might have been clearer. Based on these notes, write better expressions of your ideas by using more precise and specific/concrete language and by dating and indexing generalizations.

Replay the tape. This time take notes on any racist, sexist, or biased expression that you used. Based on these notes, write more appropriate expressions for the ones you used.

Write a paragraph or two that describes what you have learned from this experience about your use of language. ■

Language in Unique Message Contexts

While we use language in every context or situation in which we are involved, there are two specific contexts we will examine in this chapter because of the unique role of words in each context. Words perform quite uniquely in the language of humor and the language of cyberspace.

Language of Humor

Humor can be considered a shared interpersonal experience, which frequently depends upon sharing a common language (Foot, 1997). Many types of humor rely upon words to achieve the comedic effect. Puns, for instance, use two words that sound alike where one is substituted for the other. Humor can derive from a "play on words," which refers to words with more than one meaning. The humor comes from the interchange between meanings. Ironic or sarcastic humor also depends upon words where the speaker says one thing but wants listeners to understand just the opposite. There are many other language features that contribute to humor, such as exaggerated language, understatements, verbal pictures, turns of phrases, double entendres, and poking fun at the ways we use words through dialects and accents. In order to fully understand humor, we must understand all the aspects of a language. Sometimes people who speak a second language have trouble understanding some forms of humor in that language because they are not familiar with all the subtle aspects of that language. As you read humorous writing, listen to comedians, or appreciate humor shared in interpersonal exchanges, notice the important role of language in achieving humorous effect.

Language of Cyberspace

There is a new type of language developing with digital and Internet technology. Experts in computer-mediated communication (Thurlow, Lengel, & Tomic, 2004) explain the unique features of this language, which goes by various names including Weblish, netlingo, e-talk, techspeak, wired style, and netspeak. Used mostly in real-time online chatting, this language emphasizes speed and informality, which are not characteristics typically associated with written language. Usually, written language takes longer than spoken language and is more formal. Because of the need for speed in instant messaging, for example, many of the rules of grammar, style, and spelling are broken. In the interest of speed, people avoid using capitalization, punctuation, and hyphenation in text or instant messages. Many people adopt a phonetic type of spelling, which increasingly is understandable to this speech community.

Consider the language used in cyberspace versus traditional wording for the following question: wen wud u b hm (When would you be home?) New abbreviations have emerged, such as jk (just kidding), bbl (be back later), and lol (laugh out loud). In addition to these verbal communication characteristics, instant messaging includes distinct conversational features such as multiple conversational strands with very short turns that defy traditional turn-taking rules. Some communication experts who emphasize traditional styles of communication regard this new language of cyberspace as incorrect, deficient, or inferior. It is natural that people in cyberspace would develop their own language with unique vocabulary, grammar, and style.

A Question of Ethics

Pam and Christine had been best friends in high school and had decided to room together when they both chose to go to State U for college. Late in the fall semester Pam began seeing Matt, who was in a fraternity. Early on Pam and Matt had tried fixing Christine up with a series of Matt's fraternity brothers, but none of the relationships had panned out. Matt's friends each thought that Christine was just a little too "needy" and expected them to quickly form a serious relationship with her. So after a time, Matt told Pam he wouldn't help her fix Christine up any more.

As Matt and Pam's relationship intensified, Christine, who had not made many other friends at school, became more and more demanding of Pam. She wanted to know what Pam's schedule was and where Pam was going. She wanted to know the details of Pam's relationship with Matt. She asked about Matt's friends and why she hadn't heard from them. Pam felt very conflicted. She really treasured her friendship with Christine and didn't want to hurt her feelings, and she also felt that she had a right to some privacy. So when Christine would ask her a question, she found herself giving deliberately vague answers.

On Thursday when Christine asked her what she was doing that weekend, Pam said, "Well, there are a number of things going on campus and I think I'll probably hang around and see what looks good," even though she knew that she and Matt would be going to the football game and then to a fraternity party afterward. Later that day as Pam and Christine were walking across campus toward their dorm after class, they ran into Matt, who smiled broadly at Pam and said, "How about if I pick you up about 11 on Saturday so we can get a bite to eat before the game?" After they left Matt, Pam noticed that Christine was acting kind of cold and distant, and answering her with one-word answers. When they got to their room, Christine slammed her books down on her desk, jerked her coat off and threw it on the floor, and sat down at her desk with her back to Pam.

1. Was it ethical for Pam to withhold her plans for the weekend from Christine?

2. Was it ethical for Christine to expect Pam to share information about her relationship, her plans, and what she knew about Matt's friends?

3. What can be done to repair the relationship?

Summary

Language is the body of words and the systems for their use in messages that are common to a group of people. Through language, we discuss things outside our immediate experience; we reflect upon ourselves, and we talk about language itself.

You will be a more effective communicator if you understand that language affects perception in that it shapes what we are able to see and not see. Assigning meaning to others' words is not simple. Interaction with others shapes the meanings that we develop for words. When we are involved in a communication exchange, we must coordinate with the other person, so that we are agreed on the rules that shape the meaning of that interaction. The two levels of meaning attached to all words further complicate the interpretation of words. The denotation of a word is its dictionary meaning, which is complicated by the problem of many words having more than one dictionary meaning. The connotation of a word is the emotional and value significance the word has for the listener in a particular situation. Expectations of low-context and high-context cultures and high and low power-distance cultures affect language use.

Words are arbitrary, ambiguous, abstract, and ever changing. They can reveal attitudes and reinforce control. You can improve your language skills by choosing specific language while considering the use of strategic ambiguity, by adapting language to listeners, by dating information, by indexing generalizations, by practicing communication accommodation, and by demonstrating linguistic sensitivity. Words perform quite uniquely in the contexts of cyberspace and humorous situations.

Chapter Resources

Communication Improvement Plan: Verbal Communication

How would you like to improve your use of language as discussed in this chapter?

Increase specific language

Dating

Communication accommodation

Indexing

Adapting language to listeners (vocabulary, jargon, and slang)

Linguistic sensitivity (avoiding sexist and racist language)

Pick one of these topics and write a communication improvement plan. You can find a communication improvement plan worksheet on our website at www.oup.com/us/interact

Key Words

Language, *p. 85*
Sapir–Whorf hypothesis, *p. 86*
Polarized language, *p. 86*
Symbolic interactionism, *p. 87*
Coordinated management of meaning, *p. 87*
Denotation, *p. 88*
Connotation, *p. 88*
Low-context cultures, *p. 88*
High-context cultures, *p. 88*
Power distance, *p. 90*

High power-distance culture, *p. 90*
Low power-distance culture, *p. 90*
Theory of muted groups, *p. 92*
Specific words, *p. 94*
Concrete words, *p. 94*
Precise words, *p. 94*
Strategic ambiguity, *p. 95*
Jargon, *p. 96*
Slang, *p. 97*
Dating information, *p. 98*

Indexing generalizations, *p. 99*
Communication accommodation theory, *p. 100*
Convergence, *p. 100*
Divergence, *p. 100*
Generic language, *p. 101*
Nonparallel language, *p. 102*
Marking, *p. 102*
Unnecessary association, *p. 104*

Skill Practice

Skill Practice exercises challenge you to master the material you have read in this chapter. For additional Skill Practice activities, visit our website at www.oup.com/us/interact

CONCRETE, PRECISE

1. For each word listed, find three words or phrases that are more specific, or more concrete.

implements	building	nice	education
clothes	colors	chair	bad
happy	stuff	things	car

2. Make the following statements clearer by editing words that are not precise, specific, or concrete:

   "You know I love basketball. Well, I'm practicing a lot because I want to get better."

   "Paula, I'm really bummed out. Everything is going down the tubes. You know what I mean?"

   "Well, she just does these things to tick me off. Like, just a whole lot of stuff—and she knows it!"

   "I just bought a beautiful outfit—I mean, it is really in style. You'll love it."

   "I've really got to remember to bring my things the next time I visit."

Inter-Act with Media

FIND MORE
on the web
Additional media entries @
www.oup.com/us/interact

C I N E M A

Nancy Meyers (Director). (2000). *What Women Want.* Mel Gibson, Helen Hunt, Marisa Tomei, Alan Alda.

> **Brief Summary:** Nick Marshall is a chauvinistic, manipulative advertising executive. After a fluke accident, he gains the power to hear what women are actually thinking. His lifelong pattern of using and manipulating women changes as he slowly learns to be more sensitive and understanding. He learns the need for honesty in his relationships.
>
> **IPC Concepts:** Relationships, gender differences, meaning, message clarity, jargon, ethics.

Randa Haines (Director). (1991) *The Doctor.* William Hurt, Christine Lahti, Elizabeth Perkins, Mandy Patimkin, Adam Arkin.

> **Brief Summary:** This film is based on Dr. Ed Rosenbaum's book *A Taste of My Own Medicine.* William Hurt plays a doctor who believes that he must maintain distance from his patients so that he can remain objective and efficient. When he develops throat cancer, he discovers what it is like to be a patient and deal with the hospital bureaucracy. A young female cancer patient helps him to learn how to empathize with patients and to cope with his own illness. He develops an innovative approach to the training of his interns.
>
> **IPC Concepts:** Language, relationships, meaning, message clarity, jargon, ethics.

W H A T ' S   O N   T H E   W E B

Jennifer Akin, The Conduit Metaphor and language in interpersonal communication

> http://www.intractableconflict.org/m/interpersonal_communication.jsp
>
> **Brief Summary:** This is an excellent discussion of the nature of language in interpersonal relationships. Akin discusses the dangers of misunderstanding the nature of language and notes the power of the misconception of the conduit metaphor.
>
> **IPC Concepts:** Meaning, misunderstanding, semantics, the nature and power of metaphor.

Terrance A. Doyle, Verbal Communication, The Interpersonal Web

> http://novaonline.nv.cc.va.us/eli/spd110td/interper/message/messageverbal.html
>
> **Brief Summary:** This wonderful site contains a rich discussion of the nature of language by offering links to several major theoreticians in the modern study of language—Sausure, Burke, I. A. Richards, Peirce.
>
> **IPC Concepts:** Meaning, denotative and connotative meaning, nature of language, importance of symbols.

Lying

> http://www.absoluteastronomy.com/encyclopedia/l/li/lie.htm
>
> **Brief Summary:** This site goes into the nature and ethics of lying. It has excellent links to other aspects of the subject and points of view. It covers the nature, morality, and, oddly, the etiquette of lying.
>
> **IPC Concepts:** Lying, etiquette, ethics, paradox.

communicating through nonverbal behaviors

After you have read this chapter, you
should be able to answer these questions:

- What are the characteristics of nonverbal communication?

- What are the functions of nonverbal communication?

- What are the major types and uses of body motions?

- What are the elements of paralanguage?

- How do we communicate through proxemics and territoriality?

- How do we communicate through artifacts and physical appearance?

- What are the communication aspects of time and smell?

- What are the most significant cultural and gender differences in nonverbal communication?

- What are ways you can improve the nonverbal messages you send and the interpretation of nonverbal messages you receive?

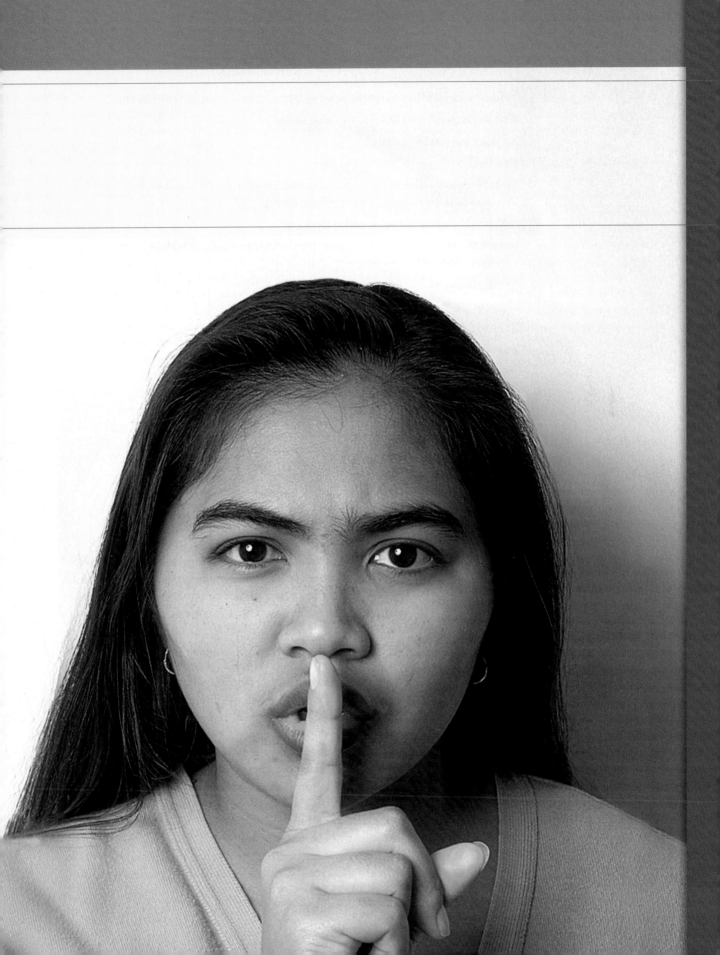

> "You don't want me to buy that denim jacket we looked at this morning, do you?" Clay asked.
>
> "What do you mean 'I don't want you to'?" Maya replied.
>
> "You've got that look on your face."
>
> "What look?"
>
> "You know the look—the one you always get on your face when you don't want me to do something I want to do. But I'm going to get that jacket anyway."
>
> "I still don't know what look you're talking about, Clay."
>
> "Sure you do. You know how I can tell you do? Because now you're embarrassed that I know and so you're acting weird."
>
> "I'm not acting weird."
>
> "Oh yes you are."
>
> "Clay, you're making me angry."
>
> "You're just saying that because I know you too well and it bothers you."
>
> "Know me too well? Clay, I don't care whether you get that jacket or not."
>
> "Of course you do. You don't have to tell me in words."
>
> "Clay, it's your decision. If you want to get the jacket, get it."
>
> "Well, I don't think I want to—but don't think you changed my mind."

We've all heard—and said—"actions speak louder than words." Actions are so important to our communication that researchers have estimated that in face-to-face communication as much as 65 percent of the social meaning is a result of nonverbal behavior (Burgoon, Buller, & Woodall, 1989, p. 155). What this means is that the meaning we assign to any communication is based on both the content of the verbal message and our interpretation of the nonverbal behavior that accompanies and surrounds the verbal message. And, as we can see from the interaction between Clay and Maya, interpreting these nonverbal actions is not always the easiest thing to do.

In the last chapter we discussed language, the verbal elements of interpersonal communication. In this chapter we provide a framework for understanding and improving nonverbal communication behavior. We begin by describing the characteristics and functions of nonverbal communication. Next we identify the types of nonverbal communication, including kinesics, paralanguage, proxemics, territoriality, artifacts, physical appearance, chronemics, and olfactory communication.

We discuss the ways that these types of nonverbal communication may vary based on cultural, sex and gender influences. Finally, we offer suggestions for improving the ways you send and interpret nonverbal communication.

In the broadest sense, the term *nonverbal communication* is commonly used to describe all human communication events that transcend spoken or written words (Knapp & Hall, 2002, p. 5). Specifically, **nonverbal communication behaviors** are the bodily actions and vocal qualities that typically accompany a verbal message.

Nonverbal communication behaviors—bodily actions and vocal qualities that typically accompany a verbal message.

Characteristics and Functions of Nonverbal Communication

To lay a foundation for a complete discussion of the specific elements of nonverbal communication, we need to consider its many characteristics and functions.

Characteristics of Nonverbal Communication

First, nonverbal communication can be *intentional* or *unintentional*. We are not consciously aware of much of what we communicate nonverbally. Perhaps Angelo smirks when he is nervous, taps his foot when he is impatient, speaks forcefully when he is angry, or stands tall when he is confident. He may be unaware of all of these mannerisms, but people close to him may be quite aware of his habits. This is why many react to seeing themselves on videotape by saying things like "I didn't know that I sounded like that, walked like that, gestured like that, or made those facial expressions." People interpret nonverbal cues as intentional, acting as if such cues are intended even if they are transmitted unconsciously or unintentionally (Burgoon, 1994, p. 231).

Second, the meaning of a particular nonverbal communication is frequently *ambiguous*. Since most nonverbal behavior is not codified, a particular behavior can have many meanings depending on the user's personality, family influences, or culture, or the context of communication or the relationship of the nonverbal behaviors to the verbal message. When François fidgets by tapping his fingers and moving in his seat, his behavior may mean he is nervous, or bored, or energetic, or impatient, or excited, or hyperactive, or feeling the effects of some cold medication he took before class. Any one of these meanings may be accurate. You may display your anger by frowning or by being poker-faced; you may speak louder or softer, quickly or slowly; you may aggressively stare at someone or avoid eye contact altogether, or you may cry. When we are in a relationship with someone, we learn to "read" their nonverbal behavior and become more accurate at decoding what their behaviors mean. When you observe the nonverbal behavior of someone who you do not know well, you are likely to interpret that behavior in light of experiences you have had with others. You are more likely to misinterpret the meaning intended by a person who is very different from others you have known.

Third, nonverbal communication is *primary*. When we communicate with others, we base our interpretation of the speaker's feelings and emotions almost totally on the nonverbal aspects of the interaction. In a classic study of nonverbal communication and emotion, psychologist Albert Mehrabian (1972) found that about 93 percent of the emotional meaning of messages is conveyed nonverbally. Nonverbal communication is perceived to be more believable than verbal communication. It is easy to deceive others with our words, but our nonverbal behavior tends to be more spontaneous and more authentic because it is harder to fake nonverbal communication. When Janelle frowns, clenches her fists, and forcefully says, "I am NOT angry!" her sister Renée knows that Janelle is angry. Renée ignores the verbal message and believes the nonverbal behavior, which indicates that Janelle is angry. Have you ever encountered a situation where your gut-level response to another was discomfort or distrust? The other person's verbal message may have seemed friendly or kind, but your reaction was based on a nonverbal cue. Though you may not have been consciously aware of what in the person's nonverbal behavior bothered you, you were reacting to it more than to the verbal message.

Fourth, nonverbal communication is *continuous*. You can never stop communicating nonverbally. This is why nonverbal communication is often called nonverbal behavior. Any time you are behaving, intentionally or not, and someone else notices that behavior and attaches meaning to it, you have communicated nonverbally. When Austin yawns and nods off during a meeting at work, his co-workers will notice this behavior and make assumptions about Austin. Some may think he is rude; others may believe he is bored; Paul may correctly recognize that his friend Austin is exhausted from studying for exams.

Fifth, nonverbal communication is *multichanneled*. When noticing someone's body language, we may get messages from posture, gestures, body movements, and body appearance factors. It is rare for nonverbal cues to come from only one source. When Adelaide meets her new neighbor Mimi, she will notice many things at once, including Mimi's smile, bright eyes, fast rate of speech, erect posture, designer suit, perfume, and apartment decor. Nonverbal behaviors come from many different sources at the same time. They rarely occur in isolation. Nonverbal behaviors can, but rarely do, occur in isolation from the verbal channel. Later in this chapter, we will discuss instances of nonverbal behaviors that stand alone. But in the vast majority of interactions, communicators use the nonverbal channel in conjunction with verbal communication.

HERB & JAMAL © Tribune Media Services, Inc. All rights reserved.

Functions of Nonverbal Communication

Nonverbal communication serves five primary purposes. While we will describe each function separately, it is important to recognize that in an interaction some of these functions overlap and nonverbal communication may fulfill more than one of these functions.

1. **To provide information.** Much information or content of a message is conveyed nonverbally. Our nonverbal cues may repeat, substitute for, emphasize, or contradict our verbal message. We may use nonverbal cues to *repeat* what we have said verbally. If you say "no" and shake your head at the same time, you have used a nonverbal cue to repeat what you have said verbally.

   Think of all the nonverbal behaviors that provide a secondary way of saying something in addition to our words. Some nonverbal cues can *substitute* for the words. A wave, for example, can stand in place of the word "hello" or "goodbye." In some cultures, curling your index finger and motioning toward yourself can substitute for the words "Come here," while in other cultures the same gesture can mean "Go away" or "good-bye." You could make a lengthy list of nonverbal symbols that take the place of words or phrases that you use frequently. For instance, pointing thumbs up may be a gesture you use to mean "everything is a go"; you may extend your first and second fingers holding them up in a V shape and mean "peace" or "victory"; you may shake your head from side to side when you mean "no" and up and down when you mean "yes"; when you shrug your shoulders you may mean "maybe," "I don't care," or "I don't know."

   Another way that nonverbal cues provide information is to *emphasize* the verbal message. Nonverbal behavior may accent, complement, or add information to the words. A teacher may smile, clap, or pat a student on the back when saying "Good job on your spelling test." The facial expression, gesture, and voice volume emphasize the verbal statement of praise. Nonverbal cues may *contradict* the verbal message. In this case, the nonverbals still provide information, but the information leads to confusion rather than clarity. When Sadie says in a quiet, monotone voice, "I am really interested in your project," while avoiding eye contact and moving away, her nonverbal message has contradicted her verbal message. The result of contradictory verbal and nonverbal messages is a mixed message. Just as people rely more on the nonverbal communication than the words of a message to determine emotional meaning, people rely more on the nonverbal cues to figure out a mixed message. Remember that it is easy for Sadie to deceive with her words, but difficult for her to fake the nonverbal behaviors.

2. **To regulate interaction.** We manage an interaction through subtle and sometimes obvious nonverbal cues. We use shifts in eye contact, slight head

inter-act with

Technology

As you watch a videotape of a movie or a television program, select a segment where two people are talking with each other for a couple of minutes. The first time you watch, turn off the sound. Based on nonverbal behaviors alone, determine the climate of the conversation (whether the people are flirting, in conflict, discussing an issue, kidding around, etc.). What nonverbal behaviors and reactions led you to that conclusion? The second time, watch nonverbals but also listen to vocal variations in volume, pitch, and rate of speed. Do any of these vocal cues add to your assessment? The third time, focus on what the characters are saying. Now analyze the segment. What percentage of meaning came from nonverbal elements? What did you learn from this? ■

movements, shifts in posture, raised eyebrows, and nodding to tell another person when to continue, to repeat, to elaborate, to hurry up, or to finish. Think of the times you have nonverbally signaled to another person that you must leave the interaction. You may decrease the amount of eye contact you give the other person, give short responses, show less facial expression, and turn or move away from the other person. Students in a classroom regularly signal to the instructor that class time is nearly over by packing away their materials, putting on their coats, fidgeting in their seats, or mumbling to each other. Effective communicators learn to adjust what they are saying and how they are saying it on the basis of others' nonverbal cues.

3. **To express or hide emotion and affect.** We have already explained that most of the emotional aspects of communication are conveyed through nonverbal means. Think of how you nonverbally show others that you care for them. You may smile, hug, kiss, sit closer to, gaze at, and spend more time with those you care deeply about. Alternatively, we can use nonverbal behavior to mask our true feelings. More often than not, however, we show our true emotions nonverbally rather than describing our emotions with words. Sometimes we try to hide our emotions or feelings, but they may unintentionally leak out. Blushing when one is embarrassed is a prime example of the inadvertent display of emotion.

4. **To present an image.** In Chapter 2, we discussed how people try to create impressions of themselves through the ways they appear and act. Much of impression management occurs through the nonverbal channel. People may carefully develop an image through clothing, grooming, jewelry, and other personal possessions. Not only do people use nonverbal communication to communicate a personal image, but two people may use nonverbal cues to present a relational image or identity. At a party, Martina and Jacob may signal to others that they are together by displaying nonverbal cues such as postures that turn in toward each other, being physically close in spacing, talking in hushed tones, and touching each other. Couples in a distressed marriage may publicly project a positive image by holding hands or being attentive to each other through facial expressions (Patterson, 1994).

5. **To express power and control**. Many nonverbal behaviors are signs of dominance, regardless or whether they are intended to convey power and control. Think of how a high-level manager conveys status and how subordinate employees acknowledge that status through nonverbal behavior. The manager may dress in the style of an executive, have a large and expensively furnished office, and walk and speak authoritatively. Subordinates show respect to managers by giving eye contact and listening attentively when a manager speaks, not interrupting, and seeking permission (appointments) to enter the manager's office. Imagine a parent who says to a child, "Look at me when I'm speaking to you." Parents expect that children will nonverbally accept parental dominance by using steady eye contact as a sign of respect. Expressions such as, "She's looking down her nose at me," or "He's talking to me like I'm a child," show the role of nonverbal behavior in expressing power, control, and dominance.

Types of Nonverbal Communication

There are many types of nonverbal communication, including kinesics (body motions), paralanguage, proxemics (use of space) and territory, artifacts, physical appearance, chronemics (use of time), and olfactory communication (use of smell).

Kinesics

Of all the research on nonverbal behavior, you are probably most familiar with **kinesics**, the technical name for the study of body motions used in communication. Body motions are nonverbal behaviors in which communication occurs through the movement of one's body or body parts. Body motions include eye contact, facial expression, gesture, posture, and touch.

Kinesics—the technical name for the study of body motions used in communication.

Eye Contact. Eye contact, also referred to as **gaze,** is how and how much we look at people with whom we are communicating. Eye contact conveys many meanings. It indicates whether we are paying attention. How we look at a person can convey a range of emotions such as anger, fear, or affection. For instance, we describe people in love as looking "doe-eyed." Intense eye contact may also be used to exercise dominance (Pearson, West, & Turner, 1995, p. 121). So we comment on "looks that could kill," and we talk of someone "staring another person down."

Eye contact or gaze—how and how much we look at people with whom we are communicating.

Moreover, through our eye contact, we monitor the effect of our communication. By maintaining your eye contact, you can tell when or whether a person is paying attention to you, whether a person is involved in what you are saying, and whether what you are saying is causing anxiety.

What meanings are revealed through facial expressions?

Although the amount of eye contact differs from person to person and from situation to situation, studies show that talkers hold eye contact about 40 percent of the time and listeners nearly 70 percent of the time (Knapp & Hall, 2002, p. 350). We generally maintain better eye contact when we are discussing topics with which we are comfortable, when we are genuinely interested in a person's comments or reactions, or when we are trying to influence the other person. Conversely, we tend to avoid eye contact when we are discussing topics that make us uncomfortable, when we lack interest in the topic or person, or when we are embarrassed, ashamed, or trying to hide something.

Eye contact often signals status and aggression. Holding a gaze for too long, or staring at someone, tends to be interpreted as a sign of dominance or aggression. Indeed, in some segments of society, a prolonged stare may be an invitation to a physical fight. Yet, not giving someone eye contact at all, ironically, can also be seen as a sign of dominance. The dominant person in an exchange, such as a boss, an interviewer, a teacher, or a police officer, has the freedom to give eye contact or look away at will; but the subordinate person in the situation is expected to give steady and respectful eye contact.

Facial expression—the arrangement of facial muscles to communicate emotional states or reactions to messages.

Facial Expression. Facial expression is the arrangement of facial muscles to communicate emotional states or reactions to messages. The three sets of muscles that are manipulated to form facial expressions are the brow and forehead; the eyes, eyelids, and root of the nose; and the cheeks, mouth, remainder of the nose, and chin. Our facial expressions are especially important in conveying the six basic emotions of happiness, sadness, surprise, fear, anger, and disgust. Facial expressions are so important to interpersonal communication that people have invented a system of conveying facial expressions online.

Emoticons—typed symbols that convey emotional aspects of online messages.

Emoticons. Typed symbols that convey emotional aspects of an online message are called emoticons. For example, : -) conveys a smile, : -(conveys a frown, { } symbolizes a hug, and ALL CAPS means emphasis or shouting (Walther & Parks, 2002). Facial expressions are important in conveying feedback during an interpersonal exchange. Think of the times you have used a quizzical look to signal that you do not understand someone or a frown to convey your disagreement.

Gestures—movements of hands, arms, and fingers that we use to describe or to emphasize.

Gesture. Gestures are the movements of our hands, arms, and fingers that we use to describe or to emphasize. Thus, when a person says "about this high" or "nearly this round," we expect to see a gesture accompany the verbal description. Likewise, when a person says, "Put that down" or "Listen to me," a pointing finger, pounding fist, or some other gesture often reinforces the point. People do vary, however, in the amount of gesturing that accompanies their speech—some people "talk with their hands" far more than others. Some gestures, called **emblems**, can stand alone and substitute completely for words. A hitchhiker's gesture is an emblem that needs no words to accompany it. A finger placed vertically across the lips automatically means "Be quiet." Emblems have automatic meanings in particular cultures but can vary greatly across cultures. Some gestures, called **adaptors**, occur unconsciously in order to respond to a physical need. For example, you may scratch an itch, adjust your glasses, or rub your hands together when they are cold. You do not mean to communicate a message with these gestures, but others do notice them and attach meaning to them.

Emblems—gestures that can substitute for words.

Adaptors—gestures that respond to a physical need.

Posture. Posture is the position and movement of the body. Posture often conveys information about attentiveness, respect, and dominance. **Body orientation** refers to your posture in relation to another person. Facing another person squarely is called direct body orientation. When two people's postures are at angles to each other, this is called indirect body orientation. In many situations, direct body orientation signals attentiveness and respect, while indirect body orientation shows nonattentiveness and disrespect. Think of how you would sit in a job interview. You are likely to sit up straight and face the interviewer directly because you want to communicate your interest and respect. Interviewers tend to interpret a slouched posture and indirect body orientation as inattentiveness and disrespect.

Posture—the position and movement of the body.

Body orientation—posture in relation to another person.

Yet, in other situations, such as talking with friends, a slouched posture and indirect body orientation may be appropriate and may not carry messages about attention or respect. This difference in meaning based on various situations shows the ambiguous nature of nonverbal communication. It is rare that any one posture absolutely means any one thing. Posture can also convey notions of power by subtly signaling dominance or submissiveness. Standing erect, especially for a tall person, and facing someone directly, can be seen an intimidating. There are certain walks that convey confidence and power and other styles of walking that signal weakness, uncertainty, and submissiveness.

Touch. Formally known as **haptics,** touch is putting part of the body in contact with something. It is the first form of nonverbal communication that we experience. For an infant, touch is a primary means of receiving messages of love and comfort. Touching behavior is a fundamental aspect of nonverbal communication in general and of self-presentation in particular. We use our hands, our arms, and other body parts to pat, hug, slap, kiss, pinch, stroke, hold, embrace, and tickle. Through touch we communicate a variety of emotions and messages. In Western

Haptics—putting part of the body in contact with something; touch.

What does indirect body orientation communicate?

Ritualized touch—touch that is scripted rather than spontaneous.

Task-related touch—touch used to perform a certain function.

Paralanguage or vocalics—the nonverbal "sound" of what we hear—how something is said.

How does the meaning of task-related touch differ from regular touch?

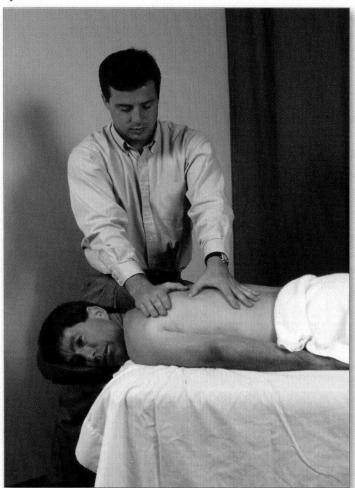

culture, we shake hands to be sociable and polite, we pat a person on the back for encouragement, we hug a person to show love, we clasp raised hands to demonstrate solidarity. There are many forms of **ritualized touch,** meaning that the type of touch is scripted rather than spontaneous in a society. Handshakes or high-five slaps of the hands are automatic forms of touch that have rather definite meaning as greeting rituals. Our touching can be gentle or firm, perfunctory or passionate, brief or lingering. Like many of the other types of body motion, touch can convey messages about power. Usually, the higher-status person in a situation is the one to initiate touch. Managers are more likely to touch their employees, and faculty are more likely to touch their students, than vice versa.

There is another type of touch, called **task-related touch,** in which touch is used to perform a certain function. A doctor may touch a patient during a physical examination or a personal trainer may touch a client during a workout at the gym. We do not attach the same meanings to task-related touch as we do to spontaneous touch. We see task-related touch as part of the professional service for which we are contracting. There is also a type of spontaneous task-related touch that can convey messages of closeness. Someone who, in public, adjusts your coat collar for you or removes some lint from your clothing is not only doing a task-related favor for you, but is signaling, perhaps inadvertently, a degree of closeness between the two of you. It would not be appropriate, for instance, to perform those functions for a complete stranger or a casual acquaintance.

People differ in their touching behavior and in their reactions to unsolicited touch from others. Some people, because of individual preference, family background, or culture, like to touch and be touched; other people do not. Although American culture is relatively non-contact-oriented, the kinds and amounts of touching behavior within our society vary widely. Touching behavior that seems innocuous to one person may be perceived as overly intimate or threatening by another. Moreover, the perceived appropriateness of touch differs with the context. Touch that is considered appropriate in private may embarrass a person when done in public or with a large group of people.

Paralanguage

Paralanguage, or **vocalics,** is the nonverbal "sound" of what we hear—how something is said. We begin by describing the four vocal characteristics that comprise paralanguage and then discuss how vocal interferences can disrupt message flow. By controlling the four major vocal characteristics—pitch, volume, rate, and quality—we can complement, supplement, or contradict the meaning conveyed by the language of our message.

Pitch is the highness or lowness of vocal tone. People raise and lower vocal pitch and change volume to emphasize ideas, indicate questions, and show nervousness. They may also raise the pitch when they are nervous or lower the pitch when they are trying to be forceful. Voices that are lower in pitch tend to convey more believability and credibility.

Volume is the loudness or softness of tone. Whereas some people have booming voices that carry long distances, others are normally soft-spoken. Regardless of their normal volume level, however, people do vary vocal volume depending on the situation and topic of discussion. For example, people talk loudly when they wish to be heard in noisy settings; they may raise their volume when they are angry, or speak more softly when they are being romantic or loving.

Rate refers to the speed at which a person speaks. People tend to talk more rapidly when they are happy, frightened, nervous, or excited and more slowly when they are problem-solving out loud or trying to emphasize a point.

Quality is the sound of a person's voice. Each human voice has a distinct tone: Some voices are raspy, some smoky, some have bell-like qualities, while others are throaty. Moreover, each of us uses a slightly different quality of voice to communicate a particular state of mind. We may associate complaints with a whiny, nasal quality, seductive invitation with a soft, breathy quality, and anger with a strident, harsh quality.

Intonation is the amount of variety, melody, or inflection in one's voice. Some voices have little intonation and sound monotonous. Other voices have a great deal of melody and may have a childlike melody to them. People prefer to listen to voices with a moderate amount of intonation.

Vocal Interferences

Although most of us are occasionally guilty of using some **vocal interferences**—extraneous sounds or words that interrupt fluent speech—these interferences become a problem when they are perceived by others as excessive and when they begin to call attention to themselves and so prevent listeners from concentrating on meaning. The most common interferences that creep into our speech include "uh," "er," "well," "OK," and those nearly universal interrupters of American conversations, "you know" and "like."

Vocal interferences may initially be used as "place markers" designed to fill in momentary gaps in speech, to indicate that we are not done speaking and it is still our "turn." So we may use an "um" when we need to pause momentarily to search for the right word or idea. The use of an excessive number of fillers can lead to the impression that you are unsure of yourself or confused in what you are attempting to say.

Equally prevalent, and perhaps even more disruptive than "uh" and "um," is the overuse of "you know" and "like." The "you know" habit may begin as a

Pitch–the highness or lowness of vocal tone.

Volume–the loudness or softness of tone.

Rate–the speed at which a person speaks.

Quality–the sound of voice.

Intonation—variety, melody, or inflection of voice.

Vocal interferences–extraneous sounds or words that interrupt fluent speech.

genuine way to find out whether what is being said is already known by others. For some, "you know" may be a source of identification—a way to establish common ground with the person being spoken to. Similarly, the use of "like" may start from making comparisons such as "Tom is hot; he looks like Denzel Washington." Soon the comparisons become shortcuts, as in "He's like really hot!" Finally, the use of "like" becomes pure filler: "Like, he's really cool, like I can't really explain it, but I'll tell you he's like wow!"

Spatial Usage

We communicate through our use of the informal space around us, our use of the spaces that we own and protect, and the ways we use objects and decorate our space.

Proxemics—the study of informal space. **Proxemics** is the study of informal space—the space around the place we are occupying at the moment. Managing informal space requires an understanding of attitudes toward space and personal territory. Have you ever been speaking with someone and become aware that you were uncomfortable because the other person was standing too close to you? Or maybe you've found yourself starting a conversation and then moving closer to someone as you begin to share an embarrassing story. If you have experienced either of these situations, you are already aware of the way that the space between conversational partners influences their interaction. Edward T. Hall (1969) suggests that in the dominant U.S. culture four distinct distances are comfortable, depending on the nature of the conversation.

- *Intimate distance*, up to eighteen inches, is appropriate for private conversations between close friends.
- *Personal distance*, from eighteen inches to four feet, is the space in which casual conversation occurs.
- *Social distance*, from four to twelve feet, is where impersonal business such as job interviews is conducted.
- *Public distance* is anything more than twelve feet.

These distance categories, based on Hall's research, represent descriptions of what most people consider appropriate or comfortable in various situations.

Of greatest concern to us is the intimate distance—that which we regard as appropriate for very personal conversation with close friends, parents, and younger children. People usually become uncomfortable when "outsiders" violate this intimate distance. For instance, in a movie theater that is less than one-quarter full, people will tend to leave one or more seats empty between themselves and others whom they do not know. If in such a setting a stranger sits right next to you, you are likely to feel uncomfortable or threatened and may even move away.

Intrusions into our intimate space are acceptable only in certain settings and then only when all involved follow the unwritten rules. For instance, people will tolerate being packed into a crowded elevator or subway and even touching others they do not know, provided the others follow the "rules." The rules may include standing rigidly and looking at the floor or the indicator above the door, but not making eye contact with others. The rules also include pretending that they are not touching or ignoring the situation.

spotlight on scholars

Judee K. Burgoon, Professor of Communication, University of Arizona, on
Nonverbal Expectancy Violation Theory

With seven books and more than 150 articles and book chapters to her credit, Judee K. Burgoon is a leading scholar who has helped to shape how we now think about nonverbal communication. Her fascination with nonverbal behavior dates back to a graduate school seminar assignment at the University of West Virginia, where she was asked to find out what was known about proxemics, the study of space. From that assignment, she says, "I just got hooked. Nonverbal is more elusive and difficult to study and I've always enjoyed a challenge!"

In the early 1970's, scholars believed that the road to interpersonal success lay in conforming one's behaviors to social norms about the distances that are appropriate for certain types of interaction and the types of touch that are appropriate for certain people in certain relationships. Thus, people would be successful in their interactions as long as they behaved in accord with these norms. Encouraged by one of her professors to "look for the counterintuitive," Burgoon's research showed that there were situations where violations of these norms resulted in positive, rather than negative consequences. For example, in settings where two people were not well acquainted and one of them

began "flirting" by moving closer to the other thus "violating" that person's space, the other person did not always react by moving away from the violator as expected. In fact, at times the person seemed to welcome the violation and at times may even have moved closer. Similarly, she noticed that touching behavior that violated social norms was sometimes rejected and at other times accepted.

To explain what she saw happening, Burgoon developed and began to test what she named "expectancy violation theory," which is based on the premise that we have strong expectations about how people ought to behave when they interact with us. Whether they meet our expectations affects not only how we interact with them, but also affects such outcomes as how competent, credible, and influential we perceive the other to be and what we think of our relationship. She found that how we interpret a violation depends on how we feel about that person. If we like the person we are likely to read the nonverbal violation as positive ("Gee, she put her arm around me—that means she's really interested in me"), if we don't like the person we are likely to read the same nonverbal violation as negative ("He better take his arm off of me—this is a clear case of harassment"). And, because we

have become sensitized to the situation, the violations will be subject to strong evaluations ("Wow, I really like the feel of her arm around my waist" vs "He's making me feel really uncomfortable"). As Burgoon continued to study violations, she discovered that when a person we really like violates our expectations, we are likely to view the interaction as even more positive than we would have if the person had conformed to our expectations. Over the years, in numerous research studies, Burgoon and her students have provided strong support for expectancy violation theory.

Burgoon's scholarship has developed like a river. Her first work, a narrow stream with a focus on proxemics, grew with expectancy violations theory to include all of nonverbal behavior and continues to branch. Presently, in one stream of work, she is studying what determines how people adapt their behavior when they experience any type of communication violation. Why and when do they reciprocate the violation (e.g., if someone shouts, you shout back) or compensate for it (e.g., if someone comes to close to you, you step back)? In a second stream Burgoon is focusing on a specific type of expectancy violation: deception. Here she is trying to sort out the role that nonverbal behavior plays in deceitful interactions. Finally, she has begun a stream of work whose purpose is to identify the essential properties of interpersonal communication that are different from the properties of media communication. Whatever branch her research takes, Judee Burgoon brings the same readiness to challenge the current thinking that has been the hallmark of her work. For complete citations of many of her recent publications in these areas, see the references for this chapter at the end of the book.

In addition to teaching a number of courses, Burgoon serves as director of graduate studies, where her role of helping students learn how to conduct research and formulate theory gives her great satisfaction. "Mentoring others is among the major gratifications of doing research. The fun is to teach others what I was taught: Always challenge the current assumptions." ∎

Only occasionally will people who are forced to invade each other's intimate space acknowledge the other as a person. Then they are likely to exchange sheepish smiles or otherwise acknowledge the mutual invasion of intimate distance. In the Spotlight on Scholars, we have featured Judee Burgoon, who has focused a great deal of her research on the effects of such intrusions into our intimate space. Her findings develop and test what she calls "expectancy violation theory."

Territory—space over which we may claim ownership.

Territory refers to the space over which we claim ownership. Sometimes we do not realize the ways that we claim space as our own, and in other instances we go to great lengths to use visible markers of our territory. If Marcia decides to eat lunch at the company cafeteria, the space at the table she occupies becomes her territory. Suppose that during lunch Marcia leaves her territory to get butter for her roll. The chair she left, the food on the table, and the space around that food are "hers," and she will expect others to stay away. If, when she returns, Marcia finds that someone at the table has moved a glass or a dish into the area that she regards as her territory, she is likely to feel resentful.

Many people stake out their territory with markers. For example, Ramon arrives early for the first day of class, finds an empty desk, and puts his backpack next to it on the floor and his coat on the seat. He then makes a quick trip to the restroom. If someone comes along while Ramon is gone, moves his backpack and coat, and sits down at the desk, that person has violated what Ramon had marked as his territory. If you regularly take the same seat in a class, that habit becomes a type of marker signaling to others that a particular seat location is yours. Other students will often leave that seat empty because they have perceived it as yours.

Sometimes we purposefully and directly communicate to others that we own certain space. People use locks, signs, and fences to communicate ownership of certain territory. Graham may have his chair in the family room; because he has announced it as his chair, other members of the family will avoid using it. Rex may "control" the kitchen, and others know that he decides where objects are placed and will be upset if anyone in the family rearranges the kitchen layout.

Territoriality can have a power dimension to it. Higher-status people generally claim larger, more prestigious, and more protected territory (Henley, 1977). A top-level executive at work may have a large, expensively decorated, top-floor office with a breathtaking view and one or more people to protect the space from intruders. The entry-level employee in the same organization may have a small cubicle that is not private or protected. Anyone at work can enter the space of the lower-level employee. Think of all the messages that we get from the amount and type of territory that someone claims, whether it be a large mansion in a gated community, a crowded inner-city apartment, a downtown loft shared by several students, or a section of a city park claimed by a homeless person.

Artifacts. Artifacts refer to our possessions and the ways we decorate our territory. People buy objects not just for their function but also for the message that each object conveys about them. Think of all the types of cars and the image that a car projects of its owner. Many advertisements for automobiles emphasize the nonverbal messages that a car conveys. People may customize their cars with gold rim hubcaps, stripes, or hood ornaments in order to send a message about themselves. Whether you carry your books and papers in a backpack or briefcase says something about you, whether or not you intend it to. People get messages about you based on whether you write notes in class with a stubby pencil, a name-brand pen, or a neon marker. People who walk down a street talking on a cell phone or listening to an MP3 player through personal headphones send messages about themselves and their image.

Think of all the ways we manage objects in our living or work space by arranging and rearranging them to create the desired atmosphere. We select and place furnishings and decorations to achieve certain effects. The chairs in a room

observe & analyze

Intruding on Personal Space

Find a crowded elevator. Get on it and face the back. Make direct eye contact with the person you are standing in front of. Note their reaction. On the return trip, introduce yourself to the person who is standing next to you and begin an animated conversation. Note the reaction of others around you. Get on an empty elevator and stand in the exact center. Do not move when others board. Note their reactions. Be prepared to share what you have observed with your classmates. ■

Artifacts—objects we own and decorations of our territory and body.

What do our artifacts communicate about us?

may approximate a circle and contribute to conversation. Or the seating in a room may face the television and discourage interaction. A supervisor's office with a chair facing the supervisor across the desk leads to formal conversation. It says, "Let's talk business—I'm the boss and you're the employee." A supervisor's office with a chair at the side of the desk (absence of a physical barrier) leads to more informal conversation. It says, "Don't be nervous—let's just chat."

The use of color is another way that we may affect our territory to send a nonverbal message. Color stimulates both emotional and physical reactions. For instance, red excites and stimulates, blue comforts and soothes, yellow cheers and elevates moods. Knowing this, professional interior designers may choose blues when they are trying to create a peaceful, serene atmosphere for a living room, whereas they may decorate a playroom in reds and yellows.

Self-Presentation Cues

We communicate through our physical appearance, our use of time, and our use of smells and scents.

Physical Appearance. We learn a great deal about others and make judgments about others based on how people look. We control some parts of our physical appearance, while other parts we inherit from our families. Physical appearance includes body type, physical features such as hair and eyes, and our choices of clothing, personal grooming, and body decorations. The size and shape of one's body sends powerful messages in our society. There are three general classifications of body type: **endormorph,** round and heavy; **mesomorph,** muscular and athletic; **ectomorph,** tall and thin. While not everyone fits perfectly into one of these categories, each person tends toward one body type. Think of the impressions, or stereotypes, that people get based on body types. Generally, people regard endomorphs as kind, warm, relaxed, and sluggish. Mesomorphs are considered to be energetic, outgoing, cheerful, and confident. Stereotypes associated with ectomorphs include anxious, serious, cautious, and tactful. We are not saying that people necessarily act these ways based on their body types. Rather, people tend to attribute certain characteristics to others based on body type.

Physical features such as height, weight, skin color, hair color and style, and facial features also convey nonverbal messages. People form impressions of others based on all of these features. First impressions frequently depend on such nonver-

Endomorph—round and heavy body type.

Mesomorph—muscular and athletic body type.

Ectomorph—tall and thin body type.

bal aspects of physical features. American society places much emphasis on physical appearance, and entire industries are devoted to changing one's physical appearance through cosmetic surgery, weight loss, and grooming products. Many people go to great lengths to select clothing to manage the impressions they portray. Particular brands of clothing convey certain images. Whether your hair is spiked, cut short, in dreadlocks, or shaved will convey a particular image, which is also affected by your own sex, race, ethnicity, and age. Tattoos and piercings convey nonverbal messages. Often institutions in society such as a workplace or a school will establish rules of dress and appearance in order to convey a certain image of that establishment. Since choice of clothing and personal grooming will communicate a message, it is important to determine what messages you want to send and then dress and groom accordingly. Of course, dress and personal grooming is highly situational, with certain formal contexts like job interviews, court appearances, or funerals expecting more uniform styles of appearance than informal situations like parties.

Time. The use of time, or **chronemics**, is another way of conveying nonverbal messages. There are several aspects of how we think about and use time which convey impressions to others. Are you a person who is focused on the past, the present, or the future? Some people and cultures think mostly about the past, while others focus on the present, and others emphasize the future (Chen & Starosta, 1998). Someone with a *past orientation* emphasizes tradition, relives the past, and is nostalgic about earlier times. If you have a *present orientation*, you live for the moment, concentrate on the here and now, and focus on what you are doing or feeling right now. Having a *future orientation* means looking ahead and planning what will happen later. While it is rare for someone to have only one of these orientations, many people use one of these approaches more than the others. One's orientation to time tends to be a psychological state that is manifested in nonverbal behavior. One style is not necessarily better than another. Relationship challenges may develop, however, if one person greatly emphasizes one orientation to time and the partner focuses on a different orientation.

Imagine if Bettina and Nadia are business partners who have different time orientations. Bettina thinks quite a bit about the future, wants to develop a five-year plan, and saves money for a long-range goal of expanding the business. Perhaps Nadia focuses on the present time, by spending to create a professional business environment, making quick decisions, and taking immediate action. The partners' different orientations to time would lead them to behave differently, perhaps with Bettina behaving cautiously, slowly, and deliberately and Nadia engaging in risk-taking, as well as spontaneous and impulsive behavior. Their different approaches to time and their resulting behaviors would be conflicting, which would make it very difficult to make joint business decisions.

Another aspect of chronemics relates to how you use your time. Some people and some cultures take a **monochronic** approach to time, meaning they do one thing at a time, adhere strictly to schedules, value punctuality, and resist interruptions. Other people and cultures use a **polychronic** approach, which involves multitasking, or doing several things at once, being flexible with time, not worrying about punctuality, and welcoming interruptions (Chen & Starosta, 1998). People who take a polychronic approach to time may not even perceive interruptions as

Chronemics—the use of time.

Monochronic—doing one thing at a time.

Polychronic—doing several things at once.

such; instead, they may be pleased to have the opportunity to do one more thing in a period of time. These are general tendencies, not absolutes, found in cultures or practiced by certain people. There is no right or wrong approach. Some relationships, families, or workplaces favor one of these approaches to time.

Sometimes, relationship problems develop if one person expects you to use one approach to time and you actually use the other approach. If Sid and Aaron are going on vacation together, Sid may want a planned itinerary with one activity scheduled at a time and set times for meals, while Aaron may want to take it as it comes, jump from activity to activity, do lots of things as the opportunity arises, and not pay attention to a clock. They would have much negotiating and compromising to do in order to have a vacation that meets the needs of both.

Olfactory Communication. The last general type of nonverbal communication is **olfactory communication**, which involves the meanings attached to smells and scents. Your intentional or unintentional display of odor, scents, and smells

Olfactory communication—meanings attached to smells and scents.

learn about yourself

Take this short survey to learn something about yourself and your orientation toward time. Answer the questions based on your first response. There are no right or wrong answers. Just be honest in reporting your true behaviors. For each question, select one of the following numbers that best describes your behavior.

1 = Always false	2 = Usually false	3 = Sometimes true, sometimes false	4 = Usually true	5 = Always true

_____ **1.** I do many things at the same time.

_____ **2.** I stick to my daily schedule as much as possible.

_____ **3.** I prefer to finish one activity before starting another one.

_____ **4.** I feel like I waste time.

_____ **5.** I would take time out of a meeting to take a social phone call.

_____ **6.** I separate work time and social time.

_____ **7.** I break appointments with others.

_____ **8.** I prefer that events in my life occur in an orderly fashion.

_____ **9.** I do more than one activity at a time.

_____ **10.** Being on time for appointments is important to me.

Scoring the survey: To find your score, first reverse the responses for the odd numbered items (if you wrote a 1, make it a 5; 2 = 4; leave 3 as is; 4 = 2, 5 = 1). Next add the numbers for each item. Scores can range from 10 to 50. The higher your score, the more monochronic you are. The lower your score, the more polychronic you are.

Adapted from Gudykunst, W. B., Ting-Toomey, S., Sudweeks, S., & Stewart, L. P. (1995). *Building Bridges: Interpersonal Skills for a Changing World.* Boston: Houghton Mifflin.

on your body or in your territory sends messages to others. If you do not think that smells and scents have the power to communicate, think of the burgeoning industry in the United States designed to manufacture and market scent-related products. Not only do we buy perfumes and colognes, but there are scented soaps, shampoos, air fresheners, candles, cleaning products, and pet products, to name a few. Often we go to great lengths to affect the smells associated with our body, our car, and our home. Aromatherapy is used to relieve stress and alter mood (Furlow, 1996). The meanings attached to certain odors and scents are very firmly based in cultures as we will see in the next section.

Cultural and Gender Variations in Nonverbal Communication

Kinesics

As we have said, the use of body motions and the meanings they convey differ among cultures. Several cultural differences in body motions are well documented.

Eye Contact. A majority of people in the United States and other Western cultures expect those with whom they are communicating to "look them in the eye." In their review of research, however, Samovar and Porter (2001) conclude that direct eye contact is not universally considered appropriate (p. 178). For instance, in Japan people direct their gaze to a position around the Adam's apple and avoid direct eye contact. Chinese, Indonesians, and rural Mexicans lower their eyes as a sign of deference—to them, too much direct eye contact is a sign of bad manners. Middle Easterners, in contrast, look intently into the eyes of the person with whom they are talking for longer periods—to them direct eye contact demonstrates keen interest.

Likewise, there are differences in use of eye contact among co-cultures within the United States. For instance, African Americans use more continuous eye contact than European Americans when they are speaking but less when they are listening (Samovar & Porter, 2001, pp. 178–179). A recent study of black kinesics (Johnson, 2004) reports that some blacks may be reluctant to look authority figures in the eye, because to do so would be a sign of disrespect recalling expectations during slavery, when for blacks to look directly at whites signaled an inappropriate assumption of equality. Likewise, Johnson describes the nonverbal cue of "rolling the eyes" by black youth as way to communicate hostility or disapproval. In the United States women tend to have more frequent eye contact during conversations than men do (Cegala & Sillars, 1989). Moreover, women tend to hold eye contact longer than men regardless of the sex of the person they are interacting with (Wood, 2001, p. 150). It is important to note that these differences, while described according to biological sex, are also related to notions of gender and standpoint in society. In other words, people (male or female) will give more eye contact when they are displaying feminine-type behaviors than when they are displaying masculine-type behaviors. Since, as we have mentioned, eye contact can convey status, it follows that in comparable situations, lower-status people (male or female) will give more eye contact to those of higher status.

Facial Expression and Gestures. Studies show that there are many similarities in nonverbal communication across cultures, especially in facial expressions. For instance, several facial expressions seem to be universal, including a slight raising of the eyebrow to communicate recognition, and wriggling one's nose paired with a disgusted facial look to show social repulsion (Martin & Nakayama 2000, pp. 183–184). In fact, at least six facial expressions (happiness, sadness, fear, anger, disgust, and surprise) carry the same basic meaning throughout the world (Samovar & Porter, 2001, p. 177).

Across cultures, people also show considerable differences in the meaning of gestures. For instance, the forming of a circle with the thumb and forefinger, which signifies "OK" in the United States, means zero or worthless in France, is a symbol for money in Japan, and is a vulgar gesture in Germany and Brazil (Axtell, 1998, pp. 44, 143, 212).

Displays of emotion may also vary. For instance, in some Eastern cultures people have been socialized to downplay emotional behavior cues, whereas members of other cultures have been socialized to amplify their displays of emotion. Research has shown some sex and gender effects in facial expressions and gestures. Women and men using feminine style of communication tend to smile frequently. Gender differences in the use of gestures are so profound that people have been found to attribute masculinity or femininity on the basis of gesture style alone (Pearson, West, & Turner, 1995, p. 126). For instance, women are more likely to keep their arms close to the body and less likely to lean forward with the body; they play more often with their hair or clothing, and tap their hands more often than men.

Haptics

According to Gudykunst and Kim (1997), differences in touching behavior are highly correlated with culture. In some cultures lots of contact and touching is normal behavior, while in other cultures individual space is respected and frequent touching is not encouraged. "People in high-contact cultures evaluate 'close' as positive and good, and evaluate 'far' as negative and bad. People in low-contact cultures evaluate 'close' as negative and bad, and 'far' as positive and good" (p. 235). Latin America and the Mediterranean countries are high-contact cultures, northern European cultures are medium to low in contact, and Asian cultures are for the most part low-contact cultures. The United States, which is a country of immigrants, is generally perceived to be in the medium-contact category, though there are wide differences among individual Americans due to variations in family heritage.

Women tend to touch others less than men do, but women value touching more than men do. Women view touch as an expressive behavior that demonstrates warmth and affiliation, whereas men view touch as instrumental behavior, so that touching females is considered as leading to sexual activity (Pearson, West, & Turner, 1995, p. 142).

Paralanguage

There are a few cultural and gender variations in use of paralanguage. In the Middle East, speaking loudly signifies being strong and sincere. People from Hong Kong use high-pitched, expressive voices. What we call vocal interferences in the United States are not considered to be interferences in China, where using fillers signals wisdom and attractiveness (Chen & Starosta, 1998).

In the United States, there are stereotypes about what are considered to be masculine and feminine voices. Masculine voices are expected to be low pitched and loud, with moderate to low intonation, while feminine voices are expected to be higher pitched, softer in volume, and more expressive. The voice characteristic of breathiness is associated with femininity. While both sexes have the option to portray a range of masculine and feminine vocalics, most people probably do conform to the expectations for their sex. One voice feature, pitch, does have a physical basis to it. Men's vocal cords, on average, are larger and thicker than women's, and this accounts for the lower pitch of men's voices and the higher pitch of women's voices. Despite this physical reason for voice pitch differences between the sexes, societal expectations about masculinity and femininity still play a part. Before puberty, the vocal cords of males and females do not differ. Yet, even before there is a physical reason for sex differences in pitch, little boys frequently speak in a lower pitch than little girls (Wood, 2003).

Proxemics and Territory

Interpersonal problems occur when one person's use of space violates the behavioral expectations of another. For instance, Lorenzo may come from a family that conducts informal conversations with others at a range closer than the eighteen-inch limit that many European Americans place on intimate space. When he talks to a colleague at work and moves in closer than eighteen inches, the co-worker may back away during the conversation. Unfortunately, there are times when one person intentionally violates the space expectations of another. When the violation is between members of the opposite sex, it may be considered sexual harassment. Glen may, through violations of informal space, posture, movements, or gestures, "come on" to Donnice. If Donnice does not welcome the attention, she may feel threatened. In this case, Glen's nonverbal behavior may be construed as sexual harassment. To avoid perceptions of harassment, people need to be especially sensitive to others' definitions of intimate space.

As you would expect, the environments in which people feel comfortable depend on cultural background. In the United States, many people live in single-family homes or in large apartments. In other countries, where population densities in inhabited regions are high, people live in closer quarters and can feel "lonely" or isolated in larger spaces. In Japan and Europe, most people live in spaces that by our U.S. standards would be called cramped. Similarly, people from different cultures have different ideas about what constitutes appropriate distances for various interactions. Recall that in the dominant culture of the United States, the boundary of personal or intimate space is about eighteen inches. In Middle Eastern cultures, however, men move much closer to other men when they are talking (Samovar &

Porter, 2001, p. 186). Thus, when an Egyptian man talks with an American man, one of the two is likely to be uncomfortable. Either the American will feel uncomfortable and invaded or the Egyptian will feel isolated and too distant for serious conversation.

But we don't have to go off the North American continent to see variations in the way uses of space may differ. In the Diverse Voices feature on pages 135–136, notice how Latin American and Anglo American use of space differs.

Artifacts and Physical Appearance

There are cultural and gender influences regarding artifacts and physical appearance. Certainly the use and types of cars as status symbols vary greatly by culture. In some cultures a motor scooter or bicycle is a prestigious artifact. Of course, there are great differences in clothing and body adornment by culture. Different clothing styles signify masculinity and femininity within a culture. In the United States, women's and feminine clothing is more decorative, while men's and masculine clothing is more functional. Think of the variety of decorative accessory products aimed at women: shoes and purses in every color and style; jewelry for ears, neck, wrists, ankles, toes, and clothing; decorations for the hair; decorative belts and scarves; patterned hose and colorful socks; not to mention the enormous variety of clothing itself. While the accessory options for men are increasing, the emphasis on decorative accessories for men remains minimal. Standards of beauty vary by culture, and the emphasis on physical appearance as an aspect of self-esteem varies widely between women and men in the United States. Women have great pressure to conform to an idealized standard of weight and to wear makeup. Men are expected to be tall and muscular.

Even the meanings that we assign to colors vary by national culture and religion. In India white, not black, is the color of mourning, and Hindu brides wear red. In Latin America, purple signifies death, and in Japan, green denotes youth and energy.

Chronemics

Like the other aspects of nonverbal communication, we see cultural variations in chronemics. Some cultures, like China, are oriented very much toward the past, while the orientation in the United States is considered to be toward the present and near future.

The dominant culture of the United States is monochronically oriented. We compartmentalize our time and schedule one event at a time. In this culture, being even a few minutes late may require you to acknowledge your lateness. Being ten to fifteen minutes late usually requires an apology, and being more than thirty minutes late is likely to be perceived as an insult, requiring a great deal of explanation (Gudykunst & Kim, 1997, p. 161).

People from other cultural backgrounds, such as those from Latin America, Africa, Asia, and the Middle East, tend to view time polychronically. Cultural dif-

diverse voices

Latin American and Anglo American Use of Personal Space in Public Places

How we use space and how we expect others to treat the space around us are determined by our culture. In this excerpt the author focuses our attention on the ways in which the body is understood and treated by Latin Americans and Anglo Americans, and the cultural differences that become apparent when these two cultural groups find themselves sharing common space.

It is 6:00 P.M. The Bayfront, a shopping mall near a Miami marina, reverberates with the noise and movement of people, coming and going, contemplating the lights of the bay, sampling exotic juice blends, savoring the not-so-exotic foods from Cuba, Nicaragua, or Mexico, and listening to the bands. The Bayfront provides an environment for the exercise of two different rituals: the Anglo American visit to the mall and the Latin American paseo, the visit to the outdoor spaces of the city.

Some of the people sitting in the plaza look insistently at me, making comments, laughing, and whispering. Instead of feeling uneasy or surprised, I find myself looking back at them, entering this inquisitive game and asking myself some of the same questions they might be asking. Who are they, where are they from, what are they up to? I follow their gaze and I see it extend to other groups. The gaze is returned by some in the crowd, so that a play of silent dialogue seems to grow amidst the anonymity of the crowd. The crowd that participates in this complicity of wandering looks is not Anglo American. The play of looks described above has a different

"accent," a Hispanic accent, which reveals a different understanding of the plaza and public space.

The Anglo American passers-by understand their vital space, their relationship with strangers, and their public interactions in a different manner. If I address them in the street, I better assume that I am confronting them in an alley. But when I am walking by myself along the halls of a Hispanic mall, I am not alone. I do not expect, therefore, to be treated by others as if they were suddenly confronting me in a dark alley. I am in a crowd, with the crowd, and anyone there has access to my attention.

Anglo Americans are alone (even in the middle of the crowd) if they choose to be, for they have a guaranteed cultural right to be "left alone" on their way to and from anywhere. To approach or touch someone without that person's consent is a violation of a fundamental right within Anglo-Saxon, Protestant cultural tradition. This is the right to one's own body as private property. Within this tradition, touching is understood as an excursion into someone else's territory. With this in mind then, it is understandable that Anglo Americans excuse themselves

when they accidentally touch someone or come close to doing so. To accidentally penetrate someone else's boundary (especially if that person is a stranger) demands an apology, and a willingness to repair the damage by stepping back from the violated territory.

One can see how rude a Latin American might appear to an Anglo American when the former distractingly touches another person without apologizing or showing concern. But within Latino and Mediterranean traditions, the body is not understood as property. That is, the body is not understood as belonging to its owner. It does not belong to me or to anyone else; it is, in principle, public. It is an expressive and sensual region open to the scrutiny, discipline, and sanction of the community. It is, therefore, quite impossible to be "left alone" on the Latin American street. For Latin Americans, the access to others in a public space is not restricted by the "privacy" of their bodies. Thus, the Latin American does not find casual contact a form of property trespassing or a violation of rights. Walking the street in the Anglo United States is very much an anonymous activity to be performed in a field of unobstructive and invisible bodies. Since one is essentially carrying one's own space into the public sphere, no one is actually ever in public. Given that the public is private, no intimacy is granted in the public space. Thus while the Latin American public look or gaze is round, inquisitive, and wandering, the Anglo American is straight, nonobstructive, and neutral.

Civility requires the Anglo American to restrict looks, delimit gestures, and orient movement. Civility requires the Latin American to acknowledge looks, gestures, and movement and actively engage with them. For the Latin American, the unavoidable nature of shared space is always a demand for attention and a request to participate. An Anglo American considers "mind your own business" to be fair and civil. A Latin American might find this an unreasonable restriction. What takes place in public is everybody's business by the very fact that it is taking place in public.

One can understand the possible cultural misunderstandings between Anglo Americans and Latin Americans. If Anglo Americans protest the "impertinence" of Latin Americans as nosy and curious, Latin Americans would protest the indifference and lack of concern of Anglo Americans. The scene in the Miami mall could happen just as easily in Los Angeles, Chicago, Philadelphia, or New York, cities in which Latin Americans comprise an important segment of the population. The influence of this cultural heritage is going to have growing influence in the next few decades on the Anglo American scene, as Hispanics become the largest ethnic and linguistic minority in the United States. The more knowledge we can gain from what makes us culturally diverse, the more we will be able to appreciate what unifies us through the mixing and mutual exchanges of our cultures. ■

Excerpted from Lozano, E. (2000). The cultural experience of space and body: A reading of Latin American and Anglo American comportment in public. In A. Gonzalez, M. Houston, & V. Chen (Eds.), *Our Voices: Essays in Culture, Ethnicity, and Communication: An Intercultural Anthology* (pp. 228–234). Los Angeles: Roxbury Publishing Company.

ferences in perception of time can cause misunderstanding. For instance, a naive U.S. sales representative with a business appointment in Latin America may be very frustrated with what he or she regards as a "cavalier" attitude toward time; likewise, a Latin American with a business appointment in the United States may be frustrated by the perceived rigidity of time schedules there.

observe & analyze

Cultural Differences in Self-Presentation

Interview or converse with two international students from different countries. Try to select students whose cultures differ from each other and from the culture with which you are most familiar. Develop a list of questions related to the self-presentation behaviors discussed earlier. Try to understand how people in the international students' countries differ from you in their use of nonverbal self-presentation behaviors. Prepare to share what you have learned with your classmates. ■

Olfactory Communication

While cultural and gender variations are not great in the olfactory aspect of nonverbal communication, there are some points worth noting. The fact that certain scents are marketed differently to men and women in colognes and perfumes does show different expectations or stereotypes for male and female preferences. In some cultures, artificial scents from colognes and perfumes are considered annoying, while in other cultures, natural body odors are offensive.

Improving Nonverbal Communication Skills

Because nonverbal communication varies by situation, culture, and gender, it is difficult to exactly prescribe how you should communicate nonverbally. There are some general suggestions, however, that we can make that will help you to be more effective at sending and receiving messages.

Sending Messages

As we explained in Chapter 1, encoding consists of the cognitive thinking processes you use to transform ideas and feelings into symbols and to organize them into a message. To improve your sending of messages, consider the following guidelines.

1. **Be conscious of the nonverbal behavior you are displaying.** Remember that you are always communicating nonverbally. Some nonverbal cues will always be out of your level of consciousness, but you should work to bring more of your nonverbal behavior into your conscious awareness. It is a matter of just paying attention to what you are doing with your eyes, face, posture, gestures, voice, appearance, and use of objects, as well as your handling of time and scents. If you initially have difficulty paying attention to your nonverbal behavior, ask a friend to point out the nonverbal cues you are displaying.

2. **Be purposeful or strategic in your use of nonverbal communication.** Sometimes, it is important to control what you are communicating nonverbally. For instance, if you want to be persuasive, you should use nonverbal cues that demonstrate confidence and credibility. These may include direct eye contact, a serious facial expression, a relaxed posture, a loud and low-pitched voice with no vocal interferences, and professional-style clothing and grooming. If, on the other hand, you want to communicate empathy and support, you might select different nonverbal behaviors including moderate gaze, caring facial expressions, leaning toward the other, a soft voice, and touch. While there are not absolute prescriptions for communicating nonverbally, there are strategic choices we can make to convey the message we desire.

3. **Make sure that your nonverbal cues do not distract from your message.** Sometimes, when we are not aware of what nonverbal cues we are displaying or when we are anxious, certain nonverbal behaviors will hinder our communication. Fidgeting, tapping your fingers on a table, pacing, mumbling, using vocal interferences, and using physical adaptors can hinder the other person's interpretation of your message. It is important to control extraneous nonverbal cues that get in the way of effective interpersonal communication.

4. **Make your nonverbal communication match your verbal communication.** When we presented the functions of nonverbal communication earlier

in this chapter, we explained how nonverbal communication may contradict the verbal communication, causing a mixed message to occur. Effective interpersonal communicators try to avoid mixed messages. Not only is it important to have your verbal and nonverbal communications match, but various aspects of nonverbal communication should match each other also. If you are feeling sad, your voice will be softer and less expressive, but you should not let your face contradict your voice with a smile. People get confused and frustrated when they receive inconsistent messages.

5. **Adapt your nonverbal behavior to the situation.** Situations vary in their formality, familiarity among the people, and purpose. Just as you would select different language for different situations, you should adapt your nonverbal messages to the situation. Assess what the situation calls for in terms of body motions, paralanguage, proxemics and territory, artifacts, physical appearance, and use of time and scents. Of course, you already do some situational adapting with nonverbal communication. You wouldn't dress the same way for a wedding as you would to walk the dog. You would not treat your brother's space and territory the same way you would treat your doctor's space and territory. But the more you can consciously adapt your nonverbal behavior to what seems appropriate to the situation, the more effective you will be as a communicator.

Receiving Messages

Decoding is the process the receiver uses to transform the messages that are received into the receiver's own ideas and feelings. To improve your receiving of messages, consider the following guidelines.

1. **When interpreting others' nonverbal cues, do not automatically assume that a particular behavior means a certain thing.** Except for the category of emblems, there is no universal meaning of nonverbal behavior. And even the meaning of emblems varies culturally. There is much room for error when people make quick interpretations or draw rapid conclusions about an aspect of nonverbal behavior. Instead of making automatic interpretations of nonverbal cues, we should consider the influences on nonverbal behavior of cultural, gender, and individual personality.

2. **Consider cultural, gender, and individual influences when interpreting nonverbal cues.** We have shown how nonverbal behavior varies widely based on one's culture, sex, or expectations of masculinity and femininity. The more you know about intercultural and gender aspects of nonverbal communication, the more accurate you will be in interpreting others' nonverbal cues. Note also that some people are totally unique in their display of nonverbal behavior. You may have learned over time that your friend grinds her teeth when she is excited. You may never encounter another person who uses this behavior in this way. Remember from Chapter 2 the importance of getting to the psychological level of prediction based on a person's uniqueness.

3. **Pay attention to multiple aspects of nonverbal communication and their relationship to verbal communication.** You should not take nonverbal cues out of context. In any one interaction, you are likely to get simultaneous messages from a person's eyes, face, gestures, posture, voice, and use of space and touch. Even in electronic communication, where much of the apparatus of nonverbal communication is absent, facial expression and touch can be communicated through emoticons, paralanguage through capitalization of words, and chronemics through the timing and length of electronic messages. All nonverbal cues will occur in conjunction with words. By taking into consideration all of the channels of communication, you will more effectively interpret the messages of others.

4. **Use perception checking.** As we discussed in Chapter 2, the skill of perception checking lets you see if your interpretation of another person's message is accurate or not. By describing the nonverbal behavior you have noticed and tentatively sharing your interpretation of it, you can get confirmation or correction of your interpretation. For instance, suppose a person smiles and nods her head when you tell her about a mistake she has made. Before you conclude that the person agrees with your observation and accepts your criticism, you might say, "From the smile on your face and your nodding, I get

what would you do?

A Question of Ethics

After the intramural mixed-doubles matches on Tuesday evening, most of the players adjourned to the campus grill to have a drink and chat. Although the group was highly competitive on the courts, they enjoyed socializing and talking about the matches for a while before they went home. Marquez and Lisa, who had been paired together at the start of the season, sat down with another pair, Barry and Elana, who had been going out together for several weeks.

Marquez and Lisa had played a particularly grueling match that night against Barry and Elana, a match that they lost largely because of Elana's improved play.

"Elana, your serve today was the best I've seen it this year," Marquez said.

"Yeah, I was really impressed. And as you saw, I had trouble handling it," Lisa added.

"And you're getting to the net a lot better too," Marquez added.

"Thanks, guys," Elana said in a tone of gratitude, "I've really been working on it."

"Well, aren't we getting the compliments today," sneered Barry in a sarcastic tone. Then after a pause, he said, "Oh, Elana, would you get my sweater? I left it on that chair by the other table."

"Come on Barry, you're closer than I am," Elana replied.

Barry got a cold look on his face, moved slightly closer to Elana, and said emphatically, "Get my sweater for me, Elana—now."

Elana quickly backed away from Barry as she said, "OK Barry—it's cool," and she then quickly got the sweater for him.

"Gee, isn't she sweet?" Barry said to Marquez and Lisa as he grabbed the sweater from Elana.

Lisa and Marquez both looked down at the floor. Then Lisa glanced at Marquez and said, "Well, I'm out of here—I've got a lot to do this evening."

"Let me walk you to your car," Marquez said as he stood up.

"See you next week," they said in unison as they hurried out the door, leaving Barry and Elana alone at the table.

1. Analyze Barry's nonverbal behavior. What was he attempting to achieve?

2. How do you interpret Lisa's and Marquez's nonverbal reactions to Barry?

3. Was Barry's behavior ethically acceptable? Explain.

the impression that you had already recognized a problem here, or am I off base?" It may be helpful to use perception checking when faced with gender or cultural variations in nonverbal behavior. It is especially important to use perception checking when you receive mixed messages from others.

Summary

Nonverbal communication refers to how people communicate through bodily actions and vocal qualities typically accompanying a verbal message. We opened this chapter by looking at various characteristics and functions of nonverbal communication. Nonverbal communication varies in intentionality; it is ambiguous, primary, continuous, and multichanneled. Nonverbal communication functions to provide information, regulate interaction, express or hide emotions, present an image, and convey power.

The major focus of the chapter has been on types of nonverbal communication. Perhaps the most familiar methods of nonverbal communication are what and how a person communicates through kinesics such as eye contact, facial expression, gesture, posture, and touch. A second form of nonverbal communication is paralanguage, which includes our use of pitch, volume, rate, quality, and intonation to give special meaning to the words we use. Whereas these vocal characteristics help us interpret the meaning of a verbal message, vocal interferences ("ah," "um," "you know," and "like") often impede a listener's ability to understand and become annoying.

People communicate through the use of personal space, how close or far away they stand, as well as by how they claim and defend their territory. We also communicate through artifacts, such as personal possessions and the ways we arrange and decorate our space. Likewise, our self-presentation cues are communicated through our personal appearance, use of time, and choice of scents and smells.

The many types of nonverbal communication we may use may vary depending on the individual's culture and gender portrayals. As a result, our body motions, touch, paralanguage, use of space and territory, and self-presentation cues through physical appearance, use of time, and olfactory communication may differ considerably.

You can improve your encoding of nonverbal communication by being conscious of the nonverbal behavior you are displaying, by being purposeful or strategic in your use of these cues, by making sure that your nonverbal cues do not distract people from your message, by making your nonverbal communication match your verbal communication, and by adapting your nonverbal behavior to the situation. You can improve your decoding by not misinterpreting others' nonverbal cues, by considering cultural and gender differences, by paying attention to aspects of nonverbal communication and their relationship to verbal communication, and by perception checking.

Chapter Resources

Communication Improvement Plan: Nonverbal Communication

Would you like to improve your use of the following skills or aspects of perception discussed in this chapter?

Eye contact	Touch
Facial expression	Paralanguage
Gesture	Vocal interferences
Posture	Proxemics
Territory	Artifacts
Chronemics	Olfactory communication

Pick a skill or an area, and write a communication improvement plan. You can find a communication improvement plan worksheet on our website at www.oup.com/us/interact

Key Words

Nonverbal communication behaviors, *p. 115*	**Haptics,** *p. 121*	**Proxemics,** *p. 124*
Kinesics, *p. 119*	**Ritualized touch,** *p. 122*	**Territory,** *p. 126*
Eye contact or gaze, *p. 119*	**Task-related touch,** *p. 122*	**Artifacts,** *p. 127*
Facial expression, *p. 120*	**Paralanguage or vocalics,** *p. 122*	**Endomorph,** *p. 128*
Emoticons, *p. 120*	**Pitch,** *p. 123*	**Mesomorph,** *p. 128*
Gestures, *p. 120*	**Volume,** *p. 123*	**Ectomorph,** *p. 128*
Emblems, *p. 120*	**Rate,** *p. 123*	**Chronemics,** *p. 129*
Adaptors, *p. 120*	**Quality,** *p. 123*	**Monochronic,** *p. 129*
Posture, *p. 121*	**Intonation,** *p. 123*	**Polychronic,** *p. 129*
Body orientation, *p. 121*	**Vocal interferences,** *p. 123*	**Olfactory communication,** *p. 130*

Inter-Act with Media

CINEMA

Gary Winick (Director). (2004) *13 Going on 30.* Jennifer Garner, Mark Ruffalo, Andy Serkis, Christa B. Allen.

Brief Summary: Jenna Rink is a preteen who wants to be grown up very badly. On the night before her thirteenth birthday, she makes a wish to get older faster. When she wakes up, her world is very different. She is 30 years old, with a career as a magazine editor and a live-in boyfriend. She goes in search of Matt, her best friend from when she was younger, to try to find out what happened. He helps her learn how to behave in her new world and life.

IPC Concepts: Meaning, types of body motions, cultural and gender differences.

WHAT'S ON THE WEB

Psychology at Salford

http://www.chssc.salford.ac.uk/healthSci/psych2000/psych2000/Interpersonal.htm

Brief Summary: This site has an excellent review of areas of nonverbal communication, including a detailed section on research dealing with interpersonal touch and links to other informative and interactive sites. The site discusses nonverbal cues, types of nonverbal communication, attribution theory, bias, and stereotyping based on nonverbal behavior.

IPC Concepts: Meaning, types of body motions, cultural and gender differences.

Microexpression

http://www.absoluteastronomy.com/encyclopedia/M/Mi/Microexpression.htm

Brief Summary: This site offers an excellent and concise discussion of the nature and importance of microexpression. The site also has numerous links for additional material on related aspects of nonverbal communication.

IPC Concepts: Facial expressions, nonverbal communication of emotional states.

holding effective conversations

After you have read this chapter, you should be able to answer these questions:

- What is a conversation?
- What are appropriate ways to start a conversation?
- How do small talk, casual social conversations, and problem-consideration conversations differ?
- What are the characteristics of a conversation?
- What are conversational rules?
- What are guidelines for effective conversationalists?
- What are significant cultural variations in conversation?

"Hey Josh, I'm glad you're home. Where have you been?"

"Out."

"What do you mean 'out'? Where did you go?"

"It's no big deal, Mom. We all went over to Jeff's and just hung out."

"Hung out doing what?"

"You know, just hung out and chilled."

"No, I don't know. What did you do while you were hanging out?"

"Nothing. We just sat around and talked."

"About what?"

"Stuff."

"Josh, you've been gone more than four hours! Tell me something that you talked about."

"I can't remember much. Oh, Jeff told us about a movie he saw and Carrie talked about her cousin's wedding that she went to. And, oh yeah, Becca told us that the Jeffersons are getting a divorce and that Meg, who we thought would be over to chill with us, is going to have to live with her dad. So we talked about how well she would deal with that and. . ."

"Whoa! That doesn't sound like you did nothing. It sounds as if you were talking about some important happenings."

"Yeah, I guess so."

Conversations are the stuff of which our relationships are made. In fact, as Steve Duck, a leading researcher on relationships, has pointed out, "If you were to sit and list the things that you do with friends, one of the top items on the list would surely have to be 'talking'" (1998, p. 7). When conversations go well, they are interesting, informative, stimulating, and just good fun. Yet, many conversations, like the one between Josh and his mom, are like pulling teeth. By understanding how a conversation works, we can see how its effectiveness and its value depend on the willingness of participants to share, and we can learn to use conversational skills that increase the informative value and the enjoyment of participating.

In this chapter, we start by describing ways to begin a conversation. Then we explain the components of the body of a conversation—small talk, casual social conversations, and problem-consideration conversations—and offer ways to disengage from a conversation. Next we present six characteristics of conversations: formality, turn-taking, topic change, talk time, scriptedness, and audience. We then discuss basic rules of conversation, including specific characteristics and the cooperative principle, as well as basic guidelines for effective conversationalists. The chapter ends with a discussion of cultural variations in conversations.

The Structure of Conversations

Conversations are locally managed, sequential interchanges of thoughts and feelings between two or more people that are interactive and largely extemporaneous. This definition highlights several key features mentioned by Jan Svennevig (1999) that distinguish conversations from other forms of communication such as speech making and debating (p. 8). First, conversations are *locally managed*. This means that only those involved in the conversation determine the topic, who will speak, the order of speaking, and the length of time each will speak in a turn. Second, conversations are *sequentially organized*; that is, they have openings, middles, and closings. Third, conversations are *interactive*; that is, they involve at least two people speaking and listening. Fourth, conversations are *largely extemporaneous*, which means the participants have not prepared or memorized what they will be saying.

All conversations have identifiable openings, bodies, and conclusions. How obvious or formal each part is will vary depending on how long the conversation lasts, how well the participants know each other, and the context of the conversation.

Conversations–locally managed, sequential interchanges of thoughts and feelings between two or more people.

Beginning to Converse

One of the most stressful times for many people is having to converse with a complete stranger. Many people are so uncomfortable that even if they are seated next to a person whom they find attractive, they are unwilling or afraid to say a word. As Thomas Holtgraves points out, people who wish to converse must indicate their availability and willingness to talk, and a topic that is mutually acceptable must be considered (2002, p. 100).

Suppose Marge and Jan (who don't know each other) are waiting for a bus. If neither is busy with another activity, both are of course available. After a few minutes of standing there, Marge says, "Beautiful day, isn't it?" to which Jan replies,

"Yeah," and then looks up the street for the bus. Although Jan is available, she shows no willingness to talk—so unless Marge pursues it, there will be no conversation. But if in response to "Beautiful day, isn't it?" Jan says, "Sure is—a great day to be outdoors, isn't it?" she indicates a willingness to continue the conversation. In essence all conversations begin with two utterances, spoken by different people. The first person initiates a topic. The second reacts to the first in a way that suggests that the participant is interested or uninterested in continuing the interaction.

How do you go about talking with a stranger in a way that will make a positive first impression? For those of us who find talking with strangers difficult, the following five strategies may be useful. Notice that each of these strategies results in question asking. A cheerful answer to your question followed by a question to you suggests that the person is interested in continuing a conversation. A refusal to answer or a curt reply may mean that the person isn't really interested in talking at this time.

1. **Begin by introducing yourself.** "Hi, my name is Gordon. What's yours?"

2. **Refer to the physical context.** "This is awful weather for a game, isn't it?" "I wonder how they are able to keep such a beautiful garden in this climate," or "Darlene and Verne have sure done a great job of remodeling this home. Did you ever see it before the renovation?"

3. **Refer to your thoughts or feelings.** "I really like parties, don't you?" "I live on this floor, too—do these steps bother you as much as they do me?" or "Doesn't it seem stuffy in here?"

4. **Refer to another person.** "Larry seems to be a great cook—have you known him long?" or "I don't believe I've met you before—do you work with Evan?"

How do we begin and sustain a conversation?

5. **Use humor or a light-hearted remark.** "Isn't it great that college tuition just keeps getting cheaper and cheaper?" Researchers have found that a shared humorous experience can ease the awkwardness of initial conversations between strangers (Fraley & Aron, 2004).

The Body of a Conversation

The body or the substantive part of a conversation may involve various types of information: small talk, casual social conversations, or problem-consideration conversations.

Small Talk. Once two people have begun a conversation, they are likely to engage in small talk (conversation that meets social needs with relatively low amounts of risk) characterized by idea exchange and gossip.

Small talk—conversations that meet social needs with low amounts of risk.

Idea exchange messages focus on conveying facts, opinions, and beliefs. Idea exchange is a common type of communication between new acquaintances and friends alike. At the office Dan may ask Walt about last night's sports scores, Maria may talk with Louise about new cars, and Pete may discuss an upcoming event with Teresa. Or, on a more serious level, Jan may talk with Gloria about the U.S. role in the Middle East or Dave may seek Bill's views on abortion. Although the discussion of foreign policy and abortion is "deeper" than the discussion about sports or cars, both discussions represent idea exchanges. During early stages of a relationship, this type of communication is important because through it you learn what the other person values and how he or she thinks. Based on this information you can assess how much effort you want to put into developing and sustaining this relationship.

Idea exchange messages—speech that conveys facts, opinions, and beliefs in a conversation.

Gossip, talking about other people who are not present, is one of the most common forms of interpersonal communication. On one hand, it's an easy way to talk with people without sharing much information about yourself. Statements such as "Do you know Bill? I hear he has a really great job," "Would you believe that Mary Simmons and Tom Johnson are going together? They never seemed to hit it off too well in the past," and "My sister Eileen is really working hard at losing weight. I saw her the other day, and all she talked about was the diet she's on" are all examples of gossip. Gossip is benign when what is discussed is common knowledge. People do break up, lose their jobs, get in accidents, win prizes, and so on. In these circumstances, there's nothing secret—and if the person were there he or she would likely talk about what happened.

Gossip—talking about other people who are not present.

On the other hand, gossip can be unethical and malicious. Gossip that discloses information that is private or inaccurate is not appropriate. Perhaps the most malicious kind of gossip is that which is engaged in for the purpose of hurting or embarrassing a person who is not present.

Casual Social Conversations. Casual social conversations are interactions between people whose purpose is to enhance or maintain a relationship through spontaneous interactions about general topics. For instance, when Connie, Jeff, Wanda, and Trevor have dinner together, they might hold conversations on multiple topics, some in which all four participate and others in which two sets of two con-

Casual social conversations—interactions between people whose purpose is to enhance or maintain a relationship through spontaneous interactions about general topics.

Figure 6.1 Casual Conversation

CONVERSATION	COMMENTARY
As they look around the theater, Donna says,"They really did an Art Deco thing with this place didn't they?"	Donna introduces a possible topic.
"Yeah … Hey," Juanita says as she surveys the audience,"it looks as if this is going to be a sellout."	Juanita acknowledges Donna's statement, chooses not to discuss it, and introduces a different topic.
"Certainly does—I see people in the last row of the balcony."	Donna accepts the topic and extends discussion with a parallel comment.
"I thought this would be a popular show. It was a hit when it toured Louisville … and I hear the attendance has been good all week."	Juanita continues the topic by providing new information.
Agreeing with Juanita, Donna adds,"Lots of people I've talked with were trying to get tickets."	Donna and Juanita continue the topic for two more turns.
"Well, it's good for the downtown."	
"Yeah," Donna says as she glances at the notes on the cast. After a few seconds she exlaims,"I didn't know Gloria VanDell was from Cincinnati!"	Donna acknowledges Juanita's reply and then introduces a different topic.

verse on different topics. During dinner they might spend nearly their entire time talking about an important upcoming election, or they might talk about a series of topics including a new movie, a television series, last week's football game, politics, or they might gossip about what different people wore to a party they had attended.

You've noticed that gossip is included as a typical casual social conversation topic. And, although at times gossip is malicious and unethical, most of the time it is a harmless form of casual social conversation that has at least some redeeming value. As Eggins and Slade point out, gossip is a powerful socializing force. It reflects a sociocultural world and at the same time helps to shape that world (1997, p. 279). So, casual conversations are held primarily to meet the participants' interpersonal needs, and their sole function is to build or maintain the relationships.

Problem-Consideration Conversations. Problem-consideration conversations are interactions between people in which the goal of at least one of the participants is to elicit the cooperation of another in meeting a specific goal. At times this specific goal is known before the conversation begins. For instance, if Glen is concerned about the fairness of workloads, he may ask Susan, his co-worker, to meet with him to generate some ideas about what can be done to better balance the jobs assigned to each person on the team. At other times, the need to consider a particular topic or problem may arise spontaneously during the discussion. For instance, while office mates are talking over lunch, one of them might say, "Garret has really been stressed out lately." This might stimulate the group to consider possible ways to help alleviate Garret's stress.

Problem-consideration conversations—interactions between people in which the goal of at least one of the participants is to elicit cooperation in meeting a specific goal.

inter-act with

Technology

Think of times that you've made a call outside your home using a cell phone. How do your conversations differ from those you have from a land line? Are they longer? Shorter? More focused on pragmatic problem considerations than on casual social exchanges? More or less private? Why do you think this is true? What differences do you see in the way you handle such conversations in comparison to the way you would handle the same topics face to face? ■

A problem-consideration conversation is much more structured than casual social conversation because it requires the participants to deliberate and reach a conclusion. As a result, these conversations may appear to be more orderly than casual social conversations and can have as many as five distinguishable parts.

1. **Greeting and small talk.** Pragmatic problem-consideration conversations may begin with a greeting followed by very brief exchange on social topics in order to develop rapport.

2. **Topic introduction and statement of need for discussion.** In the second stage, one participant introduces the problem or issue that is the real purpose for the conversation. How this topic is presented or framed affects how the discussion will proceed.

3. **Information exchange and processing.** Once it has been established that a problem should be discussed, the conversation will proceed to a series of speaking turns where participants share information and opinions, generate alternative ideas for solutions, and present the advantages and disadvantages of different options.

   Because conversations are spontaneous, they are unlikely to follow a textbook problem-solving format. The conversationalists may begin by generating some alternatives; then, while discussing advantages and disadvantages, they may share information that might lead to the suggestion of additional alternatives, and so on. In the midst of this discussion, they may digress by changing the topic to something unrelated to the problem at hand before circling back to identifying and evaluating alternatives. So while problem-solving conversations will include certain messages, the discussion may not be linear.

4. **Summarizing decisions and clarifying next steps.** As the partners approach the end of their conversation, one person will usually try to obtain closure by summarizing what has been agreed to. The other person will either accept the summary as accurate or will amend it to clarify the areas of agreement as well as any disagreements. At times conversational partners skip this step. Doing so is risky, since one partner will act on what he or she perceives has been agreed to, which may not match the other partner's perception.

5. **Formal close.** Once the conversationalists have discussed the issue and clarified the next steps that will be taken, they end the discussion of the problem. The ending statements provide a transition that enables conversationalists to move to a social conversation topic, begin a new problem consideration, or simply disengage from one another. The formal closing often includes showing appreciation for the conversation, such as "I'm glad we took some time to share ideas. I think we'll be far more effective if the two of us are on the same line." The closing might also leave the door open for later conversation, such as "If you have any second thoughts, give me a call."

observe & analyze

Problem-Consideration Conversations

Identify two recent problem-consideration conversations that you have had—one that was satisfying and one that was not. Try to recall exactly what was said. Write the scripts for these conversations. Then try to identify each of the five parts of a problem-consideration conversation. Were any parts missing? Retain these scripts for further use later in the chapter. ■

Disengaging from a Conversation

Conversations are usually ended when one person indicates a need or desire to disengage from the interaction. For instance, a person might say, "Oh, look what time it is . . ." or "This has been great, we'll have to get back together and talk some more." Sometimes, the close is not formally discussed; the parties just stop talking. After an unusually long pause indicating closure, a person might say, "Well, it's been great talking with you." At times, one or the other will attempt to extend conversation with a new approach, such as, "Just a second, I wanted to ask you. . . ." A statement like this may lead to a lengthy exchange, or may result in a minimal response before the person who wished to disengage echoes the closure statement and ends the conversation. In a face-to-face conversation, nonverbal signs of leaving, such as putting on a coat, gathering one's belongings, or moving away from the person may be used to signal the end.

Characteristics of Conversations

There are many aspects or elements that go into a conversation, though rarely do we consciously think about these elements. Conversations often are so routine or habitual that we do not think about their individual elements. There are six characteristics to a conversation: formality, turn-taking, topic change, talk time, scriptedness, and audience.

Formality

Formality—the degree to which a conversation must follow rules and procedures.

Formality refers to the degree to which a conversation must follow rules, procedures, or rituals. Two factors, status and familiarity, influence expectations of formality in a conversation. Often, status differences between the communicators lead to more formality in a conversation. If you were speaking to the president of your college or your company, the conversation would be a formal one. Because of the status differences between the two of you, there would be lots of rules for how you should communicate. You would shake hands rather than hug or slap hands when greeting; you would allow the other person to select the topics; you would be careful not to interrupt or use profanity; and certain topics of conversation would be off-limits. If you were speaking to a new neighbor, even though the two of you are strangers, the situation would be informal because you are equal in status. There would be fewer rules or procedures to follow. Each of you would feel free to select and change topics. Interruptions or mild profanity might be used. The two of you could speak about a greater range of topics. Basically, neither of you would be especially cautious or tentative in your conversation.

When speaking with a stranger or a casual acquaintance, you are expected to be more formal in the conversation than when you are conversing with a good friend. Various rules would apply such as those about avoiding interrupting, profanity, and abrupt topic changes. Certain topics would not be appropriate to discuss. You would be more cautious in your conversation.

Turn-taking

Turn-taking refers to how people alternate between speaking and listening in a conversation. A turn can be one word or a long monologue. Researchers note that in ordinary conversation people often speak at the same time, and turns are not always easy to identify. As Ford, Fox, and Thompson (2002) point out, however, the fact is that participants in interaction treat the concept of "turn" as "relevant, real, and consequential in an individual's speaking time/space" (p. 8).

Turn-taking is more predictable when two people are conversing because when one person stops speaking, then it is the other person's turn to speak. But turn-taking can be challenging when a conversation involves three or more people. R. K. Sawyer's book, *Creating Conversations* (2001), offers some unwritten norms of conversation. A speaker can select the next person to talk by directing a question to that person. Or we can become the next person to talk by being the first person to make an utterance once the first speaker has finished. Sometimes, we nonverbally signal our desire to be the next speaker by nodding, saying "uh hum," leaning forward, smiling, or giving eye contact, or by using a combination of nonverbal cues. Sometimes the speaker may nonverbally signal the next turn-taker by turning toward that person, nodding, smiling, or touching. Anyone can get a turn at speaking by interrupting another speaker. Generally, interruptions are considered inappropriate and should be avoided. There are times and situations, however, when interruptions are inevitable and appropriate. We will discuss appropriate interruptions later, in the section entitled Guidelines for Effective Conversationalists.

Turn-taking—the process by which people alternate between speaking and listening in a conversation.

How do turn-taking and topic change vary by the nature of a situation?

When two people try to take a turn speaking at the same time, various behaviors can occur. One person may back down and let the other person speak. Or both may back down through a polite negotiation where each says, "I'm sorry. You go ahead." Or both may continue trying to speak until the more persistent one wins a turn. Another person may intervene to select the next speaker by remarking, "Go ahead, Ike, you were trying to say something." The point here is that turn-taking is a complicated type of exchange that can be compared to a dance. Some people lead and some follow, the movements may be slow or fast, and we don't know when or where it will end.

A unique approach to turn-taking is emerging through the use of instant messaging. Instant messaging allows a person to converse in real time with many people at once. However, not all of those people are conversing with each other. Therefore, the conventional rules of turn-taking do not apply. Let's say that Anika is instant messaging with five different friends one afternoon. She may pose a question to her friend Howie, but before the question appears on Howie's computer or cell phone screen, he has sent a question on a different topic to her. Now, this defies the typical process of conversation, where you are expected to answer a person's question before you can ask a question of your own. Anika may be taking turns conversing online with five different people on five or more different topics at the same time, yet keeping track of what conversations go with what people. If instant messaging becomes prevalent, it may, in time, affect the very process by which we conduct face-to-face conversations.

Topic Change

Topic change is the method by which people introduce new topics into a conversation. In casual social conversations, topics are introduced and changed quite randomly. Unlike structured meetings, we do not have an agenda that lists the order of topics or tells how long we will converse on each topic. Topic change is negotiated informally and spontaneously between the participants. Imagine that Hector and Desirée are chatting casually before class. Desirée may introduce a topic based on common ground between the two of them, such as the upcoming exam. They may converse about that for a short while before subtle nonverbal cues signal that this topic is winding down. Each person's voice may become softer and less animated, and there may be shorter remarks and more pauses between turns. Perhaps Hector notices this and makes a conscious decision to introduce the topic of another student in the class. They may converse on that topic until nonverbal cues indicate the need for a change. Or Desirée may abruptly change the topic in the middle of the discussion of the classmate by asking, "Have you had lunch yet?" Topic change can be gradual or abrupt, following a natural progression from one topic to the next, or it can be quite unpredictable, changing from one unrelated issue to the next. It is best when all participants contribute equally to topic selection, though as we described earlier, higher-status people in a conversation usually have more control over topics discussed.

Talk Time

Conversations are most satisfying when all participants feel that they have had their fair share of speaking, or talk time. Generally, we should balance speaking and listening in a conversation, and all participants should have roughly the same opportunity for talk time. Of course, some people are more outgoing and others are naturally quiet, so talk time need not be completely equal among participants. The key is to give everyone who wants to talk the opportunity to do so.

Like other elements of a conversation, talk time is also affected by the status of the people conversing. We tend to defer to higher-status people, and out of respect, allow them to have more talk time. Sometimes the higher-status person will work to ensure that everyone can participate as much as each one would like.

People are likely to tune out or become annoyed at conversational partners who make speeches, filibuster, or perform monologues rather than engage in the ordinary give-and-take of conversation. Similarly, it is difficult to carry on a conversation with someone who makes one- or two-word replies to questions that are designed to elicit meaningful information. Of course, turns do vary in length depending on what is being said. However, if your statements average much longer or much shorter than those of your conversational partners, you need to adjust.

If you discover that you are speaking more than your fair share, try to restrain yourself by mentally checking whether everyone else has had a chance to talk once before you talk a second time. Similarly, if you find yourself being inactive in a conversation, you can decide to increase your participation level. Remember, if you have information to contribute, you're cheating yourself and the group when you do not share it.

If you find others are wanting to talk but can't seem to get enough talk time, you can help by saying something like, "Donna, I get the sense that you've been wanting to comment on this point" or "Gee, Tyler, you haven't had a chance to comment on this. What do you think?"

Does it bother you when one person speaks more often than others?

Scriptedness

Some types of conversation have happened so often and are so routine that they follow a basic script (Berger, 2002). A script involves the use of conversational phrases that we have learned from past encounters and judge appropriate to a given situation. Think of the habitual ways that we greet others or say good-bye. If

Kimiko and Jesse, who have not seen each other for a while, bump into each other while jogging, the conversation is likely to sound like this:

> Jesse: *Hey, it's been a long time. How are you doing?*
> Kimiko: *Yes, it's been forever since we've seen each other. I'm doing fine. How about you?*
> Jesse: *I'm good. Can't complain. How is work going?*
> Kimiko: *Work's keeping me busy. Are you still with KDC Software?*

Notice how there is a reciprocal exchange of topics in a greeting conversation. Jesse greets Kimiko and asks a question; after acknowledging the greeting and answering the question, Kimiko asks the same question of Jesse. Certain topics are standard in a greeting conversation. We are likely to chat about health, work, school, and common friends rather than world politics, serious crises, or our financial status. Notice also how turns are very short. Greeting conversations have a quick give-and-take to them. Other scripted conversations might relate to giving and receiving compliments or the annual phone call to your great aunt to thank her for your birthday present.

Sometimes we script a very important conversation, perhaps a problem-consideration conversation, by rehearsing our remarks and anticipating what our partner might say. For example, it would be appropriate to have some scripts ready when asking your boss for a raise or when breaking up with your intimate partner. We do more planning in conversations of these types because the goal and outcomes are much more important than in casual social conversations. It is important to prepare scripts as a guide, but we must be flexible in using them so that we do not sound stilted or rehearsed and so that we are able to adapt to what the other person says.

Co-narration—two people finishing each other's sentences in a conversation.

There is a unique type of conversational scripting that occurs between two individuals who have been interacting for a long time. Called **co-narration** (Sawyer, 2001), it involves two people finishing each other's sentences because they know each other's style of conversation so well. Perhaps Dana and Pat have lived together for many years and often tell stories from their shared experiences in a collaborative fashion. When Pat says, "In 1999, we went out West for a trip," Dana joins in and says, "It was spring and we drove our RV." Pat adds, "That RV always gave us trouble because. . . " and Dana finishes, "the engine would overheat when you drove fast." They are collaboratively telling a story and altering the rules of turn-taking. Because this conversation is so routine and follows a basic two-person script, Pat and Dana do not perceive that they are interrupting each other.

Conversational Audience

Most of the time, we are well aware of who is participating in a conversation and who is not. This is especially clear in a two-person interaction. Imagine a conversation among a group of people at a party, however. Perhaps everyone is standing and moving in and out of the circle of conversation. You may have been talking in a such a group conversation when you noticed a couple of people near the group listening and appearing interested in joining in. In a way, these outsiders are an audience to the conversation; but they are also candidates to join the discussion, and the group may or may not allow this. Perhaps you move to widen the circle so that the newcomers can join, or you may address a remark to them, thereby bringing them into the conversation. Alternatively, you may tighten the distance between you and your conversational partners, or move to another space, so that the candidates continue to be excluded.

Eavesdropping is another way that people become an audience to others' conversations. In some situations, we become unwilling eavesdroppers, as it becomes impossible not to overhear what others are discussing. Servers in restaurants cannot help but hear parts of the diners' conversations. Some people speak loudly in the dentist's waiting room or at the gym and we cannot help becoming an audience. This is especially true with the prevalent use of cell phones. Some people speak loudly on cell phones in public, and it is inevitable that an audience of more than one will hear. So at times, we find ourselves part of an unwilling audience to other's face-to-face or cell phone conversations.

At other times what we inadvertently overhear from another conversation interests us and we become willing eavesdroppers. Sometimes we may signal our interest in becoming part of the conversation, while at other times we may be content to simply listen without making our silent participation known.

Rules of Conversations

Although conversations may seem to have little form or structure, they are actually conducted based on implicit **rules,** which are "unwritten prescriptions that indicate what behavior is required, preferred, or prohibited in certain contexts" (Shimanoff, 1980, p. 57). These unwritten rules specify what kinds of messages and behavior will be seen as appropriate in a given physical or social context or with a particular person or group of people. We use these rules to guide our own behavior and as a framework within which to interpret the behavior of others.

Rules–unwritten prescriptions that indicate what behavior is required, preferred, or prohibited in certain contexts.

Characteristics of Rules

What makes a rule a rule? As we answer this, let's use a common conversational rule as an example: "If one person is talking, then another person should not interrupt."

1. **Rules specify appropriate human behavior.** This means that rules focus on what to do or not do.
2. **Rules are prescriptive.** A rule tells you what to do or say to be successful or effective. If you choose to break the rule, you risk being viewed as incompetent or you risk damaging your relationship. For example, if you interrupt, you may be viewed as rude and the speaker may glare at you or verbally upbraid you.

3. **Rules are contextual.** This means that conversational rules that apply in some situations may not apply under different conditions. So most of the time the rule is "Don't interrupt." But if there is a true emergency—like a fire—this rule doesn't apply. Because rules are contextual, some conversational rules differ by culture. So, when we communicate with people of different cultural backgrounds, we may unintentionally break the conversational rules that guide their behavior and vice versa. For example, cultures differ in how eye contact is used during conversations. In some cultures this rule is to look directly at a speaker, while in others the rule is to avoid direct eye contact with a speaker.

4. **Rules must allow for choice.** This means that a conversational rule by nature allows participants the freedom to comply with or violate the expectation. So, not interrupting is a rule, since you can hear a person out or choose to interrupt. Exhibit 6.1 presents several conversational rules that are common to many cultures.

The Cooperative Principle

Not only are conversations structured by the rules that participants follow or violate, but they also depend on how well conversational partners follow the cooperative principle. H. Paul Grice (1975, pp. 44–46) described the **cooperative principle,** which states that conversations will be satisfying when the contributions made by conversationalists are in line with the purpose of the conversation. Based on this principle, Grice identified four conversational **maxims,** or rules of conduct, that cooperative conversational partners follow.

1. The **quality maxim** calls for us to provide information that is truthful. When we purposely lie, distort, or misrepresent, we are not acting cooperatively in

Cooperative principle–states that conversation will be satisfying when the contributions made by conversationalists are in line with the purpose of the conversation.

Maxims–rules of conduct that cooperative conversational partners follow.

Quality maxim–the requirement to provide information that is truthful.

E X H I B I T   6 . 1

The following are common conversational rules. Notice that many rules that we use are framed in an "if … then" format:

- If your mouth is full of food, then you must not talk.
- If someone is talking, then you must not interrupt.
- If you are spoken to, you must reply.
- If another does not hear a question you ask, then you must repeat it.
- If you are being spoken to, you should direct your gaze to the speaker.
- Or, from a different cultural perspective, if you are being spoken to, you should look at the floor.
- If more than two people are conversing, then each should have equal time.
- If your conversational partners are significantly older than you, then you should refrain from using profanities and obscenities.
- If you can't say something nice, then you don't say anything at all.
- If you are going to say something that you don't want overheard, then drop the volume of your voice.

the conversation. Being truthful means not only avoiding deliberate lies or distortions but also taking care to avoid misrepresentation. Thus, if a classmate asks you what the prerequisites for Bio 205 are, you should share them if you know them, but you should not guess and offer your opinion as though it were fact. If you don't know or if you have only a vague recollection, you follow the quality maxim by honestly saying, "I'm not sure."

2. The **quantity maxim** calls for us to tailor the amount of information we provide so that what we offer is sufficient and necessary to satisfy others' information needs and to keep the conversation going. But we are not supposed to speak at such length and in such detail that we undermine the informal give-and-take that is characteristic of good conversations. So, when Sam asks Randy how he liked his visit to St. Louis, Randy's answer, "Fine," is uncooperatively brief because it makes it difficult for Sam to continue the conversation. On the opposite extreme, should Randy launch into a twenty-minute monologue that details everything he did including recounting what he ate each day, he would also be violating the maxim.

> **Quantity maxim**—the requirement to provide a sufficient or necessary amount of information—not too much and not too little.

3. The **relevancy maxim** calls for us to provide information that is related to the topic currently being discussed. Comments that are only tangential to the subject or seek an abrupt subject change when other conversational partners are still actively engaged with the topic are uncooperative. For example, Hal, Corey, and Li-Sung are in the midst of a lively discussion about the upcoming 5K walk/run for the local homeless shelter when Corey asks whether either Hal or Li-Sung has taken Speech 101. Since Corey's change of subject disrupts an ongoing discussion, he is violating the relevancy maxim.

> **Relevancy maxim**—requirement to provide information that is related to the topic being discussed.

4. The **manner maxim** calls for us to be specific and organized when communicating our thoughts. We cooperate with our conversational partners when we choose specific language so that it is easy for our partners to understand our meaning. When D'wan asks Remal how to download a computer file, Remal will comply with the manner maxim by explaining the process one step at a time, using language that D'wan can understand. Obviously, observing the manner maxim doesn't mean that you have a specific outline for every comment you make. Conversations, after all, are informal. But following the manner maxim does mean that you organize what you are saying thoughtfully so that others don't have to work too hard to understand you.

> **Manner maxim**—requirement to be specific and organized when communicating your thoughts.

While these four maxims are important markers of conversational cooperation, as Thomas Holtgraves points out, "Conversationalists rarely abide by these maxims. They are often irrelevant, they sometimes say too much or too little, and so on. But it is usually the case that people will mutually assume adherence to the CP (cooperative principle) and maxims, and this assumption serves as a frame for interpreting a speaker's utterances. That is, a speaker's utterances will be interpreted *as if* they were clear, relevant, truthful, and informative" (2002, p. 24).

In addition to the four maxims identified by Grice, Bach and Harnish (1979, p. 64), we have proposed two additional maxims that cooperative partners follow.

5. The **morality maxim** calls for us to be moral and ethical when we speak. For example, in the United States violations of the morality maxim would include

> **Morality maxim**—the requirement to meet moral/ethical guidelines.

Conversational Maxims

Refer back to the two conversation scripts you prepared in the exercise on problem-consideration conversations (p. 149). Can you identify specific conversational rules that were used? Which of these were complied with? Which were violated? How does this analysis help you understand your satisfaction with the conversation? ■

Politeness maxim—the requirement to show respect for others by acting with courtesy.

repeating information that had been disclosed confidentially, purposefully deceiving someone about the truthfulness or accuracy of another's statements, and persuading someone to do something that the speaker knows is wrong or against the other's personal interests.

6. The **politeness maxim** calls for us to demonstrate respect for other participants by behaving courteously. In our conversations we should attempt to observe the social norms of politeness in the dominant culture and not purposefully embarrass others or ourselves during the interaction. In the next section we will discuss means of practicing politeness.

Guidelines for Effective Conversationalists

Since conversations have a life of their own and move spontaneously according to the wishes of the participants, we cannot give absolute rules for being an effective conversationalist. There are some general guidelines to consider, however. Through practice and self-monitoring, you will become more skilled about following and adjusting these guidelines in particular conversations.

Develop an Other-Centered Focus

Skilled communicators do not talk about themselves and their interests too much. Instead they focus on others by asking questions, listening carefully, following up on what's been said, and being fully involved with the other person. Being fully involved also means resisting distractions—for example, by not looking around the room at others or taking cell phone calls during a face-to-face conversation. Focusing on the other does not mean that you should completely avoid talking about yourself. If others ask you questions, or if the conversation naturally moves to your interests, then it is appropriate to focus on yourself somewhat.

Engage in Appropriate Turn-Taking

Skillful turn-takers use conversation-directing behavior to balance turns between those who speak freely and those who may be more reluctant to speak. Similarly, effective turn-takers remain silent and listen politely when the conversation is directed to someone else. By paying attention to the turn-taking process, without being too preoccupied with it, you can become skilled at smooth turn-taking.

Generally, effective conversationalists do not interrupt others. Some people are chronic interrupters and do not realize it. Pay attention to your turn-taking behavior to make sure that you do not abruptly seize the floor from others. Culture and status do affect the perceived appropriateness of interruptions, however. In some cultures, turn-taking occurs frequently through interruption. Likewise, higher-status people typically have freedom to interrupt those lower in status. A physician on a tight schedule may repeatedly interrupt a patient with questions in order to understand the patient's symptoms. But a patient who frequently interrupted a physician would be seen as rude.

Although interruptions are generally considered inappropriate, interrupting for "clarification" or "agreement" (confirming) is interpersonally acceptable (Kennedy & Camden, 1983, p. 55). For instance, interruptions that are likely to be accepted include relevant questions or paraphrases intended to clarify, such as "What do you mean by 'presumptuous'?" or "I get the sense that you think presumptuous behavior is especially bad," and reinforcing statements such as "Good point, Max" or "I see what you mean, Suzie." Interruptions that are likely to be viewed as disruptive or impolite include those that change the subject or seem to minimize the contribution of the interrupted person.

Maintain Conversational Coherence

Conversational coherence is the extent to which the comments made by one person relate to those made previously by others (McLaughlin, 1984, pp. 88–89). Littlejohn (2003) pointed out that conversational coherence is "how communicators create clear meaning" in conversation (p. 83). The more directly messages relate to those that precede them, the more coherent or meaningful is the conversation. What we say should be related to what was said before. If what we want to say is only tangentially related or is unrelated, then we should yield the turn to someone else, who may have more relevant comments. If there are only two of us conversing, then the listener should respond to the speaker's message before introducing a change in topic.

Conversational coherence—the extent to which the comments made by one person relate to those made by others earlier in the conversation.

skill builders

TURN-TAKING

SKILL	USE	PROCEDURE	EXAMPLE
Engaging in appropriate turn-taking.	Determining when a speaker is at a place where another person may talk if he or she wants to.	1. Take your share of turns. 2. Gear turn length to the behavior of partners. 3. Give and watch for turn-taking and turn-exchanging cues. Avoid giving inadvertent turn-taking cues. 4. Observe and use conversation-directing behavior. 5. Limit interruptions.	When John lowers his voice as he says, "I really thought they were going to go ahead during those last few seconds," Melissa, noticing that he appears to be finished, says, "I did, too. But did you notice …"

Conversational Coherence

Refer once again to the two scripts that you prepared in the exercise on problem-consideration conversations (p. 149). Analyze each to see how coherent the conversations were. Count the number of times that someone did not directly respond to the statement that immediately preceded it. Was one conversation more coherent than the other? ■

Politeness—relating to others in ways that meet their need to be appreciated and protected.

Face-saving—helping others preserve self-image or self-respect.

Practice Politeness

Politeness—relating to others in ways that meet their need to be appreciated and protected—is universal to all cultures (Brown & Levinson, 1987). A way of showing politeness is to engage in face-saving. **Face-saving** means helping others to preserve their self-image or self-respect. It is helping another avoid embarrassment. There are many ways that we engage in face-saving during conversations. These may involve the topics we consciously avoid and the ways in which we speak to others. If Chad knows that Charlie just lost his job, Chad is not likely to bring up that topic in a casual conversation among a group of friends at the coffee shop. To say, "Hey, Charlie my man, I hear you just got canned at work," would cause embarrassment to everyone. Similarly, if Chad gives a really poor presentation in class, Charlie may help him save face by saying, "Hey man, we all get nervous and sometimes lose our place when we're making a presentation. That can happen to the best of speakers."

Sometimes face-saving occurs by the way we say something. Suppose your professor returned a set of papers and you believe the grade you received does not accurately reflect the quality of the paper. You could say, "You didn't grade my paper fairly. It deserves a much higher grade." Saying something like this, which implies that the professor was wrong, is likely to threaten the professor with a loss of face and lead to defensive behavior. You might, instead, say something like, "I would appreciate it if you could look at my paper again. I honestly thought I did a better job than what the grade shows. I've marked the places on the paper where my comments come from our textbook, and I've noted the textbook pages. I'm not sure why these sections were marked wrong. I wonder if you would consider regrading the paper or at least helping me understand the reasons for this grade."

Balance Appropriateness and Efficiency

Appropriateness—being polite and following situational rules of conversation.

Efficiency—being direct in the interest of achieving conversational goals in a short amount of time.

In every conversation, people must balance two primary considerations: the need to be appropriate and the need to be efficient (Kellerman & Park, 2001). **Appropriateness** refers to being polite and following the rules of the situation. **Efficiency** means being direct in achieving your goal in a relatively short amount of time. Depending on the situation, the amount of each factor will vary. Imagine that Vince is meeting a very important client regarding a major business deal. While he has business goals to achieve in this conversation, there are rules that he must follow. He cannot begin by asking the client to sign a contract. He may begin with small talk by asking about the client's company and sharing information about his company. Then Vince may move the conversation to a deeper level by discussing how the client likes to conduct business. Only after gradual, polite conversation can Vince directly get to the point of asking for the client's business.

In a different situation however, concern for efficiency may outweigh concern for appropriateness. If Vince calls a supplier to his company, he can immediately ask a question about when the supplies were shipped. He need not work up to the question gradually and cautiously. The balance of appropriateness and efficiency in a conversation will vary by the relationship of the participants, the topics being discussed, the context of the conversation, and the channel by which the conversation is occurring.

Formal situations or conversations with strangers usually call for more appropriateness and less efficiency. Think of all the rules of conversation you must follow during a job interview, at a funeral, or with an acquaintance at a fancy restaurant. Informal situations, routine interactions, and conversations with close friends and family usually call for more efficiency and less appropriateness. Think of how you can get right to the point when conversing with your best friend or with the pharmacist at your local drugstore. Keep in mind the dual challenges of following social norms and achieving your goal in a conversation. By analyzing the context, the status of the people involved, and the formality of the situation, you will be able to decide how to balance politeness and directness. It is important to make a conscious decision about what levels of politeness and directness are needed and then to make comments that reflect both goals.

Protect Privacy

Pay attention to who may be an audience to your conversation. Think about your needs for privacy and others' needs not to overhear your personal conversation. You may choose to move the conversation to a more private location, to speak more softly, or to have the conversation at another time. To be an effective communicator when using a cell phone means being aware of your surroundings and not imposing your conversation on others.

Keeping confidences is another way of protecting privacy. If someone reveals private information in a conversation and asks you not to share this information with others, it is important to honor this request.

Engage in Ethical Dialogue

The final guideline followed by effective conversationalists is to engage in ethical dialogue. According to Johannesen (2000), ethical dialogue or conversation is characterized by authenticity, empathy, confirmation, presentness, a spirit of mutual equality, and a supportive climate.

CATHY © 2001 by Cathy Guisewite. Reprinted with permission of UNIVERSAL PRESS SYNDICATE. All rights reserved.

When should conversations be held in public or in private?

Authenticity—direct, honest, straightforward communication of all information and feelings that are relevant and legitimate to the subject at hand.

Empathy—demonstrated by comments that show you understand another's point of view without giving up your own position or sense of self.

Confirmation—nonpossessive expressions of warmth that affirm others as unique persons without necessarily approving of their behaviors or views.

Presentness—a willingness to become fully involved with another person, demonstrated by taking time, avoiding distraction, being responsive and risking attachment.

Equality—achieved by treating conversational partners on the same level, regardless of the status differences that separate them from other participants.

Authenticity is demonstrated by the direct, honest, straightforward communication of all information and feelings that are relevant and legitimate to the subject at hand. To sit in a discussion, disagreeing with what is being said but saying nothing, is inauthentic. It is also inauthentic to agree verbally with something that you really do not believe in.

Empathy is demonstrated by comments that show you understand's another's point of view without giving up your own position or sense of self. Comments such as " I see your point" or "I'm not sure I agree with you, but I'm beginning to understand why you feel that way" demonstrate empathy. Because of the importance of empathy in making effective responses, we will consider it in more detail in Chapter 8.

Confirmation is demonstrated through nonpossessive expressions of warmth for others that affirm them as unique persons without necessarily approving of their behaviors or views. Examples of confirmation might include "Well, Keith, you certainly have an interesting way of looking at things, and I must say, you really make me think through my own views" or "Well, I guess I'd still prefer that you didn't get a tattoo, but you really have thought this through."

Presentness is demonstrated by becoming fully involved with the other person through taking time, avoiding distractions, being responsive, and risking attachment to the person. The most obvious way to exhibit presentness in a conversation is by listening actively. You can also demonstrate presentness during a conversation by asking questions that are directly related to what has been said.

Equality is demonstrated by treating conversational partners as peers, regardless of the status differences that separate them from other participants. To lord one's accomplishments, one's power roles, or one's social status over another during conversation is unethical.

Supportiveness is demonstrated by encouraging the other participants to communicate by praising their worthwhile efforts. You will recall from our discussion of relationships in Chapter 3 that positive communication climates are characterized by an exchange of messages that are descriptive, open, and tentative, as well as equality oriented.

When we engage in ethical dialogue, we improve the odds that our conversations will meet our needs and the needs of those with whom we interact.

Supportiveness—encouraging the other participants to communicate by praising their worthwhile efforts.

learn about yourself

Take this short survey, a test of your satisfaction with a conversation, to learn something about yourself. You should complete this survey in relation to an actual conversation. Answer the questions based on your first response. There are no right or wrong answers. Just be honest in reporting your true reactions to a particular conversation. For each question, select one of the following numbers that best describes your attitudes toward a particular conversation.

1 = Strongly agree	2 = Agree somewhat	3 = Neutral	4 = Disagree somewhat	5 = Strongly disagree

_____ **1.** I would like to have another conversation like this one.

_____ **2.** I was very dissatisfied with this conversation.

_____ **3.** During this conversation, I was able to present myself as I wanted the other person to view me.

_____ **4.** The other person expressed a lot of interest in what I had to say.

_____ **5.** We talked about things I was not interested in.

_____ **6.** I was annoyed by the others person's interruptions of me.

_____ **7.** Turn-taking went smoothly in this conversation.

_____ **8.** There were many uncomfortable moments during this conversation.

_____ **9.** I did not get to say what I wanted to in this conversation.

_____ **10.** I was very satisfied with this conversation.

SCORING THE SURVEY: To find your score, first reverse the responses for the odd-numbered items (if you wrote a 1, make it a 5; 2 = 4; leave 3 as is; 4 = 2, 5 = 1). Next add the numbers for each item. Scores can range from 10 to 50. The lower (closer to 10) your score, the more satisfied you were with the conversation. The higher (closer to 50) your score, the less satisfied you were with the conversation.

NOTE: After an important conversation, it would be useful for both you and your partner to separately complete this survey, then compare and discuss your scores.

* Adapted from Hecht, M. L. (1978). Measures of communication satisfaction. *Human Communication Research, 4,* 350–368.

Cultural Variations in Conversations

Throughout this chapter, we have assumed a Western cultural perspective on having effective conversations, specifically the perspective of a low-context Anglo. But just as various verbal and nonverbal rules vary from low-context to high-context cultures, so do the guidelines for effective conversation. Gudykunst and Matsumoto (1996, pp. 30–32) explain four differences in conversational patterns between people of low-context and high-context cultures.

First, while low-context culture conversations are likely to include greater use of such categorical words such as *certainly*, *absolutely*, and *positively*, high-context culture conversations are likely to see greater use of qualifiers such as *maybe*, *perhaps*, and *probably*.

Second, low-context cultures strictly adhere to the relevancy maxim by valuing relevant comments that are perceived by listeners to be directly to the point. In high-context cultures, however, individuals' responses are likely to be more indirect, ambiguous, and apparently less relevant, because listeners rely more on nonverbal cues to help them understand a speaker's intentions and meaning.

Third, in low-context cultures, the quality maxim operates through truthtelling. People are expected to verbally communicate their actual feelings about things regardless of how this affects others. Effective conversationalists in high-context cultures, however, employ the quality maxim differently. They define quality as maintaining harmony, and so conversationalists will sometimes send messages that mask their true feelings. Finally, in low-context cultures, periods of silence are perceived as uncomfortable, since when no one is speaking little infor-

the gray zone

Conversation as Argument

Though the guidelines we have presented for effective conversation generally apply, there are some types of conversation that may defy such guidelines. Often, these different types of conversation may stem from cultural variations in what constitutes a good conversation. Sawyer (2001) describes a conversational type in which several participants of Jewish background may converse by yelling, confronting, interrupting, abruptly changing topics, and being quite emotional. This style of conversation may occur among some people in southern Europe and the Middle East as well. People who are not familiar with this conversational style perceive that an argument is taking place. But for the participants, this is not an argument. It is a lively, engaging conversation. To follow rules of politeness, turn-taking, topic change, and conversational coherence would be boring. You would appear uninvolved or rude if you followed such rules. Instead, as a good conversationalist, you are expected to discuss multiple topics at once, to jump into the conversation without waiting for a turn, to speak in a loud, emotional tone, and to disagree strongly with others. This is an acceptable style of conversation within these cultural groups. By understanding and appreciating cultural variation in conversations, we can avoid judging others' conversational styles if they do not conform to our own rules. While some members of an ethnic group may employ this style of conversation, not all people of Jewish, southern European or Middle Eastern background would necessarily do so. There are many ways to have a conversation. ■

Conversational Ballgames   By Nancy Masterson Sakamoto

Nancy Masterson Sakamoto *is professor of American Studies at Shitennoji Gakuen University, Hawaii Institute, and coauthor of* Mutual Understanding of Different Cultures *(1981). A former English teacher and teacher trainer in Japan, she cowrote (with Reiko Naotsuka) a bilingual textbook for Japanese students called* Polite Fictions: Why Japanese and Americans Seem Rude to Each Other *(1982); "Conversational Ballgames" is a chapter from* Polite Fictions.

After I was married and had lived in Japan for a while, my Japanese gradually improved to the point where I could take part in simple conversations with my husband and his friends and family. And I began to notice that often, when I joined in, the others would look startled, and the conversational topic would come to a halt. After this happened several times, it became clear to me that I was doing something wrong. But for a long time, I didn't know what it was.

Finally, after listening carefully to many Japanese conversations, I discovered what my problem was. Even though I was speaking Japanese, I was handling the conversation in a western way.

Japanese-style conversations develop quite differently from western-style conversations. And the difference isn't only in the languages. I realized that just as I kept trying to hold western-style conversations even when I was speaking Japanese, so my English students kept trying to hold Japanese-style conversations even when they were speaking English. We were unconsciously playing entirely different conversational ballgames.

A western-style conversation between two people is like a game of tennis. If I introduce a topic, a conversational ball, I expect you to hit it back. If you agree with me, I don't expect you simply to agree and do nothing more. I expect you to add something—a reason for agreeing, another example, or an elaboration to carry the idea further. But I don't expect you always to agree. I am just as happy if you question me, or challenge me, or completely disagree with me. Whether you agree or disagree, your response will return the ball to me.

And then it is my turn again. I don't serve a new ball from my original starting line. I hit your ball back again from where it has bounced. I carry your idea further, or answer your questions or objections, or challenge or question you. And so the ball goes back and forth, with each of us doing our best to give it a new twist, an original spin, or a powerful smash.

And the more vigorous the action, the more interesting and exciting the game. Of course, if one of us gets angry, it spoils the conversation, just as it spoils a tennis game. But getting excited is not at all the same as getting angry. After all, we are not trying to hit each other. We are trying to hit the ball. So long as we attack only each other's opinions, and do not attack each other personally, we don't expect anyone to get hurt. A good conversation is supposed to be interesting and exciting.

If there are more than two people in the conversation, then it is like doubles in tennis, or like volleyball. There's no waiting in line. Whoever is nearest and quickest hits the ball, and if you step back, someone else will hit it. No one stops the game to give you a turn. You're responsible for taking your own turn.

But whether it's two players or a group, everyone does his best to keep the ball going, and no one person has the ball for very long.

A Japanese-style conversation, however, is not at all like tennis or volleyball. It's like bowling. You wait for your turn. And you always know your place in line. It depends on such things as whether you are older or younger, a close friend or a relative stranger to the previous speaker, in a senior or junior position, and so on.

When your turn comes, you step up to the starting line with your bowling ball, and carefully bowl it. Everyone else stands back and watches politely, murmuring encouragement. Everyone waits until the ball has reached the end of the alley, and watches to see if it knocks down all the pins, or only some of them, or none of them. There is a pause, while everyone registers your score.

Then, after everyone is sure that you have completely finished your turn, the next person in line steps up to the same starting line, with

Conversational Ballgames   *continued*

a different ball. He doesn't return your ball, and he does not begin from where your ball stopped. There is no back and forth at all. All the balls run parallel. And there is always a suitable pause between turns. There is no rush, no excitement, no scramble for the ball.

No wonder everyone looked startled when I took part in Japanese conversations. I paid no attention to whose turn it was, and kept snatching the ball halfway down the alley and throwing it back at the bowler. Of course the conversation died. I was playing the wrong game.

This explains why it is almost impossible to get a western-style conversation or discussion going with English students in Japan. I used to think that the problem was their lack of English language ability. But I finally came to realize that the biggest problem is that they, too, are playing the wrong game.

Whenever I serve a volleyball, everyone just stands back and watches it fall, with occasional murmurs of encouragement. No one hits it back. Everyone waits until I call on someone to take a turn. And when that person speaks, he doesn't hit my ball back. He serves a new ball. Again, everyone just watches it fall.

So I call on someone else. This person does not refer to what the previous speaker had said. He also serves a new ball. Nobody seems to have paid any attention to what anyone else has said. Everyone begins again from the same starting line, and all the balls run parallel. There is never any back and

forth. Everyone is trying to bowl with a volleyball.

And if I try a simpler conversation, with only two of us, then the other person tries to bowl with my tennis ball. No wonder foreign English teachers in Japan get discouraged.

Now that you know about the difference in the conversational ballgames, you may think that all your troubles are over. But if you have been trained all your life to play one game, it is no simple matter to switch to another, even if you know the rules. Knowing the rules is not at all the same thing as playing the game.

Even now, during a conversation in Japanese I will notice a startled reaction, and belatedly realize that once again I have rudely interrupted by instinctively trying to hit back the other person's bowling ball. It is no easier for me to "just listen" during a conversation, than it is for my Japanese students to "just relax" when speaking with foreigners. Now I can truly sympathize with how hard they must find it to try to carry on a western-style conversation.

If I have not yet learned to do conversational bowling in Japanese, at least I have figured out one thing that puzzled me for a long time. After his first trip to America, my husband complained that Americans asked him so many questions and made him talk so much at the dinner table that he never had a chance to eat. When I asked him why he couldn't talk and eat at the same time, he said that Japanese do not customarily think that dinner, especially on fairly formal occasions, is a suitable time for extended conversation.

Since westerners think that conversation is an indispensable part of dining, and indeed would consider it impolite not to converse with one's dinner partner, I found this Japanese custom rather strange. Still, I could accept it as a cultural difference even though I didn't really understand it. But when my husband added, in explanation, that Japanese consider it extremely rude to talk with one's mouth full, I got confused. Talking with one's mouth full is certainly not an American custom. We think it very rude, too. Yet we still manage to talk a lot and eat at the same time. How do we do it?

For a long time, I couldn't explain it, and it bothered me. But after I discovered the conversational ballgames, I finally found the answer. Of course! In a western-style conversation, you hit the ball, and while someone else is hitting it back, you take a bite, chew, and swallow. Then you hit the ball again, and then eat some more. The more people there are in the conversation, the more chances you have to eat. But even with only two of you talking, you still have plenty of chances to eat.

Maybe that's why polite conversation at the dinner table has never been a traditional part of Japanese etiquette. Your turn to talk would last so long without interruption that you'd never get a chance to eat. ■

Excerpted from Sakamoto, N. M. (1995). Conversational ballgames. In R. Holton (Ed.), *Encountering Cultures* (pp. 60–63). Englewood Cliffs, N.J.: Prentice-Hall.

A Question of Ethics

Tonia is her Uncle Fred's only living relative, and he has been her favorite relative for as long as she can remember. About three years ago, Fred was diagnosed with lung cancer that eventually led to surgery and a round of chemotherapy and radiation. At that time Fred made out his will, naming Tonia as his executor and giving her his medical power of attorney. Recently he also signed a waiver so that his medical team would be able to disclose all of his medical information to Tonia even though he has been feeling great.

Uncle Fred has worked hard all of his life and has talked about, dreamed about, and saved to take a trip to visit his mother's hometown in northern Italy. Last week he called Tonia very excited and told her that he had just finished making all of his reservations and was scheduled to leave for Italy in two weeks. While Tonia was really happy for him, she wondered if his doctor had approved his trip.

Unwilling to "rain on his parade," Tonia phoned the doctor to see if Uncle Fred had told him about the trip. She was alarmed to find not only that Uncle Fred had not mentioned the trip to his doctor but that Fred's latest follow-up CT scan showed that the cancer was growing aggressively. The doctor believed that Fred needed to cancel his trip and immediately begin another round of chemotherapy. When Tonia asked the likelihood that the treatments would bring the cancer back into remission the doctor said, "To be perfectly honest, there is only a 10% chance that the chemo will work. But without treatment the cancer is sure to kill him in less than six months." Then the doctor implored Tonia to talk with her uncle and convince him to cancel his plans and begin treatment.

1. Is it ethical for Tonia to try to convince her uncle to stay and have chemotherapy?

2. Should Tonia agree to talk with her uncle? If so, what ethical issues will she confront?

3. If she chooses to have this conversation with her uncle, how can Johannesen's guidelines for ethical dialogue help her create an effective conversation?

mation is being shared. In high-context cultures, silences in conversation are often meaningful. When three or four people sit together and no one talks, the silence may indicate agreement, disapproval, embarrassment, or disagreement, depending on context.

Summary

Conversations are locally managed, sequential interchanges of thoughts and feelings between two or more people that are interactive and largely extemporaneous. After some opening exchanges, the body of a conversation develops; it is likely to involve various types of information. Small-talk conversations meet social needs with relatively low risk. Casual social conversations occur between people when they desire to enhance or maintain a relationship. Problem-consideration conversations occur when the goal of at least one of the participants is to solicit the cooperation of the other in meeting a goal. The characteristics of a conversation include formality, turn-taking, topic changes, talk time, scriptedness, and audience.

Conversations are guided by unwritten prescriptions/rules that indicate what behavior is required, preferred, or prohibited. Conversational rules specify appropriate behavior. They are prescriptive, they are contextual, and they allow for choice.

Effective conversations are governed by the cooperative principle, which suggests that conversations "work" when participants join together to accomplish conversational goals and make the conversation pleasant for each participant. The cooperative principle gives rise to maxims relating to quality, quantity, relevancy, manner, morality, and politeness. Good communicators follow guidelines for having effective conversations, which include focusing on others, taking turns appropriately, avoiding interruptions, maintaining conversational coherence, practicing politeness, balancing appropriateness and efficiency, and protecting privacy. It is also important to realize there are cultural variations in the conduct of conversations.

Interaction Dialogue:
CONVERSATIONS

Conversations that are likely to be casual social or problem-solving interactions tend to follow unwritten rules. Conversations are most effective when they adhere to the quality, quantity, relevancy, manner, morality, and politeness maxims. Skills of effective conversation include focusing on the other, appropriately taking turns, avoiding interruptions, maintaining conversational coherence, helping others save face, and considering privacy needs.

Here's a transcript of Susan and Sarah's conversation, with analysis of the conversation in the right-hand column. As you read the dialogue, determine the type of conversation that is taking place. Look for the signs of effective conversation just mentioned. You may want to write down some of your observations before you read the analysis in the right-hand column.

Susan and Sarah are close friends who share the same religious background and the occasional frustrations related to their family beliefs.

CONVERSATION	ANALYSIS
SUSAN: *So how are you and Bill getting along these days?*	Susan initiates the conversation with a meaningful question.
SARAH: *Oh, not too well, Suze. I think we've got to end the relationship. There are so many issues between us that I just don't have the same feelings.*	Sarah answers the question and gives "free information" about her changed feelings and the presence of multiple problems.
SUSAN: *Yeah, you know, I could tell. Is there one specific thing that's a problem?*	Susan poses a question that focuses on Sarah and suggests the potential for problem consideration.
SARAH: *Yes, and it's ironic because early on I didn't think it would be problem, but it is. You know he's not Jewish, and since we've started talking about marriage, I've realized that it is a problem. While Bill's a great guy, our backgrounds and beliefs just don't mesh. I never realized how important my Jewishness was to me until I was faced with converting. And Bill feels similarly about the issue.*	Sarah accepts Susan's willingness to discuss a problem by sharing specific information that becomes the topical focus of the rest of the conversation—information that meets Grice's conversational maxims.

SUSAN: *I think I'm kind of lucky, well, in the long run. Remember in high school my parents wouldn't let me go out with anybody who wasn't Jewish? At the time I resented that and we both thought they were reactionary, but now I'm kind of glad. At the time my parents said, "You never know what's going to come out of a high school relationship." Well, they never got that far, but it did force me to think about things.*

SARAH: *Yes, I remember that. You hated it. It's amazing to realize your parents can actually be right about something.*

SUSAN: *Right, it was the pits at the time, but at least it spared me the pain you and Bill are going through. It must be awful to be in love with someone that you realize you don't want as a life partner.*

SARAH: *Exactly, but I'm glad that my parents didn't restrict my dating to Jewish guys. I've learned a lot by dating a variety of people, and I know that I've made this decision independently.*

Bill's a great guy, but for me to be me, I need to partner with a Jewish man—and Bill knows he can't be that. Making this choice has been hard, but it's helped me to grow. I guess I understand myself better.

SUSAN: *So where have you guys left it? Are you going to still see each other? Be friends?*

SARAH: *We hope so. But right now, it's too fresh. It hurts to see him, so we're trying to give each other some space. It will really be tough when I hear he's seeing someone else. But I'll get by.*

SUSAN: *Well, you know I'm here for you. And when you're ready there are some real hotties at Hillel. I'll be glad to introduce you.*

SARAH: *Thanks Suze. So how's your new job?*

SUSAN: *Oh, it's great. I really like my boss and I've gotten a new assignment that fits right in with my major. Plus my boss has been flexible in assigning my hours. I just wish that it wasn't so far away.*

SARAH: *I thought it was downtown.*

SUSAN: *It is, but it takes me over an hour because I have to change buses three times.*

SARAH: *Wow—are you at least able to study while you ride?*

SUSAN: *Not really. I get carsick.*

Susan shifts the topic a bit by speaking about her experiences. This seems to violate the relevancy maxim, but in so doing, she lays the groundwork for later exchanges.

Sarah shows that she recalls what was said. She keeps the conversation flowing.

Susan confirms that her parents' wisdom spared her pain. She then makes a statement that stimulates further discussion from Sarah.

Sarah agrees, but then explains her perception of the value of being free to date a variety of people.

Here Sarah confirms that it was her decision not to partner with a man outside her religion. But she also confirms that the decision was difficult.

Susan pursues the topic by asking questions to probe the consequences of Sarah's decision.

These questions lead Sarah to disclose the difficulties she's experienced as a result of her decision.

Here Sarah opens the door for Susan's support.

Susan picks up on Sarah's need by stating that she stands by her and is willing to help.

Sarah's thanks serve as a close to the topic. She then asks a question suggesting a change of topic.

Although Susan could probe further, she accepts the change of topic by giving information to support her generalization of "It's great."

Sarah continues the side issue by asking another question.

Susan shows why she can't study.

SARAH: *Oh I forgot. Bummer.*	*Sarah tries to save face.*
SUSAN: *Yeah, but I'll survive. Listen, I hate to leave, but I've got a class in ten minutes and if we're late the professor glares when we walk in. I don't need that.*	*Susan sees no value in continuing this discussion, so she cites a reason for ending the conversation.*
SARAH: *What a jerk.*	
SUSAN: *Yeah, well I've got to run.*	
SARAH: *Same time tomorrow?*	*The girls agree to meet again the next day. As we can see, discussion of the second issue was far less productive than discussion of the first.*
SUSAN: *Sure.*	

Chapter Resources

Communication Improvement Plan: Conversation

How would you like to improve your conversational skills as discussed in this chapter?

Developing an other-centered focus

Engaging in appropriate turn-taking

Maintaining conversational coherence

Practicing politeness

Protecting privacy

Pick one of these topics and write a communication improvement plan. You can find a communication improvement plan worksheet on our website at www.oup.com/us/interact

Key Words

Conversations, *p. 145*	**Cooperative principle,** *p. 156*	**Face-saving,** *p. 160*
Small talk, *p. 147*	**Maxims,** *p. 156*	**Appropriateness** *p. 160*
Idea exchange messages, *p. 147*	**Quality maxim,** *p. 156*	**Efficiency,** *p. 160*
Gossip, *p. 147*	**Quantity maxim,** *p. 157*	**Authenticity,** *p. 162*
Casual social conversations, *p. 147*	**Relevancy maxim,** *p. 157*	**Empathy,** *p. 162*
Problem-consideration conversations, *p. 148*	**Manner maxim,** *p. 157*	**Confirmation,** *p. 162*
Formality, *p. 150*	**Morality maxim,** *p. 157*	**Presentness,** *p. 162*
Turn-taking, *p. 151*	**Politeness maxim,** *p. 158*	**Equality,** *p. 162*
Co-narration, *p. 154*	**Conversational coherence,** *p. 159*	**Supportiveness,** *p. 163*
Rules, *p. 155*	**Politeness,** *p. 160*	

Skill Practice

Skill Practice exercises challenge you to master the material you have read in this chapter.

For additional Skill Practice activities, visit our website at www.oup.com/us/interact

IDENTIFYING PARTS OF PROBLEM-SOLVING CONVERSATIONS

Identify each part of the problem-solving conversation structure in the following script.

APRIL: *Hi, Yolanda. How are you doing?*

YOLANDA: *Oh, can't complain too much.*

APRIL: *I'm glad I ran into you—I need to check something out with you.*

YOLANDA: *Can we do this quickly? I've really got to get working on the speech I'm doing for class.*

APRIL: *Oh, this will just take a minute. If I remember right, you said that you'd been to The Dells for dinner with Scot. I'd like to take Rob there to celebrate his birthday, but I wanted to know whether we'd really feel comfortable there.*

YOLANDA: *Sure. It's pretty elegant, but the prices aren't bad and the atmosphere is really nice.*

APRIL: *So you think we can really do dinner on fifty or sixty dollars?*

YOLANDA: *Oh, yeah. We had a salad, dinner, and a dessert and our bill was under sixty even with the tip.*

APRIL: *Thanks, Yolanda. I wanted to ask you 'cause I know you like to eat out when you can.*

YOLANDA: *No problem. Gotta run. Talk with you later—and let me know how Rob liked it.*

Inter-Act with Media

FIND MORE
on the web
Additional media entries @
www.oup.com/us/interact

CINEMA

Lasse Hallstrom (Director). (2000). ***Chocolat.*** Juliette Binoche, Alfred Molina, Carrie-Anne Moss, Aurelien Parent Koenig, John Wood, Lena Olin, Leslie Caron, Johnny Depp, Judith Dench.

Brief Summary: A young woman with a preteen daughter opens a chocolate shop in a village in rural France. She immediately encounters resistance and disapproval from the mayor, who is a strict Catholic and upholds the town's religious mores. As Vianne runs counter to the town's rules by opening the shop on Sunday and by encouraging all manner of sensual delights as a result of her chocolates and the corresponding conversations that go along with them, the mayor tries to raise the village against her. Her primary weapon of response, apart from her seemingly magical chocolates, is her ability to lure those around her into very engaging and connecting conversation.

IPC Concepts: Casual and problem-solving conversation, cooperative principle, turn-taking, politeness, free information, face-threatening acts, and ethical dialogue.

Jordan Roberts (Director). (2004). ***Around the Bend.*** Christopher Walken, Michael Caine, Jonah Bobo, Josh Lucas.

Brief Summary: Four male members of a dysfunctional family are reunited by the dying patriarch. The father's death triggers the start of a process of dialogue, argument, and exploration of discovery of the secrets of the family's past. As the movie argues, "The skeletons in the family closet just came out to play."

IPC Concepts: Casual and problem-solving conversation, cooperative principle, turn-taking, politeness, free information, face-threatening acts, and ethical dialogue.

WHAT'S ON THE WEB

Conversation Cafés

http://www.conversationcafe.org/

Brief Summary: As the Web site explains, a Conversation Café is "a one-and-a-half hour hosted conversation, held in a public setting like a café, where anyone is welcome to join. A simple format helps people feel at ease and gives everyone who wants it a chance to speak." The site offers those interested access to safe, interesting, and fun places to meet other people and learn how to engage in conversation about a variety of topics.

IPC Concepts: Casual and problem-solving conversation, cooperative principle, turn-taking, politeness, free information, face-threatening acts, and ethical dialogue.

Conversation Analysis

http://www.conversation-analysis.net/

Brief Summary: This Danish Web site is for those with a professional interest in conversation analysis. The site contains valuable abstracts on a wide range of conversation topics, such as patient–physician turn-taking, medical terminology in medical consultations, symmetry and asymmetry in medical consultations, and designing questions for survey conversations.

IPC Concepts: Casual and problem-solving conversation, cooperative principle, turn-taking, politeness, free information, face-threatening acts, and ethical dialogue.

listening effectively

After you have read this chapter, you should be able to answer these questions:

- What is listening?
- How can you focus your attention?
- What are five types of listening?
- What are techniques you can use to understand?
- What are techniques used in remembering information?
- How do you critically evaluate information?
- How can listening skills be used in communicating in cyberspace?

"Garret, do you have an extra key to the media cabinet? I forgot mine, and I have to get into it right away."

"No, I don't have a key, but it doesn't matter because . . ."

"I can't believe it. I was sure that when I left home this morning I had it."

"Bart, it's OK . . ."

"I pulled out my keys—but of course I just had my car key and main door key. I always carry two sets of keys."

"Bart, I've been trying to tell you, just try the . . ."

"It's just like me. I think I've got everything, but just before I check the last time Salina will say something to me and I get sidetracked. Then I just take off . . ."

"Bart, chill out. The door's . . ."

"Chill out?! If I can't get the DVD for the meeting, I'll get torn apart. We've got six advertising people coming from all over the city just to see this DVD. What am I supposed to say to them?"

"Bart, you don't have to say anything. I've been trying to . . ."

"Oh, sure—I just go in there and say, 'By the way, the DVD of the new ad campaign is locked up in the cabinet and I left my key at home.' Come on, Garret—how am I going to get into the cabinet?"

"Bart, listen!!! I've been trying to tell you—Miller was in the cabinet and, knowing you'd be along in a minute, he left the door open."

"Well, why didn't you tell me?"

Are you a good listener—even when you're under pressure like Bart? Or do you sometimes find that your mind wanders when others are talking to you? How often do you forget something that someone says to you? Do you sometimes feel that other things get in the way of your listening effectiveness? Have any of your close friends or intimates ever complained that you just don't seem to listen to them?

Listening is a fundamental communication skill that affects the quality of our conversations and shapes the course of our relationships. First, listening creates reality. "We listen and create reality based on what we hear in each moment" (Ellinor & Gerard, 1998, p. 99). Second, listening plays an important role in the enactment, development, and maintenance of a variety of social and personal relationships (Halone & Pecchioni, 2001). Third, of the basic communication skills (reading, writing, speaking, and listening) we use listening the most. "From 42 to 60 percent (or more) of our communication time is spent listening, depending on whether we are students, managerial trainees, doctors, counselors, lawyers, or nurses" (Purdy, 1996, p. 4). Unfortunately, after forty-eight hours many listeners can remember only about 25 percent of what they heard (Steil, Barker, & Watson, 1983). Considering its importance and how little attention most of us pay to it, listening may be the most underrated of all communication skills.

What is listening? In her book on the subject, Judi Brownell reports that members of the International Listening Association favor the following definition: "**Listening** is the process of receiving, constructing meaning from, and responding to spoken and/or nonverbal messages" (Brownell, 2002, p. 48). In this chapter we will look at the four active listening processes of understanding, remembering, responding, and critically evaluating information, as well as applying various listening processes to communicating in cyberspace.

Listening—the process of receiving, constructing meaning from, and responding to spoken and/or non-verbal messages.

learn about yourself

LISTENING BEHAVIORS

How frequently do you find yourself engaging in each of the following listening behaviors? On the line, indicate 5 for frequently; 4 for often; 3 for sometimes; 2 for rarely; and 1 for never.

_____ **1.** I listen differently depending on whether I am listening for enjoyment, understanding, or evaluation.

_____ **2.** I stop listening when what the person is saying to me isn't interesting to me.

_____ **3.** I consciously try to recognize the speaker's purpose.

_____ **4.** I pretend to listen to people when I am really thinking about other things.

_____ **5.** When people talk, I differentiate between their main points and supporting details.

_____ **6.** When the person's manner of speaking annoys me (such as muttering, stammering, or talking in a monotone), I stop listening carefully.

_____ **7.** At various places in a conversation, I paraphrase what the speaker said in order to check my understanding.

_____ **8.** When I perceive the subject matter as very difficult, I stop listening carefully.

_____ **9.** When the person is presenting detailed information, I take good notes of major points and supporting details.

_____ **10.** When people use words that I find offensive, I stop listening and start preparing responses.

SCORING THE SURVEY: In this list, the even-numbered items indicate negative listening behaviors, so to score yourself, you need to reverse the scoring of these items. If you gave yourself 5 count it as 1, 4 count it as 2, 3 count it as 3, 2 count it as 4, 1 count it as 5. The odd-numbered items indicate positive listening behaviors. Count each as given. Sum all your scores. There are 50 points possible. If you score over 40, you are effective in your listening. If you score below 40, identify the questions that seemed to cause your lowest scores. You will want to give particular attention to the sections of this chapter that relate to these areas.

Attending

Attending—the perceptual process of selecting to concentrate on specific stimuli from the countless stimuli reaching the senses.

The first active listening process is attending to what is happening. **Attending** is the perceptual process of selecting to concentrate on specific stimuli from the countless stimuli reaching the senses. When attending, we focus our attention in such a way that we are aware of what people are saying and disregard extraneous sounds and other distractions.

Stop reading for a minute, and try to become conscious of all the sounds around you. Perhaps you notice the humming of an electrical appliance, the rhythm of street traffic, the singing of birds, footsteps in the hall, a cough from an adjoining room. Yet while you were reading, you may have been unaware of these sounds. Although we physically register any sounds emitted within our hearing range, we exercise psychological control over the sounds we attend to. Ineffective listeners exercise insufficient control over which sounds they attend to. Improving your listening skills begins with learning to "pay attention" by bringing some sounds to the foreground while keeping others in the background. People who have developed this skill are able to focus their attention so well that only such really intrusive sounds as a fire alarm, a car crashing into a post, or the cry of their child can intrude on their attention.

Let's consider three techniques for consciously attending.

Get Physically and Mentally Ready to Listen

Physically, good listeners create an environment conducive to listening and adopt a listening posture. Creating a physical environment conducive to listening means eliminating distractions. For instance, if the radio is playing so loudly that it competes with your roommate who is trying to talk with you, you will turn it down. The physical posture that is most helpful when listening is one that moves the listener toward the speaker, allows direct eye contact, and stimulates the senses. For instance, when the professor tells the class that the next bit of information will be on the test, effective listeners are likely to sit upright in their chairs, lean slightly forward, cease any extraneous physical movement, and look directly at the professor. They are ready to listen.

Likewise, effective listening requires mental preparation. Effective listeners focus their attention by blocking out miscellaneous thoughts that pass through their minds. In the study of college students' descriptions of "really listening to others," the good listeners emphasized the importance of putting your own thoughts aside. Attending to competing thoughts and feelings rather than the message is one of the leading causes of poor listening.

Choose the Type of Attending Appropriate for the Listening Situation

The way in which you begin to attend to a message should depend on the type of listening you think is appropriate. At least five different types or levels of listening have been identified (Purdy, 1997).

Which of these people are listening? Which are not? How can you tell?

1. **Appreciative listening.** In an appreciative listening situation, your goal is to enjoy what is being said. With appreciative listening, you do not have to focus as closely or as carefully on specifics as you do in other listening situations. You might use appreciative listening during a casual social conversation while watching a ball game with friends or when listening to your son describe the fish he caught on an outing with his grandpa.

   Appreciative listening—focusing on a message in order to enjoy what is said.

2. **Discriminative listening.** In a discriminative listening situation your goal is to accurately understand the meaning of the message by focusing on the aspects or details of a message. This involves attending closely to both its verbal and nonverbal aspects. It demands a specific focus designed to determine the meaning. You might choose discriminative listening when you are helping a customer who is explaining a service problem or when meeting with your doctor who is explaining the results of your recent physical.

   Discriminative listening—focusing on verbal and nonverbal messages in order to notice details.

3. **Comprehensive listening.** In a comprehensive listening situation your goal is not only to understand, but also to learn, remember, and be able to recall information. Of course, we seek some kind of understanding whenever we listen. But comprehensive listening goes beyond merely understanding. It focuses on learning and remembering. You should use comprehensive listening whenever an instructor gives a lecture or when a work colleague teaches you new procedure.

   Comprehensive listening—focusing on verbal and nonverbal messages in order to learn, remember, and recall information.

4. **Critical–evaluative listening.** In a critical–evaluative listening situation, your goal is to understand a message and to judge its merits. You may listen between the lines to try to determine what is not being said. You might use this type of

   Critical-evaluative listening—focusing on verbal and nonverbal messages in order to judge or evaluate information.

listening when talking to a salesperson or listening to an apology from someone who has violated your trust.

Empathic listening—focusing on verbal and nonverbal messages in order to understand another's feelings.

5. **Empathic listening.** In an empathic listening situation your goal is to understand a person's feelings. This is also called therapeutic listening, since it is used in most counseling settings. You might choose this style when someone talks with you about a recent personal loss or when counseling an employee at work.

Make the Shift from Speaker to Listener a Complete One

In conversation, you are called on to switch back and forth from being the speaker to being a listener so frequently that you may find it difficult at times to make these shifts completely. If, instead of listening, you spend your time rehearsing what you're going to say as soon as you have a chance, your listening effectiveness will suffer. Especially when you are in a heated conversation, take a second to check yourself: Are you preparing your next remark instead of listening? Shifting from the role of speaker to that of listener requires constant and continuous effort.

Understanding—accurately decoding a message so that you share its meaning with the speaker.

observe & analyze

Adjusting to Listening Goals

Select an information-oriented program on your public television station (such as *NOVA*, *News Hour with Jim Lehrer*, or *Wall Street Week*). If possible, videotape it before you watch it. Watch at least fifteen minutes of the show while lounging in a comfortable chair or while stretched out on the floor with music playing in the background. After about fifteen minutes, stop the tape and quickly outline what you have learned. Now, make a conscious decision to use the guidelines for increasing attentiveness during the next fifteen minutes of the show. Turn off the music and sit in a straight-back chair as you watch the program. Your goal is to increase your listening intensity in order to learn, so you need to eliminate distractions and put yourself in an attentive position. After this fifteen-minute segment, you should again outline what you remember. Watch the program a second time and make note of how your attentiveness affected your memory.

Compare your notes from the two listening sessions. Is there any difference between the amount and quality of the information you retained? Be prepared to discuss your results with your classmates. Are their results similar or different? Why? ■

Understanding

The second active listening process is to understand what is being said. **Understanding** is accurately decoding a message so that you share its meaning with the speaker. This involves paying close attention to the other person's verbal and nonverbal messages so that you can understand or accurately comprehend the message. Let's examine five specific techniques you can use to increase your understanding.

Resist Tuning Out

Far too often, we stop listening before the person has finished speaking because we "know what a person is going to say." Yet until the person has finished, we don't have all the data necessary to form an appropriate response—our "knowing" what a person is going to say is really only a guess. Even if we guess right, the person may still feel that we weren't really listening, and the communication will suffer as a result. Accordingly, cultivate the habit of always letting a person complete his or her thought before you stop listening or begin to respond. At times attentive listening may be the best response you can make. Most of us need to learn the value of silence in freeing others to think, feel, and express themselves. As the old Hebrew adage goes, "The beginning of wisdom is silence."

diverse voices

American Indian Students and the Study of Public "Communication"

By Donal Carbaugh

Some Blackfeet people, upon some occasions, use a cultural model of "communication" that presumes, *sui generis,* a patterned way of living. A primary mode of this "communication," from the Blackfeet view, is what might be called a "deeply communicative silence," a listener-active form of non-verbal co-presence in which all is presumably interconnected.... That form of "communication" [is] something taught by "grandparents," and discussed in this way: you are "able to communicate spiritually and physically ... you are in tune with something long enough, to a point that you know it inside-out." ...

This Blackfeet model of "communication," when realized, involves a scene of "harmony," of silently connective co-presence, a nonlinguistic togetherness in which one is knowingly integral to and communing with the actual persons, animals, spirits, and things with which one dwells. This is both an ideal for "communication" that is especially apparent in some special Blackfeet ceremonies (e.g., sweat lodge rituals), and, it is a desirable condition of "every day" communicative action. For this kind of "communication" to be forceful in social living, it presumes (and thus recreates) an unspoken consensus of interconnection that is largely non-verbal and non-linguistic, yet shared and publicly accessible, if one just listens.

This cultural model of "communication" creates a special significance for nonlinguistic channels of messages, and an important duty for communicants as listeners. Participants in this communication must therefore become active *listeners,* and observers of that which they are already a part....

Through this mode, the Blackfeet are saying something about people being already connected (or seeking a holistic connectedness), about people, spirits—and ancestors—being an inherent part of this grand picture, about natural features and animals being figured into this interconnected realm, with all of this providing a cultural scene of Blackfeet "communication." A primary mode of some Blackfeet communication is thus to "communicate spiritually and physically" through a listener-active silence with a cultural premise (a belief and value) of this mode being the inheritance of a holistic world of intricate interconnections....

In the alternate model of communication ... called a "whiteman" or "white people's" model, ... The primary mode of communication is not a listener-active silence, but verbal speaking. The "white people's" primary mode of action is verbal and is based at least partly upon these "other" cultural premises: Speaking makes something public that was heretofore private, personal, or internal; speaking helps create (or construct) social connections among those who were presumably different or separate; and, connecting through speech is the principal way a society is made, and made to work. From the "white people's" view, the primary mode of communication is verbal speaking, with this mode being important for the actual "constructions" of personal, social, and societal life (Carbaugh, 1988).

A secondary mode of communication in the "white people's" system is silence. Communicative silence is figured upon the primary mode of verbal speaking and its premises. Silence plays upon the primary mode, however, by risking its negation, or by signaling the absence of the very premises that are presumably being activated in "white people's" actions of verbal speaking. Silence as a communicative action can mean, to "white people," a negation of one's personal being (as in "the silent treatment"), a failure to "connect" with others in "relationship," and a sign that social institutions have been ruptured or broken or corrupted (e.g., "a conspiracy of silence"). Without speaking, and with silence, one can hear (or feel) being amplified not an interconnectedness as among the Blackfeet, but a separateness, and disconnectedness that is present between presumably different individuals or peoples. Silence, then, is a prominent way to accentuate the different, separate, and even disconnected states of affairs which are so often presumed as a basis for many public American (i.e., multicultural) events and scenes. ■

Excerpted from Carbaugh, D. (2002). American Indian students and the study of public "communication." In J. N. Martin, T. K. Nakayama, & L. A. Flores (Eds.), *Readings in Intercultural Communication* (pp. 138–148). New York: McGraw-Hill.

In addition to prematurely ceasing to listen, we often let certain mannerisms and words interfere with hearing a person out, perhaps to the extent of "tuning out."

Are there any words or ideas that create bursts of semantic noise for you, causing you to stop listening attentively? What is your reaction when people speak of *gay rights, skinheads, conservative Christians, political correctness,* or *rednecks?* Do you tune them in or out? When semantic noise threatens to interfere, counteract this effect and try to let a warning light go on when a speaker trips the switch to your emotional reaction. Instead of tuning out or getting ready to disagree, be aware of this "noise" and work that much harder to listen objectively. If you can do it, you will be more likely to understand what the person is saying.

Identify the Speaker's Purpose and Key Points

Even in casual social conversations, speakers have some purpose or point they are trying to make. Sometimes people's thoughts are spoken in well-organized messages whose purposes and key ideas are easy to follow and identify. Other times, however, we must work harder at understanding the speaker. As you listen, ask yourself "What does the speaker want me to understand?" and "What is the point being made?" For example, if Manuel spends two minutes talking about how much he likes the Cubs and asking Corella about her interest in baseball, casually mentioning that he has tickets for the game this weekend, Corella may recognize that he would like her to go with him.

Observing Nonverbal Cues

Listeners interpret messages more accurately when they observe the nonverbal behaviors accompanying the words, because meaning may be shown as much by the nonverbals as by the spoken words. In Chapter 5 we noted that up to 65 percent of the meaning of a social message might be carried nonverbally. When Deborah says "Go on, I can walk home from here," we have to interpret cues such as tone of voice, body actions, and facial expression to tell whether she is sincerely interested in walking or whether she'd really like a ride.

Listening means paying attention to nonverbal as well as verbal cues. What messages are being conveyed by each person's facial expression and gesture?

So, whether you are listening to a co-worker explaining her stance on an issue, a friend explaining the process for hanging wallpaper, or a loved one explaining why he or she is upset with you, you must listen to how something is said as well as to what is said.

In the Diverse Voices selection on p. 179-180, author Donal Carbaugh explains how silence creates a nonverbal connection among members of the Blackfeet community.

Avoid Interrupting

One of the most common interferences with understanding is interrupting. In the Halone and Pecchioni study (2001), college students cited interrupting as a behavior that most interferes with really listening to another person. Remember in the last chapter we discussed the typical process of appropriate turn-taking. It is especially important when trying to be a good listener that you let the other person finish before you take your turn to speak. This is quite challenging when there is a group of people talking, when you are in a heated conversation, or when you are excited and enthusiastic about what you have just heard. With concentration and practice, you can become better at waiting until a speaker is finished before you begin talking.

Ask Questions

When we don't have enough information to fully understand a person's message, one effective way to obtain the information is to ask a **clarifying question.** A

Clarifying question—a response designed to get further information, to clarify information already received, or to encourage another to continue speaking.

question is, of course, a response designed to get further information, to clarify information already received, or to encourage another to continue speaking. In addition, good questions may also help speakers sharpen their thinking about the points they've made. Although you may have asked clarifying questions for as long as you can remember, you may notice that at times your questions either don't get the information you want, or they provoke an unwanted response—perhaps the other person becomes irritated, flustered, or defensive. You can increase the chances that your questions will get you the information you want and reduce the likely defensiveness that others might feel if you observe the following guidelines.

1. **Note the kind of information you need to increase your understanding.** Suppose Maria says to you, "I am totally frustrated. Would you stop at the store on the way home and buy me some more paper?" At this point, you may be a bit confused and need more information to understand what Maria is telling you. Yet if you respond "What do you mean?" you are likely to add to the confusion, because Maria, who is already uptight, won't know precisely what it is you don't understand. To increase your understanding, you might ask Maria one of these three types of question:

   Questions to get more information on important details. "What kind of paper would you like me to get, and how much will you need?"

   Questions to clarify the use of a term. "Could you tell me what you mean by 'frustrated'?"

   Questions to clarify the cause of the feelings the person is expressing. "What is it that's frustrating you?"

   Determine whether the information you need is more detail, clarification of a word or idea, or information on the cause of feelings or events, then phrase your question accordingly.

2. **Deliver questions in a sincere tone of voice.** Ask questions with a tone of voice that is sincere—not a tone that could be interpreted as bored, sarcastic, cutting, superior, dogmatic, or judgmental. We need to constantly remind ourselves that the way we speak can be even more important than the words we use. Sometimes asking several clarifying question in a row can seem like an interrogation. If you need to ask several clarifying questions, you might explain why you are asking them. For instance, Sally could say to her Dad, "I really want to understand what you are saying, so I need to ask a few questions to get more information. Is that OK?"

3. **Put the "burden of ignorance" on your own shoulders.** In order to minimize defensive reactions, especially when people are under stress, phrase your clarifying question in a way that puts the burden of ignorance on your own shoulders. Preface your questions with a short statement that suggests that any problem of misunderstanding may be the result of *your* listening skills. For instance, when Drew says "I've really had it with Malone screwing up all the time," you might say, "Drew, I'm sorry, I'm missing some details that would help me understand your feelings better. What kinds of things has Malone been doing?"

Here are two more examples that contrast inappropriate with more appropriate questioning responses.

> **Tamara:** They turned down my proposal again!
> **Art:** *(inappropriate)* Well, did you explain it the way you should have? (This question is a veiled attack on Tamara in question form.) *(appropriate):* Did they tell you why? (This question is a sincere request for additional information.)
> **Renée:** With all those executives at the party last night, I really felt weird.
> **Javier:** *(inappropriate)* Why? (With this abrupt question, Javier is making no effort to be sensitive to Renée's feelings or to understand them.) *(appropriate):* What is it about your bosses being there that made you feel weird? (Here the question is phrased to elicit information that will help Javier understand, and may help Renée understand as well.)

Note how the appropriate, clarifying questions are likely to get the necessary information while minimizing the probability of a defensive reply. The inappropriate questions, on the other hand, may be perceived as an attack.

Paraphrase What You Heard

A second way to assure your understanding is to paraphrase what you heard. When you ask a **paraphrasing question,** you are putting your understanding of a message into words, so that the other person can verify your understanding. Paraphrasing is not mere repetition of what the speaker has said; rather, it is a message that conveys and seeks to verify the images and emotions you have perceived from another's communication. It describes in your own words, the idea or image that has been sparked in your mind by another's statement. For example, during an argument with your sister, after she has stated her concern about your behavior, you might paraphrase what she said as follows: "So you are saying that you think I try to act better than you when I talk about my successes at work." Your sister can respond by saying, "Yes, exactly! It feels like you are trying to put me down when you do that." Or she may correct your paraphrase by saying, "No, I'm not feeling

Paraphrasing question—an attempt to verify your understanding of a message by putting it in your own words.

skill builders   QUESTIONING

SKILL	USE	PROCEDURE	EXAMPLE
Phrasing a response designed to get further information, to clarify information already received, or to encourage another to continue speaking.	To help get a more complete picture before making other comments; to help a shy person open up; to clarify meaning.	1. Note the kind of information you need to increase your understanding of the message. 2. Deliver questions in a sincere tone of voice. 3. Put the burden of ignorance on your own shoulders.	When Connie says, "Well, it would be better if she weren't so sedentary," Jeff replies, "I'm not sure I understand what you mean by 'sedentary'—would you explain?"

that you are trying to act better than me. It just makes me feel bad about the fact that I'm not doing so well at work right now." A paraphrase seeks to verify our understanding of a message and helps us to listen really closely to the subtle parts of a message. Many people do not spell everything out when they speak. Instead, they hint at things and allude to feelings. Paraphrasing lets us verify what we think we have heard.

Paraphrasing may focus on content, on feelings underlying the content, or both. Whether a content or feelings paraphrase is most useful for a particular situation depends on whether you perceive the speaker's emphasis to be on the content of the statement or on his or her feelings about what was said. In real-life settings we often don't distinguish clearly between content and feelings paraphrases, and our responses might well be a combination of both. All three types of paraphrase for the same statement are shown in this example.

Statement: "Five weeks ago, I gave the revised paper for my independent study to my project advisor. I felt really good about it because I thought the changes I had made really improved my explanations. Well, yesterday I stopped by and got the paper back, and my advisor said he couldn't really see that this draft was much different from the first."

Content paraphrase: "Let me see if I'm understanding this right. Your advisor thought that you hadn't really done much to rework your paper, but you put a lot of effort into it and think this draft was a lot different and much improved."

Feelings paraphrase: "I sense that you're really frustrated that your advisor didn't recognize the changes you had made."

Combination: "If I have this right, you're saying that your advisor could see no real differences, yet you think your draft was not only different but much improved. I also get the feeling that your advisor's comments really bother you."

Content paraphrase—A response that conveys your understanding of the denotative meaning of a verbal message.

Feelings paraphrase—A response that conveys your understanding of a speaker's state of mind—the emotions behind the words.

skill builders   PARAPHRASING

SKILL	USE	PROCEDURE	EXAMPLE
A response that conveys your understanding of another person's message.	To increase listening efficiency; to avoid message confusion; to discover the speaker's motivation.	1. Listen carefully to the message. 2. Notice what images and feelings you have experienced from the message. 3. Determine what the message means to you. 4. Create a message that conveys these images and/or feelings.	Grace says, "At two minutes to five, the boss gave me three letters that had to be in the mail that evening!" Bonita replies, "If I understand, you were really resentful that your boss dumped important work on you right before quitting time, when she knows that you have to pick up the baby at daycare."

Now the question becomes, when are paraphrases appropriate? Common sense suggests that we need not paraphrase every message we receive; nor would we paraphrase after every few sentences. So when should you think of paraphrasing? We suggest that you paraphrase in the following circumstances:

- When you need a better understanding of a message in terms of content, feelings, or both.
- When misunderstanding the message will have serious consequences.
- When the message is long and contains several complex ideas.
- When the message seems to reflect emotional strain.
- When you are talking with people whose native language is not English.

Remembering and Retaining Information

The third active listening process is remembering and retaining information. Too often people forget almost immediately what they have heard. For example, you can probably think of many times when you were unable to recall the name of a person to whom you were introduced just moments earlier. How well we remember can be measured by carefully prepared standardized tests. Robert Bostrom is a leader in the field of listening tests. The accompanying Spotlight on Scholars features his work, showing how he became interested in listening and how his effectiveness in testing evolved.

Improving remembering requires conscious application of three techniques that imprint ideas on your memory: repetition, mnemonics, and note taking.

Repetition

Repetition, saying something two, three, or even four times, helps you store information in long-term memory (Estes, 1989, p. 7). If information is not reinforced, it will be held in short-term memory for as little as twenty seconds and then forgotten. So, when you are introduced to a stranger named Jack McNeil, if you mentally say "Jack McNeil, Jack McNeil, Jack McNeil, Jack McNeil," you increase the chances that you will remember his name. Likewise, when a person gives you the directions "Go two blocks east, turn left, turn right at the next light, and it's in the next block," you should immediately repeat to yourself "two blocks east, turn left, turn right at light, next block—that's two blocks east, turn left, turn right at light, next block."

Repetition—saying something two, three, or even four times.

Mnemonics

Constructing mnemonics helps listeners put information in forms that are more easily recalled. A **mnemonic device** is any artificial technique used as a memory aid. One of the most common ways of forming a mnemonic is to take the first letter of each of the items you are trying to remember and form a word. For example,

Mnemonic device—any artificial technique used as a memory aid.

spotlight on scholars

Robert Bostrom, Professor of Communication, University of Kentucky, on
Listening

Robert Bostrom's interest

in listening began when he was a child, but his career took many turns before he was able to focus his research on listening. As a young man, Bostrom taught high school and coached debate. He returned to do advanced study at the University of Iowa, in part to study with his hero, the foremost authority on listening at the time, Ralph Nichols. Because Bostrom was not assigned to work with Nichols, his early scholarship was focused in a different direction. Still, he continued to read the scholarly literature on listening and became convinced that the listening tests then in use were not really measuring listening; instead, they seemed to be measuring general intelligence. So Bostrom began to work on a test that would do a better job of measuring how well someone listens.

According to Bostrom, although there are a number of behaviors that might assist listening, it is primarily a mental process. When people listen well, they accurately retain or remember what has been said. So, he reasoned, understanding how memory works is important to understanding listening. Those who have studied memory differentiate between short-term memory and long-term memory; so too, Bostrom believes, people engage in short-term listening and

long-term listening. We engage in long-term listening when we are trying to absorb information that we will need to recall at a later time. This is sometimes called "lecture listening" because one of the dominant contexts for this type of listening is one person providing information to another by lecturing. Bostrom believes that when we are participating in interpersonal conversations, we are likely to be engaging in short-term listening. We remember what the other person has said long enough to respond to it, but then we are likely to forget what was said. Perhaps you have experienced this. When asked to recall a recent conversation, have you ever had trouble remembering what you'd discussed? Yet you know that during the conversation you knew what the other person was saying, and you responded appropriately. Listening also requires one to interpret what has been said, so Bostrom believes that part of a valid listening test should measure how accurately a person interprets what has been said.

Bostrom's first listening test, called the Kentucky Comprehensive Listening Test (KCLT), has now been given to more than twenty thousand people. While it was originally designed to help scholars conduct research on listening, the test has been found to be a

useful diagnostic tool and a motivator for those seeking to improve their listening. Some instructors use this test in classes and find that students enjoy comparing their scores to those of their classmates.

In addition to conducting basic research on listening using the KCLT, Bostrom serves as a consultant to various organizations interested in assessing how well people listen. His work with the Educational Testing Service (ETS) includes designing the listening portion of the Praxis Exam, which is the national certification examination for teachers, and a portion of the subject area certification exam for college graduates in communication. He has worked with the National Defense Language Institute to figure out what influences how well people listen to a second or third language.

Bostrom believes that the next step in listening research is to assess our abilities to decode and interpret nonverbal behavior. Now that good research has enabled us to understand how the fundamentals of nonverbal signals operate, it is time to examine the interaction of these signals with memory and retention. Intriguing possibilities stem from the lateral asymmetry of hearing, since left and right sides of the brain engage themselves differently. Another promising area of investigation lies in basic psychobiological differences in persons, such as sensation seeking. Fundamental research in the communicative process is vital to understanding listening. For example, if individuals tend to talk too much, do they then not listen? Or do they listen better? For complete citations of many of Bostrom's publications, see the references for this chapter at the end of the book.

Bostrom is now retired from the University of Kentucky but continues to teach communication theory and research methods at both the graduate and undergraduate levels. He particularly enjoys his work with undergraduates, who he believes seem to get better each year. ■

---

an easy mnemonic for remembering the five Great Lakes is HOMES (Huron, Ontario, Michigan, Erie, Superior).

When you want to remember items in a sequence, try to form a sentence with the words themselves or assign words using the first letters of the words in sequence and form an easy-to-remember statement. For example, when you studied music the first time, you may have learned the notes on the lines of the treble clef (EGBDF) with the saying "Every good boy does fine." (And for the notes on the treble clef spaces, FACE, you may have remembered the word *face.*)

Do you remember information better and longer if you take notes?

Note Taking

Although note taking would be inappropriate in most casual interpersonal encounters, it represents a powerful tool for increasing your recall of information when you are involved in telephone conversations, briefing sessions, interviews, and business meetings. Note taking provides a written record that you can go back to, and it also enables you to take a more active role in the listening process (Wolvin & Coakley, 1996, p. 239). In short, when you are listening to complex information, take notes.

What constitutes good notes will vary depending on the situation. Useful notes may consist of a brief list of main points or key ideas plus a few of the most significant details. Or the notes may consist of a short summary of the entire concept (a type of paraphrase), written after the message has been delivered. For lengthy and rather detailed information, however, good notes likely will consist of a brief outline of what the speaker has said, including the overall idea, the main points of the message, and key developmental material. Good notes are not necessarily very long. In fact, many classroom lectures can be reduced to a short outline of notes.

Critically Evaluating Information

The fourth active listening process is to critically evaluate the information. **Critically evaluating** information is the process of judging what you have understood and interpreted in order to determine how truthful, authentic, or believable you judge the meaning to be. This may involve judgements about the accuracy of facts, the amount and type of evidence supporting a position, and how a position relates to your own values. For instance, when a person tries to convince you to vote for a particular candidate for office or to sign a petition to add a skateboard park to the neighborhood, you will want to listen critically to the message. This means judging the facts and evidence and determining how much you agree with the speaker. Critical listening requires that you separate facts from inferences and probe for information.

Separate Facts from Inferences

Factual statements are those whose accuracy can be verified or proven; **inferences** are claims or assertions based on observation or fact. Separating factual statements from inferences requires us to be able to tell the difference between a verifiable observation and an opinion related to that observation. Too often people treat inferences as factual.

Let's clarify this distinction with an example. If we can document that Cesar received an A in geology, then saying that Cesar received an A in geology is a factual statement. If we go on to say that Cesar studied very hard, the statement is an inference. Cesar may have studied hard to receive his grade; but it is also possible that geology comes easily to Cesar or that Cesar had already learned much of the material in his high school physical science course. If you identify a speaker's statement as an inference, be sure to look for the data on which the inference is based.

The reason for separating factual statements from inferences is that inferences may be false, even if they are based on verifiable facts. Making sound judgments entails basing our opinions and responses to messages on facts or on inferences whose correctness we have evaluated. So, when we encounter such statements as "Better watch it; Carl is really in a bad mood today. Did you see the way he was scowling?" or "I know you're hiding something from me; I can tell it in your voice," or "Olga and Kurt are having an affair—I've seen them leave the office together nearly every night," we know that each one contains an inference. Each of them may be true, but none is necessarily true.

observe & analyze

Effective Listening

Describe five situations during the past day or two in which you were cast as a "listener" (only one of these can be a classroom setting). Was your listening behavior the same or different in each of the instances? What, if anything, determined differences in your approach to your listening in each of these situations? In which of the situations did you do the most effective listening? On what basis do you make this evaluation? What behaviors discussed in this chapter seem to best explain how your "effective" listening differed from your "ineffective" listening? ■

Probe for Information

Sometimes, after listening to a message, we need to encourage the speaker to delve deeper into the topic. Or we need to challenge the information. In order to do this, we can ask **probing questions,** questions by which we are searching for more information or trying to resolve perceived inconsistencies in a message.

What questions should listeners ask themselves as they listen to some-one who is trying to influence them?

Suppose that Jerrod's landlord was talking with him about the need to sign a lease. Examples of probing questions would be Jerrod asking a prospective landlord such questions as the following:

"You said that I would need to sign a lease, but you did not state the term of the lease. What's the shortest lease I could get?"

"Your ad in the paper said that utilities would be paid by the landlord, but just now you said that the tenant pays the utility bill. Which way will it work with this apartment?"

With both of these questions Jerrod is expecting the landlord to supply information that Jerrod needs before he can evaluate the suitability of an apartment.

When asking probing questions, your nonverbal communication is especially important. You must pay attention to your tone of voice and body language so you do not appear arrogant or intimidating. Too many probing questions accompanied by inappropriate nonverbal cues can lead the other person to become defensive.

By separating facts from inferences and probing for necessary information you are then in a position to judge the value of the information before you.

Applying Skills to Listening in Cyberspace

Thus far in this chapter we have looked at four active listening processes. In this last short section we consider important elements of applying the skills of these processes to communicating in cyberspace. **Cyberspace** is the electronic system of

Cyberspace—the electronic system of interlinked networks of computers, bulletin boards, and chat rooms.

interlinked networks of computers, bulletin boards, chat rooms, etc. Since we treat electronic writing as if it were speech, people refer to instant messaging and communication in chat rooms as talking, not writing. Thus, real-time communication in cyberspace involves listening.

There are many things we attend to during online communication: the content of a message, the tone of the message, the emotions accompanying a message, the speed of response, and how formal or informal the language is. While much of the information in this chapter pertains to online listening as well as to listening to actual speech, there are a few unique challenges of listening online. R. Anderson (1997) was one of the first experts in computer-mediated communication to offer suggestions for being an effective listener in cyberspace.

1. **Give extra effort to attending and understanding.** Because of the speed of online chatting in real time, as well as the brevity of messages and the limited range of nonverbal cues, it is easy to make mistakes in paying attention and interpreting messages. It is important to focus carefully by asking questions and paraphrasing statements before jumping to conclusions during cyberspace interactions.

2. **Practice critical evaluation.** A study of teenage interactions in cyberspace showed that deceptions about age, appearance, occupation, and life circumstances do occur online. The study also revealed that people develop identification with others more quickly online than in face-to-face interaction (Pew Internet and American Life Project, 2001). Because it is easy to fake identities online or to post inaccurate and misleading information, it is important to be able to critically evaluate information you receive. Ask clarifying and probing questions after receiving online messages. Be sure to separate facts from inferences.

3. **Don't become overdependent on cyberspace listening.** Because of the convenience of interacting in cyberspace, some people become so immersed in online interactions that they sacrifice some face-to-face interaction. Research has revealed that people heavily involved in online relationships tend to be shyer than others (Ward & Tracey, 2004). Both kinds of interaction have their place, and one should not replace the other.

Summary

Listening is the process of receiving, constructing meaning from, and responding to spoken and/or nonverbal messages. In this chapter we have looked at the four active listening processes and have presented suggestions for applying listening skills to cyberspace interactions. Attending is the perceptual process of selecting, from the countless stimuli reaching the senses, specific stimuli on which to concentrate. Three common techniques of attending are to get physically and mentally ready to listen, to choose what type of listening the situation requires, and to make the shift from speaker to listener a complete one.

A Question of Ethics

Janeen always disliked talking on the telephone—she thought that it was an impersonal form of communication. Thus, college was a wonderful respite because when her friends would call her, instead of staying on the phone she could quickly run over to their dorm or meet them at a coffeehouse.

One day, during reading period before exams, Janeen received a phone call from Barbara, an out-of-town friend. Before she was able to dismiss the caller with her stock excuses, Janeen found herself bombarded with information about old high school friends and their whereabouts. Not wanting to disappoint Barbara, who seemed eager to talk, Janeen tucked her phone under her chin and began straightening her room, answering Barbara

with the occasional "Uh huh," "Hmm," or "Wow, that's cool!" As the "conversation" progressed, Janeen began reading through her mail and then her notes from class. After a few minutes she realized there was silence on the other end of the line. Suddenly very ashamed, she said, "I'm sorry, what did you say? The phone...uh, there was just a lot of static."

Barbara replied with obvious hurt in her voice, "I'm sorry I bothered you, you must be terribly busy."

Embarrassed, Janeen muttered, "I'm just really stressed, you know, with exams coming up and everything. I guess I wasn't listening very well, you didn't seem to be saying anything really important. What were you saying?"

"Nothing 'important,'" Barbara answered. "I was just trying to figure out a way to tell you. I know that you were friends with my brother Billy, and you see, we just found out yesterday that he's terminal with a rare form of leukemia. But you're right, it obviously isn't really important." With that, she hung up.

1. Which guidelines for ethical dialogue are relevant to this case? What is the central ethical concern here? Why?

2. Identify ways in which both Janeen and Barbara could have used better and perhaps more ethical interpersonal communication skills. Rewrite the scenario incorporating these changes.

Understanding is the process of accurately decoding a message so that you share its meaning with the speaker. To increase your level of understanding, you need to resist taking your mind off what the speaker is saying. It's also critical to try to identify the speaker's purpose and key points, to attend to nonverbal cues to help your interpretation, to ask questions to assure the accuracy of your understanding, to paraphrase what has been said to give the speaker a chance to verify your understanding, and to avoid interrupting. Remembering is the active listening process of retaining information through repetition, use of mnemonic devices, and note taking. Critically evaluating information is the process of judging what you have understood and interpreted in order to determine how truthful, authentic, or believable you judge the meaning to be. In addition to these active listening processes, we have also considered the application of various techniques to listening in cyberspace.

Inter-Action Dialogue:
LISTENING EFFECTIVELY

Good listening requires getting ready to listen, listening actively, and responding after listening. Use your Inter-Act CD to view the dialogue between Gloria and Jill and analyze the listening behaviors of each.

A transcript of Gloria and Jill's conversation follows. You can analyze their conversation using the Inter-Action Analysis feature on your CD. From the Dialogue page click "Analysis for Gloria and Jill" to compare your comments to the analysis provided by the authors.

Gloria and Jill meet for lunch on campus.

CONVERSATION

GLORIA: *I'm really hungry—I don't know whether I've been working out too hard or what.*

JILL: *I know. There are some days when I can't figure out what happened, but I just feel starved.*

GLORIA: *Thanks for meeting me today. I know you're up to here in work, but ...*

JILL: *No problem Gloria. I feel bad that we haven't gotten together as much as we used to, so I've been really looking forward to seeing you.*

GLORIA: *Well, I need to talk with you about something that's been really bothering me. (She notices that Jill is fumbling with something in her purse.) Jill—are you listening to me?*

JILL: *I'm sorry, Gloria. For a minute I couldn't find my cell phone. I wanted to turn it off while we talked, and then I worried that I might have dropped it. But everything's OK. I apologize—that was rude of me. (She then sits up straight and looks directly at Gloria.) I'm ready.*

GLORIA: *Well, you know I'm working with Professor Bryant on an independent research project this term.*

JILL: *I recall you mentioning something about it, but remind me of the details.*

GLORIA: *Last semester when I took her course on family communication I wrote a term paper on how shared dinnertime affected family communication. Well, she really liked it and asked me if I wanted to work with her on a study this term. She said I could get credit.*

JILL: *How?*

GLORIA: *I had permission to sign up for four credit hours of independent study.*

JILL: *That sounds good—so what's the problem?*

GLORIA: *Well, since she videotapes actual family discussions and then interviews family members, I thought I'd get to help with some of the interviews. But so far all I've been assigned to do is transcribe the tapes and do some library research.*

JILL: *So you're disappointed because you're not being challenged?*

GLORIA: *It's more than that. I thought Dr. Bryant would be a mentor: there'd be team meetings, we'd talk over ideas and stuff. But I don't really even get to see her. Her graduate assistant gives me my assignments, and he doesn't even stop to explain why I'm being asked to do stuff. I'm not really learning anything.*

JILL: *So, if I understand, it's not only the type of assignments you're getting but it's also that instead of really being involved, you're being treated like a flunky.*

GLORIA: *Exactly.*

JILL: *So when she asked you to work on her study, did she ever sit down and discuss exactly what the independent study would entail?*

GLORIA: *Not really. I just signed up.*

JILL: *Well since the term began, have you had any contact with Dr. Bryant?*

GLORIA: *No. Do you think I should make an appointment to see her?*

JILL: *I think so, but if you did, what would you say to her?*

GLORIA: *Well, I'd just tell her how disappointed I am with how things are going. And I'd explain what I hoped to learn this term and ask if she could help me understand how the assignments I'd been given were going to help me learn about family communication research.*

JILL: *So the purpose of your meeting wouldn't be to get different assignments, but to understand what you are supposed to be learning from the assignments you've done so far?*

GLORIA: *Right. But I think I'd also like her to know that I really expected to have more contact with her.*

JILL: *Well, it sounds as if you're clear on what you'd like to ask her.*

GLORIA: *Yes, but I don't want to get her angry with me. Four credit hours is a lot and it's too late to drop the independent study.*

JILL: *So you're concerned that she would be offended and take it out on your grade.*

GLORIA: *A little. But that's probably ridiculous. After all, she's a professional, and all the students I know who have gone to see her say that she's really understanding.*

JILL: *Well, then what do you want to do?*

GLORIA: *Hm.... I'm going to make an appointment to see her. In fact, I'll stop by her office on my way to my next class. Jill, thanks for listening. You've really helped me.*

Chapter Resources

Communication Improvement Plan: Listening

Would you like to improve your use of the following skills discussed in this chapter?

    Questioning

    Paraphrasing

Pick a skill and write a communication improvement plan.

Key Words

Listening, *p. 175*	**Understanding,** *p. 178*	**Mnemonic device,** *p. 185*
Attending, *p. 176*	**Clarifying question,** *p. 181*	**Critically evaluating,** *p. 188*
Appreciative listening, *p. 177*	**Paraphrasing question,** *p. 183*	**Factual statements,** *p. 188*
Discriminative listening, *p. 177*	**Content paraphrase,** *p. 184*	**Inferences,** *p. 188*
Comprehensive listening, *p. 177*	**Feelings paraphrase,** *p. 184*	**Probing questions,** *p. 188*
Critical–evaluative listening, *p. 177*	**Repetition,** *p. 185*	**Cyberspace,** *p. 189*
Empathic listening, *p. 178*		

Skill Practice

WRITING QUESTIONS AND PARAPHRASES

Provide an appropriate question and paraphrase for each of the following statements. To get you started, the first conversation has been completed for you.

1. **Luis:** It's Dionne's birthday, and I've planned a *big* evening. Sometimes, I think Dionne believes I take her for granted—well, I think after tonight she'll know I think she's something special!

   Question: What specific things do you have planned?

   Content paraphrase: If I'm understanding you, you're planning a night that's going to cost a lot more than what Dionne expects on her birthday.

   Feelings paraphrase: From the way you're talking, I get the feeling you're really proud of yourself for making plans like these.

2. **Angie:** Brother! Another nothing class. I keep thinking one of these days he'll get excited about something. Professor Romero is a real bore!

   Question:

   Content paraphrase:

   Feelings paraphrase:

3. **Jerry:** Everyone seems to be talking about that movie on Channel 5 last night, but I didn't see it. You know, I don't watch much that's on the "idiot box."

   Question:

   Content paraphrase:

   Feelings paraphrase:

4. **Kaelin:** I don't know if it's something to do with me or with Mom, but lately she and I just aren't getting along.

   Question:

   Content paraphrase:

   Feelings paraphrase:

5. **Aileen:** I've got a report due at work and a paper due in management class. On top of that, it's my sister's birthday, and so far I haven't even had time to get her anything. Tomorrow's going to be a disaster.

   Question:

   Content paraphrase:

   Feelings paraphrase:

Inter-Act with Media

FIND MORE
on the web
Additional media entries @
www.oup.com/us/interact

CINEMA

James L. Brooks (Director). (1997). *As Good as It Gets.* Jack Nicholson, Helen Hunt, Greg Kinnear, Cuba Gooding Jr., Shirley Knight.

> **Brief Summary:** An obsessive–compulsive writer (Melvin Udall) living in New York City must learn to overcome his illness and his homophobia as he struggles to form a relationship with a waitress (Carol Connelly), a single mother who serves him breakfast at his favorite restaurant, his gay neighbor (Simon Bishop), and Simon's dog, Verdell, with whose care Melvin is suddenly entrusted.

Randa Haines (Director). (1991). *The Doctor.* William Hurt, Christine Lahti, Elizabeth Perkins, Mandy Patimkin, Adam Arkin.

> **Brief Summary:** This film is based on Dr. Ed Rosenbaum's book *A Taste of My Own Medicine.* William Hurt plays a doctor who believes that he must maintain distance from his patients so that he can remain objective and efficient. When he develops throat cancer, he discovers what it is like to be a patient and deal with a hospital bureaucracy. A young female cancer patient helps him to learn how to empathize with patients and to cope with his own illness. He also learns the importance of listening to his wife as their relationship is severely tested.

WHAT'S ON THE WEB

The Positive Way. *Listening Skills Evaluation.*

http://www.positive-way.com/listenin.htm

Brief Summary: This listening skills rating is a self-evaluation of the current level of your listening skills as well as what you perceive your partner's listening skills to be. The evaluation can be taken manually or via an automated version. The test is taken from the book by Steven C. Martin and Catherine A. Martin, *Talk to Me: How to Create Positive Loving Communication.*

IPC Concepts: The site illustrates every aspect of communication with special details on barriers, listening, feedback, and nonverbal communication.

Carter McNamara. *Interpersonal Listening Skills*

http://www.managementhelp.org/commskls/listen/listen.htm

Brief Summary: The site offers a series of links that offer practical extensions of this chapter on distinguishing good from bad listening, secrets of listening skills, empathy and listening, and a self-evaluation.

IPC Concepts: The site offers concrete examples of a number of concepts in the communication process, such as feelings, needs, thoughts, attitudes, and inner conflict as they function in the process of message creation and they influence our response to messages.

supporting *and* comforting others

After you have read this chapter, you should be able to answer these questions:

- How do people respond to the emotional situations of others?

- What is empathy?

- What role does empathy play in building and maintaining relationships?

- What are three approaches to empathizing?

- What cultural considerations affect the ability to empathize well?

- What is the process of providing emotional support to another?

- What are the characteristics of effective and ineffective emotional support messages?

- What are the skills you will want to learn in order to provide comfort to others?

"Kristy, I'm really disappointed and I need to tell you about it. For almost a year now at work," Tara explained, "the regional manager has been telling me that I'm gonna get my own store to run. They sent me to a three-day training session in February about store management. I've even been working at the Eastlake store a couple of days a week to help me to get to know that store. Everyone has pretty much told me that I would become the manager at Eastlake. Now you can probably guess what happened today."

"You didn't get the promotion?" Kristy guessed.

"Exactly! I just found out that the company brought in a manager from the West Coast and I'm not getting the promotion after all."

"You're kidding! That's too bad." said Kristy. "Oh, did I tell you that I've got an appointment to get a massage tomorrow? Well, I just can't wait. And I've got a coupon so it's only gonna cost thirty-five dollars for the hour treatment. The masseuse is supposed to be the best. Why don't you come too? I think I can get another coupon."

"Kristy, what's with you? Here I am telling you I am devastated about not getting the promotion I've expected and all you can talk about is your massage."

"Well, Tara, I was just trying to cheer you up. I thought if we talked about massages it would take your mind off work."

"Kristy, just forget it. I've got to go to class."

"All right, so you can't get that excited about my massage, then let's talk about something else."

Can you recall a situation when you went to a friend and shared how hurt you were with an incident that had just happened to you? Did you feel that the person really listened? Did your friend seem to understand and try to help you? Or was your conversation like the one between Tara and Kristy? Notice how Kristy's first response ("You're kidding!") was followed by changing the topic, what Barbee and Cunningham (1995) refer to as an "escape" strategy, where in effect one person dismisses the importance of another's concerns. So how should Kristy have responded in order to be helpful and comforting? In a research study, Barbee and Cunningham found that instead of escaping and dismissing, using comforting responses that provide solace and solve problems is perceived by recipients to be supportive—the kind of responses that Tara needed from Kristy (Cunningham & Barbee, 2000).

We often find ourselves in situations where our partner is emotionally distressed and in need of a therapeutic listener who can offer support and comfort. How well we respond in these situations not only affects how well our partner copes with the situation but also affects the relationship itself. In this chapter, we will study the concepts and skills of effective supportive communication. We begin by explaining empathy processes and describing how to improve your ability to empathize. Then we discuss the process of providing emotional support to another and the characteristics of effective and ineffective emotional support messages. Finally, we describe the specific skills you will want to learn in order to provide comfort to others.

Empathy

Appropriate supportive responses depend on our ability to empathize with our communication partner. **Empathy** is the cognitive process of identifying with or vicariously experiencing the feelings, thoughts, or attitudes of another. Scholars recognize that empathy is an important element in understanding and maintaining good interpersonal relationships (Omdahl, 1995, p. 4). When we empathize, we are attempting to understand and/or experience what another understands

Empathy–the cognitive process of identifying with or vicariously experiencing the feelings, thoughts, or attitudes of another.

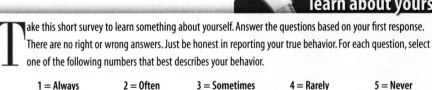

learn about yourself

Take this short survey to learn something about yourself. Answer the questions based on your first response. There are no right or wrong answers. Just be honest in reporting your true behavior. For each question, select one of the following numbers that best describes your behavior.

    1 = Always   2 = Often   3 = Sometimes   4 = Rarely   5 = Never

_____ 1. I try to consider the other person's point of view.

_____ 2. When I am upset with someone, I try to put myself in his or her shoes for a while.

_____ 3. I find it difficult to see things from the other person's point of view.

_____ 4. I try to imagine how it would feel to be in another person's place.

_____ 5. I dislike listening to other people's feelings.

_____ 6. I can easily identify with another person's feelings.

_____ 7. I would rather talk about myself than the other person in a conversation.

_____ 8. I get impatient when people talk about their own concerns and problems.

_____ 9. I like to help others feel better.

_____ 10. People spend too much time talking about their own feelings and problems.

SCORING THE SURVEY: This is a test of empathic tendency—your capacity to feel empathy for others. Each score separately ranges from 5 to 25. The lower (closer to 5) your score on Total 1, the more you tend to feel empathy toward others. The lower (closer to 5) your score on Total 2, the less you tend to feel empathy toward others.

    Add scores for questions 1, 2, 4, 6, and 9   Total 1: _____

    Add scores for questions 3, 5, 7, 8, and 10   Total 2: _____

Empathic responsiveness—experiencing an emotional response parallel to another person's actual or anticipated display of emotion.

Perspective taking—imagining yourself in the place of another.

Sympathetic responsiveness—a feeling of concern, compassion, or sorrow for another because of a distressing situation.

and/or experiences. It obviously requires more effort to empathize with someone who is very different from us or to empathize with someone who is experiencing something that is out of our realm of experience. But the goal of empathy is to understand the experiences of another person.

Approaches to Empathy

Scholars who study empathy have identified three different approaches that people can use when empathizing: empathic responsiveness, perspective taking, and sympathetic responsiveness (Weaver & Kirtley, 1995, p. 131).

Empathic responsiveness is experiencing an emotional response parallel to another person's actual or anticipated display of emotion (Omdahl, 1995, p. 4; Stiff, Dillard, Somera, Kim, & Sleight, 1988, p. 199). For instance, when Jackson tells James that he is in real trouble financially, and James senses the stress and anxiety that Jackson is feeling and feels anxious himself, we would say that James has experienced empathic responsiveness.

The empathic responsiveness approach is most easily used when there is a close or intimate relationship with the other person. Because of the strong relational bond, you may identify more easily with the other's emotion and experience it along with the other person. If you have just recently met someone, it may be more difficult to feel the emotion of his or her situation. In general, we can use empathic responsiveness most easily with those people who are our intimates.

Our ability to detect and identify the feelings of others may come from our own experiences in similar situations.

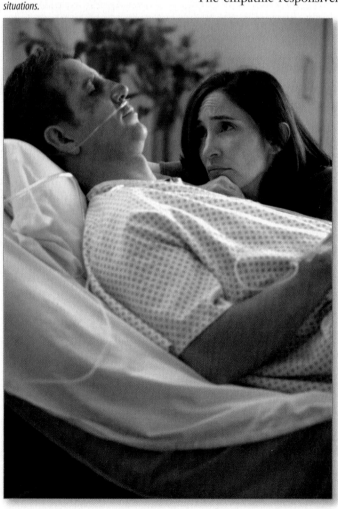

Perspective taking—imagining yourself in the place of another—is the most common form of empathizing (Zillmann, 1991). While empathic responsiveness stems from feeling what another feels, in perspective taking we imagine ourselves in the situation described, anticipate how we would feel, and then assume that the other person's feelings are similar. Although perspective taking is difficult for many of us (Holtgraves, 2002, p. 122), with conscious effort we can learn to imagine ourselves in the place of another. In our example, if James personalizes the message by picturing himself in serious financial debt, anticipates the emotions he might experience if this were to occur, and then assumes that Jackson must be feeling the same way, then James is empathizing by perspective taking.

Sympathetic responsiveness is your feeling of concern, compassion, or sorrow

diverse voices

Black and White *By Linda Howard*

Today we tend to label people as black, white, Asian, Hispanic, and so on. But what if you are half one and half another? Linda Howard is a recent high school graduate who has been awarded a four-year scholarship to a prominent university in New England. Based on the following transcript of an interview with her, in what ways can you empathize?

My parents are Black and

White American. I come from a long heritage. I am of French, English, Irish, Dutch, Scottish, Canadian, and African descent.

I don't really use race. I always say, "My father's Black, my mother's White, I'm mixed. But I'm American; I'm human. That's my race; I'm part of the human race."

It's hard when you go out in the streets and you've got a bunch of White friends and you're the darkest person there. No matter how light you are to the rest of your family, you're the darkest person there and they say you're Black. Then you go out with a bunch of Black people and you're the lightest there and they say, "Yeah, my best friend's White." But I'm not. I'm both.

I don't always fit in—unless I'm in a mixed group. That's how it's different. Because if I'm in a group of people who are all one race, then they seem to look at me as being the other race ... whereas if I'm in a group full of [racially mixed] people, my race doesn't seem to matter to everybody else.... Then I don't feel like I'm standing out. But if I'm in a group of totally one race, then I sort of stand out, and that's something that's hard to get used to.

It's hard. I look at history and I feel really bad for what some of my ancestors did to some of my other ancestors. Unless you're mixed, you don't know what it's like to be mixed.

I've had people tell me, "Well, you're Black." I'm not Black; I'm Black and White. I'm Black and White American. "Well, you're Black!" No, I'm not! I'm both. It's insulting, when they try and ... bring it right back to the old standards, that if you have anybody in your family who's Black, you're Black ... I mean, I'm not ashamed of being Black, but I'm not ashamed of being White either; and if I'm both, I want to be part of both. And I think teachers need to be sensitive to that.

See, the thing is, I mix it at home so much that it's not really a problem for me to mix it outside.

I don't think [interracial identity is] that big of a problem. It's not killing anybody, at least as far as I know, it's not. It's not destroying families and lives and stuff. It's a minor thing. If you learn how to deal with it at a young age, as I did, it really doesn't bother you the rest of your life, like drugs....

I think we're all racist in a sense. We all have some type of person that we don't like, whether it's [a

person] from a different race, or from a different background, or [a person with] different habits.

But to me a serious racist is a person who believes that people of different ethnic backgrounds don't belong or should be in their space and shouldn't invade our space: "Don't come and invade my space, you Chinese person. You belong over in China or you belong over in Chinatown."

Racists come out and tell you that they don't like who you are. Prejudiced people [on the other hand] will say it in like those little hints, you know, like, "Oh, yes, some of my best friends are Black." Or they say little ethnic remarks that they know will insult you but they won't come out and tell you, "You're Black. I don't want anything to do with you." Racists, to me, would come out and do that.

Both racists and prejudiced people make judgments, and most of the time they're wrong judgments, but the racist will carry his one step further.... A racist is a person that will carry out their prejudices.

I had a fight with a woman at work. She's White, and at the time I was the only Black person in my department. Or I was the only person who was at all Black in my department. And she just kept on laying on the racist jokes. At one point, I said, "You know, Nellie, you're a racist pig!" And she got offended by that. And I was just joking, just like she'd been joking for two days straight—all the racist jokes that she could think of.

I've got a foot on both sides of the fence, and there's only so much I can take. I'm straddling the fence, and it's hard to laugh and joke with you when you're talking about the foot that's on the other side.

She couldn't understand it. We didn't talk for weeks. And then one day, I had to work with her. We didn't say anything for the first like two hours of work. And then I just said, "Smile, Nellie, you're driving me nuts!" and she smiled and laughed. And we've been good friends ever since. She just knows you don't say ethnic things around me; you don't joke around with me like that because I won't stand for it from you anymore. We can be friends; we can talk about anything else—except race. ■

for another because of a distressing situation. Some scholars call this "emotional concern" (Stiff et al., 1988), while others use the more common term "sympathy" (Eisenberg & Fabes, 1990). Sympathetic responsiveness differs from the other two approaches in that you don't attempt to experience the feelings of the other; rather, you focus on intellectually understanding what the speaker has said and experience feelings of concern, compassion, or sorrow for that person. James has sympathy for Jackson when he understands that Jackson is embarrassed and worried, but instead of trying to feel Jackson's emotions or imagine how he himself would feel in a similar situation, James might instead feel concern and compassion for his friend Jackson.

Improving Our Ability to Empathize

Although people vary in their ability to empathize, most of us have to learn to increase our empathy and then decide to practice it. Especially those of us who are overly "I" oriented find it difficult to see the world from others' points of view, and as a result, our ability to empathize is often underdeveloped. If we are to increase our interpersonal effectiveness, we may need to exert extra effort to develop our capacity to empathize.

Though it may seem trite, the first step is to take the time and make the effort to understand the person who is speaking. This does not mean that we need to have a deep, personal relationship with others in order to empathize with them. It means that we pay serious attention to what others are saying and what they seem to feel about what they are saying. Understanding others focuses your attention on the other, not on the self. In this chapter's Diverse Voices selection (see pages 201-202), "Black and White," Linda Howard describes what she has experienced as a person who is multiethnic and biracial. As you read this excerpt from an interview with Ms. Howard, see how well you can discern, understand, and feel what she thinks and feels.

How well you empathize also depends on how observant you are of others' behavior and how clearly you "read" the nonverbal messages they are sending. How accurately can you read others' emotions from their nonverbal behavior? Research studies have shown that when people concentrate, they can do quite well. People are especially adept at recognizing such primary emotions as happiness, sadness, surprise, anger, and fear (greater than 90 percent accuracy) and rather good at recognizing contempt, disgust, interest, determination, and bewilderment (80 to 90 percent accuracy) (Leathers, 1997, p. 41). The research also suggests that recognizing facial expressions is the key to perceiving emotion (Leathers, 1997, p. 25).

In order to improve your observations, try the following. When another person begins a conversation with you, develop the habit of silently posing two questions to yourself: "What emotions do I believe the person is experiencing right now?" and "What are the cues the person is giving that I am using to draw this conclusion?" Consciously raising these questions can help you focus your attention on the nonverbal aspects of messages, where most of the information on the person's emotional state is conveyed. To ensure that you understand another's emotions accurately, use the skill of perception checking.

In summary, to become more effective at empathizing with others, try the following: (1) Show respect for the person by actively attending to what the person is saying. (2) Concentrate on observing and understanding both the verbal and

skill builders   EMPATHIZING

SKILL	USE	PROCEDURE	EXAMPLE
The cognitive process of identifying with or the vicarious experiencing of the feelings, thoughts, or attitudes of another.	To prepare yourself for making an appropriate comforting response.	1. Show respect for the person by actively attending to what the person says. 2. Concentrate on observing and understanding both the verbal and nonverbal messages, using paraphrases and perception checking to aid you. 3. Experience an emotional response parallel to another person's actual or anticipated display of emotion. Imagine yourself in the place of the person, and feel concern, compassion, or sorrow for the person because of his or her situation or plight.	When Jerry says, "I was really hurt when Sarah returned the ring I had given her," Mary experiences an emotional response parallel to Jerry's, imagines herself in Jerry's situation, or feels concern, compassion, or sorrow for Jerry.

observe & analyze

Empathizing Effectively

1. Describe the last time you effectively empathized with another person. Write a short summary of the episode. Be sure to cover the following: What was the person's emotional state? How did you recognize it? What were the nonverbal cues? Verbal cues? What type of relationship do you have with this person? How long have you known the person? How similar is this person to you? Have you ever had a real or vicarious experience similar to the one the person was reporting? Did you use empathic responsiveness, perspective taking, or sympathetic responsiveness? Why? What was the outcome of this communication episode?

2. During the next two days, make a conscious effort to use empathy guidelines in your interactions with others. At the end of each day, assess your progress. How well did you do on each guideline? Where do you need to continue to exert effort? ■

Comforting—helping people feel better about themselves and their behavior.

Supporting response—a statement whose goal is to show approval, bolster, encourage, soothe, console, or cheer up.

nonverbal messages, using paraphrases and perception checking to aid you. (3) Experience an emotional response parallel to another person's actual or anticipated display of emotion; imagine yourself in the place of the person, and feel concern, compassion, or sorrow for the person because of his or her situation or plight.

Understanding Emotional Support

Many times in our conversations with others, we may feel a need to provide emotional support—in effect to comfort the speaker. **Comforting** means to help people feel better about themselves and their behavior. Comforting occurs when one feels respected, understood, and confirmed.

Research on comforting messages suggests that people who use a relatively high percentage of sophisticated comforting strategies are perceived as more sensitive, concerned, and involved (Burleson & Samter, 1990; Kunkel & Burleson, 1999; Samter, Burleson, & Murphy, 1987).

Some comforting responses are statements that show approval of a person's feelings or acknowledge the person's right to have those feelings. Other comforting responses are efforts to commiserate with a person when bad things have happened. Under these circumstances, the comforting messages are efforts to reassure, bolster, encourage, soothe, console, and cheer up. In this section we label all these efforts as *supporting*.

Supporting

Supporting responses are comforting statements whose goal is to reassure, bolster, encourage, soothe, console, or cheer up. They show that we care about people and what happens to them; they demonstrate that the listener empathizes with a person's feelings, whatever their direction or intensity (Burleson, 1994, p. 5). Supporting is not the same as making statements that aren't true or telling people what they want to hear. Effective supportive statements must be in touch with the facts. Let's look briefly at two supportive approaches, one that supports positive feelings and another that supports negative feelings.

Supporting (Approving) Positive Feelings. We all like to treasure our good feelings; when we share them, we don't want them dashed by listeners' inappropriate or insensitive responses. Supporting positive feelings is generally easy, but still requires some care. Consider the following example.

Kendra *(hangs up the telephone, does a little dance step, and turns to Selena): That was the bank. He said that I've been approved for the loan. Can you believe it? I'm going to have my own pottery studio.*

Kendra's statement requires an appropriate verbal response. To provide one, Selena must appreciate the feeling people get when they receive good news, or she must envision how she would feel under the same circumstances. Selena responds:

Selena: *Kendra, way to go, girl! That's terrific! I am so happy for you. You've worked so hard—you deserve this.*

In this case, Selena's response gives her approval for Kendra to be excited. Her response also shows that she is happy because Kendra seems happy.

Supporting responses like Selena's are much needed. Think of the times when you have experienced an event that made you feel happy, proud, pleased, soothed, or amused and you needed to express those feelings. Didn't it make you feel even better when others recognized your feelings and affirmed your right to have them?

Supporting (Giving Comfort) When a Person Experiences Negative Feelings. When a person has had an unfortunate experience and is in the midst of or is recalling unpleasant emotional reactions, an effective supporting statement provides much-needed comfort. By acknowledging the person's feelings and affirming the person's right to the feelings, you can help the person further his or her progress at working through the feelings.

For some people, making appropriate responses to painful or angry feelings is very awkward and difficult. But when people are in pain, or when they are feeling justifiably angry, they need to be comforted by appropriate supporting statements.

The new responsibilities of parenthood can seem daunting. How might doctors, family, and friends provide positive support during the first days?

Because it can be difficult to provide comfort when we are ill at ease, we need to practice and develop skill in making supporting statements.

An appropriate comforting statement shows empathy and sensitivity, and may show a willingness to be actively involved if need be. Consider the following example.

> **Bill:** *My sister called today to tell me that Mom's biopsy came back positive. She's got cancer, and it's untreatable.*
>
> **Dwight:** *Bill, you must be in shock. I'm so sorry that this is happening. Is there anything I can do for you?*

Notice how Dwight begins by empathizing: "Bill, you must be in shock." He continues with statements that show his sensitivity to the seriousness of the situation: "I'm so sorry that this is happening." Finally, he shows that he really cares: He is willing to take time to talk about it, and he asks whether he can do anything for Bill.

We offer the exchanges between Kendra and Selena and between Bill and Dwight as an introduction to skill development. Later in the chapter we'll see that these are examples of just two approaches or skills that can be learned and used to provide support.

One of the leading scholars on comforting behavior is Brandt Burleson, who is featured in this chapter's Spotlight on Scholars section (see page 207). Over the years Burleson and his colleagues have provided a great deal of scholarship that informs the development of supportive skills.

To better understand just why some comforting messages help people feel better while others don't do anything—or even make people feel worse—Burleson has recently studied theories and research on emotion and the factors that lead to emotional distress. This study of emotion dynamics led to a new understanding of comforting as a conversational process that, at its best, helps distressed others make sense of what has happened to them, work through their feelings, and reappraise the upsetting situation. This view of the comforting process emphasizes the role of empathic listening and the importance of getting upset people to talk about their feelings and experiences in detail. People seem to make sense of their distressing experiences by expressing their thoughts and feelings in narratives or stories.

Characteristics of Effective and Ineffective Emotional Support Messages

Supportive messages–create a conversational environment that encourages the person needing support to talk about and make sense of the situation that is causing distress.

A great deal of research has been directed at understanding what types are perceived by receivers as supportive and what types are perceived as unsupportive. **Supportive messages** are helpful and provide comfort because they create a conversational environment that encourages the person needing support to talk about and make sense of a distressing situation. Nonsupportive messages are those that

Brant Burleson, Professor of Communication, Purdue University, on
Comforting

The seeds for Brant

Burleson's interest in comforting behavior were sown during his undergraduate days at the University of Colorado at Boulder, where he was taught that all communication was persuasion. This proposition did not square with Burleson's own experiences. As a child of the 1950s, who came of age during the emotion-filled 1960s, Burleson had witnessed lots of hurt and conflict. But he had also seen people engaging in altruism and acts of comforting. These comforting acts, he reasoned, were not aimed at changing anyone's opinion or behavior, but were simply done to help the other person. So when he entered graduate school at the University of Illinois, Burleson began to study formally how individuals comfort others. He wanted to establish scientifically whether comforting messages were important and whether they made a difference. Since graduate school Burleson's work has done much to affirm both propositions.

In his research Burleson has carefully defined comforting strategies as messages that have the goal of relieving or lessening the emotional distress of others. He has limited his work to looking at how we comfort others who are experiencing mild or moderate sadness or disappointment that happens as a result of everyday events. He has chosen not to study comforting in situations where there is extreme depression or grief because of extraordinary events. He has also chosen to limit his work to the verbal strategies that we use when we comfort. Burleson's care in defining the "domain" of his work is important. By carefully stating the type of emotional distress he is concerned with, and by clearly identifying the limits of his work, Burleson enables those who read his work to understand the types of comforting to which his findings apply.

Early on, Burleson worked with James L. Applegate, who had developed a way of judging the sophistication of particular comforting messages. Sophisticated messages were seen as those that acknowledged, elaborated, and legitimized the feelings of another person. Sophisticated comforting strategies are also more listener centered (aimed at discovering how the distressed person feels), less evaluative, more feeling centered, more likely to accept the point of view of the other person, and more likely to offer explanations for the feelings being expressed by the other person.

Lately, Burleson and others who study comforting have turned their attention to understanding the results of comforting. Early research judged comforting messages only on the extent to which they reduced the immediate distress that a person is feeling. But more recent research shows that the effects of comforting extend beyond this simple instrumental outcome. Effective comforting also helps the other person cope better in the future, improves the quality of personal relationships, and may even enhance physical health. Moreover, skilled comforting should also benefit the comforter. Burleson believes that when we effectively comfort others, we both increase our own self-esteem and become better liked by those we comfort and by those who see us effectively comfort others. Finally, Burleson believes that those who are effective at comforting others are likely to have better long-term relationships. There is a growing list of research studies, some conducted by Burleson and his colleagues, that provides support for his theory. For complete citations of some publications by Burleson and his colleagues, see the reference list for this chapter at the end of the book. ■

fail to meet these goals. In his recent studies, Burleson (2003, pp. 565–568) identified several effective and ineffective supportive message types. Effective and helpful supportive messages are those that:

1. Clearly state that the speaker's aim is to help the other ("I'd like to help you, what can I do?" or "You know that I'm going to be here for you for as long as it takes").

2. Express acceptance, love, and affection for the other ("I love you and understand how upset this makes you" or "I understand that you just can't seem to accept this").

3. Demonstrate care, concern, and interest in the other's situation ("What are you planning to do now?" or "Gosh, tell me more. What happened then?").

4. Indicate that the speaker is available to listen and support the other ("Say, if you need to talk more, please call" or "Sometimes it helps to have someone to listen, and I'd like to do that for you").

5. State that the speaker is an ally ("I'm with you on this" or "Well, I'm on your side—this isn't right").

6. Acknowledge the other's feelings and situation as well as express sincere sympathy ("I'm so sorry to see you feeling so bad, I can see that you're devastated by what has happened" or "You have my sympathy, I couldn't work for a jerk like that either, no wonder you're frustrated").

7. Assure the other that feelings of distress are legitimate ("With what has happened to you, you deserve to be angry" or "I'd feel exactly the same way if I were in your shoes").

8. Encourage the other to elaborate on the story ("Uh huh, yeah," or "I see. How did you feel about that?" or "Well, what happened before that? Can you elaborate?").

Ineffective and unhelpful supportive messages are those that:

1. Condemn and criticize the other's feelings and behavior ("I think you're wrong to be angry with Paul" or "That's dumb. Why do you feel like that?").

2. Imply that the other's feelings are not warranted ("You have no right to feel that way. After all, you've dumped men before" or "Don't you think you're being a bit overdramatic?").

DOONESBURY © 1990 G. B. Trudeau. Reprinted with permission of UNIVERSAL PRESS SYNDICATE. All rights reserved.

3. Tell the other how to feel or advise ignoring justifiable feelings about the situation ("You should be really happy about this" or "Hey, you should just act as if you don't care").

4. Focus attention on yourself by a lengthy recount of a similar situation you once faced ("I know exactly how you feel because when I . . .").

5. Intrude because they represent a level of involvement or concern greater than the type of relationship would indicate to be appropriate ("I know we've just met, but I know how to help you here").

observe & analyze

Emotional Support

Recall the last time you received emotional support from a partner. Describe the situation. Did you feel better because of this conversation? Which of the characteristics of effective support and ineffective support were used in the messages of your partner? Does this explain how comforted you felt? Next, consider each of the characteristics again. Which of these do your messages exhibit? ■

Supportive Interaction Phases

Although we can attempt to comfort a person with a single supportive statement, complete comforting is rarely accomplished with one message. Rather, in many situations we provide emotional support and comfort over numerous turns in a conversation. In some situations we will have several conversations spread over days, weeks, or even months in which our role is to give emotional support to someone who is having difficulty achieving a cognitive reappraisal and so continues to need our comfort. In our chapter-opening conversation, Tara had been anticipating a promotion for a year. It is likely to take her weeks, if not months, to "talk out" her feelings and develop a reappraisal that allows her to accept the disappointment. So too, a person facing financial ruin or grieving the death of someone they loved is likely to need ongoing supportive interactions.

Whether a distressed person is comforted in one conversation, or requires many conversations, Barbee and Cunningham (1995) identify four well-ordered phases that supportive interactions seem to progress through.

Phase One: Support Activation. Comforting interactions begin when something happens to trigger a supportive response. Supportive activation can be triggered by the words or behaviors of the person needing support/comforting. So in the chapter opener, Tara overtly seeks support when she self-discloses, "Kristy, I'm really disappointed and I need to tell you about it." Alternatively, a relational partner who perceives a need for comforting can trigger support activation. For example, Brianne comes home, walks into the kitchen, and finds her mother slumped over the sink silently sobbing into her arm. Brianne rushes over, puts her arms around her mom and asks, "Mom are you all right? What's happened?" Support, then, can be activated either by the person needing comforting or by one who has offered to be the comforter.

Phase Two: Support Provision. During the second phase of a supportive interaction, comforters enact messages that are designed to support/give comfort to the partner by focusing on the emotions being displayed or on the problem that has been expressed. Although Kristy avoided dealing with Tara's feelings in the chapter opener, once Brianne's mother has shared that she's lost her job, Brianne may provide solace by saying, "I'm so sorry, I can understand why you're terrified about how we'll pay this month's rent." In this way Brianne supports her mother's feelings.

Phase Three: Target Reaction. Once a comforter has responded to the person needing support, that person will react to what the helper has said or done. This reaction will indicate how successful the helper's message was at comforting the partner. Rather than being comforted by Tara's offer of escape from the topic, Tara was obviously distressed with Kristy's response. "Kristy, what's with you? Here I am telling you I am devastated about not getting the promotion and all you can talk about is your massage." In contrast, Brianne's mother may be somewhat soothed by the solace Brianne has offered. So she calms down a bit and responds, "I'm not just worried about the rent, but there's the car payment, and I just finished paying off the credit card bill. I don't know if I can face going into debt again."

Phase Four: Helper Responses. The subsequent messages of the comforter respond to what the partner has expressed. If the partner who needs comfort has reached a more stable emotional level, the helper may respond by changing the focus of the conversation. In Kristy's response to Tara, she reinterprets her initial response as "trying to cheer you up" by taking "your mind off work." To Kristy's way of thinking, her previous response was supportive. In this response to Tara she tries to demonstrate her support and soothe Tara through by explaining the reason for her earlier remark. Since Brianne's first message provided support, her mother regained some of her composure and disclosed her fears about going into debt. So now Brianne might refocus the discussion into problem solving the family's finances.

If the partner remains in need of comforting, the interaction will cycle back to a previous phase and continue until one of the partners changes the subject or ends the conversation. When the two meet again, they may begin another supportive interaction on the same subject, cycling through the same identifiable phases, but fashioning unique messages that, while related, are different from the ones shared during the previous conversation.

As you have probably experienced during your own supportive interactions, these conversations are not always smooth. There may be false starts, interruptions, topic changes, and other disruptions during the course of the discussion. And the messages themselves will vary from very brief nonverbal cues to short verbal messages to lengthy narratives complete with subplot digressions. Nonetheless, you will be more effective in providing support/comforting if the messages you use during phases two and four incorporate the supportive message skills presented next.

inter-act with

Technology

In a conversation, emotional tone is generally shared through nonverbal behavior such as voice, facial expression, and bodily movements. Professional counselors have relied on such clues to help them respond appropriately to the needs of their clients. Today, modern technology often replaces such face-to-face counseling and comforting interactions, as various crises are attended to via such high-tech interfaces as telephone support centers.

When you talk on the phone to someone who is in need of comfort or understanding, what nonverbal cues do you use to (a) determine their needs, (b) assess the accuracy of your comforting efforts, and (c) assess the efficacy of your words? ■

Supportive Message Skills

According to Burleson (2003), most people could benefit from training in emotional support skills. He cites numerous research studies that have found "support attempts that fail," "miscarried helping," and "unsupportive responses." From this Burleson concludes that we "don't offer each other emotional support as often as [we] might, and when [we] do, much of what [we] offer is of poor quality" (p. 562). Based on his analysis, Burleson has identified six supportive message skills. Forming messages that are sensitive to the emotional needs of the person calls for four of these skills: clarifying supportive intentions, buffering threats to face (which takes two skills, positive and negative facework) and other-centeredness. The other two skills, framing information and giving advice, provide support by helping the person problem-solve. Depending on the circumstances and the complexity of the situation, you may find that using a single skill will provide the necessary support. More likely, in order to be effective, you will use a combination of the skills as you provide comfort. Let's take a look at each of these individual skills.

Clarifying Supportive Intentions

When people are experiencing emotional turmoil, they can have trouble under-standing the motives of those wishing to provide support. We **clarify supportive intentions** (indicate that we are trying to give support) when we openly state that our goal in the conversation is to support and help our partner. Messages based on this skill may be a prelude to using other support skills. If our partners interpret our messages in a way that makes them doubt our motives, they may be guarded in what they disclose. When we clarify supportive intentions, our partners interpret our messages properly and are less likely to search for a hidden agenda. In addition, stating that our objective is to give support may help our partners feel a little better, because they know that someone is "on their side." Finally, once our partners

Clarify supportive intentions— openly state that our goal in the conversation is to support and help our partner.

Although you may be able to use a single skill to provide the necessary support, you are likely to need a combination of skills over time.

know our intentions, they have a context for understanding our comments. When we don't overtly make our intentions known, our partners—who are in the midst of emotional turmoil—may misinterpret our attempts to comfort. Thus, when Julie says to Kathie, "I'd really like to help you work through this situation you've described," she begins to clarify her supportive intentions.

To clarify supportive intentions (1) directly state your intentions by emphasizing your desire to help; (2) remind your partner of your commitment to your relationship (if necessary); (3) indicate that helping is your only motive; (4) and phrase your clarification in a way that reflects helpfulness.

Let's consider a more complete example.

> **David** (noticing Paul sitting in his cubicle with head in his lap and his hands over his head): Paul, is everything OK?
> **Paul** (sitting up with a miserable but defiant look on his face): Like you should care. Yeah, everything's fine.
> **David:** Paul, I do care. You've been working for me for five years. You're one of our best analysts, so if something's going on, I'd like to help, even if all I can do is to listen.

With his second response, David conveys his supportive intentions and desire to help. He then assures Paul that he is interested in his well-being. Then he points out the continuing nature of their relationship and Paul's importance to him. Finally, he directly states his willingness to help. Will this statement be enough to convince Paul to open up? Maybe it will. But if not, David can restate supportive intention and hope that a second expression will be effective.

> **Paul:** Look, you've got a lot to do without listening to my sad story. I can take care of this myself, so just forget it.
> **David:** Paul, I do have lots to do, but I always have time to listen and to help you. I don't want to pry, I just want to help.

In his second message, David further emphasizes that Paul is important to him and that his only intention is to help.

People needing comforting can feel vulnerable and may not be comfortable about disclosing until you have given several reassurances of your supportive intentions. So you may use several supportive intention messages as you interact. But you will also need to be sensitive to your partner's right to privacy. Repeated statements of supportive intentions can become counterproductive and coercive if your partner ends up disclosing information that he or she would have just as soon withheld. Supporters need to be sensitive to the fine line that exists between helping someone to "open up" and invading that person's privacy. If your only motive is to help the other, then there will be times when your own curiosity must be unsatisfied. Sometimes we can provide emotional support without knowing the full details of a situation.

Buffering Face Threats

Once you've clarified your intentions to provide support, you may discover that the very act of providing emotional support can be threatening to the face needs of your partner (recall our discussion of saving face in Chapter 6). On the one

skill builders   CLARIFYING SUPPORTIVE INTENTIONS

SKILL	USE	PROCEDURE	EXAMPLE
Openly stating that your goal in the conversation is to support and help your partner.	To enable your partner to easily interpret messages without searching for a hidden agenda. To communicate that someone is "on their side" and to provide a context for understanding supportive comments.	1. Directly state your intentions, emphasizing your desire to help. 2. Remind your partner about your ongoing relationship. 3. Indicate that helping is your only motive. 4. Phrase your clarification in a way that reflects helpfulness.	After listening to Sonja complain about flunking her geology midterm, her friend Deepak replies: "Sonja, you're a dear friend, and I'd like to help if you want me to. I did well enough on the midterm that I think I could be of help; maybe we could meet once a week to go over the readings and class notes together."

hand, providing emotional support can threaten face if your partner fears being respected, liked, or valued less because of the distressing situation. For example, Brianne's mother wants her daughter to respect her. So she is likely to be embarrassed and ashamed when telling her daughter that she has lost her job.

On the other hand, providing emotional support can also threaten people's face needs if they feel that our intrusion is a threat to their needs to be independent and self-sufficient. Support messages carry a hidden meaning. They say to our partners, "You are needy and require my help." So if Anne tells Cindy that she'd like to help her, Cindy may say, "I can take care of this myself, so just forget it." Here Cindy is reacting to the face-threatening act (FTA) that Anne unwittingly committed in stating her supportive intention message.

Because supportive messages are also FTAs, comforters need to "buffer" or cushion the effect of their words by utilizing both positive and negative politeness skills. **Positive facework** messages protect the partner's need to be respected, liked, and valued by verbally affirming the person or the person's actions in the present difficulty. **Negative facework** messages support the partner's need for independence and autonomy by verbally using indirect methods when offering information, opinions, or advice.

To perform positive facework (1) describe and convey positive feelings about what the other has said or done in the situation; (2) express your admiration for the person's courage or effort in the situation; (3) acknowledge how difficult the situation is; and (4) express your belief that the other has the qualities and skills to endure or succeed.

In the examples we have been looking at, David is performing positive facework when he says to Paul, "You're one of our best analysts." In Brianne's conversation with her mom, positive facework could be done in several ways. For instance, Brianne could acknowledge how difficult it must be to be fired. Or she might say how much she admires her mom's determination to stay out of debt. Or she might indicate her firm belief that her mother is talented and resourceful enough to quickly find a new job. Each of these statements (and countless others) can help Brianne protect her mom's self-esteem as she provides comfort.

Positive facework—messages that protect the partner's need to be respected, liked, and valued by verbally affirming the person or the person's actions in the present difficulty.

Negative facework—messages that support the partner's need for independence and autonomy by verbally using indirect methods when offering information, opinions, or advice.

skill builders   POSITIVE FACEWORK

SKILL	USE	PROCEDURE	EXAMPLE
Messages affirming a person or a person's actions in the face of a difficult situation.	To protect the other's positive face needs (to be respected, liked, and valued) in situations where other messages are perceived to be FTAs.	1. Describe and convey positive feelings about what the other has said or done in the situation. 2. Express your admiration for the person's courage or effort in the situation. 3. Acknowledge how difficult the situation is. 4. Express your belief that the other has the qualities and skills to endure or succeed.	Jan has learned that Ken has suffered his brother's anger because of an intervention by which Ken had intended to help his sibling. Jan says:"I really respect you for the way you have acted during this. It takes a lot of guts to hang in there like you've been doing, especially when you've been attacked for doing so. I know that you've got the skills to help you get through this."

Just as positive facework can mitigate the effects of FTAs to positive face needs, so too messages can be formed that reduce the effects that FTAs have on negative face needs.

To perform negative facework, form messages that (1) ask for permission before making suggestions or giving advice, (2) verbally defer to the opinions and preferences of the other person, (3) use tentative language to hedge and qualify opinions and advice, and (4) offer suggestions indirectly by telling stories or describing hypothetical options.

The simplest, yet often overlooked means for performing negative facework is to ask whether someone wants to hear your opinions or advice before you offer such assistance. For example, you might say, "Would you like to hear my ideas on this?" At times, our partners are not interested in having us solve their problems, but instead want someone to commiserate. When we brazenly offer unsolicited opinions or advice, the FTAs to our partner's negative face needs may undermine the very support we are trying to provide.

Even when our partners have indicated that they are receptive to hearing our opinions and advice, we should word our messages carefully. Our opinions and advice should be conveyed in a way that acknowledges that our partner is a competent decision maker who is free to accept or reject the advice. Messages such as "This is just a suggestion, You are the one who has to make this decision" express deference to our partner's opinion. Our messages should use language that hedges and qualifies our opinions, making it easier for our partner to disagree with what we have said. For instance, "I'm not sure this will work or that you would want to proceed this way, but if I were in a situation like this, I might think about doing. . . ." Finally, our supportive messages will be less threatening when we indirectly hint at advice and opinions by relating what others have done in similar situations or by offering hypothetical suggestions. For instance, we might say, "You know, when my friend Tom lost his job, he . . ." or "Maybe one option to try might

skill builders   NEGATIVE FACEWORK

SKILL	USE	PROCEDURE	EXAMPLE
Using verbally indirect methods when offering information, opinions, or advice.	To protect the other's negative face needs (for independence and autonomy) when presenting opinions or advice.	1. Ask for permission before making suggestions or giving advice. 2. After stating the advice verbally, defer to the opinions and preferences of the other person. 3. Use tentative language to hedge and qualify opinions and advice. 4. Offer suggestions indirectly by telling stories or describing hypothetical options.	Judy has learned that Gloria has really been hurt by rejection from a best friend. Judy says: "Would you like any advice on this?" Gloria says that she would, and Judy then offers suggestions: "These are just a few suggestions, and I think you should go with what you think is best. Now, I'm not sure that these are the only way to go, but I think…." After stating her opinions, Judy says, "Depending on what you want to accomplish, I can see a couple ways that you might proceed…."

be. . . ." When we use positive and negative facework in our supportive messages, we create a climate in which our partners can receive comfort without feeling threats to their self-esteem or autonomy.

Other-Centered Messages

In their theory of conversationally induced reappraisals, Burleson and Goldsmith (1998) suggest that people experience emotional stress when they believe that their current situation is at odds with their life goals. These authors believe that to reduce emotional distress, a person must "make sense" of what has happened. People feel better if they can re-evaluate specific aspects of the problem situation or change their opinion about how the situation relates to their goals. An important way that people form a reappraisal is by repeatedly telling the story of what happened to them and elaborating on it. In this case, the role of the comforter is to create a supportive conversational environment in which the emotionally distressed person can tell and elaborate on the story and discuss feelings about what has happened.

During the comforting process a person may show his or her inability to "make sense." By developing the skill of **other-centered messages,** you can utilize active listening, express compassion and understanding, and encourage partners to talk about what has happened, elaborate on it, and explore their feelings about distressing situations.

For many of us, other-centeredness is difficult to master. We may have been raised in families or come from cultures that taught us not to dwell on problems

Other-centered messages—utilize active listening, express compassion and understanding, and encourage partners to talk about what has happened, elaborate on it, and explore their feelings about the situation.

or that it is rude to pry into other people's business. Consequently, even when a friend or intimate starts the conversation, our gut reaction is to change the topic or make light of the situation. When Kristy switched topics and began discussing massages, she might have thought she was being helpful by taking Tara's mind off her troubles, or she might have been trying to relieve her own discomfort. Regardless, her topic change was not supportive. It took the focus away from Tara and didn't allow Tara the "space" to work through this painful situation. In our rush to help another, we may also inadvertently change the focus to ourselves.

The following guidelines are used in creating other-centered messages: (1) Ask questions that prompt the person to tell and elaborate on what happened ("Really, what happened then?"). (2) Emphasize your willingness to listen to an extended story ("You've simply got to tell me *all* about it, and don't worry about how long it takes. I want to hear the whole thing from start to finish"). (3) Use vocalized encouragement ("Uh huh . . . ," "Wow . . . ," "I see . . .") and nonverbal

skill builders — OTHER-CENTERED MESSAGES

SKILL	USE	PROCEDURE	EXAMPLE
Expressing compassion and understanding and encouraging partners to talk about what has happened and to explore their feelings about the situation.	To help partners in their efforts to cognitively reappraise an emotionally disturbing event.	1. Ask questions that prompt the person to tell and elaborate on what happened. 2. Emphasize your willingness to listen to an extended story. 3. Use vocalized encouragement and nonverbal behavior to communicate your continued interest without interrupting your partner as the account unfolds. 4. Affirm, legitimize, and encourage exploration of the feelings expressed by your partner. 5. Demonstrate that you understand and connect with what has happened but avoid changing the focus to you.	Angie begins to express what has happened to her. Allison says: "Really, what happened then?" As Angie utters one more sentence and then stops, Allison says: "You've simply got to tell me *all* about it, and don't worry about how long it takes. I want to hear the whole thing from start to finish." During Angie's discussion, Allison shows her encouragement: "Go on . . . ,""Wow . . . ,""Uh huh . . . ," and she nods her head, leans forward, etc. To affirm, Allison says: "Yes, I can see that you're disappointed. Most people would be disappointed in this situation. Is this as difficult as when. . . ?" Allison then continues: "I know that I felt angry when my sister did that to me. So what happened then?"

behavior (head nods, leaning forward, etc.) to communicate your continued interest without interrupting your partner as the account unfolds. (4) Affirm, legitimize, and encourage exploration of the feelings expressed by your partner ("Yes, I can see that you're disappointed. Most people would be disappointed in this situation. Is this as difficult as when . . . ?"). (5) Demonstrate that you understand and connect with what has happened but avoid changing the focus to yourself ("I know that I felt angry when my sister did that to me. So what happened then?").

In the conversation between Rob and James that is on your CD and at the end of this chapter you will see Rob using a series of other-centered messages to help James tell and make sense of what has happened.

During supportive interactions, there are times when our partners lack awareness or may have trouble understanding some aspect of the problem situation. At these times, you can provide information, opinions, or advice that can help them understand or improve the situation. The supportive message skills of framing and advising assist us in forming messages that convey the information or advice in a supportive manner.

Framing—the skill of providing comfort by offering information, observations, and opinions that enable the receiver to better understand or reinterpret an event or circumstance.

Framing

Framing is the skill of providing comfort by offering information, observations, and opinions that enable the receiver to better understand or to see their situation in a different light. Especially when people's emotions are running high, they are likely to perceive events in very limited ways. Many times by sharing information, observations, and opinions, we provide a different "frame" through which someone can "see" an event—thus supplying a different (and perhaps less painful) way of interpreting what took place. Consider the following situation.

Travis returns from class and tells his roommate, Abe, "Well, I'm flunking calculus. It doesn't matter how much I study or how many of the online problems I do, I just can't get it. This level of math is above me. I might as well just drop out of school before I flunk out completely. I can ask for a full-time schedule at work and not torture myself with school anymore."

Travis has not only described a situation, he has interpreted it to mean that he is not smart enough to handle college-level math courses. Yet, there could be information that Travis doesn't have or hasn't thought about that would lead to other interpretations. For example, Abe might

Sometimes the best way to provide comfort is to provide a different "frame" through which someone can "see" an event, giving the other person a different (and perhaps less painful) way of interpreting what took place. What might the coach be saying to reframe the situation for the player?

remind Travis that he has been putting in a lot of hours at work this term and maybe the work schedule is interfering with his schoolwork. Or Abe might tell Travis that he heard that the calculus instructor likes to scare the class by grading really hard, but that he curves the grades at the end of the semester. In this way, Abe provides Travis with ways of reframing what has happened in the light of alternative interpretations. There are interpretations other than inability to understand math that may account for Travis's poor grade.

Our framing statements are supportive when they soothe our partners' feelings by helping them look at what has happened in ways that are less threatening to their self-esteem. To form framing messages: (1) Listen to how your partner is interpreting events. (2) Notice information that your partner may be overlooking or overemphasizing in the interpretation. (3) Clearly present relevant, truthful information, observations, and opinions that enable your partner to reframe what has happened.

Notice how the framing statements in the next two examples provide comfort by suggesting less painful interpretations for events.

Karla: *I'm just furious with Deon. All I said was "We've got to start saving money for a down payment or we'll never get a house," and he doesn't say a word, he just gets angry and stomps out of the room.*

Shelby: *Yes, I can see what you mean, and I'd be frustrated too. It's hard to work through issues when someone up and leaves. But perhaps Deon feels guilty about not being able to save. You know his dad. Deon was raised to believe that the measure of a man is his ability to provide for his family. So, when you said what you did, unintentionally, you may have hurt his male ego.*

Micah: *I just don't believe Bradford anymore. We had my annual evaluation last week and she says my work is top-notch, but I haven't had a pay raise in over two years.*

skill builders   FRAMING

SKILL	USE	PROCEDURE	EXAMPLE
Offering information, observations, and opinions with the goal of helping the receiver to understand or reinterpret an event or circumstance.	To support others when you believe that people have made interpretations based on incomplete information or have not considered other viable explanations that would be less threatening to the individuals' self-esteem.	1. Listen to how your partner is interpreting events. 2. Notice information that your partner may be overlooking or overemphasizing in the interpretation. 3. Clearly present relevant, truthful information, observations, and opinions that enable your partner to develop a less ego-threatening explanation of what has happened.	Pam:"Katie must be really angry with me. Yesterday she walked right by me at the market and didn't even say 'Hi.'" Paula:"Are you sure she's angry? She hasn't said anything to me. And you know, when she's mad I usually hear about it. Maybe she just didn't see you."

Khalif: *I can see that you're discouraged. No one in my department has gotten a raise either. But have you forgotten that we're still under that salary freeze? At least Bradford is continuing to do performance reviews, so you know where you stand and what you should be eligible for when the freeze is over.*

Giving Advice

Sometimes, we can also support others by giving advice. **Advice-giving** messages present relevant suggestions and proposals that a person could use to satisfactorily resolve a situation. Advice can comfort our partners when we offer it in a well-established supportive climate. Unfortunately, we often rush to provide advice before we really understand the problem or before we have developed a rapport that allows our partner to see the advice as helpful.

Advice giving—presenting relevant suggestions and proposals that a person could use to satisfactorily resolve a situation.

In general, advice messages (and to a lesser extent, framing messages) should not be expressed until our supportive intentions are understood, facework has been performed, and we have sustained an other-centered focus to the interaction. Only when we believe that our partners have had enough time to understand, explore, and make their own sense out of what has happened to them, should we offer advice to help them with unresolved issues.

Suppose Shawn is aware that his boss relies on him to help solve major problems that confront the firm. Yet, twice when positions that pay much more than Shawn's have opened up, his boss has recommended others who have done much less for the firm. When Martino becomes aware that Shawn is very concerned and doesn't know what to do, he takes the time to talk with his co-worker and says, "Shawn, we've helped each other a lot over the years. May I offer some advice?" When Shawn nods, Martino goes on, "I know you have many choices—one of which is to get a different job. But if I were in your shoes, before I did anything radical I would make a point of seeing the boss and carefully stating what you've told me about his reliance on you and how you appreciate his confidence in you. And then I'd describe my disappointment at not being promoted, and then ask him why he hasn't suggested me for these jobs. Now this could irk him, but it seems to me that you might need to run that risk under the circumstances. Still, it's your decision. But I believe my suggestion is worth thinking about."

This example illustrates some rules for giving advice: (1) ask for permission to give advice; (2) word the message as *one* of many suggestions in a way that the recipient can understand; (3) present any potential risks or costs associated with the following the advice; and (4) indicate that you will not be offended, should your partner choose to ignore your recommendation or look for another choice.

As you probably noticed, by its very nature, advice is an FTA to your partners' negative face needs. Advice implies that your partners are not competent to solve their own problems and thus need your help. So several of the guidelines help you form advice messages incorporating negative facework. Asking permission, phrasing advice as suggestions, framing the advice as only one alternative, and acknowledging your partner as a capable decision maker act to mitigate the face-threatening nature of advice.

Recall the earlier example of Brianne, who was providing emotional support for her mother in the wake of her job loss. Suppose that as the older woman calms down, she begins to discuss how she will provide for the family's financial needs. After she has considered and rejected several ideas, Brianne might offer some thoughts of her own:

Brianne: *Mom, I have an idea if you'd like to hear it.*

Mom: *Well, OK.*

Brianne: *Well, this is just one alternative. If you don't like it, I'll understand. It's up to you. But here goes. Thomas and I can start helping with the family expenses. We could each take a part-time job after school and on weekends. . . . Maybe you could even take a short computer course at City Community College so you'd have more technology skills and wouldn't be intimidated when you were asked to work on the computer. We'd all be a little busier with either part-time jobs or the computer course, but I'm sure we could fit these extra things into our schedules. What do you think?*

Notice how Brianne "front-loads" her advice with negative facework. She presents her ideas and how her advice will solve the problem. Then she mentions the costs of this plan. Finally, she refocuses the discussion by asking her mother to comment on this proposal. Although Brianne's mother may reject the plan, she is likely to perceive that Brianne was sincerely trying to be helpful rather than perceiving her daughter as inappropriately bossy.

skill builders   GIVING ADVICE

SKILL	USE	PROCEDURE	EXAMPLE
Presenting suggestions and proposals a partner could use to satisfactorily resolve an emotionally difficult situation.	To comfort our partners when we have established a supportive climate and they are unable to find their own solutions.	1. Ask for permission to give advice. 2. Word the message as one suggestion in a way that the recipient can understand. 3. Present any potential risks or costs associated with the following the advice. 4. Indicate that you will not be offended, should your partner choose to ignore your recommendation or look for another choice.	After a friend has explained a difficult situation she faces, Felicia might say something like the following: "I have a suggestion if you'd like to hear it. As I see it, one way you could handle this is to . . . ." "This is just one idea—you may come up with a different solution that's just as good. So think this one over, and do what you believe is best for you."

Social Support in Cyberspace

While giving and receiving support and comfort through face-to-face interpersonal communication is most common, online support groups, chat rooms, e-mail, and instant messages from distant cyber friends provide another context for supportive communication. Researchers have identified several advantages of cyber support (Walther & Parks, 2002). First, for some people, not being face-to-face creates social distance that makes it easier to disclose problems. There might be more face-saving in sharing your troubles and getting comfort from a stranger than from a close friend. Furthermore, there is a degree of anonymity in exchanging messages online.

A second feature of cyber support is the capacity to hear from people around the world who actually have experienced your situation. For those coping with uncommon chronic or terminal diseases, online support groups provide access to people who can empathize because they have experienced the same crisis or trauma. While friends and loved ones can try to put themselves in your place, if you are dealing with an uncommon problem, being able to chat with many people who are also dealing with it can provide much comfort and emotional support.

Third, cyber support can be especially important for people who are extremely introverted, shy, or prone to loneliness (Segrin, 1998). For people who have difficulty initiating social activity and making friends, relationships developed online many be the primary means of receiving supportive and comforting messages. Finally, supportive communication online is easier to manage. As comforters, we can carefully choose our words and craft our messages so that they comply with the guidelines for effective comforting. And, unlike our face-to-face relationships, as people seeking support, we can choose when to enter and exit comforting interactions in cyber space. Our privacy is not likely to be invaded by well-meaning people whose comfort we do not want.

Gender and Cultural Similarity and Differences in Comforting

It is popular to believe that men and women differ in the value they have for emotional support, with the common assumption that women expect, need, and provide more comfort. One view holds that men and women differ intrinsically in needing comfort, while another view holds that their differences are due to how they have been socialized. Yet, in a recent article, Burleson (2003, p. 572) reports on a growing body of research indicating that both men and women of various ages place a high value on emotional support from their partners in a variety of relationships (siblings, same-sex friendships, opposite-sex friendships, and romantic relationships). Studies also find that men and women have similar ideas about what messages do better and worse jobs of reducing emotional distress. Both men and women find messages that encourage them to explore and elaborate on their feelings to provide the most comfort.

Unfortunately, while both men and women value other-centered comforting messages, research has also found that men are less likely to use other-centered messages when comforting. According to Kunkel and Burleson (1999), this suggests that "we need more efforts directed at enhancing men's abilities in the comforting realm—both in school and in the home" (p. 334).

Research has also been directed to understanding cultural differences in comforting. While studies have found some differences, Burleson reports (2003, p. 574) that for members of all social groups, solace strategies, especially other-

what would you do?

A Question of Ethics

Danny, who had been living with his parents for the two months following graduation from college, spent much time alone and at home. Many of his old friends had left town, and he had not met many new people. One Friday, Sharon, one of his co-workers, invited him to a party she was attending. He told his mom that he would be out, but probably would not be too late because he wasn't feeling that well.

The party turned out to be great. Danny met a lot of new people and really enjoyed their company. It was 3 in the morning when four of the people he'd met asked him to join them for a while at an all-night coffee shop. Once there, the group got into a heated political discussion. It was nearly 5 A.M. when Danny finally headed home.

At about noon he awoke and went downstairs to get something to eat. His mother was working in the kitchen, and he noticed she had dark circles under her eyes. "How you doing today, Mom?"

"If you must know, I barely slept last night. I was worried sick about you. What time did you get in anyway?"

"I don't know, 5 or so. Look, Mom, you can't worry about me all the time. I was having a good time for the first night since I've been home. You know, I've been really lonely around here and would think that you'd be glad that I was out with people my own age."

"Oh, so that's all the appreciation I get. Your father and I aren't any fun, huh?"

"That's not what I said—"

"We don't charge you rent, we feed you, and this is the thanks we get? I'm sorry I'm not as good as some college friends, but the least you could have done was call."

"I thought about calling," he lied, "but it was after one o'clock and I didn't want to wake you. Of course I do appreciate what you've done and are doing for me. Can't you understand, though, how I must feel? I'm a grown man and I need some space."

"Fine, maybe you better start looking for your own 'space', then. But if you are going to live here, you have to respect that I worry about you and

can't have you out at all hours of the night. You are disrespectful and...."

"Mom, this is ridiculous. We shouldn't be having this conversation now—you're tired, and I just got up. I'm not thinking clearly or expressing myself well. Can we talk about this later?"

"Whatever, Danny. You'll have your own way like always. But if you get into an accident or something next time, don't expect me to be there to pick up the pieces."

With that, his mother stormed out of the room. Danny was left with a cold piece of toast, wondering how his mother had misinterpreted everything he had said.

1. What ethical interpersonal guidelines did Danny and his mother violate during their conversation?

2. How was Danny responsible for what happened? His mother? What could either of them have said or done to make the situation easier?

centered messages, are the most sensitive and comforting ways to provide emotional support. Burleson mentions four differences that have been found in studies. (1) European Americans, more than other American ethnic groups, believe that openly discussing feelings will help a person feel better. (2) Americans are more sensitive to other-centered messages than are Chinese. (3) Both Chinese and Americans view avoidance strategies as less appropriate than a direct approach, but Burleson's Chinese respondents saw these as more appropriate than the Americans did. (4) Both Chinese and American married people viewed the emotional support provided by their spouse to be the most important type of social support they received.

Overall, it appears that we are more than likely different when it comes to our desire to be supported by our partners and what types of messages we find to be emotionally comforting.

Summary

Responding with understanding and comforting others begins with being able to empathize. Empathy is shown through empathic responsiveness, perspective taking, and sympathetic responsiveness. When we have empathized, we are in a position to provide emotional support and comfort. Empathizing requires detecting and identifying feelings of others. We can increase our ability to empathize through caring and concentrating. Empathizing is especially difficult with strangers and/or across cultures.

Supportive responses are comforting statements that reassure, bolster, encourage, soothe, console, or cheer up another. We can be supportive of another's positive feelings and experiences as well as comforting others in difficult situations. Supportive messages provide comfort when they provide a conversational environment that encourages the other to talk about and make sense of the situation that is causing them distress.

Effective comforting or supportive messages show a desire to help others, to express acceptance, to demonstrate care, to show availability, to be an ally, and to acknowledge feelings, as well as to express sympathy.

Although we can attempt to comfort a person with a single statement, supportive interactions often go through the four phases of support: activation, support provision, target reaction, and helper response.

Research has identified the specific supportive message skills of clarifying supportive intentions, buffering face threats with positive and negative facework, using other-centered messages, framing, and giving advice. Online support groups may be one way of achieving understanding and comfort. The desire to be comforted appears to be universal, with little substantial differences reported between men and women.

Inter-Action Dialogue:
RESPONDING AND COMFORTING

Providing emotional support to someone requires empathizing, clarifying your supportive intentions, positive and negative facework, use of other-centered messages, framing, and advice giving. Use your Inter-Action CD to view the dialogue between James and Rob and analyze the comforting behaviors of each.

     A transcript of James and Rob's conversation is printed below. You can analyze the conversation online using the Inter-Action Analysis feature on your CD. From the Dialogue page, click "Analysis for James and Rob" to compare your comments to the analysis provided by the authors.

Rob and James meet after class.

CONVERSATION

ROB: *Hey man, what's up? You look rough.*

JAMES: *Well, I'm not feeling very good. But I'll get by.*

ROB: *Well, tell me what's bothering you—maybe I can help. I've got the time.*

JAMES: *Come on—you've got better things to do than to listen to my sad story.*

ROB *(sitting down and leaning toward James): Hey, I know you can take care of it yourself, but I've got the time. So humor me, spill it. What's got you so down?*

JAMES: *It's my old man.*

ROB: *Uh huh.*

JAMES: *You know I hardly ever see him, what with him living out west and all.*

ROB: *That's hard.*

JAMES *(lowering his voice and dropping his head): And, you know, I thought that now that my mom remarried and has a whole bunch of stepkids and grandkids to take care of that maybe I could go out to California to college and, you know, live with my dad.*

ROB: *Yeah, that's understandable. So, did you call him? What did he say?*

JAMES: *Oh, I called him and he said it was fine. Then he said we "could share expenses." Share expenses? I can't even afford the bus ticket out there. And I was hoping he'd pay for the college.*

ROB: *Ouch.*

JAMES: *Rob, my dad's always had lots of money. Been living the good life. At least that's what he's been telling me all these years. He never sent the support money, but that's because he said he was "building his business." My mom's always been putting him down, but I believed him. Now I don't know what to think. What a fool I was.*

ROB: *Hey, you're no fool. Why wouldn't you believe him? But it sounds like he's been lying to you, and now you're really disillusioned. Is that it?*

JAMES: *Yeah, I guess. You know, I always thought that when I was a man the two of us could, you know, get together. I love my mama. She's my hero. She raised me. But I always was proud of my dad with his business and all, and I just wanted to spend time with him. Get to know him.*

ROB: *I can relate. My dad died when I was young, but I'd sure like to have known him better. So have you told your mom about any of this?*

JAMES: *No.*

ROB: *What do you think she'd say?*

JAMES: *Oh, she'd probably just hug me and tell me to let it be.*

ROB: *Can you do that?*

JAMES: *Maybe.*

ROB: *Do you want my advice?*

JAMES: *Sure, why not.*

ROB: *Well, it's your decision, and I'm sure that there are other ways to handle it, but my advice is, do what your mom says—let it go. If he wants to see you, let him call you. You've got a great family here.*

JAMES: *Maybe you're right. I'm so tired of being let down. And my stepdad is a good guy. He's been taking me to the gym and we play a little ball in the driveway. He's not my dad, but even with all the other kids around, at least he makes time to be with me. I guess getting close to my dad is just not meant to happen. And I guess I don't really need him. If he can't even help with college then why would I want to leave here? I mean, I have great friends … right?*

ROB: *Right.*

Chapter Resources

Communication Improvement Plan: Responding

Would you like to improve your use of the following skills discussed in this chapter?

Empathizing

Clarifying supportive intentions

Positive facework

Negative facework

Other-centered messages

Framing

Giving advice

Pick a skill and write a communication improvement plan. You can find a communication improvement plan worksheet on our website at www.oup.com/us/interact

Key Words

Skill Practice

Skill Practice exercises challenge you to master the material you have read in this chapter. For additional Skill Practice activities, visit our website at www.oup.com/us/interact

BUFFERING FACE THREATS

Choose one of the following situations and write a multiturn script in which you use the five skills of supportive messages to comfort the speaker. Identify which message skills are present in each of your turns.

1. Your best friend walks into the restaurant, flops down in the booth, and sighs, "My manager is trying to fire me or get me to quit. He told me that my error rate was higher than average so he wants me to drive all the way downtown to headquarters and take another ten hours of training on my own time."

2. As you turn the corner at work, you spy your co-worker, Janet, leaning against the wall, silently sobbing into her hand.

3. Your sister (or brother) storms in the front door, throws her (or his) backpack on the floor, and stomps upstairs. You slowly follow.

Inter-Act with Media

CINEMA

Marc Forster (Director). (2004). ***Finding Neverland.*** Johnny Depp, Kate Winslet, Julie Christie, Dustin Hoffman, Freddie Highmore.

Brief Summary: The movie is about how J. M. Barrie befriended a family that helped him to create the story of Peter Pan. In the course of his developing friendship with Sylvia and her children, Barrie comes to learn much about himself and his relational needs. He learns how to offer comfort to young Peter and to his mother, Sylvia.

IPC Concepts: The film is an excellent way of illustrating the various aspects of understanding the pain that others suffer and how to offer valid and respectful forms of comfort. The triangle of Barrie, Sylvia, and Peter is filled with relational bonding, pain, and joy. Barrie's efforts to comfort mother and son also help the grandmother and the other children through very painful experiences.

Chris Weitz and Paul Weitz (Directors). (2002). ***About a Boy.*** Hugh Grant, Nicholas Hoult, Toni Collette, Rachel Weisz, Sharon Small.

Brief Summary: This film tells the story of Marcus, a young English boy in search of what he describes as "backup" for the relationships in his life. His mother is an emotionally unstable person who tries to commit suicide. She also tries to mold Marcus into a modern version of her youthful dreams of being a hippy. Consequently, Marcus encounters a great deal of abuse and isolation at school. He meets Will, an irresponsible and immature man who lives off the proceeds of his father's famous Christmas song. Will teaches Marcus how to be cool and more accepted among his peers. Marcus helps Will to grow into a responsible adult. In the process, they both find "backup."

The movie is based on a popular novel by British author Nick Hornby.

IPC Concepts: The movie illustrates various approaches to understanding and comfort, some effective, some ineffective. Will tries to appear supportive in a group of single mums so that he can find dates with vulnerable women more easily. He illustrates how easy it can be for a manipulative person to appear to be understanding and comforting. On the other hand, Will also learns how to comfort Marcus at multiple points in the story. He must help save the boy's fragile and endangered ego.

WHAT'S ON THE WEB

Comforting a Dying Person

> http://endoflifecare.tripod.com/Caregiving/id117.html
>
> **Brief Summary:** This is a short but helpful site on the kind of things to say to and to do with someone who is dying.
>
> **IPC Concepts:** Empathy, respect, comforting strategies.

Amy Patterson Neubert. *Comforting Skills Crucial in Female Relationships*

> http://www.medicalnewstoday.com/medicalnews.php?newsid=25601
>
> **Brief Summary:** This article examines the role of comforting strategies in light of Brant Burleson's research as it applies to female relationships.
>
> **IPC Concepts:** Comforting strategies.

sharing personal information:
SELF-DISCLOSURE AND FEEDBACK

After you have read this chapter, you
should be able to answer these questions:

- What do we mean by self-disclosure?
- How do we balance self-disclosure and
  privacy?
- What are cultural and gender differences in
  disclosure and privacy?
- What are guidelines for appropriate self-
  disclosure?
- When and how does one describe feelings?
- How does one own feelings and opinions?
- Why and how does one manage privacy?
- Why and how does one ask for feedback?
- How does one provide constructive criticism
  and praise?

> "Solomon, you seemed a bit frustrated with my cousin James at lunch today. You were so quiet. Didn't you like being with him?"
>
> "Not really. He's not one of my favorite people."
>
> "What? You've never told me you don't like James."
>
> "Well, . . . No, I guess I never did."
>
> "We've been married more than ten years and I'm just now learning that you don't like James."
>
> "Well, I'm sorry, Janelle," Solomon said sheepishly.
>
> "Are there other things that you haven't told me?"
>
> "Well, probably."
>
> "Solomon—why aren't you telling me about these things?"
>
> "Well, I don't know, Janelle. I guess I didn't think it was worth disappointing you."
>
> "Disappoint me? I am more disappointed that you don't tell me how you actually feel. Every Saturday for all these years we have had lunch with James and you never mentioned that you didn't like him. You know what's ironic? I've never really liked James. As a kid, he was mean to me, and now I don't enjoy his sarcasm. I only continued these lunches because I thought you really enjoyed talking with him about the stock market."
>
> "Janelle, why didn't you ever tell me that you didn't like James?"
>
> "Well, uh, . . ."

Poor Solomon and Janelle—all those years! But is their experience all that unusual? Do we take the time to tell others what we're really thinking and feeling? For a lot of people, the answer is a resounding no.

As you have read in Chapter 3, self-disclosure and feedback are means of deepening relationships because it is through these exchanges that people learn more about themselves and each other. As you disclose, you move information from the "secret" area of your Johari window to the "open" pane. Similarly, when your partner gives you feedback, information that is in the "hidden" area moves into the open area. As two people disclose and provide feedback to each other, they increase the intimacy of the relationship. Yet many of us don't really understand when self-disclosure is appropriate and how to share our feelings effectively with others. Similarly, we sometimes refrain from providing others with our observations about their behavior because we don't want to hurt their feelings or don't know how to begin politely.

Because the self-disclosure and feedback processes are fundamental to healthy relationships, in this chapter we explain these concepts and elaborate on the skills associated with each. More specifically, we discuss balancing self-disclosure and privacy, cultural differences in disclosure and privacy, owning feelings and opinions, describing feelings, and ways to maintain privacy. We conclude the chapter by discussing ways to ask for feedback and to give feedback to others.

Take this short survey to learn something about yourself. You should be thinking of a specific target person when completing this survey. Answer the questions based on your first response. There are no right or wrong answers. Just be honest in reporting your true behavior and feelings in this relationship. For each question, select one of the following numbers that best describes your behavior or your views about your partner's behavior.

1 = Strongly agree	2 = Agree somewhat	3 = Neutral	4 = Disagree somewhat	5 = Strongly disagree

_____ **1.** I often talk about my feelings.

_____ **2.** I often reveal undesirable things about myself.

_____ **3.** I can show my innermost self.

_____ **4.** I do not hesitate to disclose personal things about myself.

_____ **5.** I feel safe in sharing any personal information.

_____ **6.** My partner shares personal information with me.

_____ **7.** My partner reveals personal feelings to me.

_____ **8.** I am completely sincere in revealing my own feelings.

_____ **9.** My partner expresses personal beliefs and opinions.

_____ **10.** I can be honest about anything.

This is a test of your self-disclosure in a relationship.

SCORING THE SURVEY: Add all of your scores for the ten items. Your total score will range from 10 to 50. The lower (closer to 10) your score, the more you and your relational partner engage in self-disclosure. The higher (closer to 50), your score, the less you and your relational partner engage in self-disclosure.

Self-Disclosure

Developing and maintaining relationships requires some degree of self-disclosure. In the broadest sense, **self-disclosure** is the process of revealing your biographical data, personal ideas, and feelings to another person. Statements such as "I was 5 foot 6 inches tall in seventh grade" reveal biographical information—facts about you as an individual. Usually, biographical disclosures are the easiest to make, for they are, in a manner of speaking, a matter of public record. By contrast, statements such as "I think people should have the right to die with dignity through physician-assisted suicide" disclose deeply personal ideas and reveal what and how you think. And statements such as "I get anxious when I think about what I'm going to do after graduation" disclose personal feelings. In terms of accuracy in understanding of self and others, it is this last sense in which most people think of self-disclosure—that is, revealing personal information that the other person does not know.

Self-disclosure—divulging biographical data, personal ideas, and feelings.

Balancing Self-Disclosure and Privacy

Self-disclosure is the heart of what is called social penetration theory. The term *social penetration* was coined by Irwin Altman and Dolman Taylor (1973). Initially, they thought that in a relationship the patterns for self-disclosure moved steadily from shallow disclosures to deeper, more personal ones. Their research, however, has shown that levels of self-disclosure are cyclical. Relational partners go back and forth between achieving greater intimacy by disclosing more and developing distance by refraining from disclosure. This cycle allows partners to manage the dialectical tension between the need for privacy and protection (or closedness) and the need to be known and connected with each other (or openness) (Altman, 1993, p. 27). So in relationships we are constantly choosing either to increase our level of disclosure or to maintain our privacy.

Why is the decision to begin self-disclosure difficult? When we self-disclose, we "give" knowledge about ourselves to someone else. Since information is power, the more someone knows about us, the greater is that person's potential to do us harm. So, for most of us, deeper disclosures occur only when we have developed trust that the other person will not use what we have disclosed to hurt us. This is why we disclose biographic and demographic information early in a relationship and more personal information in a more developed relationship (Dindia, Fitzpatrick, & Kenny, 1997, p. 408).

Although knowing a person better may well result in closer interpersonal relations, learning too much too soon about a person may result in alienation. If what we learn about another person causes us to lose trust in the person, our affection is likely to wane—hence the saying "Familiarity breeds contempt." Because some people fear that their disclosures could have negative rather than

Through self-disclosure, people move their relationship from non-intimate levels to deeper, more personal ones.

positive consequences for their relationships, they refrain from disclosing.

So, although self-disclosure can help people become more intimate with each other, unlimited self-disclosure may have negative effects. By far the most consistent finding of the research on self-disclosure is that self-disclosure is most positive when it is reciprocated (Berg & Derlega, 1987, p. 4). That means that each partner in a relationship should engage in approximately the same amount of self-disclosure.

It is equally important to decide when not to disclose and when to disclose in a relationship. Managing self-disclosure must be balanced with managing privacy, not only in developing relationships, but in long-term relationships as well. Privacy is the right of an individual to keep biographical data, personal ideas, and feelings secret. **Managing privacy** is a conscious decision to withhold information or feelings from a relational partner. Individuals may chose privacy over self-disclosure for many legitimate reasons including protecting another person's feelings, avoiding unnecessary conflict, helping another save face, and protecting the relationship.

For example, imagine that Will knows that his partner Celeste gets extremely anxious about their financial security. In the past, Celeste's worrying has caused her to lose weight and sleep over minor unpaid bills. If Will hears through the grapevine that, as a result of a merger with another company, there is a slight possibility that he will lose his job, he may decide not to disclose this information to Celeste unless this rumor is confirmed. Will's decision to keep this information private is based on his desire to protect Celeste from what may turn out to be unnecessary anxiety. In a few weeks, Will learns that his job is secure. His conscious decision to maintain privacy with Celeste will have paid off. But if he had found out that he would be laid off, he would have had to decide when and how to disclose the bad news to Celeste.

While appropriate self-disclosure generally deepens a relationship, there are times when by maintaining privacy we may avoid certain disclosures in order to enhance a relationship. Studies have shown that one of the most common disclosure problems in relationships is expressing complaints about one's partner too freely (Petronio, 2002).

inter-act with

Technology

Conduct a computer search (Google, Lycos, etc.) for a chat room that asks for your personal opinions or feelings on a topic that interests you. After spending some time interacting on the site, stop and ask yourself about your own self-disclosure. How honest were you? Did you disclose more or less online than you would have disclosed in a face-to-face discussion of the same topic? What might account for the differences in your self-disclosure levels? Have you ever used a false identity in a chat room or on a blog? If so, why? ■

Managing privacy—making a conscious decision to withhold information or feelings from a relational partner.

Cultural and Gender Differences

Culture. Some people, by virtue of their culture, gender, or family upbringing, may have distinct privacy rules or boundaries, while other people are generally quite flexible and open with information. As we might expect, the level of dialectical tension created by disclosure differs from culture to culture. People from formal cultures value privacy and are less likely to disclose personal information to social acquaintances or casual friends. The level of formality in a culture can be seen in how people dress and the forms of address they use as well as the use of self-disclosure. Germany, for instance, a country that is like the United States in many ways, has a much higher degree of formality. Germans are likely to dress well even if just visiting friends or going to school. They also use formal titles in their interactions with others. And they have fewer close friends. A German proverb states, "A friend to everyone is a friend to no one." Japan is another country that has a much higher degree of formality than the United States. The United States is considered an informal culture (Samovar & Porter, 2001, p. 82). As a result, Americans tend to disclose more about themselves than people from other cultures.

Particularly in the beginning stages of a cross-cultural friendship, differences in openness and closedness can easily lead to misperceptions and discomfort. For instance, a person from the United States may perceive an acquaintance from England as reserved or less interested in pursuing a "genuine" friendship because the Briton doesn't reciprocate personal disclosure. Yet the English person may see the American's disclosures as inappropriate, discourteous, or embarrassing. When we understand how cultures vary in what is viewed as appropriate disclosure behavior, we can vary our level of disclosure so that it fits the situation.

Gudykunst and Kim report that across cultures, despite cultural differences about what types of disclosure are appropriate at a particular stage of relationship, when relationships become more intimate, self-disclosure increases. In addition, these researchers found that the more partners disclosed to each other, the more they were attracted to each other and the more uncertainty about the other was reduced (Gudykunst & Kim, 1997, p. 325).

Gender. Consistent with what you might expect, women tend to disclose more than men, are disclosed to more than men, and are more aware than men of cues that affect their amount of self-disclosure (Reis, 1998, p. 213). In their discussion of differences in disclosure, Pearson, West, and Turner (1995, p. 164) suggest that women may disclose more because they are expected to (a kind of self-fulfilling prophecy), because self-disclosing is more important to women, and because the results are more satisfying to women. Interestingly, both men and women report that they disclose more intimate information to women (Stewart, Cooper, Stewart, & Friedley, 1998, p. 110).

Differences in learned patterns of self-disclosure can create misunderstandings between men and women, especially in intimate relationships. In *You Just Don't Understand*, Deborah Tannen (1990, p. 48) argues that in their disclosure patterns men are more likely to engage in **report-talk** (sharing information, displaying knowledge, negotiating, and preserving independence), while women engage in **rapport-talk** (sharing experiences and stories to establish bonds with others). When men and women fail to recognize these differences in disclosure patterns, the stage is set for misunderstandings about whether the partners are being truly open and intimate with each other.

As with all discussions of culture and gender differences, we should remember that individuals can and do vary from the norm behavior that is exhibited by members of their group. So you may have an English friend who is very open and easily discloses personal information, or a girlfriend who is closed and values her privacy.

Report-talk—sharing information, displaying knowledge, negotiating, and preserving independence.

Rapport-talk—sharing experiences and stories to establish bonds with others.

Guidelines for Appropriate Self-Disclosure

The following guidelines will help you manage the dialectical tensions surrounding openness and closedness as you make decisions about making a self-disclosing statement.

1. **Self-disclose the kind of information you want others to disclose to you.** When people are getting to know others, they begin by sharing information that they see as normally shared freely among people in that type of relationship in that culture. At early stages in a relationship this might include information about interests such as sports, music, TV shows, movies, and schools, and views of current events. One way that people signal that a relationship may be moving to a deeper level is when one partner takes a risk and discloses something that would normally be perceived as more appropriate to a more intimate relationship. This disclosure "tests" a new level. If after some time the other person has not reciprocated, then the disclosing partner should reassess the potential for a deeper relationship.

2. **Self-disclose more intimate information only when you believe the disclosure represents an acceptable risk.** There is always some risk involved in disclosing, but as trust in the relationship grows, you may perceive that disclosing more revealing information is less threatening and, therefore, the risk becomes acceptable. Incidentally, this guideline explains why people sometimes engage in intimate self-disclosure with bartenders, and with people they meet in travel or online. Indeed, rapid or exaggerated intimacy has been found to be a feature of online relationships (Rabby & Walther, 2003). People may perceive such disclosures as safe (representing reasonable risk) because the cyber acquaintance either does not know them or is in no position to use the information against them.

3. **Continue intimate self-disclosure only if it is reciprocated.** Research confirms that people expect a kind of equity in self-disclosure (Derlega,

the gray zone

Topic Avoidance

In newly developing relationships and in relationships that are changing in type or intimacy, people tend to avoid certain topics for the sake of protecting the relationship. For instance, if a casual dating relationship seems to be moving toward greater emotional attachment, the relational partners will, for a certain period of time, avoid communicating on topics such as the state of the relationship, expectations of each other in the relationship, prior romantic relationships, and extra-relationship activity (Knobloch & Carpenter-Theune, 2004). Because of the relational uncertainty, the partners engage in topic avoidance. They will purposely evade communication on these topics until there is a clearer sense of the nature of the relationship. Imagine the embarrassment of disclosing to a relational partner that you care enough to define this relationship as a committed, exclusive dating one if she is still thinking in terms of casual dating. Such disclosure could harm the relationship beyond repair. The tendency to avoid topics related to defining the relationship makes sense and is an effective communication strategy when parties face relationship uncertainty. Of course, partners cannot avoid such disclosures forever. Rather, they will subtly seek to find a mutually satisfactory time to engage in such self-disclosure. ■

Metts, Petronio, & Margulis, 1993, p. 33). When it is apparent that self-disclosure will not be returned, you should limit the disclosures you make. Lack of reciprocity usually means that the other person does not wish for the relationship to become more intimate.

4. **Move self-disclosure to deeper levels gradually.** Listening to another's self-disclosure can be as threatening as disclosing, so it may create unsettled dialectical tension for people when disclosures continually exceed their preferences for the relationship. Over time, if a relationship matures, disclosure of very personal information is likely to be less threatening.

5. **Reserve the most personal and sensitive self-disclosure for ongoing intimate relationships.** Disclosures about your fears, past indiscretions, and intimate secrets are appropriate in very close, well-established, long-term relationships. People who disclose highly personal information to casual acquaintances are likely to be viewed as overly personal, and their disclosures may damage relationships. Making such disclosures before a bond of trust is firmly established risks alienating the other person. Moreover, people are often embarrassed by and hostile toward others who try to saddle them with personal information in an effort to establish a relationship where none exists.

Skills for Self Disclosure and Privacy Management

In this section we explain two skills you can use as you form self-disclosure messages. We also describe two strategies and one skill you can use to maintain your privacy when you are being pressured to disclose something you do not want to share.

Owning Feelings and Opinions

Owning feelings or opinions (crediting yourself)—making "I" statements to identify yourself as the source of a particular idea or feeling.

A basic skill of self-disclosure, **owning feelings or opinions** (or crediting yourself), means making "I" statements to identify yourself as the source of a particular idea or feeling. An "I" statement can be any statement that uses a first-person pronoun such as *I, my, me,* or *mine.* "I" statements help the listener understand fully and accurately the nature of the message. Consider the following paired statements:

"Advertising is the weakest department in the corporation."	"I believe advertising is the weakest department in the corporation."
"Everybody thinks Collins is unfair in his criticism."	"It seems to me that Collins is unfair in his criticism."
"It's common knowledge that the boss favors anything that Kelly does."	"In my opinion, the boss favors anything Kelly does."
"Nobody likes to be laughed at."	"Being laughed at embarrasses me."

Instead of owning their feelings and opinions and honestly disclosing them as such, people often express their thoughts and feelings in impersonal or generalized language or attribute them to unknown or universal sources. Why do people use vague referents to others rather than owning their ideas and feelings? There are two basic reasons.

1. **To strengthen the power of their statements.** Saying "Everybody thinks Collins is unfair in his criticism" implies that anyone who doubts the statement is bucking the collective evaluation of countless people. Of course, not everybody knows and agrees that Collins is unfair. In this instance, the statement really means that one person holds the belief. Yet a speaker who thinks that his or her feelings or beliefs will not carry much power may feel the need to cite unknown or universal sources for those feelings or beliefs.

2. **To escape responsibility.** Similarly, people use collective statements such as "everybody agrees" and "anyone with any sense" to escape responsibility for their own feelings and thoughts. It seems far more difficult for a person to say, "I don't like Herb" than to say, "No one likes Herb."

Being both accurate and honest with others requires taking responsibility for our own feelings and opinions. We all have a right to our reactions. If what you are saying is truly your opinion or an expression of how you really feel, let others know and be willing to take responsibility for it.

Describing Feelings

At the heart of intimate self-disclosure is sharing your feelings with someone else. And sharing feelings is a risky business. Yet, all of us experience feelings and have to decide whether and how to deal with them. Obviously, one option is to withhold or mask our feelings. But if we decide to disclose our feelings, we can display them or we can describe them.

Masking Feelings. The concealment of verbal or nonverbal cues that would enable others to understand the emotions that a person is actually feeling is considered unhealthy and is generally regarded as an inappropriate means of dealing with feelings. The behavior of masking feelings is exemplified by the good poker player

Masking feelings—concealing verbal or nonverbal cues that would enable others to understand the emotions that a person is actually feeling.

skill builders

OWNING FEELINGS AND OPINIONS

SKILL	USE	PROCEDURE	EXAMPLE
Making an "I" statement to identify yourself as the source of an idea or feeling.	To help others understand that the feeling or opinion is yours.	When an idea, opinion, or feeling is yours, say so.	Instead of saying, "Maury's is the best restaurant in town," say, "I believe Maury's is the best restaurant in town."

who develops a "poker face"—a neutral look that is impossible to decipher, always the same whether the player's cards are good or bad. To take another example, suppose Jerome feels very nervous when Anita stands over him while he is working on a report. When Anita says "That first paragraph isn't very well written," Jerome begins to seethe, yet his expression remains impassive and he says nothing.

Habitually masking feelings leads to a variety of physical problems, including heart disease, as well as psychological problems such as anxiety and depression. Moreover, people who withhold feelings are often perceived as cold, undemonstrative, and not much fun to be around.

When is masking your feelings appropriate? When a situation or relationship is inconsequential, you may well choose to mask your feelings. For instance, a stranger's inconsiderate behavior at a party may bother you, but there is often little to be gained by disclosing your annoyance. You don't have an ongoing relationship with the person, and you can deal with the situation simply by moving to another part of the room. At the other extreme, you might want to mask your feelings in situations where disclosing them would represent an unreasonable risk to your physical or emotional well-being. In the example of Jerome seething at Anita's behavior, however, masking could be costly to both parties because Jerome's feelings of irritation and tension are likely to affect a working relationship as well as Jerome's well-being.

Displaying Feelings. Displaying feelings is the expression of feelings through facial reactions, body responses, or paralinguistic reactions. Although displays of feelings may be accompanied by verbal messages, the feelings themselves are acted out in the nonverbal behavior. Spontaneous cheering over a great play at a sporting event, howling when you bang your head against the car doorjamb, and grinning widely when you get a perfect score on an exam are all displays of feelings.

Displaying feelings—expressing feelings through facial reactions, body responses, or paralinguistic reactions.

We display feelings through facial reactions, body responses, or paralinguistic reactions. What differences do you detect in the emotions being expressed by these two people?

Since displays of feeling often serve as an escape valve for very strong emotions, they can be a more healthy approach to feelings than masking because at least we "get them out of our system." Unfortunately, negative emotional displays can damage our relationships and cause stress in our relational partners and may on occasion rise to the level of verbal abuse. Since most people are not able to read other's emotional displays with consistent accuracy, there also can be room for misunderstandings when it comes to displaying feelings. Rather than just display our emotions, we can use the self-disclosure skill of describing feelings to help us communicate our feelings with others.

In most situations, **describing feelings,** which is the skill of naming the emotions you are feeling without judging them, increases the likelihood of having a positive interaction and decreases the chances of creating defensiveness. Moreover, when we describe our feelings we actually can teach other people how to treat us by explaining how what has happened has affected us. This knowledge gives our relational partners information that they can use to help us deal with our emotions. For example, if you tell Paul that you enjoy it when he visits you, your description of how you feel should encourage him to visit you again. Likewise, when you tell Tony that you are annoyed that he borrows your jacket without asking, he is more likely to ask the next time. Describing your feelings allows you to exercise a measure of control over others' behavior simply by making them aware of the effects their actions have on you.

Many times people think they are describing their feelings when they are actually displaying feelings or evaluating the other person's behavior. For instance, an outburst like "Who the hell asked you for your opinion?" is a display of feelings, not a description.

Simply beginning a sentence with "I feel" may not result in a description of feelings. In many cases such statements actually evaluate, blame, or scapegoat someone or something. Consider a statement that starts "I feel like you insulted me when you said. . . ." While the speaker may believe that he has described a feeling, this statement blames. So the use of "I feel" doesn't automatically lead to a description of an emotional state. Stop and think—if a person says something that you perceive as insulting, how might you *feel?* Perhaps you feel hurt, rejected, or betrayed. If so, then the descriptive statement might be "I feel hurt (or rejected, or betrayed) when you say. . . ." Notice how this statement would describe a particular feeling. Let's look at one more example. Suppose that your brother screamed at you for something you did. If you said, "I feel that you're angry with me," your statement echoes what the other person said, but does not describe your present feelings. To describe your feelings, you might say, "When you talk to me in an angry tone of voice, I feel scared (or hurt, pained, distressed)."

Sometimes we don't effectively describe our feelings because we lack the active vocabulary of words that describe the various feelings we experience. We may experience anger; however, we may not be able to verbalize the distinctions between feeling angry and feeling annoyed, betrayed, cheated, crushed, disturbed, envious, furious, infuriated, outraged, or shocked. Each of these words describes a slightly different feeling, related to but distinct from anger. Table 9.1 lists a surprising

Describing feelings—naming emotions you are feeling without judging them.

Table 9.1 A list of more than 200 words that can describe feelings

Words related to *Angry*			
agitated	annoyed	bitter	cranky
enraged	exasperated	furious	hostile
incensed	indignant	infuriated	irked
irritated	mad	offended	outraged
peeved	resentful	riled	steamed

Words related to *Helpful*			
agreeable	amiable	beneficial	caring
collegial	compassionate	constructive	cooperative
cordial	gentle	kindly	neighborly
obliging	supportive	useful	warm

Words related to *Loving*			
adoring	affectionate	amorous	aroused
caring	charming	fervent	gentle
heavenly	passionate	sensitive	tender

Words related to *Embarrassed*			
abashed	anxious	chagrined	confused
conspicuous	disconcerted	disgraced	distressed
flustered	humbled	humiliated	jittery
overwhelmed	rattled	ridiculous	shame faced
sheepish	silly	troubled	uncomfortable

Words related to *Surprised*			
astonished	astounded	baffled	bewildered
confused	distracted	flustered	jarred
jolted	mystified	perplexed	puzzled
rattled	shocked	startled	stunned

Words related to *Fearful*			
afraid	agitated	alarmed	anxious
apprehensive	bullied	cornered	frightened
horrified	jittery	jumpy	nervous
petrified	scared	shaken	terrified
threatened	troubled	uneasy	worried

Words related to *Disgusted*			
afflicted	annoyed	nauseated	outraged
repelled	repulsed	revolted	sickened

Table 9.1 A list of more than 200 words that can describe feelings—cont'd

Words related to *Hurt*			
abused	awful	cheated	deprived
deserted	desperate	dismal	dreadful
forsaken	hassled	ignored	isolated
mistreated	offended	oppressed	pained
piqued	rejected	resentful	rotten
scorned	slighted	snubbed	wounded

Words related to *Belittled*			
betrayed	defeated	deflated	demeaned
diminished	disparaged	downgraded	foolish
helpless	inadequate	incapable	inferior
insulted	persecuted	powerless	underestimated
undervalued	unfit	unworthy	useless

Words related to *Happy*			
blissful	charmed	cheerful	contented
delighted	ecstatic	elated	exultant
fantastic	giddy	glad	gratified
high	joyous	jubilant	merry
pleased	satisfied	thrilled	tickled

Words related to *Lonely*			
abandoned	alone	bored	deserted
desolate	discarded	empty	excluded
forlorn	forsaken	ignored	isolated
jilted	lonesome	lost	rejected
renounced	scorned	slighted	snubbed

Words related to *Sad*			
blue	crestfallen	dejected	depressed
dismal	dour	downcast	gloomy
heavyhearted	joyless	low	melancholy
mirthless	miserable	moody	morose
pained	sorrowful	troubled	weary

Words related to *Energetic*			
animated	bold	brisk	dynamic
eager	forceful	frisky	hardy
inspired	kinetic	lively	peppy
potent	robust	spirited	sprightly
spry	vibrant	vigorous	vivacious

number of words for the feelings we experience. If you are to become more effective in describing your feelings, you may first need to work to develop a more complete "vocabulary of emotions."

The ability to describe feelings requires us to develop three skills. (1) Identify what has triggered the feeling. A trigger is anything that causes a feeling or reaction. The feeling results from some behavior, so it is important to identify the behavior. (2) Mentally distinguish what you are feeling—name the emotion; be specific. This sounds easier than it sometimes is. When people experience a feeling, they will sometimes display it without thinking about it. To describe a feeling, you must be aware of exactly what you are feeling. Table 9.1 provides a vocabulary of emotions to help develop your ability to select the specific words that describe them. (3) Verbally state the specific feeling.

Here are two examples of describing feelings:

> *"Thank you for your compliment [trigger]; I [person having the feeling] feel gratified [the specific feeling] that you noticed the effort I made."*
>
> *"When you criticize my cooking on days that I've worked as many hours as you have [trigger], I [the person having the feeling] feel very resentful [the specific feeling]."*

To begin with, you may find it easier to describe positive feelings: "You know, taking me to that movie really cheered me up," or "When you offered to help me with the housework, I really felt relieved." As you gain success with positive descriptions, you can try describing negative feelings attributable to environmental factors: "It's so cloudy; I feel gloomy," or "When we have a thunderstorm, I get really anxious." Finally, you can move to negative descriptions resulting from what people have said or done: "When you step in front of me like that, I really get annoyed," or "When you use a negative tone of voice while saying that what I did pleased you, I really feel confused."

Managing Privacy

There are several reasons that people may choose to maintain privacy. First, they might believe that disclosure, especially about their true feelings, will make them

skill builders
DESCRIBING FEELINGS

SKILL	USE	PROCEDURE	EXAMPLE
Putting emotional state into words.	For self-disclosure; to teach people how to treat you.	1. Indicate what has triggered the feeling. 2. Mentally identify what you are feeling—think specifically. Am I feeling hate? Anger? Joy? 3. Verbally own the feeling. For example, "I'm (name the emotion)."	"As a result of not getting the job, I feel depressed and discouraged." "Because of the way you stood up for me when I was being put down by Leah, I'm feeling very warm and loving toward you."

too vulnerable. It is true that if you tell people what hurts you, you risk their using the information against you, should they decide to hurt you on purpose. So it is safer to act angry than to be honest and describe the hurt you feel; it is safer to appear indifferent than to share your happiness and risk being made fun of. Nevertheless, when you keep your feelings and ideas to yourself, you risk having others misunderstand you.

For instance, if Pete calls you by a derogatory nickname that embarrasses you, and you tell Pete that you're embarrassed, Pete has the option of continuing to call you by that name. But if he cares about you, he is likely to stop. On the other hand, if you don't describe your feelings to Pete, he's probably going to continue calling you by that name simply because he doesn't realize that you don't like it. By saying nothing, you may have inadvertently reinforced his behavior. While the level of risk varies with each situation, you are more likely to improve a healthy relationship by disclosing than to damage it.

Second, some people avoid disclosure out of fear that if they share their personal stories, ideas, and real feelings, others will judge them or make them feel guilty. At a tender age, we all learned about "tactful" behavior. Under the premise that "the truth sometimes hurts," we learn to avoid the truth by not saying anything or by telling "little" lies. Perhaps when you were young, your mother said, "Don't forget to give Grandma a great big kiss." At that time, you may have blurted out, "Ugh—it makes me feel yucky to kiss Grandma. She's got a mustache." If your mother then responded, "That's terrible—your grandma loves you. Now you give her a kiss and never let me hear you talk like that again!" you probably felt guilty for having this "wrong" feeling. Yet the thought of kissing your grandmother did make you feel "yucky," whether it should have or not. In this case, the issue was not your having the feelings but the way you talked about them.

Third, some people fear that disclosure will cause harm to others or to the relationship. There are disclosures that will do harm to relationship partners and to the relationship itself. Prematurely disclosing intimate information about yourself can quickly short-circuit a relationship. For example, if Jerri is recovering from substance abuse, her disclosure of information on a first date may cause her partner to re-evaluate any thought of becoming further involved. But at times we have an overblown perception of our own potency and the effect that our disclosures can have on others.

There are two strategies that you can use when you are being pressed to disclose something that you are not comfortable sharing.

1. **Change the subject.** If your partner has made a disclosure and seems to want you to make a parallel disclosure that would involve information you are unwilling to share, introduce a different topic. For example, when Pat and Eric are leaving economics class, Pat says to Eric, "I got an 83 on the test, how about you?" If Eric does not want to disclose his grade, he might simply say, "Hey, that's a B. Good going. Did you finish the homework for calculus?"

2. **Tell a "white lie."** You probably have heard that a white lie is a false or misleading statement that is acceptable when telling the truth would embar-

rass you or your partner and when the untruth will not cause serious harm to either person or to the relationship. So when Pat asks Eric about his grade on the test, Eric might respond, "I'm not sure. I got a few tests back this week."

While changing the subject and telling "white lies" may be strategies that work in one-time situations, the skill of establishing a boundary enables you to verbally confront a attempt to violate your privacy and to help your partner understand your privacy needs. So when Pat asks Eric about his test grade, Eric might reply, "I know that everyone's different and I don't mean to be rude, but I don't ask other people about their grades and I prefer not to discuss my own." When someone asks you a question about yourself that you do not want to answer: (1) Determine why you are choosing not to share the information. (2) Identify a policy statement related to your choice. (3) Form an "I"-centered message in which you briefly establish a boundary by telling the person of the policy and that you wish to keep that information private.

Asking for Feedback

We can deepen our relationships and gain self-knowledge by asking our relational partners for feedback. Just as self-disclosure moves information from the secret to the open part of a Johari window, feedback moves information from the hidden to the open pane. We can seek information from others in order to identify our strengths and weaknesses or to correct our mistakes. Although the most obvious way of getting feedback is to ask for it directly, people are often reluctant to do so because they feel threatened or embarrassed. Instead, people rely on others' nonverbal cues. Yet even when we interpret nonverbal cues accurately, they fail to help us understand why our behavior generated the reaction it did. Nor will such cues help us decide what changes are needed in order for us to improve. By using the verbal skill of asking for feedback, we can accomplish both these objectives.

So, how do you prepare to receive feedback from others?

1. **Think of feedback as being in your best interest.** No one likes to be criticized, and some people are embarrassed by praise; but through feedback we often learn and grow. When you receive a different appraisal from the one you expected, you have learned something about yourself that you did not previously know. Whether you will do anything about the feedback is up to you, but feedback you have solicited allows you to consider aspects of your behavior that you might not have identified on your own.

2. **Before you ask, make sure that you are ready for an honest response.** If you ask a friend "How do you like this coat?" but actually want the friend to say that the coat is attractive on you, you are not being honest. Once others realize that when you request an appraisal you are actually fishing for a compliment, honest appraisals will not be forthcoming.

3. **If you take the initiative to ask for feedback, you will avoid surprises.** Taking the initiative in asking for feedback prepares you psychologically to deal with what is said.

The following steps will increase the likelihood that people will give you the kind of feedback that you want and really need to hear.

1. **Specify the kind of feedback you are seeking.** Rather than asking very general questions about ideas, feelings, or behaviors, ask specific questions. If you say, "Colleen, is there anything you don't like about my ideas?" Colleen is likely to consider this a loaded question. But if you say, "Colleen, do you think I've given enough emphasis to the marketing possibilities?" you will encourage Colleen to speak openly to the specific issue.

2. **Try to avoid negative verbal or nonverbal reactions to the feedback.** Suppose you ask your roommate how he likes your rearrangement of the furniture. If when he replies "It's going to be harder for everyone to see the TV when we have people over to watch a DVD," you get an angry look on your face and exclaim, "Well, if you can do any better, you can move the furniture!" your roommate will quickly learn not to give you feedback even when you ask for it.

3. **Paraphrase what you hear.** By paraphrasing the feedback, you ensure that you do not over-generalize from what has been said.

4. **Show gratitude for the feedback you receive.** Regardless of whether what you heard makes you feel good or bad, thank people for their feedback.

skill builders — ASKING FOR FEEDBACK

SKILL	USE	PROCEDURE	EXAMPLE
Asking others for their reaction to you or to your behavior.	To get information that will help you understand yourself and your effect on others.	1. Outline the kind of feedback you are seeking. 2. Avoid verbal or nonverbal negative reactions to criticism. 3. Paraphrase what you hear. 4. Give positive reinforcement to those who take your requests seriously.	Lucy asks, "Tim, when I talk with the boss, do I sound defensive?" Tim replies, "I think so—your voice gets sharp and you lose eye contact, which makes you look nervous." "So you think that the tone of my voice and my eye contact lead the boss to perceive me as defensive?" "Yes." "Thanks, Tim. I've really got to work on this."

Giving Personal Feedback

Sometimes in our interactions and relationships it is appropriate to comment on another person's behavior by giving personal feedback.

In some relationships we will need to consider carefully whether it is our place to give feedback; in other relationships we may be expected or required to provide it. For example, you may weigh whether it is your place to tell a friend that she has had too much to drink. But if you are a bartender in a state with dramshop laws, giving patrons this type of feedback will be part of your job. Similarly, managers, parents, social workers, and others are expected to give personal feedback to employees, children, and clients. So, improving our skills in giving feedback to others about both their positive behaviors and accomplishments and their negative behaviors will have broad use.

There are three skills that we use to give personal feedback. First, effective feedback includes describing behavior. Second, when we highlight positive behavior and accomplishments, we give praise. Third, when we identify negative or harmful behavior, we can provide constructive criticism.

Describing Behavior

When giving feedback many of us have a strong impulse to form our messages around generalized conclusions and evaluations we have reached based on what someone has said or done. So, it is common to overhear feedback like "You're so stupid," "Don't act like a jerk," or "You're really cool." These statements and countless others like them are attempts to provide feedback to the other person, but as stated these messages are evaluative and vague.

Describing behavior—accurately recounting the specific actions of another without commenting on their appropriateness.

Rather than evaluating behavior, effective feedback uses the skill of **describing behavior**—accurately recounting the specific actions of another without commenting on their appropriateness. When we describe behavior, we hold ourselves accountable for our observations and any resulting conclusions we have drawn. Consider the following situation. Steve and you are discussing the performance of the college football team. After you have interrupted Steve for the third time, he could say either "You're so rude with your interruptions" or "Do you realize that you interrupted me three times before I had the chance to finish a sentence?" Which form of feedback would you feel better about receiving? The first message is a clearly an evaluative generalization, and most of us would be embarrassed and might even become defensive upon hearing it. The second message is an accurate description of our behavior. Since most of us already know that interrupting is not "good form," this feedback, describing the behavior but not voicing an evaluation of it, is more sensitive to the interrupter's face needs and so evokes less embarrassment and defensiveness.

In other cases, feedback messages that evaluate rather than describe can be frustrating to the receiver. For example, telling someone "You didn't really do a good job of leading that meeting" is not helpful, since the message doesn't inform the recipient about the specific behaviors that led to your impression. As a result, the recipient doesn't know how to change in order to improve. A statement that describes the behavior is more helpful. For example, "Sandy, the meeting lasted an hour longer than was planned. People kept bringing up and discussing topics that weren't on the agenda, but you didn't do anything to steer us back to the business at hand."

Describing behavior seems simple but can be very difficult to do, since it requires us to move backward in the perceptual process. While we may base our evaluations on a generalized perception, describing behavior requires us to identify the specific stimuli on which our general perception was based. Steve may have concluded quickly that your interruptions fit the pattern that he associates with the category "rude." But in order to describe your behavior, he must recall and verbalize the exact actions that led him to this conclusion.

The following guidelines will help you describe behavior: (1) Identify the generalized perception you are experiencing. (2) Recall the specific behaviors that have led you to this perception. (3) Form a message in which you report only what you have seen or heard without judging its appropriateness.

The skill of describing behavior is useful in a variety of feedback situations. Once you have described someone's behavior, you may want to voice your reaction to the behavior. When your reaction is positive, you can send messages of praise; when your reaction is negative, you can provide constructive criticism. As you will learn in Chapter 11, describing behavior also is used when you wish to work collaboratively to resolve an interpersonal conflict.

Giving Constructive Criticism

Research on reinforcement theory has found that people learn faster and better through positive rewards such as praise, but there are still times when you will want to give personal feedback on behaviors or actions that are negative. While it's best

skill builders   DESCRIBING BEHAVIOR

SKILL	USE	PROCEDURE	EXAMPLE
Accurately recounting the specific actions of another without commenting on their appropriateness.	Holding ourselves accountable for our observations and any resulting conclusions we have drawn.	1. Identify the generalized perception you are experiencing. 2. Recall the specific behaviors that led you to this perception. 3. Form a message in which you report only what you have seen or heard without judging its appropriateness.	Instead of saying "She is such a snob," say "She has walked by us three times now without speaking."

Constructive criticism—describing the specific negative behaviors or actions of another and the effects that these behaviors have on others.

to give this type of feedback when a person specifically asks for it, we sometimes need to address behaviors of people who haven't asked for feedback. **Constructive criticism** is describing the specific negative behaviors or actions of another and the effects that these behaviors have on others.

Although the word *criticism* can mean "harsh judgment," the skill of constructive criticism is not based on judgment. Rather, it is grounded in empathy and understanding. When we give another constructive criticism, our intention is to help. So we should begin by trying to empathize with the person and by forecasting how he or she will react to the feedback. Then we should work to formulate a message that accurately communicates our meaning while attending to the face needs of the message recipient. Unfortunately, most of us are far too free in criticizing others and not really all that constructive. At times we overstep our bounds by trying to help others "become better persons" even when they aren't interested in hearing from us. Even when the time is right for giving negative feedback, we may not always do a good job of expressing it. While research shows that well-given feedback can actually strengthen relationships and improve interactions, feedback that is not empathically grounded or is poorly understood is likely to hurt relationships and lead to defensive interactions (Tracy, Dusen, & Robinson, 1987).

In order to be effective in providing constructive criticism, you should adopt the following guidelines:

1. **Begin by describing the behavior.** Describing behavior lays an informative base for the criticism and increases the chances that the person will understand what led to your conclusion. Feedback that is preceded with detailed description is less likely to be met defensively. Your description shows that you are focusing on the behavior rather than attacking the person, and it identifies what needs to change. For example, suppose DeShawn asks "What do you think of my presentation of a fund-raising plan for the fraternity?" Instead of saying "It's not going to make us much money," a constructive critic might say, "Well, I think the idea of the guys doing spring cleanup work for a daily fee is really creative, but I think the plan to have us sell magazines could be a problem. The rowing team just did that last month and only made one-third of their goals. They found that college students don't have extra money for magazine subscriptions. " This criticism does not attack DeShawn's self-concept, and it tells him what specifically may need to change.

THE BUCKETS reprinted by permission of United Feature Syndicate, Inc.

2. **Whenever possible, preface a negative statement with a positive one.** One way to address the face needs of the recipient is to begin your comments by praising some related behavior. Of course, common sense suggests that superficial praise followed by crushing criticism will be seen for what it is. But criticism that is prefaced with valid praise can reduce defensiveness. Recall in the preceding situation the comment, "I think the idea of the guys doing spring cleanup work for a daily fee is really creative." Here the praise that is provided is relevant and balances the negative feedback that follows.

3. **Be as specific as possible.** The more specifically you describe the behavior or the actions you are going to criticize, the more effectively a person will be able to understand what needs to change and how to change it. In our example, it would not be helpful to say, "Some of your ideas won't work." This comment is so general that DeShawn would have no idea of what you believe needs to change.

4. **When appropriate, suggest how the person can change the behavior.** Since the focus of constructive criticism is helping, it is appropriate to provide the person with suggestions that might lead to positive change. So in responding to DeShawn's request for feedback, you might also have added, "Maybe we could find out what school supplies or personal care products are most often purchased and sell those instead." By including a positive suggestion, you not only help the person, you also show that your intentions are constructive.

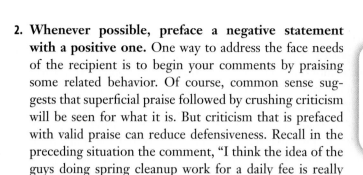

observe & analyze

Expressing Criticism

Think about the last time you criticized someone's behavior. Which, if any, of the guidelines for constructive feedback did you follow or violate? If you were to do it again, what would you say differently? ■

skill builders   **GIVING CONSTRUCTIVE CRITICISM**

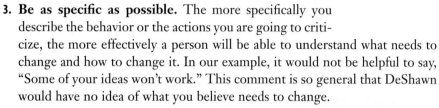

SKILL	USE	PROCEDURE	EXAMPLE
Describing the specific negative behaviors or actions of another and the effects that these behaviors have on others.	To help people see themselves as others see them.	1. Describe the person's behavior accurately. 2. Preface negative statements with positive ones if possible. 3. Be specific. 4. When appropriate, suggest how the person can change the behavior.	Carol says, "Bob, I've noticed something about your behavior with Jenny. Would you like to hear it?" After Bob assures her that he would, Carol continues, "Although you seem really supportive of Jenny, there are times when Jenny starts to relate an experience and you interrupt her and finish telling the story."

Praising

Too often, the positive things people say and do or the accomplishments that they achieve are not acknowledged by others. Yet, as you'll recall from our earlier discussion of self-concept, our view of who we are—our identity—as well as our behavior, is shaped by how others respond to us. Praise can reinforce positive behavior and help another to develop a positive self-concept. By praising we can provide to others feedback affirming that what they have said or done is commendable.

Praise—describing the specific behaviors or accomplishments of another and the positive effects that this behavior has on others.

Praising messages describe the positive behaviors or accomplishments of another and the specific effects on others of such behavior. When we praise, our compliments are sincere and reflect our positive perception of the behavior or accomplishment. When we praise, our sole purpose is to inform others, not to get on their good side or to manipulate them.

For praise to be effective, we focus the praise on specific behaviors and accomplishments and word the message to be consistent with the significance or value of the accomplishment or behavior. If a child who tends to be forgetful remembers to return the scissors he borrowed, that behavior should be praised so that it is reinforced. Saying "You're so wonderful, you're on top of everything" reinforces nothing, because this is an overly general statement that doesn't identify the particular behavior or accomplishment. An effective praise message might simply say something like, "Thanks for putting the scissors back where they belong—I really appreciate that." This response acknowledges the accomplishment by describing the specific behavior and the positive feeling of gratitude that the behavior has caused. Following are two more examples of appropriate praising.

Praise should focus on a specific action and be in keeping with the value of the accomplishment.

BEHAVIOR: *Sonya selected and bought a group wedding present for a friend. The gift is a big hit.*

PRAISE: *"Sonya, the present you chose for Steve was really thoughtful. Not only did it fit our price range, but Steve really liked it."*

ACCOMPLISHMENT: *Cole receives a letter inviting him to a reception at which he is to receive a scholarship award for academic accomplishments and community service work.*

PRAISE: *"Congratulations, Cole. I'm so proud of you! It's really great to see that the effort you put into studying, as well as the time and energy you have devoted to the Second Harvest Food Program and Big Brothers, is being recognized and valued."*

While praising doesn't "cost" much, it is valuable and generally appreciated. Not only does praising provide information and acknowledge the worth of another person, but it can also deepen a relationship by increasing its openness. To increase the effectiveness of your praise, use the following guidelines: (1) Make note of the specific behavior or accomplishment that you want to reinforce. (2) Describe the specific behavior and/or accomplishment. (3) Describe the positive feelings or outcomes that you or others experience as a result of the behavior or accomplishment. (4) Phrase your response so that the level of praise appropriately reflects the significance of the behavior or accomplishment.

skill builders   PRAISE

SKILL	USE	PROCEDURE	EXAMPLE
Describing the specific positive behaviors or accomplishments of another and the effects that the behaviors have on others.	To help people see themselves positively.	1. Make note of the specific behavior or accomplishment that you want to reinforce. 2. Describe the specific behavior and/or accomplishment. 3. Describe the positive feelings or outcomes that you or others experience as a result of the behavior or accomplishment. 4. Phrase the response so that the level of praise appropriately reflects the significance of the behavior or accomplishment.	"Marge, that was an excellent writing job on the Miller story. Your descriptions were particularly vivid."

A Question of Ethics

The Local Employee Fraud Team (LEFT) was a newly formed task force comprising four women and two men: bright, career-minded employees whose job it was to design a system to uncover theft on the job for the Comptel Corporation. Their effectiveness hinged on their ability to work closely and secretly. Obviously, each member of the team had to be completely trusted by the others or else the project could fail.

Maria Sanchos, a Mexican American graduate of Yale Law and new member of the company, was excited to be assigned to such an important task force. She put in long hours and found the company of most of her associates pleasant. However, Theresa Waterson, the leader of the group, had the social skills of the stereotypical queen bee, and Maria could not figure out why she, of all people, had been appointed to head the project. Occasionally, Theresa would make statements that were colored with stereotypical biases. Maria wondered if Theresa really knew how the statements were affecting her; and increasingly, she found herself angered by Theresa's views on issues of affirmative action and abortion, even though they had nothing to do with the team's work. Several times Maria felt like debating Theresa on these issues, but she knew herself well enough to know that when she debated, she could be verbally cruel. The harmonious relationship of the group was at stake, and Maria would not risk the group's cohesiveness.

Although Maria was able to control herself in most settings, she began to harshly point out what she considered to be illogical thinking on Theresa's part and openly upbraided the team leader for her mistakes. When one of the men on the task force privately confronted her, she considered trusting him with her problem, yet she unconsciously feared that self-disclosure would make her seem weak, particularly to a white male. Several days later, when the two other women in the group confronted her about her behavior toward Theresa, Maria broke down and told them her problem.

1. What are the ethical issues in this case?

2. Did Maria behave ethically in this situation?

3. If you were one of the women advising Maria, what would you recommend that she do?

Summary

Self-disclosure statements reveal information about you that is unknown to others. In this chapter we have discussed balancing self-disclosure and privacy as well as cultural and gender influences on issues of disclosure and privacy. There are several guidelines that can help you decide when self-disclosure is appropriate.

Skills for self-disclosure and privacy management include owning opinions and feelings, describing feelings, masking feelings, and displaying feelings. There are several reasons for maintaining privacy, which can be accomplished through changing the subject, telling "white lies," and establishing boundaries.

Asking for feedback can deepen our relationships and provide self-knowledge. We can give personal feedback to others by describing their behavior, and by giving them constructive criticism and praise.

Inter-Action Dialogue:
SELF-DISCLOSURE

Relationships move toward friendship and intimacy through appropriate self-disclosure and feedback. Disclosure includes report-talk and rapport-talk. Effective disclosures own opinions and describe feelings. Giving effective feedback requires describing specific behavior and how it affects others. When the effects are positive, praise statements are used; when effects are negative, constructive criticism can be given. Use your Inter-Act CD to view the dialogue between Maria and Mark and analyze the comforting behaviors of each.

A transcript of Maria and Mark's conversation follows below. You can record your analysis of their behavior in the right-hand column, then complete your analysis online using the Inter-Action Analysis feature on your CD. From the Dialogue page, click "Analysis for Maria and Mark," to compare your comments to the analysis provided by the authors.

Maria and Mark have coffee after seeing a movie.

CONVERSATION

MARIA: *That was a great movie! The characters were so fascinating, and I loved the way we slowly learned about their childhood.*

MARK: *Yeah, I liked it too, but at times it hit a little too close to home.*

MARIA: *Really? How do you mean?*

MARK: *Well, remember how as a little guy he spent so much time alone?*

MARIA: *Yes, that made me feel kind of sad.*

MARK: *Oh? Well, my mom and dad both had full-time jobs and my dad often worked a second one as well. So since I was an only child, and we didn't have any other family here, I spent a lot of time alone.*

MARIA: *That must have been hard on you.*

MARK: *In a way, yes, but I think it helped me to become independent, resourceful, and very competitive at games and sports.*

MARIA: *Gee, I guess I understand independent, but why do you say being alone helped you to become resourceful?*

MARK: *Well, usually no one was home when I came home from school and sometimes my mom had to work late, so I had to get my own supper.*

MARIA: *So how did that make you resourceful?*

MARK: *When there were leftovers it wasn't too hard to reheat them, but when there weren't any, I'd have to scrounge around in the cupboards and fridge. I wasn't allowed to use the stove or oven—just the microwave—so I sometimes had to be really creative.*

MARIA: *Really? What did you make?*

MARK: *I was a master of microwave black beans and rice. If you're lucky I'll make them for you someday.*

MARIA: *I think I'll pass. I ate enough beans and rice when I was growing up. My mom wanted us to identify with our "heritage" so she made a big deal of cooking recipes from her childhood a couple of times a week. Unfortunately, she's not a good cook, so we got pretty sick of it. Today, my favorite take-out is Thai—now that's cuisine!*

MARK: *I've never had Thai food. What's so great about it?*

MARIA: *Well it's very spicy-hot, with lots of complex flavoring.*

MARK: *Does it have much MSG? I'm allergic to that.*

MARIA: *I don't know. Hey, back to our previous topic. You said being alone also made you competitive. How?*

MARK: *Well, since I was alone and had no friends to play with, I'd work out ways to compete with myself.*

MARIA: *Really, like what?*

MARK: *I'd play "Horse." You play basketball, don't you?*

MARIA: *Sure. But what's "Horse"?*

MARK: *Well, Horse is usually played with two or more people: One person takes a shot and if he makes it, the other person has to attempt the same shot. If he misses he gets an "h." If he makes it, then he takes a shot and his opponent now has to try to make it. the first one to get all five letters, h,o,r,s,e, loses.*

MARIA: *So how'd that make you competitive?*

MARK: *Well, I used to play against my alter ego. Only he was a lefthander! After awhile I got so I was as good lefthanded as I was righthanded. I think that's how I made first string on my high school basketball team. I'm not very fast, but I can shoot with either hand from about anywhere on the court.*

MARIA: *So spending a lot of time alone wasn't all bad.*

MARK: *No. In truth I learned to enjoy my own company and I still like to be alone a lot. In fact, I have trouble enjoying just hanging out or partying with lots of people. It kind of seems like a waste of time. I enjoy smaller groups or one-on-one time, but the party scene leaves me cold.*

MARIA: *Yes, I've noticed that when we're with the group, you don't have much to say. I used to think you thought you were better than us, but I guess I understand why you act that way now. Still, you might want to think about being more vocal. You're really an interesting guy and I think others in the group don't know how to take you.*

Chapter Resources

Communication Improvement Plan: Developing Relationships Through Self-Disclosure and Feedback

Would you like to improve your disclosure or feedback skills discussed in this chapter?

Describing feelings	Praise
Owning feelings and ideas	Giving constructive criticism
Describing behavior	Asking for criticism

Choose the skill(s) you want to work on and write a communication improvement plan. You can find a communication improvement plan worksheet on our website at www.oup.com/us/interact

FIND MORE *on the web* Additional plans @ www.oup.com/us/interact

Key Words

Self-disclosure, *p. 231*	**Owning feelings or opinions**	**Describing feelings,** *p. 239*
Managing privacy, *p. 233*	**(crediting yourself),** *p. 236*	**Describing behavior,** *p. 246*
Report-talk, *p. 234*	**Masking feelings,** *p. 237*	**Constructive criticism,** *p. 248*
Rapport-talk, *p. 234*	**Displaying feelings,** *p. 238*	**Praise,** *p. 250*

Skill Practice

FIND MORE *on the web* Additional Skill Practice @ www.oup.com/us/interact

Skill Practice exercises challenge you to master the material you have read in this chapter.

For additional Skill Practice activities, visit our website at www.oup.com/us/interact

PROVIDING FEEDBACK

For each of the following situations, write an appropriate feedback message.

1. You have been driving to school with a fellow student whose name you got from the transportation office at school. You have known him for only three weeks. Everything about the situation is great (he's on time, your schedules match, and you enjoy your conversations), except he drives ten to fifteen miles per hour faster than the speed limit, and this scares you.

2. A good friend of yours has fallen into the habit of saying "like" and "you know" more than once every sentence. While you know she has a good vocabulary and is a dean's list student, she comes across as uneducated. She is about to graduate and has begun on-campus job interviews. Thus far she has been disappointed because every employer with whom she has spoken has rejected her. She asks why you think she is having such a hard time.

3. After being on your own for five years, for financial reasons you have returned home to live with your parents. While you appreciate your parents' willingness to take you in, you are embarrassed to be living at home. Your mother has begun to treat you the way she did when you were a child. Specifically, she doesn't respect your privacy. She routinely enters your room without knocking and opens your drawers under the guise of putting away your clean clothes. Yesterday you found her looking at your bank statement, which was in an envelope on your desk. You are becoming resentful of these intrusions.

4. Your professor in this class has asked you for feedback on his or her teaching style. Based on your experience in this class, write a message of praise and one of constructive criticism.

Inter-Act with Media

CINEMA

Richard Curtis (Director) (2003). *Love Actually.* Bill Nighy, Gregor Fisher, Colin Firth, Sienna Guillory, Liam Neeson, Emma Thompson, Kiera Knightley, Laura Linney, Alan Rickman.

Brief Summary: This movie follows the lives of eight very different couples and their children as they deal with relational problems, their struggles for love and affection, and their personal responsibilities and tragedies. The story takes place during the month leading up to Christmas. Of particular note for this chapter are the relationships between Billy Mack and Joe, Daniel and his stepson, and Jamie and his Portuguese girlfriend. Mack ultimately needs to express his love for his best friend and recording engineer; Daniel needs to get his stepson to open up to him after the sudden death of the boy's mother (Daniel's wife); and Jamie and his girlfriend must learn how to bridge the language barrier so that they can disclose their true feelings for each other.

IPC Concepts: The movie is rich in all of the basics of relationships: types, communication patterns, exchange theory, need theory, and the ethical implications of how we treat those around us.

John Hughes (Director) (1985). *The Breakfast Club.* Emilio Estevez, Judd Nelson, Molly Ringwald, Anthony Michael Hall, Ally Sheedy, Paul Gleason.

Brief Summary: Five high school students spend a Saturday in detention under the supervision of an angry, disrespect-ful, burned-out teacher. We never come to know the teens' real names. We know them only as the Jock, the Princess, the Delinquent, the Brain, and the Weirdo. While initially presented as a group of stereotyped students, eventually each discloses enough information to become a real flesh-and-blood individual to the others and to the viewer. This films transcends time and generations in its ability to resonate with a wide range of age groups.

IPC Concepts: Self-disclosure, relationship building, conflict, diversity, expression of emotion.

WHAT'S ON THE WEB

Human Relations Lab 3: *Developing Self-Disclosure and Feedback Skills*

　　http://inst.santafe.cc.fl.us/~mwehr/HumanRel/3ASelfD.html

　　Brief Summary: Web site on the relational model of communication and the role of the self, disclosure, and some useful exercises.

　　IPC Concepts: Self-disclosure, response skills.

Self-Disclosure and Openness

　　http://mentalhelp.net/psyhelp/chap13/chap13i.htm

　　Brief Summary: This material is from Clayton & Tucker-Ladd's book *Psychological Self-Help,* available on the Web at the site listed. This particular chapter offers an excellent overview of the disclosure process and is a good reinforcement to this chapter.

　　IPC Concepts: Self-disclosure, guidelines, feelings, and feedback.

The Art of Self-Disclosure

　　http://inst.santafe.cc.fl.us/~mwehr/HumanRel/3cSelfD.html

　　Brief Summary: This site offers an excellent extension to the material in this chapter. It offers a good discussion of the guidelines and risks in disclosure and has a five-level exercise on self-disclosure.

　　IPC Concepts: Disclosure, guidelines, feelings, anxiety.

using interpersonal influence ethically

After you have read this chapter, you
should be able to answer these questions:

- What does it mean to influence another?

- What is interpersonal power?

- What are the sources of interpersonal power?

- What are types of persuasive messages?

- What are effective means of gaining compliance?

- What is assertiveness?

- How can you be assertive rather than passive or aggressive?

> As Chet and Marney were sitting at the table eating their breakfast, Chet looked at Marney and said, "I'm out of shaving cream. Get me some shaving cream today."
>
> "What was that?" Marney replied.
>
> "I said, 'Get me some shaving cream today.'"
>
> "Chet, 'Get me some shaving cream today' doesn't sound like a very loving husband."
>
> "Come on, you know I love you—but I need shaving cream for tomorrow."
>
> "That's the point. You need something, but you're not sounding very considerate in the way you're trying to get it. Why don't you try this, 'Hon, would you please get me some shaving cream when you go shopping today?'"
>
> Chet paused for a second, and then said, "Hon, would you please get me some shaving cream when you go shopping today?"
>
> "I'd be delighted to— in fact I'm going to the drugstore this morning," said Marney.
>
> A few minutes later, Chet looked up from his paper and said, "Get me some toothpaste, too."

Stop for a minute and think of a time you tried to get someone to do something for you. Were you successful? Did you pay any attention to thinking about how you should proceed? Did you think about how the person you were talking with might react to the way you went about it? The opening chapter vignette is an example of a lack of real consideration for another person—and it portrays a style that is all too common, even among people who say they "really care for each other." In this chapter we consider the issue of influence and how it can be achieved effectively and ethically.

Interpersonal influence is primarily concerned with symbolic efforts to preserve or change the attitudes or behavior of others (Dillard, Anderson, & Knobloch, 2002, p. 426). It is fundamental to all human relationships and part of most conversations. The most common situations for using interpersonal influence include giving advice, gaining assistance, sharing activities, obtaining permission, changing attitudes, and altering relationships (Dillard & Marshall, 2003). Therefore, understanding influence processes and learning how to use influence ethically are fundamental to effectiveness in your relationships.

Thinkers and scholars across human history, including the Greek philosophers Socrates, Plato, and Aristotle, and the Roman orator Cicero, studied and wrote about persuasion, or having influence on others. Over the years their ideas have been elaborated upon and refined. Today, the study of influence includes not only general strategies for persuasion, but also compliance gaining and assertiveness. In this chapter we will examine each of these areas. To understand influence, we begin by discussing interpersonal power, which is the potential a person has in a relationship to influence the other.

Interpersonal influence— symbolic efforts to preserve or change the attitudes or behavior of others.

Interpersonal Power in Relationships

Interpersonal power is the potential that one person has for changing the attitudes, beliefs, and behaviors of a relational partner. John French and Bertram Raven (1968) proposed that people who have strong power bases will be effective in influencing others. Research has continued to support the claim that people "who are perceived as more expert, attractive, trustworthy, and credible" are likely to be more persuasive (Tedeschi, 2001, p. 116).

Interpersonal power—a potential for changing attitudes, beliefs, and behaviors of a relational partner.

French and Raven (1968) identified five major sources of power in relationships: coercive, reward, legitimate, expert, and referent. In 1980 T. R. Hinken and C. A. Schriesheim published a study that sharpened our understanding of these sources.

Perception of Coercive Power

People have **coercive power** if they can harm their partners physically and/or psychologically, should the partners resist the influence attempt. As with other types of power, a person can have coercive power and yet never intentionally attempt to use it to influence others. Nonetheless, the potential for influence is there. This is humorously illustrated in the old vaudeville joke: "Where does a gorilla sit when it enters the room? Anywhere it wants to."

Coercive power—derives from the perception that people can harm their partners physically and/or psychologically, should the partners resist an influence attempt.

Whether a person actually tries to coerce a partner is not important. What is important is the partner's awareness that the potential is there. Thus, when we recognize that a person can harm us, we may accept their influence.

Reward Power

People have **reward power** when they are able to provide their partners with monetary, physical, or psychological benefits that the partners desire. So if children perceive that their parents will praise them for cleaning their rooms, they are likely to comply when the parents request them to do so.

Reward power—derives from providing partners with monetary, physical, or psychological benefits that the partners desire.

Your reward power is based on how much your partner values the rewards you control, how likely you are to bestow the rewards regardless of your partner's compliance with your influence attempt, and how easily your partner can obtain these rewards from someone else. For example, Wendy really wants to attend the White Stripes concert, but it has sold out (highly valued, not easily obtained elsewhere). Mitchell, her brother, has an extra ticket to this concert (physical benefit that could be provided). Wendy knows that Mitchell has several friends who would also like to go (other competitors for already scarce reward). And she knows of no one else with an extra ticket (no alternative source). Should Mitchell ask Wendy to clean up the dishes after dinner, she may comply, hoping to ingratiate herself so that Mitchell will "reward" her by taking her to the concert.

So, when the rewards you control are of great value to your partner, if your partner believes that you will not bestow the rewards unless he or she complies with your influence attempt, and if your partner does not have other sources for this reward, then there is a high probability that if you try to influence your partner he or she will comply because of the reward power you have. Likewise, if the rewards you control are not valued by your partner, if your partner believes that you will give the benefits even if he or she does not comply with your influence attempts, or if the benefit can be obtained from some other source, then you will have lower reward power.

Legitimate Power

Legitimate power—derives from using the status that comes from being elected, being selected, or holding a position to influence a partner.

People have **legitimate power** when they use the status that comes from being elected, being selected, or holding a position to influence a partner. The power is called "legitimate" since, in many situations, failure to exercise authority has legal consequences. Teachers have legitimate power with respect to their students, parents with their minor children, older siblings with their younger brothers and sisters, managers with employees, and government officials with specific constituents. So speeders stop by the side of the road when they catch sight of the flashing red light on the top of a police car. Likewise, students may complete lengthy projects because they understand that their teachers have the right to make these assignments.

Expert Power

Expert power—derives from people having knowledge that their relational partners don't have.

People have **expert power** when they have knowledge that their relational partners don't have. Expert power is both subject and relationship specific. Because of her expertise, a friend who is an attorney has the potential to influence decisions about my divorce settlement; but since she is childless, her opinions on how I should raise my kids are not persuasive.

In the classroom, which sources of power are most commonly available to professors?

We believe people who appear to know more than we do. In your classes, your instructors can influence your thinking because they usually have more subject-specific knowledge and expertise than you do. Similarly, when a physician tells you to take medication for your high blood pressure, you are probably persuaded, because your doctor has the medical knowledge and you do not.

At times we can be blinded by the perception of expert power. For instance, when shopping for clothing, a person can be intimidated into buying something by an aggressive sales associate. Salespeople, however, are not always fashion mavens; rather, they are hired to sell, and their product knowledge may be sketchy. As salespeople gain experience with a line of goods, they may acquire specific product knowledge that is valuable to their clients. We are always grateful to have a knowledgeable sales associate when we have to buy an expensive item like a TV or computer.

Referent Power

People have **referent power** when their partners are attracted to them because of their physical appearance, image, charisma, or personality. Let's face it, we want to get along with and impress those we are attracted to and like. So we are likely to allow them to influence our ideas. If your best friend raves about a movie, you are likely to go and see it. The concept of "peer pressure" acknowledges the potency of referent power for adolescents. And corporations hire celebrities to endorse products knowing that they can draw on the referent power of the star in selling their product. Thus Pepsi hired P. Diddy to advertise Diet Pepsi not because he has reward, coercive, legitimate, or expert power, but because of his referent power.

We are also attracted to those we find agreeable. Since we tend to like those who pay attention to us and treat us well, improving your interpersonal communication skills, especially your listening, supporting, and conversational skills, is likely to increase your referent power.

> **Referent power**—derives from people being attracted to others because of their physical appearance, image, charisma, or personality.

Types of Persuasive Messages

Persuasion is the skill of crafting verbal messages to influence the attitudes or behaviors of others using ethical means. It is an ethical means of influence because it relies on verbal arguments rather than force and allows others freedom to resist the influence attempt (Trenholm, 1989, p. 5). Crafting persuasive messages involves giving good reasons, presented by a credible source, in a way that arouses emotions.

> **Persuasion**—the intentional use of verbal messages to influence the attitudes or behaviors of others using ethical means.

Giving Good Reasons

Because people pride themselves on being "rational"—that is, they seldom do anything without some real or imagined reason—you increase the likelihood of persuading them if you can provide them with good reasons. **Reasons** are statements

> **Reasons**—statements that provide the basis or cause for some behavior or action.

Claims—statements of belief or requests for action.

that provide the basis or cause for some behavior or action. They answer the question "Why?" As you think about your efforts to influence, you can probably think of many times that you made a **claim** (a statement of belief or a request for action), and the person you were talking to said, in effect, "I can't accept what you've said on face value—give me some reasons!" Suppose I'm talking with a friend about movies. I might ask, "Have you seen *Napoleon Dynamite?*" If my friend says "No," I might then say, "You really need to see it." If my friend says why, I might then go on to explain, "Well, first, it's a really quirky comedy with some great slapstick scenes. And it's got a low-key sense of humor." My reasoning could be diagrammed as follows:

CLAIM: *You need to see* Napoleon Dynamite. *(Why?)*
REASON 1: *Because it's a quirky comedy with some great slapstick scenes.*
REASON 2: *Because it uses a low-key sense of humor.*

Ethically, giving reasons is important because when people are provided with a rational basis for your particular claim, they are able to weigh and evaluate for themselves the substance of the influence attempt. Then they are free to accept or reject the argument. If they deem the reasons to be good enough, they may believe that thinking or behaving in a particular way is reasonable. So they may decide to comply with what has been requested. It doesn't matter whether you're trying to persuade someone to take a specific course, select a particular restaurant, go to a particular movie, or vote for a particular candidate, they'll want to know "why?"

Now let's consider the elements of good reasons.

1. **Good reasons are relevant to the claim.** As you think of the reasons that you might give, you'll find that some reasons are better than others because they relate more directly to the issue at hand. For example, the reasons offered

You increase the likelihood of persuading people when you can provide them with good reasons.

for seeing *Napoleon Dynamite*, "quirky," "great slapstick," and "low-key sense of humor" are relevant reasons. Why? Stop and think for a moment. Ask yourself: "When people go to a movie that's supposed to be funny, what are the criteria they are likely to use in order to evaluate the comedic quality of that movie?" Quirkiness, use of slapstick, and low-key humor are likely to be criteria that people look for in comedic movies.

2. **Good reasons can be and are well supported.** So we've decided that some reasons are more relevant to making a decision than others. But can we gain belief or action solely by stating good reasons? For instance, if all I say is "You should see *Napoleon Dynamite* because it is really quirky and it has some great slapstick scenes," am I likely to convince my friend? Maybe. But it's more likely that my friend will want additional information that justifies these two reasons. So, I'll have to provide some specific support. For instance, in support of the reason "It's a quirky comedy" I might say, "Throughout the movie, Napoleon has to deal with his geeky brother and pitiful uncle who's stuck in 1982."

   Any time you're trying to persuade by using reasons, you need accurate specific information to support the reasons you present. You are likely to be most effective in using good reasons when you have expertise. In fact, the persuasiveness of your reasoning often depends on your listener's acknowledgment of your expert power.

3. **Focus on reasons that will have the greatest impact on the person(s) you're trying to influence.** We've said that you want to select relevant reasons, that is, reasons that make the most sense in terms of the subject. But there are times when you know something about your conversational partner that calls for you to give more weight to a particular reason than you ordinarily would. For instance, suppose the friend to whom I recommended seeing *Napoleon Dynamite* has a geeky, computer-nerd brother. In this case, I might want to mention that he'll love the scenes with the brother.

In summary, good reasons are relevant to the claim, can be well supported, and are meaningful to the person you're talking with.

Personal Credibility

Good, well-supported reasons alone may be persuasive, but they are even more powerful when presented by a credible source. **Credibility** is the extent to which the target believes in the speaker's expertise, trustworthiness, and likability. In effect, how persuasive you are may depend on whether your conversational partner has confidence in you as a person.

You may be able to recall times when no matter how logical the information presented to you appeared to be, you didn't believe it because you lacked confidence in the person presenting it. On the flip side, of course, are situations where people believe or do anything that a highly charismatic person asks even when that person provides no reasons or argues illogically.

Why do we *ever* allow our opinion of another to be the sole factor in important decisions? In this chapter's Spotlight on Scholars, Richard Petty, who has stud-

Credibility—the extent to which the target believes in the speaker's expertise, trustworthiness, and likability.

ied attitude change, argues that as receivers of information we follow cognitive and peripheral routes in our consideration of persuasive requests. The cognitive route requires us to weigh and consider the reasons and evidence. We often reserve this route for issues about which we are highly motivated, issues that are really important to us. We use the peripheral route for issues about which we are not motivated and believe are less important. So, although selecting a movie or a restaurant has some importance to us, we feel a need to engage in cognitive effort in making our choice. As a result, we may well rely on the word of a friend even without a great deal of support for the judgment.

Numerous research studies have confirmed that people are more likely to accept messages whose source is perceived to be credible (Chebat, Filiatrault, & Perrien, 1990, p. 165). So when we are considering how to vote on a sales tax proposal, our thinking may go something like this: "I don't want to spend the time to learn about the sales tax proposal. Since Joe is a bright enough guy and has studied the issues, and he and I think a lot alike on many other issues, I'll trust what he recommends." Generally, however, we allow others to influence us in this way only if we believe they are truly credible.

Characteristics of Credibility. Credibility is not the same as blind faith. People will consider your messages to be credible when they believe that you are competent, trustworthy, and likable.

1. **Competence.** When people seem to know what they're talking about, have good information, and are perceived as clear thinkers, we say that they are **competent.** If Alan sees his friend Gloria as unusually well informed on local political issues, Alan may be persuaded to vote for a tax levy simply because Gloria is supporting it. So, the more people perceive you as knowledgeable on a particular subject, the more likely they will pay attention to your views on that subject.

2. **Trustworthiness.** When people seem to be dependable and honest, keep the promises they have made, and are perceived to be acting for the good of others more than for self, we say that they are **trustworthy.** A speaker's intentions or motives are particularly important in determining whether others will view the person as trustworthy. For instance, if you are trying on a pair of slacks and a sales clerk you know is working on commission says to you "Wow, you look terrific in those," you may well question that person's intentions. However, if a bystander who is fashionably dressed looks over at you and comments "I wish I looked as good in those; they really fit you well," you are likely to accept the statement at face value. The bystander has no reason to say anything, so you have no reason to doubt his or her intentions. The more positively you view the intentions of people, the more credible their words will seem to you.

3. **Likability.** When people seem to be congenial, attractive, warm, and friendly, we think of them as **likable.** Until proven wrong, we tend to believe people that we like. So Ron may let Jose talk him into spending the night camping out in the desert with Jose's Cub Scout troop simply because Ron likes Jose. Scam artists are unethical operators who cultivate personal characteristics

Competence—the impression made by people who seem to know what they're talking about, who have good information and are perceived as clear thinkers.

Trustworthiness—the impression made by people who seem to be dependable and honest, who keep the promises they have made, and are perceived to be acting for the good of others more than for self.

Likability—the combination of congeniality, attractiveness, warmth, and friendliness.

spotlight on scholars

Richard Petty, Professor of Psychology, the Ohio State University, on
Attitude Change

As an undergraduate

political science major, Richard Petty got so interested in how people change their attitudes that he chose to minor in psychology, where he could not only take more courses in attitude change but also learn empirical research methods. He then decided to go on to graduate work in psychology at the Ohio State University, where he could focus on studying attitude change and persuasion. Like many scholars, the subject of his doctoral dissertation laid the foundation for a career of research. Petty chose attitude change induced by persuasive communications.

When Petty began his research, the psychological scholarship of the previous forty years had been unable to demonstrate a relationship between people's attitudes and their behavior. Petty believed that the relationship between attitude change and behavior had been obscured by the complexity of the variables involved in assessing attitude change. Now Petty is in the forefront of scholars who have demonstrated that attitude change and behavior are, in fact, related, but in a complex way.

During the last twenty years, Petty has published scores of research articles on his own and with colleagues on various aspects of influence, seeking to discover

under what circumstances attitudes affect behavior. His work with various collaborators has been so successful that he has gained international acclaim. Not only have many of his works been published worldwide, but the theory of the elaboration likelihood model of persuasion (ELM) that he developed in collaboration with John Cacioppo has become the most cited theoretical approach to attitude and persuasion.

According to the ELM theory, attitude change is likely to occur from one of just two relatively distinct "routes to persuasion." The first, central route, is through a person's careful and thoughtful consideration of the true merits of the information presented in support of a claim. The second, peripheral route, is via a simple cue in the persuasion context (such as an attractive source) that induces change without necessitating scrutiny of the central merits of the claim. Following their initial speculation about these two routes to persuasion, Petty and Cacioppo developed, researched, and refined their ELM.

The ELM is a theory about the processes responsible for attitude change and the strength of the attitudes that result from those processes. The ELM hypothesizes that what is persuasive to a person

and how lasting any attitude change is likely to be are dependent on how motivated and able people are to assess the merits of a speaker, an issue, or a position. People who are highly motivated are likely to study available information about the claim. As a result, they are more likely to arrive at a reasoned attitude that is well articulated and bolstered by information received via the central route. For people who are less motivated to study information related to the claim, attitude change can result from a number of less resource-demanding processes that do not require the effort of evaluating the relevant information. Less motivated people are affected more by information through the peripheral route, but their attitude changes are likely to be weaker in endurance. The ELM explains why some attitude changes are related to behavior but others are not. Specifically, attitude changes that result from considerable thought also result in behavior change, but attitude changes that result from simple peripheral cues (e.g., agreeing simply because the source is an expert), may not.

So what can we learn about influencing others from Petty's research? First, we must recognize that attitude change results from our choices of influence tactics in combination with the choices made by our conversational partners about how deeply they wish to probe into the information. We should strive to present rational influence strategies based on good reasons and supporting evidence when we expect that our conversational partner will think deeply about what we are saying. Likewise, we should draw on our credibility and use emotional influence factors when listener thinking is expected to be superficial.

Finally, we must remember that the attitudes changed by considerable mental effort will tend to be stronger than those that were changed after little thought.

This complexity of attitude change suggests that as communicators, we must have not only the necessary information to form well-constructed arguments but must also the artistic sense to understand important aspects of those we intend to influence and the artistic power to use available persuasive means effectively.

Where is Petty going from here? He will certainly continue working on aspects of attitude change for, as he says, "I never finish a project without discovering at least two unanswered questions arising from the research." In addition, he's interested in finding out how people behave when their judg-

ments may have been inappropriate or biased. That is, sometimes it becomes salient to people that they were inappropriately biased by the mere attractiveness of the message source rather than by the substance of what was said.

Petty teaches both graduate and undergraduate courses in attitudes and persuasion, research methods, and theories of social psychology. Petty has written scores of research articles and several books, all dealing with aspects of attitude, attitude change, and persuasion. For titles of several of his publications, see the references for this chapter at the end of the book. ■

that make them likable in order to use their credibility to persuade others to do things that are not really in the best interests of those who have been influenced.

Establishing Your Credibility. Over time, you can establish your credibility. First, you can *show* that you know what you are doing and why you are doing it—that you are competent. In contrast, if you behave carelessly, take on too many tasks at one time, and do not double-check details, you're likely to be perceived as incompetent.

Second, you can show that you care about the effects on others of what you say and do. Some people develop reputations as manipulators because, though their intentions are good, they fail to state why they behave as they do. When you don't explain your behavior, others may make wrong assumptions about your intentions. Remember, people are not mind readers. Although you can't change your character or personality on the spur of the moment, you can make your actions reflect your character and personality. For instance, if you perceive yourself as hardworking, you can give yourself totally to the job at hand. Likewise, if you are friendly or likable, you can smile when you meet strangers or offer to help people with their jobs. If people do not see you as a credible person, you may be able to change your image by improving your competence and sharing your intentions.

Third, and perhaps most important, you can establish your credibility by behaving in ways that are ethical—that is, in keeping with the standards of moral conduct that determine our behavior. When you believe strongly in the rightness of your cause, you may well be tempted to say or do anything, ethical or not, to achieve your goals. Before you succumb to such temptation, think of all the people

What qualities would you ascribe to the person talking that would cause others to see him as a credible source?

in the world who have ridden roughshod over moral or ethical principles to achieve their goals. If your credibility is important to you, then you will not want to adopt the philosophy that the end justifies the means. Even if you achieve your short-term goal, it will be at the cost of satisfying relationships with others.

How you handle ethical questions says a great deal about you as a person. What is your code of ethics? The following behaviors are essentials of ethical persuasion.

1. **Tell the truth.** Of all the aspects of trustworthiness, this may be the most important. If people believe you are lying to them, they are likely to reject you and your ideas. If they think you are telling the truth but later learn that you have lied, they will look for ways to get back at you. If you are not sure whether information is true, say so. Many times an honest "I really don't know, but I'll find out" will contribute far more to your reputation for trustworthiness than trying to deflect a comment or use irrelevant information to try to make points.

2. **Resist personal attacks against those who oppose your ideas.** There seems to be an almost universal agreement that name-calling is detrimental to your trustworthiness. Even though many people resort to name-calling in their interpersonal communication, it is still unethical.

3. **Disclose the complete picture.** People can make something sound good or bad, better or worse, by the phrasing they select, but purposely putting a favorable spin on unfavorable information is unethical. For instance,

Hector's mother asks him, "Why were you out until 3:00 A.M.?" Hector replies indignantly, "It wasn't anywhere near 3:00!" (He got in at 2:20.)

Marjorie says to Allison, "I want you to know that I was not the one who told your mother that you got a speeding ticket. I'd never do that!" What Marjorie fails to say is that she did tell Brenda, suggesting that perhaps Brenda could tell Allison's mother.

Such people may tell themselves "I did not tell a lie," but their behavior is still unethical. Messages that are perceived to be ethical are more likely to persuade.

Appeals to Emotion

Messages that give good reasons from a credible source are likely to be persuasive. But when you're trying to influence others to act, you can increase the persuasiveness of your message by appealing to people's emotions (Jorgensen, 1998, p. 403). Although people can be moved to act on the basis of well-supported reasons from credible sources, some who *believe* they should do something may be reluctant to act on their belief. For instance, Jonas may believe that people should donate money to worthy causes, but he may not do so; Gwen may agree that people should exercise for forty-five minutes, three times a week, but she may not do so. What motivates people who simply believe in something to act on that belief is often the degree of their emotional involvement. Emotions are the driving force behind action, the instrument that prods or nudges us from passive belief to overt action. So, understanding and using an emotional appeal can increase effectiveness of our persuasive messages.

The effectiveness of emotional appeals depends on the mood and attitude of the person you are persuading and the language itself. Suppose you are trying to convince your brother to loan you money so that you can buy your textbooks for the semester without waiting for your grant money to be released. In addition to your rational approach, you may want to include several appeals to his emotions. "I'm sure you remember how tough it is to understand the lectures when you haven't looked at the book," or "Mom will be on my back if I don't do well in this class," or "I know you want to be a nice guy and help your little brother here."

How can you form messages with strong emotional appeal? Focus on specific examples and experiences. Describe the examples and experiences—often you can develop your descriptions in story form. So, instead of saying "I thought you might be interested in going hiking and rock climbing with me tomorrow—it will be fun," you might say, "I thought you might be interested in going hiking and rock climbing with me. I think it will be like old times when we would spend the whole day at the gorge. Just two brothers, 'bonding.' Remember how much fun we had on the hike to Clear Creek Canyon?"

Compliance-Gaining Strategies

Whereas persuasion is the art getting others to change their beliefs or actions, compliance gaining strategies focuses others to do what you want them to do. In this section we look at specific **compliance-gaining strategies** that you may consider using in your influence attempts.

In their analysis of the research on compliance-gaining strategies, Kellerman and Cole looked at 74 different lists covering over 840 strategies (1994, p. 6). From these, they identified 64 strategies that overlapped in several studies (pp. 7–10). Dan O'Hair and Michael J. Cody (1987, pp. 286–287) looked at many of the same lists and boiled them down to the seven strategy types that we will present in this section. As you will see, each of these strategy types is based on a unique combination of reasoning, credibility, and emotional appeals.

Compliance-gaining strategies—strategies for influencing others to do what you want them to do.

Supporting-Evidence Strategies

In **supporting-evidence strategies,** which draw primarily on reasoning, a person seeks compliance by presenting reasons and/or evidence. To use this strategy, you present the reasons a person should behave as you wish. So you might say, "Let me give you what I think are the three best reasons for holding onto the job you have," or "May I borrow your curling iron for a few minutes? When I wear this outfit, I think I look a lot better with just a little curl in my hair."

Supporting-evidence strategies—strategies that draw primarily on reasoning and include all those strategies in which a person seeks compliance by presenting reasons and/or evidence.

Exchange Strategies

In **exchange strategies** a person seeks compliance by offering trade-offs. Although in an exchange strategy you do not give reasons directly, you do imply the presence of a reason. To use this strategy, you might say "I'll help you with calculus if you help me with history," or "I'll agree to the price if you'll throw in free delivery." In short, you use the negotiated element as a type of a reason: Why will I help you with calculus? Because you'll help me with history. Notice that exchange strategy is also based in credibility. Your conversational partner is likely to comply based on an exchange only if he or she believes that you will carry out your part of the exchange.

Exchange strategies—strategies in which a person seeks compliance by offering trade-offs.

Direct-Request Strategies

In **direct-request strategies** a person seeks compliance by asking another to behave in a particular way. A person might say "Can I borrow your shirt?" or "Will you lend me twenty dollars?" Direct requests generally are not accompanied by reasons. They are based primarily on credibility. In effect, they are saying, "You know me. You know I'm trustworthy and cooperative, and I will return what I have asked for." These may also take the form of suggestions, such as "Why don't you think about going out for the golf team?"

Direct-request strategies—strategies in which a person seeks compliance by asking another to behave in a particular way.

Empathy-Based Strategies

In **empathy-based strategies** a person seeks compliance by appealing to another's love, affection, or sympathy. Sometimes a persuasive statement is worded in a way that tries to show the importance of how others feel about the target of

Empathy-based strategies—strategies in which a person seeks compliance by appealing to another's love, affection, or sympathy.

the persuasion. So, a person might say "If you really loved me and respected my feelings, you wouldn't try to drive when you've been drinking," or "You know we can't get along without you, and if you don't go in for treatment we're afraid we may lose you." These statements suggest that a person should behave in a certain way because of ties based on expertise, trustworthiness, or personality. Other examples are based on showing similarity of values: "Since we're in this together, why don't we join forces?" "You and I have always looked at things the same way, so it's only logical that we do this together." "If you want to get your supervisor to pay attention to your ideas, you may want to try the approach I used with my boss." These statements are saying, "Because we have so much in common or think so highly of each other, we should behave in similar ways." Empathy-based strategies are primarily grounded in credibility and may use emotional appeal as well.

Face-Maintenance Strategies

Face-maintenance strategies—strategies in which a person seeks compliance while using indirect messages and emotion-eliciting statements.

In **face-maintenance strategies** a person seeks compliance while using indirect messages and emotion-eliciting statements. A person might say "Is there something I can get for you now?" Or to make a friend more receptive to suggestions, someone might say "You know I find you really attractive, and I think we share many of the same feelings." Or one might elicit emotions indirectly by saying "Gee, I really want to look my best tonight, but I just can't seem to get my hair to work right—I wish I had a curling iron." These messages are meant to create emotional bonds between the participants, and these bonds become the basis upon which the request is complied with. So Joan offers to lend Carol her curling iron because of her affection for her friend. Of course, in these strategies one's credibility is also being tapped. Only if Joan finds Carol likable will she have positive feelings that Carol can draw on in using a face-maintenance strategy.

Other-Benefit Strategies

Other-benefit strategies—strategies in which a person seeks compliance by identifying behaviors that benefit the other person.

In **other-benefit strategies** a person seeks compliance by identifying behaviors that benefit the other person. A person might say "I think this car is just right for the kind of driving you do," or "Ken, I think that spending a semester abroad would be a great experience for you." In these cases the kindling of emotion is tied to the meeting of interpersonal needs.

Distributive Strategies

Distributive strategies—strategies in which a person seeks compliance by threatening or making the other person feel guilty.

In **distributive strategies** one person seeks compliance by making threats or causing another person to feel guilty. To use this strategy, someone might say, "I'm only asking to borrow your curling iron for a minute, not for the rest of your life" or "You better do this for me, or you've had it." These strategies are based in negative emotional appeals and, though often successful, they are generally regarded as interpersonally unethical.

Choosing a Strategy

How should you choose a compliance gaining strategy to use in a particular situation? Miller, Cody, and McLaughlin (1994) point out that situational perceptions are highly important in making these decisions. In short, your choice depends on how effective you believe a particular strategy will be in a given situation. The better you are at assessing the situation, the more likely you are to craft a message that will be effective.

Although there is no one "best" strategy, you may find the following guidelines useful in helping you make your decision.

1. **Choose the strategy that you believe is most likely to be effective.** Your first consideration is effectiveness. Since people are unique and no strategy will work equally well for everyone, you have to think about the person you want to influence. Will this person respond more favorably to a direct or an indirect method? Will he or she appreciate a logical argument or be more likely to comply on the basis of trust in you as a person? Are you in a position to offer some reward?

2. **Choose the strategy that would best protect the relationship.** Sometimes a strategy that would work will not be good for the relationship. If the relationship is one that you want to preserve, then you will want to select a strategy that will not be perceived as manipulative. Moreover, you are likely to want to select a strategy that will be perceived as polite. For instance, if you put pressure on a person by using a threat of punishment, the person may comply but is likely to be resentful. Distributive strategies are considered to be the least polite of all strategies (Kellermann & Shea, 1996, p. 154). Sometimes failing to win compliance is better than hurting the relationship.

3. **Choose the strategy that is most comfortable for you.** Sometimes a strategy that would work without necessarily hurting the relationship may be personally uncomfortable for you. There are some persuasive strategies that are a better fit with our personal communication style. Since you are more likely to be effective with a strategy that fits you, all other things being equal, choose the one that best suits you.

In addition to these three guidelines for selecting a compliance-gaining strategy, Hample and Dallinger (2002) found that people take into consideration whether an influence strategy is too distasteful or forceful, whether using it would make them look bad or threaten the other person, and whether it is relevant to the situation at hand.

Overcoming Resistance

Not all attempts to influence will be successful. Sometimes, even when we have stated well-reasoned, credible positions that should have appealed to our partner's emotions, we will encounter resistance. As Knowles, Butler, and Linn (2001) point out, "Resistance is the most important component of any social influence attempt that fails to gain compliance" (p. 57). Too often when someone resists, our tendency is to continue to use the techniques we used in the first place. This only adds to a person's resistance. Instead of redoubling our persuasive efforts, one of the easiest ways of dealing with resistance is to ask people to elaborate on their positions. By using effective listening skills, you will hear their objections. Then you may be able to answer the objections with additional information or appeals. Some research has shown that when an initial influence attempt is unsuccessful, people tend to use follow-up messages that are more forceful, more aggressive, and sometimes ruder (Hample & Dallinger, 1998). When facing resistance to our influence, it is important that we try new strategies, without becoming too aggressive or intimidating in our style, rather than just being repetitive.

Assertiveness

Many people who understand both persuasion and compliance gaining remain ineffective at exerting influence in their relationships because they are not assertive. **Assertiveness** is the art of declaring our personal preferences and defending our personal rights while respecting the preferences and rights of others. It requires us to describe our feelings honestly or to verbalize our needs and personal rights. Assertiveness messages may include describing feelings, giving good reasons for a belief, or suggesting behaviors or positions we think are fair. Assertive statements are not exaggerations made for dramatic effect, nor do assertive statements attack another individual. We can understand the specific qualities of assertive behavior best if we contrast it with other ways of interacting when we believe our rights or feelings are in danger of being violated or ignored.

Assertiveness—the art of declaring our personal preferences and defending our personal rights while respecting the preferences and rights of others.

Contrasting Methods of Expressing Our Needs and Rights

When we believe our needs or rights are being ignored or violated by others, we can choose to behave in one of three ways: passively, aggressively, or assertively.

Passive behavior—the reluctance or failure to state opinions, share feelings, or assume responsibility for one's actions.

Passive Behavior. People behave passively when they do not state their honest opinions, do not describe deeply held feelings, or do not assume responsibility for their actions. So, passive behavior is not influential, and those who use this method end up submitting to other people's demands, even when doing so is inconvenient, is against their best interests, or violates their rights. For example, suppose that when Bill uncrates the new plasma television set he purchased at a local department store, he notices a deep scratch on the left side. If he is upset about the scratch but doesn't try to get the store to replace the expensive item, he is behaving passively.

Aggressive behavior—the lashing out at the source of one's discontent with little regard for the situation or for the feelings, needs, or rights of those who are attacked.

Aggressive Behavior. People exhibit aggressive behavior when they belligerently, violently, or confrontationally present their feelings, needs, or rights with little or no consideration for the feelings, needs, or rights of others. Aggressive messages depend on coercive power; they can be judgmental, dogmatic, or faultfinding.

learn about yourself

Take this short survey to learn something about yourself. Answer the questions based on your first response. There are no right or wrong answers. Just be honest in reporting your true behavior. For each question, select one of the following numbers that best describes your behavior.

| 1 = Strongly agree | 2 = Agree somewhat | 3 = Neutral | 4 = Disagree somewhat | 5 = Strongly disagree |

_____ **1.** I am aggressive in standing up for myself.

_____ **2.** If a salesperson has gone to a lot of trouble to show me merchandise that I do not want to buy, I have no trouble saying No.

_____ **3.** If a close and respected relative were bothering me, I would keep my feelings to myself.

_____ **4.** People do not take advantage of me.

_____ **5.** If food in a restaurant is not satisfactory to me, I complain and insist upon a refund.

_____ **6.** I avoid asking questions for fear of sounding stupid.

_____ **7.** I would rather make a scene than bottle up my emotions.

_____ **8.** I am comfortable in returning merchandise.

_____ **9.** I find it difficult to ask friends to return money or objects they have borrowed from me.

_____ **10.** If I hear that a person has been spreading false rumors about me, I confront that person and talk about it.

_____ **11.** I can yell at others when I feel that I have been wronged.

_____ **12.** I get anxious before making problem-solving business phone calls.

This is a test of your passive, assertive and aggressive behavior.

SCORING THE SURVEY: Add your scores for items 3, 6, 9, and 12. Your score will range from 4 to 20. The lower (closer to 4) your score, the more you tend to engage in passive behavior.

Add your scores for items 2, 4, 8, and 10. Your score will range from 4 to 20. The lower (closer to 4) your score, the more you tend to engage in assertive behavior.

Add your scores for items 1, 5, 7, and 11. Your score will range from 4 to 20. The lower (closer to 4) your score, the more you tend to engage in aggressive behavior.

Suppose that after discovering the scratch on his new television set, Bill storms back to the store, confronts the first salesperson he finds, and loudly demands his money back while accusing the salesperson of being a racist who had intentionally sold him damaged merchandise. Such aggressive behavior may or may not result in getting the damaged set replaced, but it will certainly damage his relationship with the salesperson. Most receivers of aggressive messages are likely to feel hurt by them (Martin, Anderson, & Horvath, 1996, p. 24). Moreover, while Bill may not care about his relationship with the salesperson, if he is prone to aggression as a means of influence, he will likely damage other, more intimate relationships.

Would you say that this person is being assertive or aggressive? What leads you to your conclusion?

Assertive Behavior. People behave assertively when they openly represent their honest opinions, needs, and rights in a manner that persuades others while at the same time respects the feelings, needs, and rights of others. The difference between assertive behavior and passive or aggressive behavior is not in how individuals feel, but rather the way in which they choose to act on various feelings or needs. If Bill chooses an assertive response upon discovering that he has bought a damaged TV, he will still feel angry. But instead of either doing nothing and living with the damaged merchandise, or verbally assaulting the clerk, Bill might choose to call the store, describe the condition of the TV set to a customer service representative, share his feelings on discovering the scratch, and state what he would like to see happen now. For instance, he might ask how to return the damaged set and get a new one. He might ask that the store send out a replacement. Bill's assertive messages should accomplish his goals without annoying or hurting anyone.

observe & analyze

Passive, Aggressive, and Assertive Behavior

For the next day or two, observe people and their behavior. Make notes of situations where you believe people behaved in passive, aggressive, and assertive ways. Which of the ways seemed to help the people achieve what they wanted? Which of the ways seemed to maintain or even improve their interpersonal relationship with others? ■

Distinguishing among Passive, Aggressive, and Assertive Responses

It is inevitable that in our interpersonal relationships we will need to assert ourselves, so it is important to learn to distinguish among passive, aggressive, and assertive responses. Let's look at several examples.

At Work. Tanisha works in an office that employs both men and women. Whenever the boss has an especially interesting and challenging job to be done, he assigns it to a male co-worker whose desk is next to Tanisha's. The boss has never said anything to Tanisha or to the male employee that would indicate he thinks less of Tanisha or her ability. Nevertheless, Tanisha is frustrated by the boss's behavior.

> PASSIVE: *Tanisha says nothing to her boss. She's very frustrated by consistently being over-looked, but makes no response.*
>
> AGGRESSIVE: *Tanisha storms into her boss's office and says, "I'm sick and tired of you giving Tom the plum assignments and leaving me the garbage jobs. I'm every bit as good a worker, and I'm not going to take this anymore."*
>
> ASSERTIVE: *Tanisha arranges a meeting with her boss. At the meeting she says, "I don't know whether you are aware of it, but during the past three weeks, every time you had a really interesting job to be done, you gave it to Tom. To the best of my knowledge, you believe that Tom and I are equally competent—you've never said anything to suggest that you thought less of my work. But when you 'reward' Tom with jobs that I perceive as plums and continue to offer me routine jobs, I'm really frustrated. Do you understand my feelings about this?" In this statement, she has described both her perception of the boss's behavior and her feelings about that behavior.*

If you were Tanisha's boss, which of her responses would be most likely to achieve her goal of getting better assignments? Probably the assertive behavior. Which of her responses would be most likely to get her fired? Probably the aggressive behavior. And which of her responses would be least likely to "rock the boat"? Undoubtedly the passive behavior—but then she would continue to get the boring job assignments.

With a Friend. Dan is a doctor doing his residency at City Hospital. He lives with two other residents in an apartment they have rented. Carl, one of the other residents, is the player of the group: It seems that whenever he has time off, he has a date. But like the others, he's a bit short of cash. He doesn't feel at all bashful about borrowing clothes or money from his roommates. One evening Carl asks Dan if he can borrow his watch—a new, expensive watch that Dan received as a present from his father only a few days before. Dan is aware that Carl does not always take the best care of what he borrows, and he is very concerned about the possibility of Carl's damaging or losing the watch.

> PASSIVE: *"Sure."*
>
> AGGRESSIVE: *"Forget it! You've got a lot of nerve asking to borrow a brand-new watch. You know I'd be damned lucky to get it back in one piece."*
>
> ASSERTIVE: *"Carl, I know I've lent you several items in the past, but this watch is special. I've had it only a few days, and I just don't feel comfortable lending it. I hope you can understand how I feel."*

What are likely to be the consequences of each of these behaviors? If he behaves passively, Dan is likely to worry the entire evening and harbor some resentment of Carl even if he gets the watch back undamaged. Moreover, Carl will

observe & analyze

Assertiveness

As you observe people, notice situations in which individuals fail to behave assertively. What kind of power were they granting to other people? What kind of power might they have really had that they didn't seem to recognize? ■

continue to think that his roommates feel comfortable in lending him anything he wants. If Dan behaves aggressively, Carl is likely to be completely taken aback. No one has ever said anything to Carl before, so he has no reason for believing that his borrowing was becoming an issue. Moreover, Dan will damage the relationship. But if Dan behaves assertively, he puts the focus on his own feelings and on this particular object—the watch. His response isn't a denial of Carl's right to borrow items, nor is it an attack on Carl. It is an explanation of why Dan does not want to lend this item at this time.

In a Social Situation. Kim has invited two of her girlfriends and their dates to drop by her residence hall suite before the dance. Shortly after the group arrives, Nick, who has come with Ramona, Kim's best friend, lights a joint, takes a drag, and passes it to Kim. Kim, who doesn't smoke, knows that if they are caught she will get kicked out of the residence hall.

> PASSIVE: *Kim takes the joint, holds it for a minute, and then passes it on.*
> AGGRESSIVE: *"Nick, that's really stupid, bringing a joint into my room. Can't anybody here have a good time without getting high? Now put out that joint before somebody notices and get out of here."*
> ASSERTIVE: *"Nick, Ramona probably didn't tell you that I don't get high and you may not know that I can get kicked out of the residence hall if you get caught. So please put the joint away."*

Again, let's contrast the three behaviors. In this case, the passive behavior is not at all in Kim's interest. Kim knows what she believes, she knows the residence hall rules, and even if no one finds out, she'll feel uncomfortable because she did nothing. But the aggressive behavior is hardly better. She knows nothing about Nick, but her outburst assumes bad intentions not only from Nick but also from her friends. If Nick is at all inclined to be belligerent, her method is only going to incite him and damage her relationship with Ramona besides. The assertive behavior accurately and pleasantly presents her position in a way that respects Nick's face need.

Characteristics of Assertive Messages

As these examples demonstrate, assertive messages draw on several of the basic interpersonal communication skills you have learned in this course. These include the following.

1. **Own ideas, thoughts, and feelings.** Because the purpose of assertive messages is to represent your position or needs, the message should include "I" statements like "I think . . . ," "I feel . . . ," and "I would like. . . ."

2. **Describe behavior and feelings.** If we want others to satisfy our needs, then we should provide them with specific descriptive information to justify our requests. We do this by describing the feelings we have and the behavior and outcomes we desire.

3. **Maintain regular eye contact and a self-confident posture.** Our nonverbal behaviors should convey our convictions. When we maintain steady eye contact, we are perceived as serious; yet it important not to stare aggressively while being assertive. Repeatedly shifting our gaze away is a sign of submissiveness. A relaxed, involved body posture will convey self-confidence.

4. **Use a firm but pleasant tone of voice.** Aggressiveness is signaled with yelling or harsh vocal tones. Assertive messages should be conveyed at a normal pitch, volume, and rate.

5. **Speak fluently.** Avoid vocalized pauses and other nonfluencies that result in perceptions that you are indecisive.

6. **Be sensitive to the face needs of the other.** The goal of assertive messages is to influence the other without damaging the relationship. Messages should be formed in ways that both meet the face needs of the other and present the needs of the speaker.

It's important to recognize that you will not always achieve your goals by being assertive. And just as with self-disclosure and describing feelings, there are risks involved in being assertive. For instance, some people will label any assertive behavior as "aggressive." But people who have difficulty asserting themselves often do not appreciate the fact that the potential benefits far outweigh the risks. Remember, our behavior teaches people how to treat us. When we are passive, people will ignore our feelings because we have taught them that they can. When we are aggressive, we teach people to respond in kind. By contrast, when we are assertive, we can influence others to treat us as we would prefer to be treated.

skill builders   ASSERTIVENESS

SKILL	USE	PROCEDURE	EXAMPLE
Standing up for yourself and doing so in interpersonally effective ways that describe your feelings honestly and exercise your personal rights while respecting the rights of others.	To show clearly what you think or feel.	1. Identify what you are thinking or feeling. 2. Analyze the cause of these feelings. 3. Choose the appropriate skills necessary to communicate these feelings, as well as any outcome you desire. 4. Communicate these feelings to the appropriate person. Remember to own your feelings.	When Gavin believes that he is being unjustly charged, he says, "I have never been charged for a refill on iced tea before—has there been a change in policy?"

Useful guidelines for practicing assertive behavior are as follows: (1) identify what you are thinking or feeling; (2) analyze the cause of these feelings; (3) choose the appropriate skills to communicate these feelings, as well as the outcome you desire, if any; and (4) communicate these feelings to the appropriate person. If you have trouble taking the first step to being more assertive, try beginning with situations in which your potential for success is high (Alberti & Emmons, 1995). In addition, try to incorporate the six characteristics of assertive behavior listed at the outset of this section.

Assertiveness in Cross-Cultural Relationships

Assertiveness is valued and practiced in Western cultures. As Samovar and Porter (2001) point out, "Communication problems arise when cultures that value assertiveness come in contact with cultures that value accord and harmony" (p. 85). Thus, as the following paragraphs demonstrate, the standard of assertiveness considered appropriate in the dominant American culture can seem inappropriate to people whose cultural frame of reference leads them to perceive it as either aggressive or weak.

Whereas North American culture is known for its assertive communication style, Asian and South American cultures value accord and harmony. For instance "to maintain harmony and avoid interpersonal clashes, Japanese business has evolved an elaborate process called 'nemawashii,' a term that means binding the roots of a plant before pulling it out. In this process, any subject that might cause disorder at a meeting is discussed in advance. Anticipating and obviating interpersonal antagonism allow the Japanese to avoid impudent and discourteous behavior" (Samovar & Porter, 2001, p. 85).

In fact, in collectivist societies, "a style of communication in which respecting the relationship through communication [is paramount] is more important than the information exchanged" (Jandt, 2001, p. 37). Jandt goes on to explain that these societies use group harmony, avoidance of loss of face to others and oneself, and a modest presentation of oneself as means of respecting the relationship. "One does not say what one actually thinks," Jandt continues, "when it might hurt others in the group" (p. 37).

On the other hand, in Latin and Hispanic societies, men, especially, are frequently taught to exercise a form of self-expression that goes far beyond the guidelines presented here for assertive behavior. In these societies, the concept of "machismo" guides male behavior.

Thus when we use assertiveness—as with any other skill—we need to be aware that no single standard of behavior ensures that we will achieve our goals. Although what is labeled appropriate behavior varies across cultures, the results of passive and aggressive behavior seem universal. Passive behavior can cause resentment, and aggressive behavior leads to fear and misunderstanding. When talking with people whose culture, background, or lifestyle differs from your own, you may need to observe their behavior and their responses to your statements before you can be sure of the kinds of behavior that are likely to communicate your intentions effectively.

A Question of Ethics

Cassandra and Pete had been very lucky. They both had well-paying jobs that they dearly loved. During college they had both worked hard and saved money so that two years after graduating they had enough money to buy a house. Their first home needed a lot of remodeling, but Cassie and Pete found that they enjoyed working together and learning how to do various projects. So far they had refinished the floors, repaired some drywall, and removed wallpaper and repainted every room in the house. Now it was time to tackle the kitchen.

The current kitchen was a mess. The cabinets were scratched and several doors were loose, the flooring was discolored and coming up in places, and the appliances were from the 1950s. The more they discussed the kitchen, the more they found that they disagreed on what needed to be done. Pete wanted them to tackle the project themselves and believed that they could make the kitchen serviceable by removing the current floor,

putting down ceramic tile, painting the current cabinets, and buying new appliances, phasing in the purchases over several years. Cassie, who loved to cook, wanted the kitchen to be the centerpiece of the home. She wanted to hire a kitchen designer to plan and execute a complete kitchen remodel. Pete adamantly refused to consider spending the twenty thousand dollars or more that this would take. Having stated his position, Pete considered the conversation over, walked out of the room, and turned on the TV. Cassandra continued talk to his retreating back until she gave up in frustration.

Several days later on their long commute to work, Cassandra decided to take a different approach. So she asked Pete, "Do you really love me?" to which Pete replied, "Of course I love you, do you really need to ask?"

"Well, I was wondering if for our anniversary we could take a couple of weeks and go to Europe? It would be expensive, but it would be such a wonderful treat."

"Hey, that's a great idea," Pete replied, "I'll talk to a travel agent tomorrow."

"Well, are you sure?" Cassandra asked, "I mean, it's going to cost a lot, since we already used up our frequent flier miles."

"Don't worry, babe, we've got the money in the bank, and you know I only live to make you happy."

"Really," Cassandra pounced, "then why can't we hire a designer and have the kitchen done first class? You know I hate to travel, but I love to cook. Why are you willing to pay for an expensive trip but not pay for my dream kitchen?"

1. What are the ethical issues that Cassandra and Pete confronted in this situation?

2. Analyze the conversation that Cassandra and Pete. Was Cassandra's approach an ethical use of interpersonal persuasion, or was it a manipulative trap?

Summary

Influence is the ability to affect people's attitudes and behaviors. Conscious efforts to influence others are accomplished through persuasion, compliance gaining, and assertiveness.

Influence is possible when people believe that they have power over their fate. Interpersonal power is the potential ability to influence another person's attitude or behavior. The sources of power are described as coercive, reward, legitimate, expert, and referent.

Persuasion is the skill of crafting verbal messages to influence the attitudes or behaviors of others through ethical means. Persuasion can be accomplished through giving good reasons, by drawing on personal credibility, and by appeals to emotion. Compliance-gaining messages can employ seven possible strategies: supporting evidence, exchange, direct requests, empathy, face maintenance, other benefits, and distributive. The choice of strategy may depend on a communicator's perception of the situation in which compliance is being sought.

Assertiveness is the skill of stating our ideas and feelings openly in interpersonally effective ways. Passive people are often unhappy as a result of not stating what they think and feel; aggressive people get their ideas and feelings heard but may create more problems for themselves because of their forcefulness. Some of the characteristics of behaving assertively are owning ideas, thoughts, and feelings; describing behavior and feelings; maintaining eye contact and a self-confident posture; using a firm but pleasant tone of voice; speaking fluently; and being sensitive to the face needs of others.

Inter-Action Dialogue:
INFLUENCE

Influence occurs when one person attempts to change another person's attitudes or actions. Consider type(s) of power exerted in influence efforts, presence of persuasion (reasons and evidence, credibility, emotional appeal), compliance-gaining strategies, and assertiveness. Use your Inter-Act CD to view the dialogue between Hannah and Paul and notice the influence behaviors of each.

A transcript of Hannah and Paul's conversation follows. You can complete an analysis online using the Inter-Action Influence Analysis feature on your CD. On the Dialogue page, click "analysis for Hannah and Paul," and compare your comments to the analysis provided by the authors.

Paul's friend Hannah stops by his dorm to show him what she has done.

CONVERSATION

HANNAH: *Hey Paul, take a look at my term paper.*

PAUL *(quickly reading the first page): Wow, so far this looks great. You must have put a lot of time into it.*

HANNAH: *No, but it should be good, I paid enough for it.*

PAUL: *What?*

HANNAH: *I got it off the Internet.*

PAUL: *You mean you bought it from one of those term paper sites? Hannah, what's up? That's not like you—you're not a cheater.*

HANNAH: *Listen—my life's crazy. I don't have time to write a stupid paper.*

PAUL: *What's stupid about the assignment?*

HANNAH: *I think the workload in this class is ridiculous. The professor acts as if this is the only class we've got. There are three exams, a team project, and this paper. What's the point?*

PAUL: *Well I think the professor assigned this paper for several reasons, to see whether students really know how to think about the material they have studied and to help us improve our writing.*

HANNAH: *Come on, we learned how to write when we were in elementary school.*

PAUL: *That's not what I said. Sure you can write a sentence or a paragraph, but can you really express your own ideas about this subject? What the professor is doing is putting us in a position not only where we show our understanding of the material, but also where we have to show our ability to phrase our thoughts in a sophisticated* *manner. By writing a term paper we have the chance to develop our own thinking about a topic. We can read a wide variety of sources and then make up our own minds and in our writing explain our thoughts. And the neat thing is, we'll get feedback about how we did.*

HANNAH: *Yes, but you're not listening—I just don't have time.*

PAUL: *So you believe the best way to deal with the situation is to cheat?*

HANNAH: *Man, that's cold. But I'm not the only one doing this.*

PAUL: *Are you saying that since some people cheat it's OK for you to cheat? Like people take drugs or sleep around so it's OK for you?*

HANNAH: *No, don't be silly, but I told you I'm up to here in work. I've got no time.*

PAUL: *Right. So remind me what you did last night.*

HANNAH: *You know. I went to Sean's party. I deserve to have a little social life. I'm only twenty after all.*

PAUL: *Sure, point well taken. So what did you do the night before?*

HANNAH: *Well, I worked until 8:00, then Mary and I grabbed a bite to eat and then went clubbing.*

PAUL: *So, for two nights you chose to do no school work, but you had time to socialize? And you're saying you're "up to here in work." Hannah, I'm just not buying it. Your workload is no different from mine. And I manage to get my work done. It's not perfect—like your Internet paper. But it's mine. So who do you hurt when you cheat? Besides your own character, you hurt me. Thanks friend.*

HANNAH: *Hey, chill. You've made your point. But what can I do now? The paper's due in two days and I haven't even begun.*

PAUL: *Do you have to work tonight?*

HANNAH: *No.*

PAUL: *Well, then you still have time. It will be a couple of long, hard days, but I'll bring you coffee and food.*

HANNAH: *What a friend. Well, OK, I guess you win.*

PAUL: *Hey wait. Let's seal it by tearing up that bought paper.*

HANNAH: *What! You mean I can't even borrow a few ideas from it?*

PAUL: *Hannah!*

HANNAH: *OK. OK. Just kidding.*

Chapter Resources

Communication Improvement Plan: Influencing Ethically

FIND MORE
on the web
Additional plans @
www.oup.com/us/interact

Would you like to improve your use of the following skills discussed in this chapter?

  Persuading

  Gaining compliance

  Assertiveness

Pick a skill and write a communication improvement plan. You can find a communication improvement plan worksheet on our website at www.oup.com/us/interact

Key Words

Skill Practice

FIND MORE *on the web* Additional Skill Practice @ www.oup.com/us/interact

Skill Practice exercises challenge you to master the material you have read in this chapter.

For additional Skill Practice activities, visit our website at www.oup.com/us/interact

DEVELOPING ASSERTIVE RESPONSES

For each of the following situations write a passive or aggressive response and then contrast it with a more appropriate assertive response.

1. You come back to your dorm, apartment, or house to type a paper that is due tomorrow, only to find that someone is using your computer.

   Passive or aggressive response:

   Assertive response:

2. You're working at a store part time. Just as your hours are up and you are ready to leave (you want to rush home because you have a nice dinner planned with someone special), your boss says to you, "I'd like you to work overtime if you would—Martin's supposed to relieve you, but he just called and can't get here for at least an hour."

   Passive or aggressive response:

   Assertive response:

3. During a phone call to your parents, who live in another state, your mother says, "We're expecting you to go with us when we visit your uncle on Saturday."

   You were planning to spend Saturday working on your résumé for an interview next week.

   Passive or aggressive response:

   Assertive response:

4. You and your friend made a date to go dancing, an activity you really enjoy. When you meet, your friend says, "If it's all the same to you, I thought we'd go to a movie instead."

   Passive or aggressive response:

   Assertive response:

Inter-Act with Media

FIND MORE *on the web* Additional media entries @ www.oup.com/us/interact

CINEMA

Roger Mitchell (Director). (2002). ***Changing Lanes.*** Ben Affleck, Samuel L. Jackson.

> **Brief Summary:** This is the story of a lawyer and a struggling small-businessman who have an accident on a New York expressway on their way to important appointments. As a result of the accident and a degree of road rage, the men try to get even with each other. Each one fails to perceive the other accurately and, consequently, each makes false assumptions about the other. Both men subsequently try to force compliance from the other as their war continues to escalate out of control to the potential ruin of both their lives.

> **IPC Concepts:** Dysfunctional approaches to influence. Both characters resort to coercion, force, violence, and every form of power to try to force compliance.

Nancy Meyers (Director). (2000). ***What Women Want.***   Mel Gibson, Helen Hunt, Marisa Tomei, Alan Alda.

Brief Summary: Nick Marshall is a chauvinistic, manipulative advertising executive. After a fluke accident, he gains the power to hear what women are actually thinking. His life-long pattern of using and manipulating women changes as he slowly learns to be more sensitive and understanding. He learns the need for honesty in his relationships.

IPC Concepts: Relationships, gender differences, meaning, message clarity, jargon, ethics.

WHAT'S ON THE WEB

Kelton Rhoads. *Ethics of Influence*

http://www.workingpsychology.com/ethics.html

Brief Summary: This wonderful site posts chapters from *Rhoads's Working Psychology: Introduction to Influence.* It contains a rich discussion of the nature of influence in personal and societal applications, tactics, and ethics.

IPC Concepts: Influence, power, tactics, ethics.

Arpana Greenwood. *Neuro-Linguistic Programming, Alaska: Ethical Influence*

http://www.conscioussolutions.com/article-ethical-influence.html

Brief Summary: This site discusses the difference between influence and manipulation. It discusses the skills and tools that can be misused to mislead others into doing things that they really do not want to do. It also explains how the study of Neuro-Linguistic Programming can serve as a form of ethical influence.

IPC Concepts: Influence, power, means of persuasion.

managing conflict

After you have read this chapter, you
should be able to answer these questions:

- What is interpersonal conflict?
- What are the five types of conflict?
- What are withdrawal, accommodating, forcing, compromising, and collaborating?
- What are destructive behaviors to avoid?
- What skills are used in initiating conflict?
- What skills are used in responding to conflict?
- What are the skills involved in mediating a conflict?

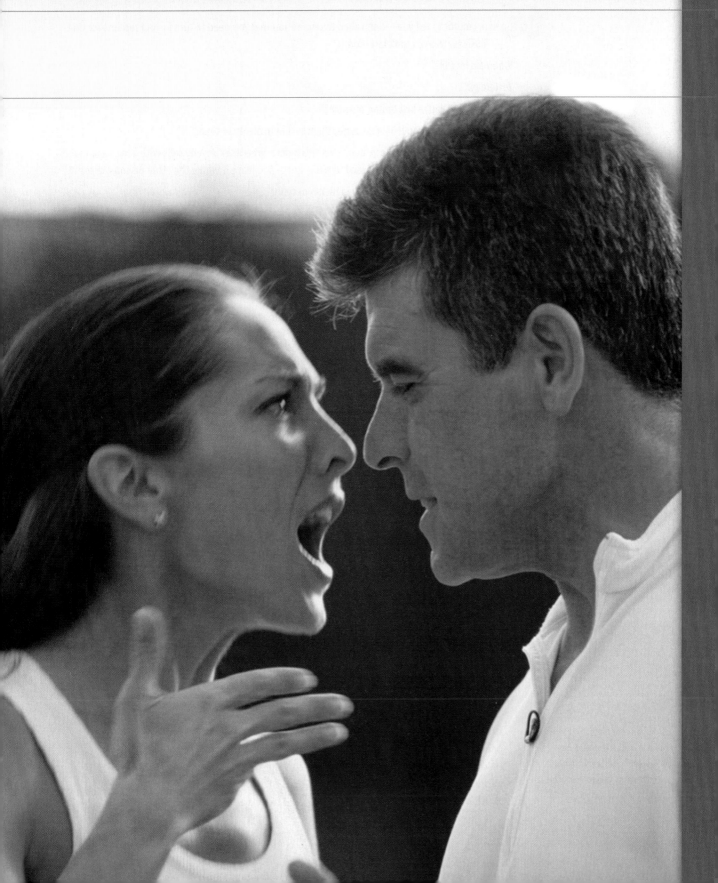

"Oh hon, I forgot to tell you—Jeff called to remind you that you need to turn in your receipts for that business trip you took last month."

"When did he call?"

"Yesterday."

"Yesterday! And you're just telling me now?"

"I told you I forgot—you'll be able to get them to him in plenty of time."

"That's not the point, Mark. We've gone over this before. Whenever anyone calls with a message that is at all important we're supposed to write a note and leave it where the other person can see it."

"Lisa, this isn't a big deal—I told you in plenty of time."

"But what if you had 'forgotten' for another couple of days? I could be in deep trouble."

"But you're not in trouble."

"Mark, that's not the issue. Remember last week you had a call from Dale about Mary being sick? I wrote you a note and put it on your planner."

"That's right, you did."

"See, if you'd just follow my lead—when I get a message for you, I write it down."

"Always?"

"Always."

"So how come this morning when I went over to Jane's for the neighborhood block watch meeting she told me that she called yesterday and told you it was canceled."

"Uh, well . . ."

"Always, huh? That's what I thought."

Sometimes in our relationships we find ourselves in serious conflict over core issues. But most of the time our conflicts occur over mundane, day-to-day issues. In either case, how we choose to deal with conflict will affect our relationships. For instance, the issue of communicating important telephone messages that Mark and Lisa are discussing may be resolved easily, or it may escalate into a serious disagreement that could damage their relationship.

Most scholars agree that conflict involves some incompatibility between people (Canary, Cupach, & Messman, 1995, p. 4). We define **interpersonal conflict** as a situation occurring when the needs or ideas of one person are perceived to be at odds with or in opposition to the needs or ideas of another.

Interpersonal conflict—a situation in which the needs or ideas of one person are perceived to be at odds with or in opposition to the needs or ideas of another.

Although many people believe that conflict is a sign of a bad relationship, the reality is that conflicts occur in all relationships. Whether conflict hurts or strengthens a relationship depends primarily on how we deal with it. Since conflict is inevitable, it should be managed in ways that maintain the relationship while satisfying important needs of both parties. As students of interpersonal communication, understanding conflict and developing conflict management skills will make you more effective in dealing with the inevitable conflict episodes you face in your relationships.

How conflict is perceived is culturally based. While you may not like conflict, in American culture, conflict is viewed as inevitable. However, in other cultures, especially in Asian cultures, conflict is viewed as dysfunctional to relationships and damaging to social face (Ting-Toomey, 2006, p. 375). In this chapter we present information that is grounded in an American perspective.

We begin by looking at types of conflict. Then we discuss five styles people use to manage conflict, indicating when each approach can be used effectively; the collaborative style is found to apply to almost any situation. Next, we describe destructive behaviors to be avoided in conflicts. Finally, we describe specific communication strategies that can be used to initiate, respond to, or mediate conflict episodes.

Types of Interpersonal Conflict

Some conflicts are easier to manage than others. When we can identify the type of conflict that is occurring, we are better equipped to manage it. Conflicts will generally fall into one of the following five broad categories.

Pseudoconflict

A **pseudoconflict** is a conflict that is apparent, not real. It occurs in a situation of apparent incompatibility between the needs or ideas of the partners.

Pseudoconflict—conflict that is apparent, not real.

A common form of pseudoconflict is **badgering**—light teasing, taunting, and mocking behavior. If badgering is a recognized part of a pair's normal interaction, then it may not signal problems to come. However, badgering becomes destructive when the unspoken goal is to goad a person into a real conflict over some other issue, or when the person being badgered is hurt.

Badgering—light teasing, taunting, and mocking behavior.

A second common form of pseudoconflict occurs when two people are confronted with goals or needs that they believe cannot be achieved simultaneously when in reality they can. For instance, Carl says, "Hey, the Bengals–49ers game is on television—I've got to see this," to which Cynthia replies, "But you said that we'd go to the park this afternoon!" Carl and Cynthia both have things they want to do, and it seems as if they are in conflict. However, with some creative adaptation it may be possible to meet both agendas. If Cynthia is willing to delay going to the park for a few hours, then Carl can watch the game; or if Carl can TiVo the game to watch later, he and Cynthia can go to the park now. In this case both parties' needs can be accommodated, so there is not a real conflict.

When the conflict is recognized to be pseudoconflict, the parties should deal with the apparent conflict before it becomes real. If they do not or cannot resolve the conflict, it may escalate and become real.

Fact Conflict

Fact conflict, often referred to as **simple conflict,** occurs when the information one person presents is disputed by the other. These conflicts are "simple" because the accuracy of the information in dispute can be verified. For example, Ken says to Marge, "Paul asked if I would go with him to the community watch meeting next Wednesday," to which Marge replies, "You can't do that; that's Parents' Night at school." "No," says Ken, "Parents' Night is the following Wednesday." At this point Marge and Ken can begin to escalate the argument into a conflict, with allusions to Ken's bad memory and Marge's acting like a know-it-all. Or, if they recognize this as a simple conflict over a fact, they can double check the dates.

If you find yourself in a conflict over a fact, agree to disengage until a source for verifying the fact can be found or until some guidelines for selecting from among competing sources can be determined.

Fact conflict or simple conflict—conflict that occurs when the information one person presents is disputed by the other.

Value Conflict

While pseudoconflicts and fact conflicts can be managed easily, when the conflict stems from differences in value systems the conflict management process is more difficult. **Value conflicts** occur when people's deeply held beliefs about what is good or bad, worthwhile or worthless, desirable or undesirable, moral or immoral are incompatible. Value conflict can occur (1) when we differ on what we believe is good or bad or (2) when we differ in the priority we assign to a value we agree on.

Suppose, for example, that Josh and Sarah are considering getting married. In their discussions, they have discovered that they have two serious areas of value conflict. First, Sarah, a conservative Jew, believes that weekly attendance at synagogue is required. Josh, who was also raised in a Jewish environment, doesn't attend temple except on major religious holidays. In this case they share a value, but each assigns it a different priority. Second, Sarah is a committed vegetarian, while Josh is an avid meat eater. Here Sarah and Josh are likely to have conflict because they value meat differently. Sarah views eating meat as socially irresponsible, while Josh sees meat as the best part of a meal.

Many times conflicts over values are not resolvable. At times we must simply be content to respect each other but "agree to disagree." However, if resolution is possible, it will begin with the recognition that the issue is a value conflict. In the Josh-and-Sarah scenario, it is important for both to realize that the other person is not "just being stubborn" or "spoiled" or "just wanting his or her own way."

Value conflicts—conflicts over the deep-seated beliefs people hold about what is good or bad, worthwhile or worthless, desirable or undesirable, moral or immoral.

Instead they must draw on the trust and mutual respect that they have established to recognize that they have incompatible values on the issues before them. Then, recognizing these differences, they may be able to discuss their emotional attachment to the issues. Once Josh and Sarah acknowledge that each of them is interested in doing what he or she thinks is "right," they can move to a respectful discussion of what to do in any specific case.

Policy Conflict

Policy conflicts occur when two people in a relationship disagree about what should be the appropriate plan, course of action, or behavior in dealing with a perceived problem. For instance, the chapter opening vignette suggests that Mark and Lisa have resolved their policy conflict over what to do about telephone messages intended for the other person.

What is perceived to be an appropriate policy is both situational and culturally based, so this type of conflict is common to most relationships. Many times conflict stems from novel situations (or problems) for which there is no existing relational policy. For instance, Tyrone and Cherise come from families that approach child rearing quite differently. Tyrone comes from a family in which children are given a lot of freedom, while Cherise comes from a family in which children's activities are closely monitored and supervised. So, Tyrone and Cherise may experience a policy conflict over whether to set a curfew for their adolescent children.

At other times policies have been agreed to, but a changing situation causes renewed policy conflict. For instance, Paul and Mary have been going out together for several months. Early on, an informal but never discussed "policy" appeared to be that Paul would pay all the expenses of their dates. Lately, however, Paul has become uncomfortable with this policy. He knows that Mary earns more than he does, and he sees their relationship escalating and expenses mounting. Thus he now sees a problem with the policy—a problem important enough to require discussion and change. Although Mary may understand the problem, her view of how to handle it may or may not agree with Paul's. If they disagree, then they will experience a policy conflict.

Because policy conflicts concern what "should" be done, there is no "right" or "wrong" way to resolve them; the policy that is followed depends on what the parties agree to. These conflicts can be successfully managed if the parties are willing to consider a plan or course of action that best deals with the perceived problem and with each party's feelings about it.

Ego Conflict

Ego conflicts occur when the people involved view "winning" the conflict as central to maintaining their positive self-image. When both people see the conflict as a measure of who they are, what they are, how competent they are, whom they have power over, or how much they know, ego conflicts occur. In these situations "winning" the conflict becomes the only means of satisfying needs.

Policy conflicts—conflicts that occur when two people in a relationship disagree about what should be the appropriate plan, course of action, or behavior in dealing with a perceived problem.

Ego conflicts—conflicts that occur when the people involved view "winning" the conflict as central to maintaining their positive self-image.

Conflicts in which values or egos are at issue often escalate. How can we manage conflicts of these types?

Ego conflicts can develop when discussion of facts or values is undermined by personal or judgmental statements. The more expert you believe yourself to be, the more likely it is that your ego will become involved when your word on your specialty is questioned. Once your sense of self-worth has been threatened, your ability to remain rational can be impaired. Before you realize it, emotions come into play, words may be said that cannot be taken back, and a conflict can be blown out of proportion.

When we recognize that we are experiencing ego conflict, we should use face work to de-escalate the conflict to the content level. For instance, suppose Grant says to Darlene, "Why are you giving me a hard time about this? We're talking about *my* family. I know a whole lot more about my brother than you ever could."

Table 11.1 Conflict types and resolution strategies

Type	Dialogue	Resolution Strategy
1. Pseudoconflict	"I've told you those pants have to go. Where's your taste?"	Recognize badgering for what it is. Don't let yourself be drawn in.
2. Fact Conflict	"We can't go to the play. I've asked Martha to come over." "Parker said that the paper has to be in today." "No, it can be turned in Tuesday."	Look for ways of meeting both needs. Stop and check the facts.
3. Value Conflict	"Tom, you've got to tell Jamison what he wants to hear." "But I don't see the world the way he does and I'm not going to say I do."	Look for areas in which both parties agree and work from there. If no agreement, may have to agree to disagree.
4. Policy Conflict	"Myrna, please write down any message you take." "Why? I remember to tell you without writing it down."	Identify the nature of the problem. Agree on a policy (a plan of action or set of behaviors) that is most likely to provide the best solution.
5. Ego Conflict	"Gloria, I don't think that this design fits the assignment." "Oh, so you think that I'm incapable of doing this job."	Look for ways to move the conflict away from an ego level and back down to a content level.

Darlene might de-escalate the conflict by replying, "Grant, I know that you understand your brother way more than I do. I've only seen him three times and you've lived with him all your life. The point I was trying to make is that your brother hasn't returned the sleeping bag he borrowed over a month ago."

learn about yourself

Take this short survey to learn something about yourself. Answer the questions based on your first response. There are no right or wrong answers. Just be honest in reporting your true behavior. For each of the following questions, select one of the following numbers that best describes your behavior.

1 = Always   2 = Often   3 = Sometimes   4 = Rarely   5 = Never

_____ **1.** I try to avoid conflicts whenever possible.

_____ **2.** I will give up my own desires in order to end a conflict.

_____ **3.** It is important to win an argument.

_____ **4.** I am willing to compromise to solve a conflict.

_____ **5.** It is important to discuss both people's point of view in a conflict.

_____ **6.** I am stubborn in holding to my position in a conflict.

_____ **7.** In conflicts, I give up some points in exchange for other points.

_____ **8.** I try to avoid conflicts.

_____ **9.** I give in to others during conflict.

_____ **10.** It is important to regard conflicts as problems to be solved together.

_____ **11.** I strongly assert my views in a conflict.

_____ **12.** I withdraw from disagreements.

_____ **13.** I try to find the middle-ground position in a conflict.

_____ **14.** I will give in to the other person in order to end an argument.

_____ **15.** I try to be cooperative and creative in finding a resolution to a conflict.

This is a test of your conflict management style.

SCORING THE SURVEY: Add your scores for items 1, 8, and 12. Your score will range from 3 to 15. The lower (closer to 3) your score, the more you tend to use withdrawal as a conflict management style.

Add your scores for items 2, 9, and 14. Your score will range from 3 to 15. The lower (closer to 3) your score, the more you tend to use the accommodating style of conflict management.

Add your scores for items 3, 6, and 11. Your score will range from 3 to 15. The lower (closer to 3) your score, the more you tend to use the forcing style of conflict management.

Add your scores for items 4, 7, and 13. Your score will range from 3 to 15. The lower (closer to 3) your score, the more you tend to use the compromising style of conflict management.

Add your scores for items 5, 10, and 15. Your score will range from 3 to 15. The lower (closer to 3) your score, the more you tend to use the collaborating style of conflict management.

Styles of Managing Conflict

Think about the last time you experienced a conflict. How did you react? Did you avoid it? Give in? Force the other person to accept your will? Did you compromise? Or did the two of you use a problem-solving approach? All these approaches differ in how much you were willing to cooperate in attempting to satisfy the other person's needs or concerns and how assertive you were in trying to satisfy your own needs and concerns. You cooperate more or less depending on how important you believe the relationship to be. You vary your assertiveness depending on how important the issue is to you. When faced with a conflict, you can withdraw, accommodate, use a forcing approach, compromise, or collaborate (Lulofs & Cahn, 2000, pp. 101–102).

Withdrawal

Withdrawal—resolving conflict by physically or psychologically removing oneself from the conflict.

One of the most common, and certainly one of the easiest, ways to deal with conflict is to withdraw or avoid the conflict. When people **withdraw,** they physically or psychologically remove themselves from the conflict. This style is both uncooperative and unassertive because at least one person is refusing to talk about the issue.

A person may withdraw physically by leaving the site. For instance, as Eduardo and Justina get into an argument about their financial situation, Eduardo may withdraw physically by saying "I don't want to talk about this" and walk out the door.

What motivates people to withdraw? What is lost as a result?

Psychological withdrawal occurs when one person simply ignores what the other person is saying. Using the same example, when Justina begins to talk about their financial situation, Eduardo may ignore her and act as though she has not spoken.

Considered from an individual-satisfaction standpoint, withdrawal creates a lose/lose situation because neither party to the conflict really accomplishes what he or she wants. Although Eduardo temporarily escapes from the conflict, he knows it will come up again. Likewise, Justina experiences frustration at two levels. First, she doesn't get an answer to her question about how to pay the bills, and second, Eduardo's refusal to talk about their finances further strains the relationship.

When used repeatedly, withdrawal hurts the relationship. Why? Because those who withdraw don't eliminate the source of the conflict, and the withdrawal actually increases the tension. As Roloff and Cloven (1990) say, "Relational partners who avoid conflicts have more difficulty resolving their disputes" (p. 49). In ongoing relationships the conflict will undoubtedly resurface. Another consequence of withdrawal is that it results in what Cloven and Roloff (1991, p. 136) call "mulling behavior." By mulling, they mean thinking about or stewing over an actual or perceived problem until one person perceives the conflict as more severe than it was and begins engaging in blaming behavior. Thus, in many cases, not confronting a problem promptly only makes it more difficult to deal with in the long run.

Although withdrawal is an ineffective style most of the time, there are at least two sets of circumstances in which withdrawing may be a useful strategy. First, withdrawing permits a temporary disengagement that allows strong emotional reactions to be checked. For example, when Pat and Bill begin to argue heatedly over going to Bill's mother's house for Thanksgiving dinner, Pat may stop and say, "Hold it a minute. Let me make a pot of coffee and calm down a bit; then we'll talk about this some more." A few minutes later, having calmed down, Pat may return, ready to approach the conflict in a different way.

Withdrawal also is appropriate when neither the relationship nor the issue is really important. Consider Josh and Mario, who work in different departments of the same company. At company gatherings, the two men have gotten into heated arguments about whether the Giants or the Cardinals is a better ball club. At the next gathering Mario may avoid sitting near Josh or may quickly change the subject when Josh begins the argument anew. In this case, Mario judges that it simply isn't worth trying to resolve the disagreement with Josh—neither the issue nor the relationship is that important.

Accommodating

When people **accommodate,** they manage conflict by satisfying others' needs or accepting others' ideas while neglecting their own. This approach is cooperative but unassertive. It preserves friendly relationships but fails to protect personal rights.

People who are insecure in their relations with others accommodate in order to ensure the continuance of relationships they perceive as fragile. For instance, as Juan and Mariana discuss their vacation plans, Mariana says that she'd like to ask

Accommodating—resolving conflict by satisfying others' needs or accepting others' ideas while neglecting our own.

two of their friends who will be vacationing the same week to join them. When Juan says that he'd like for the two of them to go alone, Mariana replies, "But I think it would be fun to go with another couple, don't you?" Juan replies, "OK, whatever you want." Even though Juan really wants the two of them to go alone, he sees that Mariana is enthusiastic about all four going together, and so he accommodates.

Considered from an individual-satisfaction standpoint, accommodation is a lose/win situation. The accommodator chooses to lose and the other person gets what he or she wants. From a relational-satisfaction standpoint, habitual accommodation has two problems. First, accommodation may lead to poor decision making because important facts, arguments, and positions are not voiced. Second, habitual accommodation results in one person's taking advantage of the other. This can damage the accommodating person's self-concept and lead to feelings of resentment that undermine the relationship.

There are situations, of course, in which it is appropriate and effective to accommodate. When the issue is not important to you, but the relationship is, accommodating is the preferred style. Hal and Yvonne are trying to decide where to go for dinner. Hal says, "I really have a craving for some Thai food tonight." Yvonne, who preferred pizza, says, "OK, that will be fine." Yvonne's interest in pizza was not very strong, and since Hal really seemed excited about Thai food, she accommodated. It may also be useful to accommodate from time to time to build "social credits" or goodwill that can be used later. It should be noted that in some cultures, accommodating is a preferred style of dealing with conflict. In Japan, for instance, it is thought to be more humble and face-saving to accommodate than to risk losing respect through conflict (Lulofs & Cahn, 2000, p. 114).

Forcing

Forcing—resolving conflict by attempting to satisfy your own needs or advance your own ideas with no concern for the needs or ideas of others and no concern for the harm done to the relationship.

A third style of dealing with conflict is forcing or competing. When people use **forcing**, they attempt to satisfy their own needs or advance their own ideas with no concern for the needs or ideas of others and no concern for the harm done to relationships. Forcing can be done through physical threats, verbal attacks, coercion, or manipulation. If the other party accommodates, the conflict subsides. If, however, the other side responds forcibly, the conflict escalates. Forcing is uncooperative but assertive. The forcer wishes to exert his or her will over the other and will argue assertively to do so.

Considered from an individual-satisfaction standpoint, forcing is I win/you lose. The person who is forcing wins—at the expense of the relational partner. From a relational-satisfaction standpoint, forcing usually hurts a relationship, at least in the short term. But there are times when forcing is an effective means to resolve conflict. In emergencies, when quick and decisive action must be taken to ensure safety or minimize harm, forcing is useful. Finally, when an issue is critical to your own or the other's welfare and you know you are right, you may find forcing necessary. If you are interacting with someone who will take advantage of you if you do not force the issue, this style is appropriate. For example, David knows that, statistically speaking, the likelihood of death or serious injury increases dramatically if one does not wear a helmet when riding a motorcycle. So he insists that his sister wear one when she rides with him, even though she complains bitterly.

Compromising

In **compromising,** people manage a conflict by giving up part of what each wants in order to provide at least some satisfaction for both parties. Under this approach both people give up part of what they really want or believe, or to trade one thing they want in order to get something else. Compromising is intermediate between assertiveness and cooperativeness. Each person has to be somewhat assertive and somewhat cooperative to get partial satisfaction. For example, Heather and Paul are working together on a class project and need to meet outside of class. If both have busy schedules, they may compromise on a time to meet.

From an individual-satisfaction standpoint, compromising creates a lose/lose situation, because both people in a sense "lose" even as they "win." From a relational-satisfaction standpoint, compromise may be seen as neutral to positive, because both parties gain some satisfaction.

Although compromising is a popular style, there are significant problems associated with it. One problem of special concern is that the quality of a decision is affected if one of the parties "trades away" a better solution in order to find a compromise. Compromising is appropriate when the issue is moderately important, when there are time constraints, and when attempts at forcing or collaborating have not been successful.

Compromising—a form of conflict management in which people attempt to resolve their conflict by providing at least some satisfaction for both parties.

Collaborating—resolving conflict by trying to fully address the needs and issues of each party and arrive at a solution that is mutually satisfying.

Collaborating

A fifth style of dealing with conflict is through problem-solving discussion, or collaboration. People are **collaborating** when they try to fully address the needs and issues of each party and arrive at a solution that is mutually satisfying. During collaboration people treat their disagreement as a problem to be solved, so they discuss the issues, describe their feelings, and identify the characteristics of an effective solution. Collaborating is both

inter-act with
Technology

Suppose you are participating in a newsgroup discussion online in which the topic of conversation is controversial. What kinds of behavior (withdrawal/avoidance, accommodating, forcing/coercing, compromising, or collaborating) do you tend to engage in most? Does your conflict management behavior online differ from your behavior in face-to-face conflicts? If so, what accounts for those differences? ■

assertive and cooperative. It is assertive because both parties voice their concerns; it is cooperative because they work together to gain resolution.

From an individual-satisfaction standpoint, collaborating is win/win, since both people's needs are met. From a relational-satisfaction standpoint, collaboration is positive because both sides feel that they have been heard. They get to share ideas and weigh and consider information. Whatever the solution, the effort has been truly collaborative.

Managing conflict through collaboration requires many of the communication skills we have discussed previously. Participants must use accurate and precise language to describe their ideas and feelings. They must empathically listen to the ideas and feelings of the other person. Using a problem-solving approach, they must define and analyze the problem, develop mutually acceptable criteria for judging alternative solutions, suggest possible solutions, select the solution that best meets the criteria, and work to implement the decision. Table 11.2 summarizes the questions that must be addressed during a collaborative discussion.

Let's consider a conflict example mentioned earlier: Justina and Eduardo's financial situation. To collaborate, both parties must honestly want to satisfy the other's concerns as well as their own. If they agree to collaborate, each may begin by describing the situation from his or her perspective while the other listens with empathy and understanding. Justina may describe for Eduardo the landlord's threats and her anxiety about not paying bills on time. Eduardo may remind her that money is tight because he recently took a pay cut in order to take a new job that has more potential. From this baseline they can work together to create a list of guidelines or criteria a solution would have to meet for it to be acceptable to them both.

What is necessary to stimulate collaboration in resolving an issue of conflict?

Table 11.2 Collaborating through problem-solving discussion

1. Define the problem.	What's the issue being considered?
2. Analyze the problem.	What are the causes and symptoms?
3. Develop mutually agreeable criteria for judging alternative solutions.	What goals will a good solution reach?
4. Generate alternative solutions.	What could we do? List before discussing each.
5. Select the solution that best fits the criteria identified.	Select one or a combination from those listed.

Table 11.3 Styles of conflict management

Approach	Characteristics	Goal	Outlook
Withdrawal	Uncooperative, unassertive	To keep from dealing with conflict	"I don't want to talk about it."
Accommodating	Cooperative, unassertive	To keep from upsetting the other person	"Getting my way isn't as important as keeping the peace."
Forcing	Uncooperative, assertive	To get my way	"I'll get my way regardless of what I have to do."
Compromising	Partially cooperative, partially assertive	To get partial satisfaction	"Ill get partial satisfaction by letting the other person get partial satisfaction as well."
Collaborating	Cooperative, assertive	To solve the problem together	"Let's talk this out and find the best solution possible for both of us."

Justina might suggest that the solution should be one that enables them to pay more than the minimum balances on their credit cards and get the payments in on time so that they avoid additional penalties. Eduardo might want the solution to be one that doesn't leave them without any way to "have fun." Then, together they might brainstorm a list of possible solutions. For example, Justina might propose that they save money by eating out only once a month and renting DVDs rather than going to movies. Eduardo might suggest that they have a yard sale to sell stuff they don't use any more and use the proceeds as a "fun fund."

Does this process sound too idealized? Or impractical? Collaboration is difficult. When two people commit themselves to trying, however, chances are they will discover that through discussion they can arrive at creative solutions that meet their needs and maintain their relationship. Later in this chapter we will focus on guidelines that can help us manage our conflicts through good collaborative discussions.

The five different styles of conflict management, with their characteristics, outcomes, and appropriate usage, are summarized in Table 11.3. If we are to become more effective at interacting in conflict situations, we need to understand each style, we need to know when and at what cost it is likely to be effective, and we need to know when and how to use it.

observe & analyze

Conflict Episodes

Describe a conflict episode you have recently experienced. How did you act, and how did the other person behave? What was the outcome of the conflict? How did you feel about it then? Now? Was there a different way the conflict might have been handled that would have resulted in a better outcome? ■

Communication Patterns that Impede Effective Conflict Management

Communicating during a conflict episode is quite challenging under any circumstances, but it can be unnecessarily complicated when partners use negative thinking and destructive behavioral patterns. Five common patterns that partners engage in that complicate effective conflict management are ascribed motives, counter blaming, demand withdrawal, spiraling negativity, and reciprocal stubbornness. During a conflict episode, it is important to monitor your own communication so that you disrupt these patterns when you see them developing and move to ones that are more effective at managing the conflict.

Ascribing motives

In conflicts, you may think you know what others are thinking or why they are behaving a certain way. Often, we look for and come up with hidden malevolent motivations in people's behavior. But assuming we know what motivates our partner involves guesswork rather than actual knowledge. If you base your comments on what you believe to be the other's motives, you engage in inference–observation confusion, which may make a conflict worse. Suppose Ben leaves a phone message to cancel playing basketball with Sol. If Sol assumes that Ben really had something better to do with another friend, Sol may harbor feelings of hurt and resentment. In actuality, Ben may have had to work late. Sol's self-inflicted hurt feelings may continue to affect his relationship with Ben and lead to further conflict. Sol's mistake was making an inference that wasn't justified on the basis of the incomplete information he had about Ben's motive.

Counterblame

Sometimes, participants become focused on proving that a problem originated from the behavior of the other. Nicole may initiate a conflict by saying to Stacey, "I can't believe you just took my green skirt and wore it without asking." Stacey may move the interaction to one of counterblame by replying, "I would not have had to borrow your skirt for work today if you had done the laundry like you promised." Nicole may take the bait and retort, "I couldn't do the laundry because you didn't buy any laundry detergent when you went shopping." And Stacey may counter, "Well, how can I know that we need detergent when you don't bother to put it on the shopping list?" Notice how counterblaming moves the discussion away from the original issue (the unauthorized borrowing) and leaves it unresolved, while escalating the potential damage to the relationship. Had Nicole chosen to avoid counterblame, she might have refocused the discussion by saying something like "Stacey, the issue is not why you needed to borrow the skirt, but that you did it without asking me."

Demand Withdrawal

Demand withdrawal can become a recurring pattern of conflict communication in long-term relationships (Caughlin & Huston, 2002). In demand withdrawal, one person chooses a forcing style that nags, blames, or criticizes, while the other partner counters the forcing behavior by using the withdrawal style. Imagine that Angelina reintroduces her continuing concern about her husband's weight by saying, "Kevin, you really need to lose a few pounds. It's not good for your health to be overweight. It's all the pop you drink and the bedtime snacks." Kevin, acting as though he did not hear a word Angelina said, looks up from the computer and says, "Hey, we could get a great deal on a digital camera that is for sale on eBay." Whenever Angelina brings up the topic of his weight, Kevin ignores her comments and changes the subject. His unwillingness to discuss the topic leads to more forcing on her part until this pattern becomes a chronic feature of the conflict in their relationship.

Spiraling Negativity

Another destructive pattern of conflict communication begins when one person interjects a mean or hostile comment into a conflict conversation and the partner matches that negative comment with one of their own. This pattern, called spiraling negativity, may result in the degeneration of a conversation into name-calling and bitter accusations that could poison the entire relationship. Although it is natural to feel defensive when you believe you have been attacked, you can halt a negative spiral by describing your feelings and refocusing the discussion on the issue. For example, you might say, "What you just said really hurts my feelings, but I think we are not going to resolve this by making personal attacks. So I'd like us to refocus on the issues. . . ."

Stubbornness

When both parties to a conflict obstinately cling to their position on an issue for the sake of maintaining face, they hinder effective discussion and conflict management. While at times holding to your position is an ethical obligation, more frequently, people stubbornly refuse to acknowledge when a partner has made a good point. When you notice yourself inflexibly maintaining your own position for the sake of winning the debate, you can modify your messages and be more flexible. Likewise, when you notice that your partner is becoming inflexible, you might engage in a discussion of what you believe to be the real issue at stake—resolving the disagreement or winning the argument.

observe & analyze

Changing Conflict Patterns

Think of a recent conflict you experienced in which an ineffective conflict pattern developed. Analyze what happened using the concepts from this chapter. What type of conflict was it? What style did you adopt? What was the other person's style? What dysfunctional patterns developed? How did styles each of you selected contribute to what happened? How might you change what you did if you could "redo" this conflict episode? ■

Communication Skills that Promote Successful Conflict Management

Your primary goal in managing conflict is to be both appropriate and effective in your own behavior and to disrupt destructive patterns by using communication skills that promote successful conflict management. In the Spotlight on Scholars on pages 300 and 301, we can see how the research of Professor Daniel Canary, at

spotlight on scholars

Conflict Management

Dan Canary, citing the personal benefit of studying conflict, stated, "I learned how to control my own behavior and become more effective in my personal relationships." Canary's initial curiosity about effective conflict management behaviors was piqued when he was in graduate school at the University of Southern California. At the time he was a classmate of Brian Spitzberg (see Spotlight on Scholars, pp. 19–20), who formulated the theory that relational competence is a product of behaviors that are both appropriate and effective, and Bill Cupach, who was studying conflict in relationships. Although Canary saw the connection between his work and theirs, it was several years later—after he experienced successful and unsuccessful resolution of significant conflict episodes in his personal life—that he began in earnest to study how the way people behave during conflict episodes affects their relationships.

Communication scholars can become well known by developing a new theory that more clearly describes what really happens when we interact, by carrying out a series of research studies that test and elaborate on the theories developed by others, or by organizing, integrating, and synthesizing the existing theories and research work in an area so that people who are not specialists can better understand what is known. Dan Canary's reputation was made largely as a result of his ability to identify and build on connections among the theories and experimental data available to scholars.

Canary's research studies are helping to identify the behaviors that lead to perceiving a person as a competent conflict manager. Canary argues that although people will view some of the communication behaviors to manage conflict as appropriate and some behaviors as effective, both are necessary if one is to be perceived as competent. Drawing on Spitzberg's competence theory, Canary's research studies are designed to identify conflict behaviors that accomplish the goals of both appropriateness and effectiveness. The results of his studies consistently show that integrative conflict strategies—problem solving, collaborative, and compromising approaches that display a desire to work with the other person—are perceived to be both appropriate and effective (i.e., competent). Furthermore, his studies have shown that when one partner in a relationship is thought to be a competent conflict manager, the other one trusts the partner more, is more satisfied with the relationship, and perceives the relationship to be more intimate.

Canary's research studies identify specific conflict management behaviors that are viewed as appropriate and/or effective. Canary has found that a person who acknowledges the arguments of others (e.g., "Uh huh, I can see how you would think that") and agrees with the arguments that others make to support their points (e.g., "Gee that's a good point that I hadn't really thought about") is viewed as having appropriately handled the conflict. To be viewed as effective, however, requires a different set of behaviors. According to Canary's findings, conflict-handling behaviors that are viewed as effective included stating complete arguments, elaborating and justifying one's point of view, and clearly developing one's ideas. Canary noticed that in a conflict situation, what was viewed as appropriate alone had the potential to be ineffective, since appropriate behaviors seemed to involve some sort of agreement with the other person.

Canary reasoned that there must be ways to be both appropriate and effective in conflict situations. This led him to consider methods of sequencing or ordering messages in a conflict episode. His preliminary results have revealed that competent communicators (those perceived to be both appropriate and effective) will begin by acknowledging the other's viewpoint, or agreeing with part of the other's argument, before explaining, justifying, and arguing for their own viewpoint. Canary believes that in using this sequence, competent communicators help "frame" the interaction as one of cooperative problem solving rather than as a situation of competing interests where only one party can "win."

Many of Canary's major contributions to the study of conflict in personal relationships are included in two books: *Relationship Conflict* (co-authored with William Cupach and Susan Messman), a synthesis of the diverse conflict literature was written for graduate students and other scholars; *Competence in Interpersonal Conflict* (also co-authored with Cupach) focuses on how readers outside the academic community can increase their competence at managing interpersonal

conflict in a variety of settings. For complete citations of these books and additional works by Canary, see the references for this chapter at the end of the book.

Canary teaches courses in interpersonal communication, conflict management, and research methods. His most recent research involves a quickly applied conflict rating system that people can use to observe conflict in an efficient yet valid way. ■

Arizona State University, has validated the importance of both appropriateness and effectiveness in conflict management. While each of the five conflict styles can be used to manage a conflict, in most interpersonal settings we are concerned about the long-term relationship, so collaboration will be the preferred style.

In the remainder of this chapter we will describe the skills that you can use to resolve a conflict collaboratively. We begin by explaining how to initiate a conflict. Then we describe how you can respond to a conflict initiated by your partner. Finally, we present guidelines to help you mediate the conflicts of others.

Communication Skills for Initiating Conflict

The following guidelines for initiating conflict (as well as those for responding to conflict in the next section) are based on work from several fields of study (Adler, 1977; Gordon, 1970; Whetten & Cameron, 2005).

1. **Recognize and state ownership of the apparent problem.** If a conflict is to be managed, it is important to acknowledge that you are angry, hurt, or frustrated. It is honest to own what is occurring by owning your own ideas and feelings, making "I" statements (see Chapter 9).

   Suppose you are trying to study for a major test in your most difficult course and your neighbor's music is so loud that your walls are shaking and you can't concentrate. As this continues, you become agitated because you can't focus on your study. Who has a problem? Your neighbor? No. You have a problem. It's your study that is being disrupted, so you decide to confront your neighbor.

   Remember, your goal is to seek collaboration in dealing with the problem. You could knock on your neighbor's door and shout, "Your music is too damn loud, turn it down—I'm trying to study!" This approach is almost guaranteed to arouse defensiveness in your neighbor and lead to an ego conflict. An appropriate way of owning your problem would be to say, "Hi, I'm having a problem that I need your help with. I'm trying to study for an exam."

2. **Describe the basis of the potential conflict in terms of behavior, consequences, and feelings.** The behavior, consequences, and feelings (b-c-f) sequence is a specific order for communicating your concerns: "When a specific behavior(s) happen(s), the specific consequences result, and I feel (a certain way)" (Gordon, 1971). It's important to include all three of these elements in order for the other person to fully understand what is happening. This is because you are describing for the other person what you see or hear, what happens to you as a result, and what feelings you experience.

Earlier in this book we discussed the skills of describing behavior and describing feelings. When the b-c-f sequence is used in initiating a conflict, it helps to communicate the problem in nonevaluative terms. Notice, then, that the b-c-f sequence combines the skills of owning feelings, describing behavior, and describing feelings.

In the example of the loud music, you begin by owning the problem: "I'm having a problem that I need your help with. I'm trying to study for an exam." Now let's see how you might follow up on that opening using the b-c-f sequence. "When I hear your music [b], I get distracted and can't concentrate on studying [c], and then I get frustrated and annoyed [f]." The loudness of the music is the behavior; the consequences are distraction and inability to concentrate; and the feelings are frustration and annoyance.

3. **Avoid evaluating the other person's motives.** Since your goal is to resolve your complaint without escalating the conflict, you want to make sure that you do nothing to create defensiveness. So be careful to avoid making accusations or distorting what the other person has done. Your neighbor is probably not intentionally undermining your study time, but rather trying to enjoy her leisure time. While using the b-c-f sequence, don't let evaluations and blaming statements creep in. For instance, you wouldn't want to say "You're being really inconsiderate of others in the building." You want the focus to be on what is happening to you.

4. **Be sure the other person understands your problem.** Even when we take the greatest care in describing our needs, others may become defensive, try to

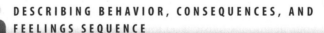

skill builders

DESCRIBING BEHAVIOR, CONSEQUENCES, AND FEELINGS SEQUENCE

SKILL	USE	PROCEDURE	EXAMPLE
Describing the basis of a conflict in terms of behavior, consequences, and feelings (b-c-f).	To help the other person understand the problem completely.	1. Own the message. 2. Describe the behavior that you see or hear. 3. Describe the consequences that result. 4. Describe your feelings.	Jason says, "I have a problem that I need your help with. When I tell you what I'm thinking and you don't respond (b), I start to think you don't care about me or what I think (c), and this causes me to get very angry with you (f)."

rationalize, or immediately counterattack. They may get the general drift of the message but misunderstand the seriousness of the problem, or they may not understand at all. At times you will need to rephrase or restate what you have said.

Suppose when you approach your neighbor about the music, she says, "Oh come on, everyone plays loud music in this neighborhood, and there have been times when I have even heard your loud music." You might reply, "Yes, I understand it's a noisy neighborhood, and loud music normally doesn't bother me. And I'm sorry if I've disturbed you in the past—I didn't mean to. But I'm still having a problem right now, and I was hoping you could help me." Notice that this doesn't accuse the noisy neighbor of not listening or of continuing to be insensitive. It merely attempts to get the focus back on the problem that you are having.

5. **Phrase your preferred solution in a way that focuses on common ground.** Once you have been understood and you understand the other's position, make your suggestion for change. This suggestion is more likely to be accepted if you can tie it to a shared value, common interest, or shared constraint. In our example you might say, "I think we both have had times when even little things got in the way of our being able to study. So even though I realize I'm asking you for a special favor, I hope you can help me out by turning down your music for a couple of hours."

6. **Mentally rehearse what you will say before you confront the other person, so that your request will be brief and precise.** Initiating a collaborative conflict conversation requires us to be in control of our emotions. Yet, by nature and despite our good intentions of keeping on track, our emotions can get the better of us, and in the heat of the moment we may say things we shouldn't, or we may go on and on and annoy the other person.

Take a minute to practice. Say to yourself, "I need to own the problem and then follow the b-c-f sequence." Then mentally rehearse a few statements until you think you can do it when your neighbor comes to the door.

7. **Keep it short.** Since problem solving requires interaction, it is important that you quickly draw the other person into the conversation. The longer you talk, the more likely it is that the other person will become defensive. Effective turn-taking during the early stages of conflict conversation will nurture the problem-solving climate.

Communication Skills for Responding to Conflict

It is more difficult to create a collaborative climate when responding to conflict initiated by another than it is to begin a conflict appropriately. Because most people do not use the behavior-consequences-feelings sequence to initiate conflict and instead express their feelings in inappropriate, evaluative terms that threaten others, it can be difficult for the other parties to overcome their defensiveness and respond appropriately. For instance, suppose you were not the one to initiate a conflict over loud music. Suppose your neighbor knocks on your door and says,

"Turn down that damn music! Quit being such a jerk to others." Even if you were playing the music very loudly, this approach might lead you to slam the door and keep listening to your music.

Your most difficult task as a responder is to take ineffectively initiated conflicts and turn them into productive, problem-solving discussions. The following guidelines will help you to respond effectively in these situations.

1. **Put your "shields" up.** When someone becomes overly aggressive in initiating a conflict, we need to learn to put our mental "shields" up to enable us to listen and improve our capacity to respond effectively rather than becoming defensive and blindly counterattacking. One method that can help you do this is to remind yourself that the other person obviously has a problem, not you. It also helps to remember that it is unlikely that anything you have said or done has led to this inappropriate overreaction. In all likelihood the anger being vented toward you is due to accumulated frustration, only part of which directly relates to the current issue. So put those shields up, and while you're "counting to ten" think of your options for turning this into a problem-solving opportunity.

2. **Respond empathically with genuine interest and concern.** A person who initiates a potential conflict, even with a bold order like "Turn down that damn music!" will be watching you closely to see how you react. If you make light of the other person's concerns, become defensive, or overreact, you will undermine the opportunity to cooperate in problem solving. Even if you disagree with the complaint, for effective collaboration to occur, you must show respect to the person by being attentive and empathizing. Sometimes you can do this by allowing the other to vent while you listen. Only when the other person has calmed down can you begin to problem-solve. In our example, you might well start by saying, "I can see you're angry. Let's talk about this."

3. **Paraphrase your understanding of the problem and ask questions to clarify issues.** Since most people are unaware of the b-c-f sequence, you may want to form a paraphrase that captures your understanding of b-c-f issues or ask questions to elicit this information. For instance, let's suppose your co-worker says, "What in the world were you thinking when you did the safety report this morning?" If information is missing, as with this initiating statement, then you can ask questions that reflect the b-c-f framework. "Can you tell me what's wrong with the report? Is there a problem that I don't realize?" It can also be helpful to ask the person if there is anything else that has not been mentioned. Sometimes people will initiate a conflict episode in relation to minor issues without mentioning what really needs to be considered.

4. **Seek common ground by finding some aspect of the complaint to agree with.** This does not mean giving in to the other person. Nor does it mean that you should feign agreement on a point that you do not agree with. However, using your skills of supportiveness, you can look for points with which you can agree. Adler (1977) says that you can agree with a message without accepting all of its implications. For example, you can agree with part of it, you can agree with it in principle, you can agree with the initiator's

perceptions of the situation, and/or you can agree with the person's feelings.

Let's return to our example: "I'm having a problem that I need your help with," a neighbor says to you. "I'm trying to study for a big exam. When I hear your music, I get distracted and can't concentrate on studying, and then I get frustrated and annoyed." In your response, you could agree in part: "I know it's hard to study for a tough exam." You could agree in principle: "I know it's good to have a quiet place to study." You could agree with the initiator's perception: "I can see that you're having trouble studying with loud music in the background." Or you could agree with the person's feelings: "I can see that you're frustrated and annoyed."

You do not need to agree with the initiator's conclusions or evaluations. You need not concede. But by agreeing to some aspect of the complaint, you create common ground from which a problem-solving discussion can proceed.

5. **Ask the initiator to suggest alternative solutions.** As soon as you are sure that the two of you have agreed on what the problem is, ask the initiator for alternative ways to handle the conflict. Since the initiator has probably spent time thinking about what needs to be done, your request for alternatives signals a willingness to listen and cooperate. You may find that one of the suggestions seems reasonable to you. If none are, you may be able to craft an alternative that builds on one of the ideas presented. In any case, asking for suggestions communicates your trust in the other person, strengthening the problem-solving climate.

Communication Skills for Mediating Conflict

Sometimes you are called on to mediate or referee a conflict between other people. A **mediator** is an uninvolved third party who serves as a "neutral and impartial

Mediator—an uninvolved third party who serves as a neutral and impartial guide, structuring an interaction that enables the conflicting parties to find a mutually acceptable solution to their problems.

It is often useful to have help in mediating conflict. What is a mediator likely to do to help people resolve conflict?

guide, structuring an interaction that enables the conflicting parties to find a mutually acceptable solution to their problems" (Cupach & Canary, 1997, p. 205). You can probably think of times when friends have disagreed and have asked for your advice. Mediators can play an important role in resolving conflicts if they observe the following guidelines (Cupach & Canary, 1997; Whetten & Cameron, 2005).

1. **Make sure that the people having the conflict agree to work with you.** If one of the parties doesn't really want your help, then you are not likely to be able to do much good. You may be able to clarify this by saying, "I'm willing to help you work on this, but only if both of you want me to." Sometimes people say they want a mediator when in reality they just want to stall discussion or resolution.

2. **Help the people identify the real conflict.** Many times people seem to be arguing over one thing when the true source of conflict has not been stated. It is important that you help the parties identify the real issue.

3. **Maintain neutrality.** Even as a mediator who listens empathically, you cannot show favoritism. Any perception of favoritism will destroy the opportunity for successful mediation.

4. **Keep the discussion focused on the issues rather than on personalities.** Because problem solving is nurtured in a supportive communication climate, the mediator must help participants to make descriptive statements. This can be done through questions that elicit b-c-f statements and by setting ground rules that encourage statements that are problem oriented and not person oriented, descriptive and not evaluative. If, during the discussion, one of the parties begins accusing or insulting, the mediator can simply remind the violator of the previously agreed to ground rules.

5. **Work to ensure equal talk time.** It's important for the mediator to control the conversation so that both parties have an equal chance to be heard. The quality of the conversation is increased if each person gives equal input. A mediator can do this by directing questions to a more reticent party and by encouraging turn-taking with statements such as "We've heard your concerns, Erin; now I'd like us to hear how Ed sees this issue."

6. **Focus the discussion on helping the parties find a solution.** A mediator is not a judge. Mediators should not let themselves be placed in the position of assessing guilt or making decisions. While some interpersonal conflicts involve issues of right and wrong, most arise from differences in perspective. The mediator should avoid making any judgmental statements. If asked for a personal opinion, the mediator might say, "I'm not in a position to judge. What I want to do is help find a way to handle this issue that both of you can feel good about." In this way, the mediator focuses the participants on managing the conflict between them rather than bringing the mediator into it.

7. **Use perception checking and paraphrasing to make sure both parties fully understand and support the agreed-upon solution.** Sometimes mediators make the mistake of believing that when one party suggests a reasonable solution to which the other party voices no disagreement, the dispute has been resolved. Silence cannot automatically be interpreted as agreement, however. A good media-

The Power of *Wastah* in Lebanese Speech   *By Mahboub Hashem*

Mahboub Hashem teaches communication at Fort Hayes State University. His research interests are in the areas of interpersonal and intercultural communication.

"Do you have any *wastah*?"

This was the only question that many of my Lebanese friends and relatives asked me when I applied for one of the Chair of Administrative Affairs positions at the Lebanese University [some years ago]. I replied that I ranked among the top five in the competency exam and they needed to hire at least ten people, so why would I need a *wastah*? They simply shrugged and warned, "Wait and you'll see."

To make the story short, I was passed over and more than 10 other people were hired. Every one of those who were hired had some type of *wastah*. I was hired three years later only after I had acquired strong *wastah,* which included several influential individuals, among them Suleiman Frangieh, the President of Lebanon at that time....

By examining the *wastah* phenomenon in Lebanon and how it is practiced, one may be able to shed some light on this very important communicative behavior not only in Lebanon but also in the rest of the Middle East. This essay addresses the power of *wastah* (i.e., mediation), considered to be one of the most important communication patterns in the Lebanese cultural system....

Wastah has been the way of life in Lebanon since before it became a republic. The term *wastah* means many things to many Lebanese people, including clout, connections, networking, recommendations, a "go-between" for two parties with different interests, and a type of contraception to prevent pregnancy.

Wastah can be used within various contexts, such as family, clan, government organizations, neighbors, villages, and nations. It is usually necessary to get a job, a wife, a date, a passport, a visa, a car, or any other commodity. It can also resolve conflicts, facilitate government decisions, or solve bureaucratic problems. For instance, I once had to wait three hours until I could find an influential person to help me pay the annual tag fee for my car. The common perception in the Arab world, particularly in Lebanon, is that "one does not do for oneself what might better be done by a friend or a friend's friend." ...

How Does the Process of Wastah Work?

Wastah is mostly used to find jobs for relatives or close friends and to solve conflicts. The extended family acts as an employment agency by searching for a *wasit* to help get a job, preferably one with high social status in the family. The *wasit* is supposed to be well "wired up," an insider who can make things happen (Hall 1984). He must also be able to use the language of persuasion ... with the elite of the religious and political groups of the nation.

In conflict situations, the *wasit's* job is to conciliate rather than to judge. Conciliation is intended to lead disputants toward a compromise through mutual concessions, as well as to re-establish their relationship on the basis of mutual respect. The *wasit* tries to talk to each disputant separately, then brings them together to reach a possible compromise that presumes to save face for everyone involved and their extended families.

Lebanese people prefer mediators from the same family or business, depending on the type and context of the conflict.... [T]he role of a *wasit* is to create a supportive climate of communication wherein conflicting parties can modify their behaviors. When a conflict is between members from two different clans, however, a *wasit* on each side tries to prevail over his or her own clan members. These mediators then come together to conciliate.

For instance, when a conflict occurred between my father and a man named Tony Ayoub, one elderly person from the Hashem clan and another one from the Ayoub clan came together to mediate and negotiate a possible settlement. Then each of the two met with their clan member to discuss the results of their meeting(s) and what the two believed to be a fair solution. After several private meetings between the two mediators, my father and Tony were asked to personally participate in the final one to announce the settlement of the problem. The common ground among mediators of different families is the mutual desire to keep the government out of the clans' affairs as much as possible. Hence, mediators seem better qualified than government agencies to resolve certain conflicts....

The knowledge of these styles and how they are used in various cultures promotes more awareness and understanding of ourselves and others and can consequently lead to more effective intercultural relationships. ■

Excerpted from Hashem, M. (2000). The power of *Wastah* in Lebanese speech. In A. González, M. Houston, & V. Chen (Eds.), *Our Voices* (pp. 150-154). Los Angeles: Roxbury Publishing Company.

support it. It is also important that mediators check their perceptions of the nonverbal messages that participants send. While a participant may voice agreement, his or her nonverbal behavior may be shouting hesitancy. If the mediator suspects that a participant's agreement is half-hearted, this should be explicitly explored through a perception check. Once convinced that both parties are satisfied with the proposed solution, the mediator can move to the final step in the process.

8. **Establish an action plan and follow-up procedure.** Unfortunately, some mediators stop short, assuming that once a solution has been agreed to in principle, the participants can work out the details unassisted. But making sure that the parties have an action plan, with clearly agreed-to responsibilities, is part of effective mediating. The action plan should specify what each party is to do and how results will be measured and monitored. A mediator can move participants to this final stage by praising them for reaching agreement on a general solution framework and asking each party to describe the specific behaviors or changes in behavior that will be performed to make the solution an actuality.

As you have seen, mediating conflict draws on a variety of basic interpersonal communication skills. Mediators must be assertive and persuasive, as well as effective at listening, paraphrasing, and questioning. At times they will use interpreting responses to reframe issues in ways that reduce defensiveness. As a mediator you can provide a useful service for friends and family as you help them repair relationships and work to create more positive communication.

Recovering from Conflict Management Failures

There are times when no matter how hard both parties try, they will not be able to manage the conflict successfully in a way that meets everyone's needs. Sillars and Weisberg (1987, p. 143) have pointed out that conflict can be an extremely complex process and that some conflicts may not be resolvable even with improved communication.

Understanding Unresolved Conflicts. Especially when the relationship is important to you, it is useful to analyze your inability to manage the conflict. Ask yourself questions such as the following: What went wrong? Did one or more of us become competitive? Or defensive? Did I use a style that was inappropriate to the situation? Did we fail to implement the problem-solving method adequately? Were the vested interests in the outcome too great? Did I initiate or respond inappropriately?

By analyzing your behavior, you will become more aware of how you can continue to improve your skills and more aware of how to handle areas of incompatibility in your relationships. And, since conflict is inevitable, you can count on using this knowledge again.

Forgiving. Whether or not you are able to effectively manage a conflict, it is important to forgive the party with whom you were in conflict, especially if it is a friend or acquaintance who is or has been a major part of your life. Forgiveness consists of letting go of feelings of revenge and desires for retaliation. Forgiveness

what would you do?

A Question of Ethics

Maria and Jose had been shopping at the outlet mall. After loading their purchases into the trunk of the car, they decided to move the car to a parking space closer to the next group of shops. Maria was backing out; she glanced in the rearview mirror and cried, "She's going to hit us!" She began to honk her horn, but the other vehicle, an SUV, continued backing and banged into Maria's rear bumper. Maria and Jose immediately hopped out of the car to check out the damage.

Three conservatively dressed women, with their hair covered by scarves, appeared to be daughter, mother, and grandmother. They slowly exited the SUV. Jose shouted, "What's wrong with you! Couldn't you see us or hear the horn?" Maria told Jose to shut up and turned to the driver, a young woman about her own age, and said, "Good grief! Just give me your information!" Rima, the other driver, turned to Jose and politely told him that she hadn't seen them or heard the horn. Then she turned to Maria and said that she needed to call her husband and immediately retreated into the SUV, pulling her cell phone out of her purse as she closed the door.

Maria exploded. She began banging on Rima's window, shouting "Why do you need to talk to your husband? He wasn't here! What does he have to do with this!" At this point the second woman, who appeared to be Rima's mother, quietly asked Maria not to yell, but her request had no effect. After a few moments, Rima opened the door and asked Maria to speak with Rima's husband, who was on the phone. Maria yelled that she had no intention of speaking to anyone and again demanded that Rima produce her license and insurance information. Rima then directed her mother and grandmother to get back in the car and said that she was going to call the police. The three women sat in the SUV until a police car arrived.

After talking with Maria and Jose, the officer who had responded to the call explained to Rima that police don't intervene in traffic accidents on private property if there are no injuries unless there is a problem with the parties exchanging information. Rima and her mother cut him off and told him that Maria had verbally assaulted them using bad words, and threatening them. The police officer replied that Maria's behavior might have been unfortunate, but her request had been legal and was actually the proper procedure at the scene of this type of accident. Rima responded that she had never had an accident before and had called her husband to find out what she should do. Had Maria simply been patient, none of this would have happened.

1. In this situation, was it ethical for each person to use the conflict style chosen?

2. Which of Johannesen's characteristics of ethical dialogue (see Chapter 6) were violated in this incident?

then paves the way for reconciliation, through which you can rebuild trust in a relationship and work toward restoration. As Lulofs and Cahn (2000) have put it, "There is virtual agreement in the literature that forgiveness is a process in which a person lets go of feelings of revenge and his or her right to retaliate against the other person. With few exceptions, forgiveness is not equated with forgetting what has happened. Nor is forgiveness equated with the immediate restoration of trust. Forgiveness is generally conceived of as a process through which people get on with their lives after experiencing some hurt" (p. 329).

Summary

Interpersonal conflict arises when the needs or ideas of one person are perceived to be at odds with the needs or ideas of another. Even in good relationships, conflicts are inevitable.

There are five types of conflict: pseudoconflicts; conflicts over facts (simple conflicts), interpretations of facts, definitions, or choices; value conflicts over competing value systems that are brought to bear on the issues; policy conflicts over ways of solving or coping with problems; and ego conflicts that personalize the conflict. Such clashes become more complicated as they escalate from conflicts of fact to those of values, then policies, then egos.

We manage conflict by withdrawing, accommodating, forcing, compromising, or collaborating. Each of these strategies can be effective under certain circumstances. When we are concerned about the long-term relationship, collaboration will be most appropriate strategy. We can also improve our chances of effectively managing conflict if we avoid the communication patterns that complicate effective conflict management, namely ascribed motives, counterblaming, demand withdrawal, spiraling negativity, and reciprocal stubbornness.

To initiate a collaborative conflict management conversation, you can use many communication skills: Own the problem; describe the potential conflict using the behavior-consequences-feelings sequence; avoid evaluating the other person's motives; be sure that the other person understands your problem; plan what you will say before you confront the other person; and phrase your request so that it focuses on common ground.

When seeking collaboration by responding to another person's initiation, put your shields up, respond empathically, paraphrase your understanding of the problem, seek common ground, and ask the person to suggest alternatives.

When you mediate a conflict, first make sure that the people agree to work with you. Then help them identify the real conflict. You should maintain neutrality, keep the discussion focused on the issues, work to ensure equal talk time, find solutions rather than placing blame, make sure parties understand what they've agreed to, and establish an action plan and follow-up procedure.

Finally, learn from failures in conflict management. Even when you cannot resolve a conflict, you can try to understand why things didn't work out and forgive the other person so that you can get on with your life.

Inter-Action Dialogue:
CONFLICT

Conflict occurs when the needs or ideas of one person are perceived to be at odds with or in opposition to the needs or ideas of another. Consider types of conflict, styles of managing conflict, and skills that promote successful conflict management.

A transcript of Brian and Matt's conversation follows. Analyze the conversation on your own, then go to the Dialogue section of your CD to read the authors' analysis.

Brian and Matt share an apartment. Matt is consistently late in paying his share of expenses. Brian has tolerated this for over six months, but has finally had enough and decides to confront Matt.

CONVERSATION

BRIAN: *Matt, I need to talk with you.*

MATT: *What's up?*

BRIAN: *Well, I have a problem. When I got home from class today, I tried to call my mom, and guess what? The phone's been disconnected.*

MATT: *You're kidding.*

BRIAN: *No, I'm not. And when I went next door and called the phone company, you know what they said?*

MATT: *I can guess.*

BRIAN: *They said the bill hadn't been paid and that this was the fourth month in a row that the bill was over two weeks late.*

MATT: *Look man, I can explain.*

BRIAN: *Like you explained not paying the utility bill on time last month? We were just lucky that it was a cool week and that we didn't fry without air conditioning. The candlelit dinner was charming and all that, but I really resented having to go the library to study for my test. Matt, I just can't go on like this. I mean, I gave you my share of the phone bill three weeks ago. I always give you my half of the utility bill the day it arrives. And I'm sick and tired of having to nag you for your share of the rent. For the last four months I've had to cover your share by taking money out of what I am saving to buy Angie's engagement ring. I know that you eventually pay me back, but I lose the interest and it's just not fair.*

MATT: *Gosh, I didn't know that you were so upset. I mean it's not like I don't pay. I always make good don't I?*

BRIAN: *Yes, so far that's true, but every month it's later and later before you pay me back. And I'm not a lending agency. Why do you expect me to loan you money each month? We work at the same place, make the same money, and we've both got the same expenses. If I can come up with the rent and other expenses on time, you can too.*

MATT: *Listen man, I apologize about the phone bill. I thought I'd mailed it. So, I'll check it out with the phone company tomorrow morning. And the utility bill was just a mistake. I lost the bill and didn't realize it hadn't been paid. I know that I've not always had the money for the rent when you asked, but you usually ask me for it a week or more before it's due. You are really good at saving ahead, but I'm not. You say we have the same expenses, but that's not true. I have a car loan and you don't. And since I got that ticket last year, my car insurance has skyrocketed. Some months I'm living really close to the edge. I know it's no excuse, but I want you to understand that I'm not just some deadbeat who's trying to suck off of you.*

BRIAN: *Matt, I'm sorry I said that we have similar expenses. You're right, yours are higher. And if I understood you correctly, our problems with the utility company and the phone company weren't due to your not having the money, but were because somehow the bills just slipped through the cracks?*

MATT: *Yeah. I'm never very organized but right now things are chaos. Between work, school, and the stuff that's going on with my family I don't know if I'm coming or going.*

BRIAN: *Well, I can understand that you are under a lot of pressure. And I hope you can understand that when you don't pay bills on time, it's not just you that suffers. Angie and I want to buy a house before we get married, so I'm really careful about paying bills on time so that I have a good credit rating. That's why I ask you for the rent so early. When you forget to pay the utility and phone bills, not only do we lose service, but since both of our names are on the bill, we both take a hit in our credit ratings. A poor credit rating will make it harder for me to get a loan. And it also will make it harder for you to get credit later. I know that you wouldn't intentionally do anything to hurt me, but the fact is, you have.*

MATT: *Whoa, I never really thought about it this way. Man, I'm sorry.*

BRIAN: *Apology accepted. So how can we work this out?*

MATT: *Well, you seem to have thought more about it than I have, do you have any ideas?*

BRIAN: *Yeah, as a matter of fact, a couple of alternatives come to mind. One, we could agree on a date each month to sit down and pay the bills together. That way, I'd know that the bills had been written and sent, and you could control my tendency to bug you for your half of the rent before it really needs to be sent. Or, with each paycheck we could each put a certain amount into a joint account. Then when the bills come in I would just write the checks out of that account, and you wouldn't have to bother with it at all.*

MATT: *Maybe we could do a combination of those things.*

BRIAN: *What do you mean?*

MATT: *Well, I don't want to totally turn control over to you. I mean, I really need to learn how to be responsible for getting stuff done on time. But I'm really jammed for time right now. So how about if we set the date for paying the bills, but also set up the joint account. That way, if something comes up and I don't have the time to sit down with you and pay the bills, you can still get them done on time. But when I do have time, we can do it together. I think I can probably learn some good budgeting habits from you.*

BRIAN: *That's fine as long as you put in your share each pay period. I really get a kick out of managing my personal finances, and I'd be glad to show you what I do. What I do may not work for you, but you might get some ideas that you can adapt to your style. In any case, I'm glad we talked. I was really getting pissed at you and now I'm feeling like things are going to be OK. So when can we get together to set our bill paying "date" and set up the joint account?*

Chapter Resources

Communication Improvement Plan: Conflict Management

Would you like to improve your use of the following aspects of your conflict resolving behavior discussed in this chapter?

    Initiating conflict

    Responding to conflict

    Mediating conflicts of others

Pick an aspect and write a communication improvement plan. You can find a communication improvement plan worksheet on our website at www.oup.com/us/interact

FIND MORE *on the web*
Additional plans @
www.oup.com/us/interact

Key Words

Interpersonal conflict, *p. 286*
Pseudoconflict, *p. 287*
Badgering, *p. 287*
Fact conflict or simple conflict, *p. 288*
Value conflicts, *p. 288*
Policy conflicts, *p. 289*
Ego conflicts, *p. 289*

Withdrawal, *p. 292*
Accommodating, *p. 293*
Forcing, *p. 294*
Compromising, *p. 295*
Collaborating, *p. 295*
Mediator, *p. 305*

Skill Practice

Skill Practice exercises challenge you to master the material you have read in this chapter.

For additional Skill Practice activities, visit our website at www.oup.com/us/interact

IDENTIFYING TYPES OF CONFLICT

Label the following as S (pseudoconflict), F (fact), V (value conflict), P (policy), or E (ego conflict).

a. Joe wants to live with Mary, but Mary wants the two of them to get married.

b. Stan believes that because he is an insurance salesman, Jerry should not dispute his position on annuities.

c. George defends his failure to present an anniversary gift to Agnes by asserting that their anniversary is not today (May 8) but May 18.

d. Martin calls to announce that he is bringing the boss home for dinner. His wife replies, "That will be impossible. The house is a mess and I need to go shopping."

e. Jane says, "Harry, pick up your clothes." "I'm not your maid!" Harry replies, "I thought we agreed that it's your job to take care of the house. I take care of the yard."

 a. V b. E c. F d. S e. P

Inter-Act with Media

CINEMA

Callie Khouri (Director). (2002). ***Divine Secrets of the Ya-Ya Sisterhood.*** Sandra Bullock, Ellen Burstyn, James Garner.

  Brief Summary: This film tells the story of a dysfunctional mother–daughter relationship. Vivi Walker is the mother and Siddalee Walker is the daughter returning home as a successful playwright. After a confrontation between mother and daughter, friends of Vivi "kidnap" Siddalee for a period of self-confrontation aimed at helping her reach a better understanding of herself and of her mother.

  IPC Concepts: Conflict types, styles of managing conflict, the need for better communication skills for more successful conflict management.

Gus Van Sant (Director). (2000). ***Finding Forrester.*** Sean Connery, Rob Brown, F. Murray Abraham, Anna Paquin, Busta Rhymes.

  Brief Summary: Jamal Wallace is an Afro-American teen writing prodigy who risks his future as he struggles with peer pressure to not excel and to fit in. He meets William Forrester, an aging recluse who is secretly a famous writer. The two become friends, and Forrester helps Jamal develop his writing skills and encourages him to attend a prestigious New York prep school. Jamal's conflicts include those within himself, with his friends, with Forrester, and with Professor Crawford at the prep school. The film illustrates all of the conflict types and styles covered in this chapter.

  IPC Concepts: Conflict types, styles. Assertiveness and ethical influence as well.

Sidney Lumet (Director). (1957). ***Twelve Angry Men.*** Henry Fonda, Lee J. Cobb, Ed Begley, E. G. Marshall, Jack Klugman, Jack Warden, Martin Balsam, John Fiedler, George Voskovec, Robert Webber, Edward Binns, Joseph Sweeney.

Brief Summary: This film unfolds the powerful story of twelve jurors in a murder trial. We see the defendant only once, at the beginning of the film, when the judge is giving instructions to the jury. The balance of the film is about the deliberations and conflicts that eventually result in a unanimous verdict.

IPC Concepts: Every type of conflict is in evidence. Also, stereotyping, emotion, styles of conflict, styles of communication, personality, listening, etc. This is a blockbuster film of communication theory—it's almost as though it was written specifically for communication classes!

WHAT'S ON THE WEB

Conflict Management Skills

http://www.cnr.berkeley.edu/ucce50/ag-labor/7labor/13.htm

Brief Summary: This is an excellent site. It does a nice job of summarizing a lot of good basic information for the student in an introductory course in interpersonal communication..

IPC Concepts: Conflict, self esteem, styles of management, mediation, arbitration, and ground rules for improved communication in conflict.

Terry Besser. *How Disagreements Become Antagonisms*

http://www.extension.iastate.edu/communities/news/ComCon03.html

http://www.extension.iastate.edu/communities/news/ComCon03.html

Brief Summary: This site offers an excellent and concise discussion of ways in which a situation can escalate from a simple difference of opinion into a full-scale conflict. It covers the role of face-saving measures, polarization, and Gresham's law of conflict.

IPC Concepts: Nature of conflict, styles, views, and skills.

communicating *in* intimate relationships:

FRIENDS, SPOUSES, AND FAMILY

After you have read this chapter, you
should be able to answer these questions:

- What are intimate relationships?

- What are the characteristics of intimate relationships?

- What types of intimate relationships are there?

- What are the purposes of family communication?

- What are the strengths and challenges of intergenerational family communication?

- What are ways to improve communication in families?

- What are ways to deal with problems of loneliness, relational uncertainty, jealousy and sex-role stereotyping in intimate relationships?

> As they walked to the door, she turned and said, "Thanks for the ride home."
>
> "Hey, no problem," Luis replied.
>
> "That Metropolis is a great club, isn't it? And it's great to dance with someone who actually knows how to dance—I was impressed!"
>
> "You think I move pretty well, huh? Maybe we could go out again?"
>
> "Sure. I'll probably be at Metropolis again next Friday."
>
> "OK, I'll look for you. . . . Listen, I've got tickets to the big concert next week. You want to go with me?"
>
> "You got tickets for that show? I thought they were sold out? That's sweet—I'll go with you."
>
> "Great! I'll pick you up about 7:30."
>
> "I'll be ready."
>
> "Then it's on," Luis said as he gave her a quick kiss. As she turned and went into the house, Luis danced down the stairs, jumped into his car, and sped up the street. "Oh yeah," he crooned to himself, "I think I'm falling in love—big time." Then in a moment of utter horror it hit him. He'd forgotten to ask her name!

Daniel Perlman and Beverly Fehr (1987) note that the personal relationship literature is "replete with evidence testifying to the importance of relationships in our lives" (p. 19). In fact, every human being has the simultaneous need for community (connection to friends) and attachment (intimacy with a spouse or lover). The absence of either causes loneliness. Yet, the vast majority of people find themselves able to make and maintain intimate relationships.

Luis's experience, at the beginning of this chapter, illustrates the beginning of the most intimate of relationships—romantic love. Yet romantic relationship are not the only kind of intimate relationships that you are likely to have.

In this chapter we will consider characteristics of intimate relationships, types and styles of intimate relationships, and problem areas in intimate communication.

Characteristics of Intimate Relationships

Intimate relationships are marked by high degrees of warmth and affection, trust, self-disclosure, and commitment, and are formalized through symbols and rituals (Prisbell & Andersen, 1980). Let's consider each of these characteristics.

Warmth and Affection

Perhaps the first, if not the most important, characteristic of intimacy is warmth and affection. Intimate friends have a great deal of liking for each other. In short, a good intimate relationship is not a trial. If being with the partner seems like work, then something is wrong. One way intimate partners express liking is through time spent with each other. Intimates always look forward to being with each other because they experience a joy in each other's company; they enjoy talking with each other, and they enjoy sharing experiences.

Trust

Another important characteristic of intimacy is trust. **Trust** is placing confidence in another in a way that almost always involves some risk. It is a prediction that if you reveal yourself to another, the result will be to your advantage rather than to your disadvantage. We trust those persons who, among other things, will not intentionally harm our interests (LaFollette, 1996, p. 116). And, as Rusbult and colleagues (2001) point out, "As partners develop increased trust in one another, they are likely to become increasingly dependent on one another—that is, they are likely to become increasingly satisfied, increasingly willing to forgo alternatives, and increasingly willing to invest in the relationship" (p. 107).

Susan Boon's research (1994, pp. 97–101) articulates four key issues that underlie the development of trust within an intimate relationship. The first of these is dependability. A **dependable partner** is one who can be relied upon at all times, under all circumstances. In effect, we must know that the person will be there for us whenever we need him or her. A second issue is responsiveness. A **responsive partner** is one whose actions are geared toward the other person's particular needs. At times this may require that one person sacrifice his or her needs for the good of the other. An **effective conflict-resolving partner** is one who can help manage conflicts in a collaborative way. If partners tend to withdraw from potential conflicts, constantly give in to preserve the peace, or force their goals on each other, trust weakens. When partners can engage in open and constructive conflict, they are exercising their trust in each other—trust that they will be able to work out the conflict in beneficial ways. The fourth issue that undergirds intimacy is faith. A **faithful partner** is one who is secure in the

Intimate relationships—relationships that are marked by high degrees of warmth and affection, trust, self-disclosure, and commitment, and are formalized through symbols and rituals.

Trust—confidence placed in another in a way that almost always involves some risk.

Dependable partner—one who can be relied upon at all times, under all circumstances.

Responsive partner—one whose actions are geared toward the other person's particular needs. At times this may require one person to sacrifice his or her needs for the good of the other.

Effective conflict-resolving partner—one who can help manage conflicts in a collaborative way.

Faithful partner—one who is secure in the belief that the other person is trustworthy and that the relationship will endure.

inter-act with

Technology

Suppose you have important information that you want to communicate to (1) a friend, (2) an acquaintance, and (3) a rival or enemy. In each instance, which means would you be *most likely* to use: face-to-face? telephone? regular mail? e-mail? Would you use the same means in all three situations? If so, why? Would you consider different means for one or two of the situations? If so, why? What is it about each means that makes it more or less desirable for each type of relationship? ■

belief that the other person is trustworthy and that the relationship will endure. When you see partners who often question whether the relationship can survive, it seems doomed to failure; when you see partners who are jealous of each other's relationships with same-sex and opposite-sex friends, again the partnership seems doomed to failure.

Self-Disclosure

Intimacy demands relatively high levels of self-disclosure. Through sharing feelings and the process of highly personal self-disclosure, people really come to know and to understand each other. Intimate friends often gain knowledge of their partner's innermost being.

As a result of this increasing amount of disclosure they increase their investment in the relationship and develop a sense of "we-ness."

Although it is unrealistic, and perhaps undesirable, to expect to share feelings with a great many others, the achievement of a feelings-sharing level of communication with a few people is a highly beneficial communication goal. When people find that they get satisfaction out of being together and are able to share ideas and feelings, their intimacy grows.

Even with intimate relationships, there may be limits to the amount of self-disclosure that is appropriate. Although communicating private information about the self and making personal observations regarding the other are necessary for intimacy to develop, on occasion unconditional openness can short-circuit an otherwise good relationship. Still, as Mills and Clark (2001) point out, "sharing and revealing personal information is so characteristic of strong mutual communal relationships that self-disclosure has been thought of as the essence of close relationships" (p. 20).

the gray zone

Positive Misunderstanding

While we generally seek to understand our partner through communication and self-disclosure, there are times when misunderstanding can actually be functional in a relationship. Research shows that in cases of irreconcilable differences in a committed relationship, such as a marriage or a sibling relationship, it is better not to truly understand one's partner (Sillars, 1998). Disclosing ideas and feelings would only emphasize the differences between the partners. For example, relational partners of different political persuasions might avoid discussing some political hot topics in order to avoid acknowledging their conflicting worldviews. In some relationships, a little bit of ignorance is bliss. By not truly understanding each other, we can have a more satisfying relationship. In some instances, misunderstanding might preserve optimism in a relationship and allow it to thrive despite a major difference between the partners. ■

Commitment

Intimate relationships also require a deep level of commitment. For instance, intimate friendships are characterized by the extent to which a person gives up other relationships in order to devote more time and energy to the primary relationship. Especially when two people are testing the suitability of an enduring relationship—going together, engagement, or marriage—they spend long periods of time together.

Intimate relationships have a great deal of strength. Sometimes when one person moves to another part of town or even to another city, the relationship remains unaffected. Some people see each other only once or twice a year but still consider themselves intimates because they share ideas and feelings freely, experience comfort and satisfaction when they are together physically, and rely on each other's counsel and support.

Types of Intimate Relationships and Relational Styles

Intimacy is an aspect of different kinds of close relationships. It is not synonymous with "love" or exclusivity. **Intimates,** then, are people who share a close, caring, and trusting relationship characterized by mutual self-disclosure and commitment. Intimates may go out of their way to help each other; they are concerned for each other's welfare. Both platonic and romantic relationships may become intimate. A **platonic relationship** is one in which the partners are not sexually attracted to each other or do not choose to act on the sexual attraction they feel. Conversely, a **romantic relationship** is one in which the partners act on their sexual attraction to each other.

From early on many of us have developed relationships with people who are likely to be there when we need them. They stand by us regardless of the circumstances, and they listen to our joys and woes nonjudgmentally. People look for same-sex and opposite-sex intimate friends with whom they can share their innermost secrets. Although we have a large number of friends and acquaintances, we are likely to have only a few relationships that we'd define as intimate. Let's consider the nature of male relationships, female relationships, and male–female relationships in order to identify some of the similarities and differences.

Intimates—people who share a close, caring, and trusting relationship characterized by mutual self-disclosure and commitment.

Platonic relationship—a relationship in which the partners are not sexually attracted to each other or do not choose to act on the sexual attraction they feel.

Romantic relationship—a relationship in which the partners act on their sexual attraction to each other.

Male Relationships

Throughout history, male relationships have been glorified as the epitome of camaraderie. Large numbers of popular books, movies, and television shows have portrayed male comradeship and romanticized the male bonding experience. Yet, using male behavior as a standard for defining intimacy has been questioned. For

Male friendship usually focuses on activities, and men regard practical help, mutual assistance, and companionship as benchmarks of caring.

instance, in 1975 sex-role expert Joseph Pleck wrote that male bonding "may indicate sociability, but does not necessarily indicate intimacy" (p. 441). During the past several years research has shown that male–male intimate behavior is qualitatively different from the standard definition of "high levels of self-disclosure." As Julia Wood and Christopher Inman (1993) have pointed out, men "appear to regard practical help, mutual assistance, and companionship as benchmarks of caring" (p. 291).

A great deal about relationships is revealed by what people talk about. Conversational topics can be classified as topical (politics, work, events), relational (the friendship itself), or personal (one's thoughts and feelings). In general, men's conversations tend to be topical, revolving around sports, sex, work, and vehicles, rather than personal, centered on issues or problems. Research with middle-aged and elderly men shows the same pattern: Men talked to same-sex friends about women, the news, music, art, and sports (Fehr, 1996, p. 119). Thus, of the three categories, men's conversations usually are topical. Likewise, much of men's friendship focuses on activities such as playing video games, attending sporting events, and helping each other with repair or renovation projects.

Men generally don't spend time with their male close friends discussing relationships and personal issues. But Wood and Inman (1993) explain that intimacy and closeness in relationships can come through many forms. Men may use an "alternate path" to intimacy by relying on shared activities and favors rather than personal disclosures as a means of developing closeness.

Julia Wood (2003) has suggested that at times men may use playful insults, competition, or mild put-downs to signal their closeness to another man. A **covert intimacy** exchange is a message or series of messages that signals closeness, trust,

Covert intimacy—messages showing closeness, trust, and equality by mild insults, competition and put-downs of a partner.

and equality by using mild insults, competition or put-downs of one's partner (Wood, 2003). These behaviors, when used with a less intimate acquaintance, would signal hostility and would be perceived as a one-up power move leading to distrust and relationship damage. But within the context of a well-established intimate male relationship, such exchanges usually signal affection. For example, Jon might playfully say to Alex, his boyhood friend and now roommate, "Hey idiot, has that girlfriend of yours realized yet that she can do better than you?" Alex might respond, "At least I have a girlfriend. When was the last time some girl was willing to go out with you?" It is through such covert intimacy that insults, competition, and put-downs become a way for male friends to implicitly say that they care about each other.

Many men, however, report that the relationships most meaningful to them are male–female relationships. Although men don't share much intimate information with each other, they still have a need for relationships with people who will give them help or counsel when they are having difficulty. As one might expect, a large sample of men rated their female friends highest in this nurturing quality but gave their male friends the lowest ratings (Fitzpatrick & Bochner, 1981). Interestingly, men not only confide more to their best women friends but also report being closer to their women friends than to their male friends (Winstead, Derlega, & Rose, 1997).

Female Relationships

Whereas men rarely communicate their feelings to their male friends, women's intimate friendships are marked by mutual disclosures. In fact, women's relationships seem to be the total opposite of male friendships. In contrast to male conversation, which we've learned is generally topical, female conversations tend to span the topic categories—topical, relational, and personal—with the focus on relational and personal. Research with middle-aged and elderly adults shows the same pattern: women talk about men, food, relationship problems, family, and fashion (Fehr, 1996, p. 119). Moreover, women's friendships develop more quickly than men's and tend to be more intense.

It would seem that female relationships are rich when measured by many of the criteria of effective interpersonal communication. Nonetheless, women are not always satisfied with their female relationships. Because women care so much about others, they tend to experience the troubles of those close to them as their own. This heavy emotional involvement can take its toll over time, leading to health costs and overdependence on the relationships. Because intimacy is an issue in all relationships, let's look at how men and women differ in this regard.

Gender Differences in Intimacy

Recent research continues to support the view that men's relationships are defined in terms of joint activities and women's in terms of shared thoughts and feelings (Reis, 1998, p. 216). Similarly, men's views of intimacy seem related to physical nearness. So, for men, intimacy is based on shared activity in male relationships and sexuality in male–female relationships. In contrast, women's intimacy is based on talking and affection, regardless of whether the friend is female or male (Reis, 1998, p. 218). Yet, despite the apparent differences in behaviors, Reis goes on to say that both men and women define intimacy using the same words: warmth, disclosure of personal feelings, and shared activity (p. 219).

Male–Female Relationships

Because men and women tend to achieve relational intimacy through different means, they can be critical of each other's styles, and frustrations can occur in cross-sex relationships.

For instance, Duck and Wright (1993) point out that women's emphasis of enacting verbal disclosures legitimizes an unfortunate stereotype of women's friendships as noninstrumental (with less emphasis on action, fun, and companion-ship) or at least less instrumental than those of men (p. 725).

Women frequently criticize men for failing to express their feelings. Men need to understand that for a woman, intimacy is defined as sharing information, feelings, secrets, and insights through such self-disclosing statements as "Our rela-tionship is really important to me. My life would be empty without you." Women need to understand that for many men intimacy is defined as practical help, mutual assistance, and companionship. Thus, statements about what the man has done for an intimate friend, such as "While you were at the meeting, I washed your car and cleaned up the kitchen," represent a male standard of showing intimacy. So, whereas female intimacy tends to be expressive, male intimacy tends to be instru-mental.

In the past, our society has valued a feminine preference for verbal disclosures as the measure of intimacy; recently more emphasis has been placed on the male tendency toward instrumental activity as equally important in determining inti-macy (Wood & Inman, 1993, p. 280). Some say that women's expressive style and men's instrumental style are complementary approaches that work well together. Still others maintain that the optimal situation is one in which all people, regardless of gender, embrace both affective and activity-oriented modes of relating to friends (Fehr, 1996, p. 141).

Interestingly, older people are less likely to have cross-sex friendships than are younger people; men are more likely to report cross-sex friendships than are women; and unmarried persons are more apt to develop cross-sex friendships than married persons (Werking, 1997, p. 394). Women more than men report that dating and marriage negatively affect friendships because women may choose to spend more time with boyfriends or husbands than with friends and because the men often object to the time their female partners spend with friends (Winstead, Derlega, & Rose, 1997).

Both cross-sex friendships and loving male–female relationships can be complicated by the fact that men and women seek intimacy in different ways. Male–female relationships are likely to run more smoothly if participants recognize and value the differing approaches. In addition, both men and women can have difficulty distinguishing between satisfying intimate friendship relationships and romantic, sexual relationships. Attempts at male–female friendships, especially when the man and the woman are married to someone else, are frequently misinterpreted. Indeed, O'Meara (1989) found that cross-sex friendships frequently encounter issues of sexuality as well as challenges of defining the relationship for others.

Marriage and Other Long-Term Committed Relationships

A substantial amount of research has been directed at understanding intimacy in marriage and other long-term, committed romantic relationships. When the relationship between life partners is a good one, it meets many tests of the ideal. Perhaps most important, in good relationships of these types, people find greatest satisfaction in being with each other. For example, in a survey of more than two thousand American married people, J. D. Bloch (1980) found that 40 percent of all respondents considered their spouse to be their best friend. In a different study of married people, 88 percent of married men and 78 percent of married women named their spouse as the person "closest" to them (Fischer & Narus, 1981, p. 449).

Nevertheless, what husbands and wives get from each other is somewhat out of balance. Although married women named their spouse as their closest friend, women still need close female friendships to satisfy all their needs. Men, on the other hand, reported that their wives offer them the most satisfaction and emotional support of all the relationships in their lives—more than neighbor, co-worker, boss, parent, sibling, or same-sex and opposite-sex friends (Argyle & Furnham, 1983, p. 490).

Despite similarities of apparent needs in marriage partners, there is no one single ideal marriage style. Mary Anne Fitzpatrick, a leading scholar of marriage, has identified characteristics or dimensions that identify different types of couples (Fitzpatrick, 1988, p. 76; Fitzpatrick & Badzinski, 1994, p. 741). Couples can be differentiated on the basis of their "independence," the extent to which they share their feelings with each other. Some couples are highly interdependent, depending on their partners for comfort, expressions of love, and fun. Other couples are more reserved and do not depend on their partners for emotional sharing and support. The second dimension on which couples can be differentiated is their ideology. Ideology is the extent to which the partners adhere to traditional belief systems and values, especially about marriage and sex roles, or hold nontraditional beliefs and values that tolerate change and uncertainty in relationships. The third dimension is one that Fitzpatrick originally called "conflict avoidance" but now calls "communication." Couple types differ in the extent to which they seek to avoid conflict as they interact.

Using these dimensions, Fitzpatrick describes three basic types of enduring couple relationships, which she labels as traditional, independent, and separate.

Traditional couples—those who have a traditional ideology but maintain some independence in the marriage.

Independent couples—those who share an ideology that embraces change and uncertainty in the marriage relationship but, like traditional couples, are interdependent and apt to engage in rather than avoid conflict to resolve differences.

Separate couples—those who share traditional ideology but differ from traditional and independent couples in that they engage in less emotional sharing.

Traditional couples have a traditional ideology, but maintain some independence in their marriages. They follow the values accepted by parents and grandparents. Their values place more emphasis on stability than on spontaneity. They hold to traditional customs: The woman takes her husband's last name in marriage; infidelity is always inexcusable. Traditional relationships show a great deal of interdependence, marked by a high degree of sharing and companionship, and they are apt to engage in rather than avoid conflict.

Independent couples share an ideology that embraces change and uncertainty in the marriage relationship but, like traditional couples, they are interdependent and apt to resolve differences by engaging in rather than avoiding conflict. They hold more nonconventional values. Independents believe that relationships should not constrain a partner's freedoms. Independent partners maintain separate physical spaces and sometimes find it difficult to maintain regular daily time schedules.

Separate couples are characterized by a shared traditional ideology, but differ from the previous two groups in that they engage in less emotional sharing and so are less interdependent. In addition, separate couples tend to avoid conflict. They are conventional in marital and family issues but, like independents, they stress the importance of individual freedom. They have significantly less companionship and sharing in their marriage than partners in either traditional or independent marriages. Separate couples indicate interdependence by keeping a regular daily schedule.

While in two-thirds of all the couples she studied, Fitzpatrick found that couples agreed about their marital type, in the remaining third the partners disagreed. When partners disagreed, the wife most frequently classified herself as a "traditional" and the husband more frequently saw himself as a "separate." Fitzpatrick

How does a traditional marriage differ from an independent one?

spotlight on scholars

Mary Anne Fitzpatrick, Dean of the College of Arts and Sciences of the University of South Carolina, on

Couple Types and Communication

The notion that not all marriages are exactly alike seems obvious. We all know of couples who seem to have marriages that "work" for them, and these marriages seem similar in "feel" to those of other couples we know. At the same time, we know some couples whose relationships are very different from the marriages of other people we know but seem to be equally effective for the people involved. As a doctoral student, Mary Anne Fitzpatrick became intrigued with the different relational patterns that she saw in marriages. In her dissertation she began work to uncover a typology or classification scheme that could describe these different relationships. Fitzpatrick's own observations of married couples suggested to her that couples of the same type showed a pattern in relating to one another, a pattern different from the one displayed by couples of a different type.

As is noted in the text, Fitzpatrick has found three distinct types of couples: traditional (both partners have a traditional ideology, are highly interdependent, and are apt to engage in rather than avoid conflict), independent (partners share an ideology that embraces change and uncertainty in the marriage relationship but,

like the traditional, are interdependent and apt to engage in rather than avoid conflict to resolve differences), and separate (couples are characterized by a shared traditional ideology, but differ from the previous two groups in that they engage in less emotional sharing, and so are less interdependent, and tend to avoid conflict).

In conducting her research, Fitzpatrick has demonstrated scholarly leadership through her methods. In all of her work, Fitzpatrick has been careful to study a broad range of couples from a wide cross section of the population. While in some research it may be permissible to study only college students (who are easy to find at a university), Fitzpatrick believes that for theories about communication in marriage and family to be accurate, the population studied must be drawn from a broader base. So she is careful to recruit participants for her studies in a variety of settings and from a variety of backgrounds.

Fitzpatrick believes that her most useful work comes from studies in which she examines the actual conversations of couples and families. Using a research technique called "discourse analysis," Fitzpatrick and other scholars study, categorize, and summarize

the flow of actual conversations. By studying the order, topics, and interaction processes through which conversations unfold, Fitzpatrick is able to understand how different types of couples negotiate their relationships. This technique is labor intensive. Each hour of conversation takes about thirty hours of study and coding to turn the conversation into data that can be compared to data from other conversations.

Finally, Fitzpatrick believes in involving her undergraduate students in her research. Along with her colleagues at the University of Wisconsin and elsewhere, Fitzpatrick is committed to the concept of "scholarship in the service of teaching," meaning that the purpose of scholarship is twofold. First, through scholarship, we create better explanations that more accurately describe the world. These up-to-date explanations should be the substance of what is taught in the modern university. Second, a goal of university teaching is to strengthen the critical thinking and lifelong learning skills of graduates. So involving students in ongoing research projects equips them to be critical of other studies they read, able to sort out well-done studies from those that are less well executed. Further, it allows students to "get their hands dirty" and in so doing gives them practice in research skills that they can use later to study problems and find valid answers on their own.

Recently, Fitzpatrick has extended her work to investigating how the family relationships differ in families headed by different types of couples. She has already completed one project that provided encouraging evidence for her belief that there is a systematic relationship between types of couples and types of families. Fitzpatrick and her students also have coded conversation data from families with adolescent children. The data will be used to discover how different types of families communicate with one another and handle misunderstandings. For some of Fitzpatrick's major publications, see the references for this chapter at the end of the book. ■

called this pattern "separate-traditionals." In these relationships, the husband and wife agree on the traditional ideology of marriage, but whereas the wife views the marriage as an interdependent relationship where conflict is expressed, the husband views the relationship as one that is more emotionally distant and where conflict should be avoided.

Using these couple types and focusing on actual conversations of couples, Fitzpatrick and her associates, as well as other scholars, have been able to understand how different couple types handle conflict, deal with compliance-gaining messages, display power and control, have casual discussions, and talk about the issues and themes that are important to a marriage.

What Fitzpatrick has concluded is that no couple type is better than the others; rather, each type has different kinds of strengths and weaknesses. To provide more insight into Mary Anne Fitzpatrick and her work, we featured her in the Spotlight on Scholars on p. 327-328.

To many of us, an important question is, what is the secret to a long and happy intimate romantic relationship? Researchers have found there are three common characteristics of married couples that have stayed together for more than fifty years (Dickson, 1995, pp. 47–48). The first characteristic is **mutual respect**—treating each other with dignity. In short, long-lasting marriages are a product of people's valuing each other for what and who they are.

The second characteristic is a **comfortable level of closeness**—spending an appropriate amount of time with a relational partner. This does not mean that longtime partners are with each other all the time. Whereas some partners desire constant companionship, others are happy with relatively low closeness. But the defining point is that both partners continue to know each other. The fact is that many couples grow apart over time—that is, they quit seeking each other's company or come to prefer the company of different people.

What we've discovered is that continuing closeness takes effort on the part of the couple. For many couples closeness is developed through such rituals as celebrations, family traditions, and patterned routines (Werner, Altman, Brown, & Ginat, 1993, p. 115). Probably the most important element in maintaining closeness in a relationship is a patterned routine. For instance, some couples make sure that at least one night a week they go out together for dinner and a movie or just sit and talk. When people regularly make time to be together, it's easy for them to remember why they were drawn to each other. But if partners let their relationship drift, before long they may lose track of what brought them together in the first

Mutual respect—treating each other with dignity.

Comfortable level of closeness—spending an appropriate amount of time with a relational partner.

place. Yet with families, as with most people, practical matters often get in the way of nurturing the relationship. That is, some families are so busy handling those things that "must be done" that they forget what it takes to keep a relationship growing. The ritual of patterned routines is designed to foster the relationship and is an essential part of any long-term relationship.

The third characteristic is the **presence of a plan or life vision.** Sometimes this is consciously negotiated. At other times it just seems to happen. But the defining point is that both partners agree on their long-term goals—and, of course, that the partners see each other in those long-term plans. Such partners talk about "we" and "us" rather than "I" or "me."

Presence of a plan or life vision—agreeing on long-term goals.

Family Relationships

A **family** is "a group of intimates who generate a sense of home and group identity, complete with strong ties of loyalty and emotion, and experience a history and a future" (Galvin & Brommel, 1996). Families are structured in different ways. The

Family—a group of intimates who generate a sense of home and group identity, complete with strong ties of loyalty and emotion, and experience a history and a future.

learn about yourself

Take this short survey, a test of respect for a partner, to learn something about yourself. Answer the questions based on your first response. There are no right or wrong answers. Just be honest in reporting your true feelings about a partner in an intimate relationship. For each question, select one of the following numbers that best describes your feeling.

| 1 = Always | 2 = Often | 3 = Sometimes | 4 = Rarely | 5 = Never |

_____ **1.** My partner is trustworthy.

_____ **2.** My partner fosters a relationship of mutual care.

_____ **3.** My partner shows interest in me.

_____ **4.** My partner is sensitive and considerate of my feelings.

_____ **5.** My partner provides unconditional love.

_____ **6.** My partner is open and receptive.

_____ **7.** My partner is honest and truthful.

_____ **8.** My partner fosters good two-way communication.

_____ **9.** My partner is committed to me.

_____ **10.** My partner is understanding and empathic.

SCORING THE SURVEY: Add the scores together for all ten questions. The score will range from 10 to 50.

The lower your score (closer to 10), the more you feel respect for your relationship partner. The higher your score (closer to 50), the less respect you feel for your relationship partner.

Adapted from: Frei, J. R., & Shaver, P. R. (2002). Respect in close relationships: Prototype definition, self-report assessment, and initial correlates. *Personal Relationships, 9,* 121–139.

traditional family consists of two opposite-sex parents living with one or more children from the union of those two parents; but today, many people live in satisfying and nurturing families whose structure is different from tradition. Exhibit 12.1 describes other common structures.

E X H I B I T 1 2 . 1

Common family structures

- Traditional: two opposite-sex parents living with one or more children from the union of those two parents
- Single-parent families: one parent lives with the children; the other is not present in the home and may or may not be actively parenting the children
- Shared-custody families: the parents have divorced; the children live alternately with each parent
- Blended families: two adults and one or more children, some of whom were born to those parents in previous relationships
- Common-law families: unmarried opposite-sex partners living with the children of their union
- Gay and lesbian couples raising children: same-sex partners raising children
- Childless couples: same- or opposite-sex couples without children
- Empty-nest couples: couples whose children are grown and live elsewhere
- Extended families: multiple generations of related people living together
- Communal families: unmarried people related by nongenetic factors who participate in cooperative living arrangements

Regardless of type, family relationships develop and change. A person's first intimate friendships are likely to be with family members. For instance, small children first rely on their parents, then perhaps on a brother or sister. Family relationships may remain intimate ones; in many families sisters or brothers continue to be each other's closest friends throughout their lives. During teen years and beyond, however, many people develop closer friendships with people outside the family.

Much of the functioning of the family system is a product of the communication within the family. Family communication serves at least three major purposes for individual family members.

Family Communication Contributes to Self-Concept Formation. In Chapter 2 we discussed the role of communication in the formation of one's self-concept. One major responsibility that family members have to one another is to "talk" (family talk includes both verbal and nonverbal communication elements) in ways that will contribute to the development of strong self-concepts in all family members, especially younger children (Yerby, Buerkel-Rothfuss, & Bochner, 1995). Research by D. H. Demo (1987) emphasized the point that self-concepts are established, maintained, reinforced, and/or modified by communication from family members. Family members' self-concepts are enhanced by the following:

1. Statements of praise: "Jason, you really did a nice job of cleaning your room," and "Mom, that was really nice of you to let Emily stay the night."

diverse voices

Performing Commitment *By Jacqueline Taylor*

Families are structured in different ways. In this excerpt, the author describes how mundane daily activities as well as rituals and public ceremonies serve as performances of commitment in her family.

For over 13 years I have created family within the context of my commitment to Carol, my partner and longtime companion. The law says we are not a couple, but two single women. No church or state has blessed or ratified our union. Although our property and our finances are by this time as entwined as our hearts and lives, the state does not apply its joint-property laws to us or give us the right to inherit from each other in the absence of a will. I cannot include her on the family insurance benefits my university offers. The only place we can purchase a family membership is at the women's bookstore.

Eight years ago we became mothers together, with the adoption of our first daughter, Lucy. One year later we adopted Grace. The law recognized us not as one family, but as two—two single mothers living in the same house with our two adopted children. No blood ties unite any of the four of us. We are a family not because but in spite of the social and legal structures that refuse to name us so. Because our status as a family has been ignored or denied by the laws and customs of our society, our existence as a family can never be taken for granted but must be constantly created and recreated. That our family differs in some significant ways from conventional notions of what constitutes a

family means that our creation of family must simultaneously affirm and critique familial structures. . . .

The process of knitting ourselves into a family has taken years and has been characterized more by daily and, yes, mundane performances of commitment than by rituals and ceremonies. Yet we have also participated in public rituals that have helped us to construct ourselves.

The arrival of our babies was greeted by four different showers thrown by friends. Each of our workplaces and two sets of friends organized parties. The various communities we participate in have worked hard to fill the gap between what the law and convention define as family and what our experience reveals. The four of us crate our own rituals, as well. . . .

Carol reminds me that the most important performance of commitment is the daily care and love we give to our daughters. Parents communicate commitment every day through the constant and repetitive tasks that children's survival depends on—changing diapers, wiping up spills, kissing "owies"—and later on, supervising homework, chauffeuring to sports and music lessons, listening to their stories. For heterosexual families perhaps this is enough. But we gay and lesbian (and adoptive) families create family outside the context of the social and legal structures

that allow traditional families to take themselves for granted, and so we must do more.

Thus, we have learned to use language consciously, carefully, and repetitively to define ourselves to each other and our social world. *"Family"* we say, over and over. "Thank you for carrying that package. You are helping our *family."* "This party is just for our *family."* "In our *family,* we don't hit." . . .

Our family doesn't fit anybody's mold. But we are a family, held together by ties of love, loyalty, commitment, and daily life. Because our family does not conform to traditional definitions of family, the performances that connect us to the social fabric and to one another take on even greater importance. Through the anniversaries, ceremonies, rituals, and holidays that mark our years and the repeated mundane actions of commitment that mark our days, we perform the bonds that make us kin. . . .

. . . [F]amily is a group of people who live together and love each other, bound by their shared commitment to the health, growth, and welfare of all. ∎

Excerpted from Taylor, J. (2002). Performing commitment. In Martin, J. N., Nakayama, T. K., & Flores, L. A. (Eds.), *Readings in Intercultural Communication* (pp. 310–318). New York: McGraw-Hill.

2. Statements of acceptance and support: "If you have good reasons to drop out of the band, we accept your decision," and "Andy doesn't see eye to eye with us, but he's welcome in our home because he's your friend, and we respect that."

4. Statements of love: "Lee, I know it hurts to play poorly in front of your family, but we love you and we'll be here again next game," and "We both love you very much, Trevor."

Family Communication Supplies Needed Recognition and Support. A second responsibility of family members is to interact with each other in ways that recognize and support individual relatives. Recognition and support help family members feel that they are important and help them get over the difficult times all of us sometimes face. The importance of this responsibility cannot be overstated. Family members are usually the people with whom we feel safest, and we often turn to them when we need praise, comfort, and reassurance. Yet in many families this important responsibility is forgotten in the rush of day-to-day living. For example, when Judith, the youngest daughter, comes home excited about the gold star she received for her spelling test, her mother and/or father need to take time to recognize the accomplishment regardless of how busy they are or what problems they may have faced that day. Likewise, when parents come home from a rough day at work, spouses and children need to behave in ways that show that home is a safe haven, where the difficulties of the workaday world can be set aside. The point is that all family members need to be told when they are doing well and assured that they can rely on each other. When people can't get recognition and support from within the family, they go outside the family for it.

Family Communication Establishes Models. A third responsibility of family members is to communicate in ways that serve as models of good communication for younger family members. Parents serve as role models, whether they want to or not. The saying "Do as I say, not as I do" hardly represents a workable model of behavior because it teaches only hypocrisy. If Julia sees her parents listening, paraphrasing, and comforting each other, Julia will be more likely to paraphrase and comfort her friends and siblings. If, however, Julia sees family members half-listening and being unsympathetic to others, Julia will learn to behave similarly. How many times have we heard a parent say, "I don't understand Tim's or Bea's behavior," when that behavior strongly resembles the parent's?

Recognition and support help family members feel valuable and help them get over difficult times they face. Recall an incident in your own life when a family member gave you support. How did that behavior affect your relationship?

Modeling behavior is especially important in managing conflict. Children react in vigorous ways when they believe they have been wronged. They will scream, cry, hit, punch, and scratch. As they become more sophisticated, they learn to manipulate, lie, and do whatever is necessary to get their own way. It's the parents' responsibility to socialize children, to teach them how to manage the conflict in their lives. But telling children how to behave and then engaging in just the opposite behavior will only reinforce aggressive or passive conflict-managing strategies. On the other hand, parents can model collaboration by discussing, weighing and considering, describing their feelings, and being supportive during their disagreements. In so doing they not only protect their own relationship but they also model for their children how loving people work through conflict.

observe & analyze

Communication in Your Family

For a few days, keep a diary of communication in your family: Report examples of language and nonverbal communication that seem to raise or lower self-concepts, to recognize and support or fail to recognize and support family members, and to provide good or bad models of communication behavior. In general, does the family communication appear to be more positive or more negative? What do you see as the effects of family communication styles on individual members of the family and on the family as a unit? ■

Intergenerational Family Communication

Communication between children, parents, and grandparents can be a source of both great joy and much frustration in families. In studying intergenerational communication across the life span, Williams and Nussbaum (2001) found many factors accounting for the strength of child–parent relationships across seventy or more years. Lifelong parent–child relationships remain satisfying when there is consistent contact, high levels of mutual affection, social support and tangible assistance, and a consensus of values, beliefs, and opinions. It is also important that each party know what topics not to discuss with the other.

Communication between older and younger family members can be challenging and frustrating as well. Adolescents and their parents often experience conflict around issues of control, autonomy, and responsibility. This is a period of great change in the relationship, and both the parents and the teens must be willing to adapt to and negotiate the changes.

Different generations of family members may find it difficult to communicate with each other because of different interests, geographic distance, the fast past of contemporary life, and stereotypes of aging (Ryan, Pearce, Anas, & Norris, 2004). One of the most frequently reported problems of communication between younger and elderly family members is young adults' manner of speaking to their elders. Gould (2004) found that younger family members often overaccommodate older relatives. They limits the topics introduced, speak in overly simple ways, talk too loudly, and tend to be repetitive in their remarks. Older adults recognize and resent this style of communication as limiting and patronizing.

Yet intergenerational communication can be rewarding as older family members transmit cultural and family values and younger family members carry on family traditions, thus providing their elders with a sense of immortality.

Improving Family Communication

In outlining the importance of effective communication in families, we have alluded to methods for improving family communication. Let's now specifically discuss five guidelines that members (as well as any people in intimate relationships) can use to improve communication in the family.

Opening the Lines of Communication. For a number of reasons, lines of communication within a family can become scrambled or broken, causing family members to feel isolated from one another. With the exception of requests and orders from other family members ("Clean up your room," "Don't play the stereo so loudly"), many people actually spend very few minutes each day genuinely communicating with other members of their family. Instead, they spend the bulk of their time interacting with people outside the home.

The first step in opening lines of communication is setting a time specifically for family members to talk. Each member of the family needs the opportunity to recount what happened that day. One good time for families to talk is during the evening meal. Unfortunately, the rush of busy lives and the ever-present television often compete for the attention of family members, even when they are physically together, and thus threaten such conversations. Recent national studies are showing that families are spending much less time together than they did a generation ago: Family dinners are down by one-third over the past twenty years, and family vacations have decreased by 28 percent (Family time, 2002). It may be difficult to have significant family time every day of the week, but the consequences of not doing so are becoming increasingly clear.

Confronting the Effects of Power Imbalances. Members of a family are dependent on one another for many things. Children depend on their parents for food, shelter, clothing, and transportation, as well as love. Children depend on one another for friendship and support. Parents need their children's love and companionship, and in many cases parents need their children to behave in ways that validate the parents' self-concept. Because of the nature of these dependencies, the distribution of power within the family is unequal. Society gives parents legitimate power over their children, and because parents usually control the family budget and are physically stronger than their children, they wield considerable reward and coercive power. Older children often have great amounts of coercive and referent power over their younger brothers and sisters in addition to the legitimate power given them by the parents. Imbalances in referent power occur between two siblings when one will go to almost any lengths to please the other (usually older) child. For instance, young Todd may endure abusive treatment from his older brother, Mark, because Todd at least has the "privilege" of being with Mark. Within any family with children, then, some of the members will have more power than others. The younger child may be placed in the position of having to please three "parents"—mother, father, and an older brother or sister. If the demands of all three are in accord, few problems should arise. If, however, the older sibling begins to abuse the power relationship, the younger sibling may react by withdrawing or becoming hostile.

Family communication is often strongly influenced by these dependencies and the power distributions that derive from them. In many families children are not treated equally. For example, parents who realize that one of their children has certain gifts or talents that the others lack, may allow this child privileges the others do not enjoy. Occasionally, parents simply make a mistake and treat one child unequally because he or she is more demanding or because the parents have forgotten how they treated the other (usually older) children under similar circumstances.

observe & analyze

Family Power Relationships and Support Systems

Analyze the power relationships between you and (a) your mother or father, (b) your siblings, or (c) your children. How do these dependencies affect your communication? Analyze the support systems in your family. Discuss who listens, who helps, and who can be counted on. ■

If lines of communication within a family are open, it is possible to identify and confront family power imbalances and the inequities they may be causing within relationships. Each member of the family should feel free to inquire about any family rule or behavior that is a problem for that family member. For instance, suppose the oldest sister in a family is unhappy because she has to be in by 10:30 on weeknights. If lines of communication are open, she will question that rule. If lines of communication are open, parents will explain why they are making and enforcing a 10:30 curfew rather than simply relying on their authority and answering "Because I said so, that's why!" If parents explain to their children and give them reasons for rules, then children are more likely to accept the rules and confide in their parents.

Recognizing and Adapting to Change. Members of a family know each other so well that they may be quick to predict how a particular family member will think, feel, or act under many different circumstances. These predictions will not always be accurate, however. All people change with time, though such changes are likely to be gradual, and family members may be the last to recognize them. For example, it isn't until Tanya returns from six weeks at summer camp that another member of the family is likely to recognize how she has changed.

Even as children grow and change, their brothers and sisters, and especially their parents, continue to see them as they once were, not as they are or are becoming. Quite often a younger member of the family will hear such statements as "Don't tell me you like asparagus—remember, I'm your brother, I know you," or "You're going to be a doctor? Come on, you faint at the sight of blood." If you are studying away at college, you may be offended when you return home and your parents continue to treat you as they did when you were in high school.

Recall our discussion in Chapter 2, where we showed that social perceptions are not always accurate. This is true even when those perceptions come from family members who "know each other like the back of their hand." The skill of perception checking is as important for family members as it is for strangers. Moreover, the skill of dating generalizations, discussed in Chapter 4, is another important one for members of a family to master. It may well be true that Maggie didn't like asparagus or that Ginger used to faint at the sight of blood, but as the years go by, Maggie and Ginger change.

Recognizing and adapting to change appear to be especially difficult as children become teens and strive to achieve independence at the same time that their parents may be experiencing the changes associated with midlife transition.

Frequently, parents who are occupied with their own adult life transition find it difficult to reexamine and change their relationship with the adolescent child to one that is better suited to the emerging needs of both of them. Thus parents continue to interact with the child in the habitual way and justify the behavior by asserting that the child must earn the right to be treated like an adult. Yet a teenager who is treated like a child will probably rebel or act out, whereas a teenager treated as an adult is likely to reason and discuss.

Recognizing change has another dimension as well. Family members need to be alert to the kinds of change that may indicate stress or emotional distress in other members. Unfortunately, people often are unable to notice gradual changes in behavior that serve as signals to problems until a family member is seriously troubled. Family members who suspect difficulty should be open in confronting relatives about their behavior. They might begin by saying something like "I've noticed that you don't seem to be yourself. You've withdrawn from most of your activities, you aren't eating well, and you look really sad. Is there something happening that we can help you with?" Family members, like people in all relationships, need to use their supportive communication skills to help other members of the family deal with change.

Respecting Individual Interests. Healthy family communication respects individual interests. Chapters 7 and 8 discussed the importance of listening, understanding, and comforting. Certainly these skills apply to family relationships; yet family communication can often be marked by indifference or apathy. Individual family members are sometimes overly concerned with themselves and fail to consider the feelings of others. When something nice happens to one member of the family, the first reaction of other family members should never be "Big deal." If

What clues suggest that this family enjoys each other's company?

other family members celebrate the accomplishments of a member and show interest in his or her activities, that person is likely to return the favor.

Managing Conflicts Equitably. Because interdependent family members have unique needs, and because power in the family is unevenly distributed, situations that lead to conflict are inevitable. Yet, families differ in their abilities to resolve conflict in effective ways. Families develop rules for how differences between members will be handled. Although these rules are generally determined by the parents' preferred conflict styles, individual children will differ in the extent to which they comply with these rules.

In some families, conflict is avoided at all costs. So members learn to avoid conversing about subjects on which there is likely to be disagreement. These families may also withdraw or defer to the position taken by the most powerful person. So children (and even young adults) obey the will of their parents in order to keep peace.

Other families develop rules that are more democratic. When family members find themselves in conflict, they may hold a family meeting to jointly work out the problem. In these meetings, one or more of the neutral members may serve as a mediator. Conflict mediation and problem solving also may occur in a less formalized process. Nevertheless, the rule in these families is to view conflict as an opportunity to promote win/win outcomes between members.

A third rule for dealing with conflict within the family is to use coercive or forcing behaviors. Such families often end conflict episodes by acceding to the wishes of the most powerful member. "As long as you're under my roof . . ." and "because I'm the mother, that's why" and "if you don't, I'll tell Mom what you did" are all examples of forcing.

In some families, forcing behaviors are not met by acquiescence but by resistance. These situations are troublesome, since they may escalate into incidents of family violence. Family violence (Yerby et al., 1995, p. 304) is a spiral of family conflict that escalates into attacks upon family members. These attacks take many forms, including wife-battering and spouse abuse, child abuse and neglect, sexual abuse of children, marital rape, sibling abuse, abuse of elderly relatives, psychological abuse of family members, and violence by children.

Unfortunately, in many families almost any conflict can grow to be physical and result in abusive behavior. Because men are generally physically stronger, physical abuse is most often perpetrated by men (Sabourin & Stamp, 1995, p. 213). But verbal aggression can be every bit as harmful to a relationship as physical abuse, and whereas physical abuse is usually a reaction of the man, both men and women engage in verbal abuse.

What causes people to resort to verbal and physical abuse of people they claim to love? While there is strong evidence to suggest that the tendency to use abusive behavior is handed down from generation to generation, those who engage in abuse are likely to lack appropriate communication skills, including those related to constructive conflict management (Sabourin, 1996, p. 213). How can you keep relationships from becoming abusive? The best advice is to reread the material in Chapter 11 and try to apply it in your family relationships.

Problems Associated with Intimacy

Intimacy in relationships is difficult to achieve. In this final section we describe four problems related to intimacy: loneliness, relational uncertainty, jealousy, and sex-role stereotyping.

Loneliness

Loneliness—the condition of a person whose desired level of social interaction is higher than the level achieved.

Loneliness can be characterized as the condition of a person whose desired level of social interaction is higher than the level achieved (Segrin, 1998). If Justin wants more social interaction than he has, then he is likely to feel lonely. Loneliness does not depend on the sheer amount of social interaction. Someone who has little interaction with others could be content with that level of interaction. Someone else who has frequent social interactions might desire even greater social contact, and would feel lonely as a result. People who have satisfying intimate relationships are rarely lonely. Conversely, people who have many superficial relationships may feel lonely even if they are continuously in others' presence.

There are several characteristics that describe lonely people. People who frequently experience loneliness tend to have difficulty introducing themselves to others, are unable to initiate social activity, have trouble making friends, and tend to be less accepting of other people in general.

Relational Uncertainty

Relational uncertainty—a feeling of doubt about the nature of a relationship.

Relational uncertainty occurs when people feel doubt about the nature of a relationship. One source of relational uncertainty is absence of clarity between partners about whether the relationship is platonic or romantic. There may be elements of both relationship types occurring simultaneously, and one or both parties may be uncertain about how to define the relationship. This type of relational uncertainty is most prevalent as a relationship moves from casual dating to serious romantic attachment (Knobloch & Solomon, 2002), since it is rare for both partners to desire to move from a casual flirtation to a serious romantic relationship at the very same time. A second source of relational uncertainty stems from the dialectical tension that has partners wanting closeness one day and more separation the next. You will recall from the discussion of relational dialectics in Chapter 3 that competing tensions pull people back and forth in their relationship needs. Such variations within and across individuals can contribute to relational uncertainty.

A third source of relational uncertainty arises from concern about the future of a relationship stemming from perceived distancing, unresolved conflicts, or life change events. Perhaps people in a committed relationship begin to notice signs that the relationship is more distant, with less sharing or less time spent on mutually enjoyable activities. Or partners may notice that tension exists because of unresolved (or irresolvable) conflicts such as differences in money management philosophies or religious beliefs. Normal life transitions can also give rise to uncertainty. When a daughter marries, her mother may experience this type of relational uncertainty as new boundaries to their relationship are developed. Or best friends may become uncertain about how their relationship will change as they prepare to leave for different colleges. A young soldier about to deploy may be concerned about how his military experience will change not only who he is but also his relationships with his friends and family. The best way to deal with relational uncertainty is to consciously acknowledge it to yourself and to discuss the nature and the future of the relationship with your relational partner. While such openness may be difficult, communicating directly about each other's feelings about and goals for the relationship can be a useful way to reduce uncertainty and to sustain the relationship.

Imagine that Dana and Jamie have been close friends their whole lives. Recently, Jamie has not been returning Dana's calls or responding to e-mails. They have not found the time to get together socially in quite a while. Dana misses the close friendship with Jamie and feels uncertain about whether the two of them have different goals for the friendship and commitment it. Perhaps Dana asks Jamie directly, "Do you think that our friendship is drifting apart? It seems to me that we have not gotten together in about six months, and we seldom talk by phone or e-mail. I wonder what the future holds for our friendship." Jamie may clarify by responding, "Hey, I feel bad about not being able to get together or to even talk once in a while. I am swamped at work right now and I'm in the middle of trying to finishing building the deck on my house before the weather turns cold. I don't want you to think that I'm blowing off our friendship. I hope that whatever happens in our separate lives, we can count on each other as friends."

Jealousy

Jealousy is the suspicion of rivalry or unfaithfulness, and it is a major destructive force in intimate relationships. According to one study, 57 percent of respondents cited a former friend's jealous feelings or critical attitude toward the respondent's other relationships as a "moderate to very important" reason for the breakup of their relationship (Marsh, 1988, p. 27). The traditional scenario under which the emotion of jealousy occurs is when person A feels that person C is getting affection or favored treatment from person B—favored treatment that A wants (LaFollette, 1996, p. 169).

Jealousy—the suspicion of rivalry or unfaithfulness.

Jealousy does not seem to be a personality trait, but low self-esteem can make a person susceptible to feeling jealous. When people question their self-worth, they are likely to be insecure in their relationships and to perceive "unfaithfulness" in their partners.

What triggers jealousy seems to differ between men and women. When women feel ignored or in other ways separated emotionally from their partners, they are likely to feel jealous. On the other hand, men are more likely to feel jealous when their partner gives positive attention to another person. Unfortunately, jealousy poisons intimate relationships by creating self-fulfilling prophesies. For example, as a woman repeatedly expresses her jealousy through accusations and complains about being ignored, isolated, and separated, her partner may seek to protect himself from these unpleasant conversations by withdrawing. By the same token, as a man becomes territorial and angrily accuses a woman of unfaithfulness for simply speaking with other men, she begins to seek more rational male companionship.

The best way to reduce jealousy in a relationship is to increase the level of trust that exists between partners. Unfortunately, the very nature of jealous behavior makes this difficult to do, especially when one partner suffers from low self-esteem. Only if both partners willingly embrace the situation as a conflict over which to collaborate will they be able to maintain intimacy through supportively discussing and resolving the issues that give rise to the jealousy. Left unresolved, jealousy will eventually choke off relational intimacy.

Sex-Role Stereotyping

Sex-role stereotyping continues to be a problem in many intimate relationships. Because intimate communication entails shared deep personal meaning, both men and women need to be able to step outside the traditional stereotypes, acquire each other's traditional skills, and become well-rounded communicators. Many men need to develop and feel comfortable using the skills that nurture and support others in times of emotional distress; many women need to acquire influence and assertiveness skills so that they present their own point of view clearly and forcefully.

A first step toward improving communication in male–female relationships is for men and women to acknowledge the effects of their early conditioning on their interpersonal communication. For example, Matt has trouble describing his feelings. Yet describing feelings, as you have learned, is one of the most important communication skills. Unless Matt is willing to probe his upbringing to find out why he is having difficulty developing this skill (perhaps he has been conditioned that "big boys don't cry"), he may never integrate this particular skill into his behavior. Similarly, unless Mary understands that the socialization process has encouraged her to be passive (perhaps she has been conditioned that "nice girls don't talk back"), she will find it difficult, if not impossible, to learn to be assertive and stand up for herself.

observe & analyze

Sex-Role Stereotypes

Brainstorm a list of "famous old sayings" on sex roles (e.g., "Big boys don't cry"). Take a poll to determine which of the sayings seemed to be the most commonly heard. Discuss your reactions to them when you first heard them and your reactions now. Any differences? ■

Another step toward improving male–female relationships is for men and women to examine the dependency relationships that result from sex-role stereotypes. Because society values traditionally masculine behaviors more highly than it does feminine behaviors, men continue to have a power advantage. Under these circumstances, as you can imagine, a climate of equality in communication between women and men is difficult to establish. A man who adopts a superior attitude toward a woman undermines the effectiveness of their communication.

The fact that society values masculine over feminine behaviors has ramifications for same-sex relationships as well. In our society, for example, Amy may cancel her plans to go shopping with Beth if Joe calls to say he'd like to stop by for lunch. Yet if Joe has plans to go out with his friend Tom, he probably will not cancel them to spend the evening with Amy—even if she has said she really wants to see him. Simply stated, a man's company is more valued than a woman's. Women will sometimes jeopardize their relationships with other women to advance what they believe to be a more socially desirable relationship with a man. Because masculine behavior is more valued, however, men don't often risk same-sex friendships in this way.

A third way to improve male–female relationships is for men and women to monitor sex-role-based tendencies toward communication dominance or passiveness.

what would you do?

A Question of Ethics

Jackie and Michael had been dating for a year and were talking about marriage when Michael's job transferred him to Columbus for six months. Two months into their separation, Jackie visited Michael's new city and had a chance to meet his co-workers at a party, including Veronica, a beautiful woman a couple of years younger than Jackie. Michael had talked to Jackie about all of his new colleagues, including Veronica, but she had had no idea how attractive Veronica was. In addition, as the evening went on, Jackie could sense that Michael and Veronica were forming a special friendship. She couldn't help but feel a twinge of jealousy for this woman who got to spend time with her boyfriend. Nevertheless, Michael seemed completely attentive to Jackie and they had a wonderful visit.

A couple of weeks later, while on a business trip to Columbus, Gwen, an acquaintance of Jackie's, happened to see Michael and Veronica having dinner together at a restaurant. The day after her return, Gwen ran into Jackie at the grocery store and casually remarked that she had seen Michael with Veronica. When Jackie commented that Michael and Veronica were co-workers, Gwen hesitantly replied, "Well, they certainly seem to have a close working relationship." Jackie blanched. Trying to soothe her, Gwen said, "I'm sure there's an explanation for everything. I mean there could be lots of reasons for him to be holding her hand. I'm sorry I said anything." But Jackie did not feel better.

Later that evening when Michael called, Jackie immediately confronted him by saying sarcastically, "So, how's Veronica?"

When Michael replied, "What do you mean?" Jackie went on, "Don't give me any of your innocent 'what do I mean' stuff—you were seen and you know it!"

"Oh, Gwen," said Michael. "So you'll take the word of some nosy, trouble-making woman and judge me before you find out the real situation. If that's all you trust me, then I'm not sure...."

"Oh, sure, defend yourself by blaming Gwen. But she did see you. You're right about one thing, this is about trust."

1. What ethical issues are involved in this situation?

2. What could/should Jackie have said to her friend Gwen and to Michael?

3. How could/should Michael have responded?

If, as a normal part of your sex role, you tend to assume either an obviously dominant or an obviously passive communication style, then you are likely to create defensiveness in your communication partners. Remember, a good communication climate results in part from equality, which is impossible to achieve if one person is dominant.

A climate of equality makes people more willing to accept nontraditional sex-role behaviors. Even though more and more women hold nontraditional jobs, many people still have trouble acknowledging their right to do so. And men who pursue nontraditional jobs may have even more trouble being accepted. "Househusband" is all too often a term of ridicule. It does not matter whether you personally wish to lead a nontraditional life. What does matter is this: If you desire successful interpersonal communication, you must be willing to accept behavior that is different from your own.

Summary

Intimate relationships are those in which a high degree of closeness occurs. They are marked by high degrees of warmth and affection, trust, self-disclosure, commitment, and expectation that the relationship will grow and endure.

Four types of intimate relationships are those of friends (same-sex and opposite-sex friendships), lovers, spouses, and families. Major kinds of intimate relationships are male, female, male–female, marriage, and family relationships.

Male friendships emphasize activities, assistance, favors, and companionship, and communications tend to be topical—related to politics, work, and events. Men may show covert intimacy through playful insults and put-downs. Women's friendships emphasize disclosure, and their talk focuses on relational and personal topics. Although male–female friendship relationships can be tremendously satisfying, they pose a special problem: Many people have difficulty distinguishing between satisfying intimate friendship relationships and romantic, sexual relationships.

Perhaps the ultimate in intimacy is a marriage relationship. Marriage relationships generally fit into three types: traditional, independent, and separate.

The family is a basic social unit composed of people who generate a sense of home and group identity, have a history and a future together, and feel strong loyalty and emotion for each other. Family communication is important because (1) it affects self-concept formation in children, (2) it supplies recognition and support, and (3) it provides models of behavior from members in positions of power for other family members. There are many factors contributing to strong intergenerational family relationships, as well as challenges and frustrations in communication across generational lines. Family relationships are improved by opening lines of communication, by confronting the effects of power imbalances, by recognizing changes in family members, by respecting individual interests, and by managing conflict.

Problems in intimate relationships often stem from loneliness, relational uncertainty, jealousy, and sex-role stereotyping.

Chapter Resources

Communication Improvement Plan: Intimate Relationships

Would you like to improve your use of the following aspects of your intimate relationship communication discussed in this chapter?

Male communication

Female communication

Male–female communication

Marriage communication

Family communication

Pick an aspect and write a communication improvement plan. . You can find a communication improvement plan worksheet on our website at www.oup.com/us/interact

Key Words

Intimate relationships, *p. 319*	**Traditional couples,** *p. 326*
Trust, *p. 319*	**Independent couples,** *p. 326*
Dependable partner, *p. 319*	**Separate couples,** *p. 326*
Responsive partner, *p. 319*	**Mutual respect,** *p. 328*
Effective conflict-resolving partner, *p. 319*	**Comfortable level of closeness,** *p. 328*
Faithful partner, *p. 319*	**Presence of a plan or life vision,** *p. 329*
Intimates, *p. 321*	**Family,** *p. 329*
Platonic relationship, *p. 321*	**Loneliness,** *p. 338*
Romantic relationship, *p. 321*	**Relational uncertainty,** *p. 338*
Covert intimacy, *p. 322*	**Jealousy,** *p. 338*

Inter-Act with Media

CINEMA

Nancy Meyers (Director). (2003). *Something's Gotta Give.* Jack Nicholson, Diane Keaton, Keanu Reeves, Frances McDormand, Amanda Peet, Paul Michael Glaser, Rachel Ticotin.

Brief Summary: Harry Sanborn is a sixty-three-year-old swinger who still chases younger women, much younger women. After a heart attack while trying to make love to Marin at the home of her mother, Erica, Harry must begin to come to terms with his aging, his real relational needs, and his growing attraction to Erica, a highly accomplished playwright much closer to his own age. Erica is also struggling with her own relational issues. She is drawn into a relationship with a younger doctor, Julian, but must ultimately decide what she wants in a serious relationship.

IPC Concepts: Characteristic of intimate relationships, types of relationships, patterns of communication in intimate relationships.

Spike Lee (Director). (1994). *Crooklyn.* Alfre Woodard, Delroy Lindo, David Patrick Kelly, Zelda Harris, Carlton Williams, Sharif Rashed, Tse-Mach Washington, Spike Lee.

Brief Summary: This is the story of an African American family in Brooklyn in the 1970s. Their strong-willed mother, Carolyn, holds the family together despite extreme poverty, a free-spirited unemployed father, Woody, and a sometimes dangerous neighborhood. The neighborhood has undergone tremendous change in terms of its racial and ethnic composition, which has fostered resentment between the groups. The story centers around Troy, the only girl in the family. When family strife becomes a serious problem, they take Troy to spend the summer with her aunt in the South. Troy strikes up a friendship with her cousin, but longs for her home in Brooklyn. Upon her return, she learns that her mother has become quite ill. Carolyn dies of cancer, and the family is filled with insecurity as well as grief.

IPC Concepts: Family, sibling rivalry, conflict, communication between parents, between parents and children, role models, coping with change.

Mira Nair (Director). (1995). *The Perez Family.* Marisa Tomei, Anjelica Huston, Alfred Molina, Chazz Palmintieri, Trini Alvarado, Celia Cruz, Diego Wallraff.

Brief Summary: In 1980, after twenty years of political imprisonment in Cuba, a former plantation owner, Juan Raul Perez, is released as part of the massive prisoner release by Castro. He dreams of being reunited with his wife and family in Miami, but when he arrives in Florida in the company of a fiery young woman, Dorita, who claims to be his wife for immigration purposes, he fails to make contact with his brother–in-law, who had been looking for a single man. His real wife, Carmela, believes that he has not been released and grieves for him. While Juan tries to find his wife, Dorita tries to create a family so that they can find a sponsor in the United States. Dorita's unlikely group slowly becomes a family. Their goal is to survive, learn how to deal with America, and find their place in it. They become interdependent and help each other deal with the constant changes in their lives. Eventually Juan is reunited with Carmela, but they realize that they have grown away from each other.

IPC Concepts: Family as social system, effective communication—illustrates family interdependence, environmental change, goals, and adaptation. Its central question is, what is the real meaning of a family?

WHAT'S ON THE WEB

Middle Way House. *Individual Rights in Intimate Relationships*

http://www.bloomington.in.us/~mwhouse/individualrights.htm

Brief Summary: This site is sponsored by a crisis center in Bloomington, Indiana. It delineates ten fundamental rights that a person has in an intimate relationship. It also offers a twenty-four-hour crisis hotline and other support services for women who are in need of protection from an abusive partner.

IPC Concepts: Casual and problem-solving conversation, cooperative principle, turn-taking, politeness, free information, face-threatening acts, and ethical dialogue.

Couple Communication Program

http://www.couplecommunication.com/

Brief Summary: This is a program that a couple approaching marriage can take in order to prepare for the many challenges of a married relationship. It is not free, but it offers a young couple an option for finding premarital counseling.

IPC Concepts: The program includes listening, couple closeness, parenting, sexuality, conflict management, personality issues, and family and friends.

Mapping of Rules, by Frederick R. Ford

http://home.pacbell.net/frccford/index.html

Brief Summary: This site features a list of rules followed by people in several different kinds of families. A Web-based test (with online scoring) measures five family systems: Two Against the World, Children Come First, Share and Share Alike, Every Man for Himself, and Until Death Do Us Part. Links provide explanations and a bibliography.

IPC Concepts: Relationships and commitments, priorities, support, trust, caring.

communicating
in the workplace

After you have read this chapter, you
should be able to answer these questions:

- What should you do to prepare for a job interview?

- What are the important elements of a well-
  written résumé?

- What are some typical questions used by job
  interviewers?

- How do managers and subordinates develop
  fair exchanges?

- How can you communicate effectively with
  co-workers?

- What are the characteristics of an effective
  work team?

- What roles are needed in team decision-
  making communication?

- How do you effectively lead a team meeting?

- What are communication issues of a diverse
  workplace?

At 3:30 sharp Chas arrived at the door of the human resources director of Grover Industries for his inter-view. The secretary led him into the office and introduced him to Michele Beddington.

"Sit down," Beddington said, "and we'll get started.

"Well, I've looked over your résumé, and now I have just a few questions. How did you get interested in Grover Industries?"

"Our student placement office said you were hiring."

"And for what kind of position do you think you would be most suited?"

"One where I could use my skills."

"What skills do you have to offer our company that would make you a good hire for us?"

"Well, I'm a hard worker."

"Are you familiar with our major products?"

"Not really. I haven't had time yet to look you up."

"I see. Well, how do you know that you could be helpful to us?"

"Well, because I work really hard."

"What kinds of experience have you had in business?"

"Um, let's see. Well, I sold magazines for my high school. And my sister-in-law owns her own business and I hear her talking about it a lot."

"OK, what do you see as some of your major skills?"

"I told you, I can work really hard!"

"Well, Chas, companies are impressed by hard workers. We're talking to other applicants, of course. So, I'll be in touch."

When Chas got home Tanya asked, "How did the interview go?"

"Great," Chas replied. "Ms. Beddington was impressed by the fact that I'm a hard worker."

What do you think Chas's chances are for getting the job?

Adults spend approximately half their waking hours at work. Thus, many of the relationships that adults maintain are on the job. These relationships differ from friendships and family rela-tionships because, for the most part, they serve different purposes and are not voluntary—you usually don't choose the people you work for or with. In this chapter we'll explore the interpersonal com-munication challenges that we face at work. Of course, the first challenge is getting a job. The interpersonal communication process of interviewing is the most frequently used hiring practice, and getting an interview often depends on having an effective cover letter and résumé. So, we'll begin by discussing both cover letter and résumé preparation. Then we'll describe how to communicate effectively in an interview.

Once hired, we have relationships to manage at work, including communication with managers and co-workers. Since many employees these days work in teams, we will describe the characteristics of effective work teams, discuss roles to be performed when teams communicate to make decisions, and provide suggestions for leading a team meeting as well as participating in a team meeting. Finally, we discuss issues of diversity at work including organizational romance, sexual harassment, culture-based work styles and intergenerational differences.

Presenting Yourself During the Hiring Process

Because most organizations use interviews as part of their selection process, you have probably already been an interviewee and so you know how stressful interviews can be. In this section, we describe strategies and tactics you can use to make your next job search more successful and less stressful.

Getting the Interview

Because interviewing is time consuming, most organizations do not interview all the people who apply for a job. Rather, they use a variety of screening devices to eliminate people who don't meet their qualifications. Chief among these is evaluating the qualifications presented on your résumé and in the letter that accompanies it. The goal of your résumé and cover letter then is to "sell yourself and get an interview" (Schmidt & Conaway, 1999, p. 92).

It All Begins with Research. In order to write an effective cover letter and résumé that highlights your qualifications for a particular job, you need to know something about the job requirements and about the company. The career center advisors at your college or university can assist you with your research.

Write an Effective Cover Letter. A cover letter is a short, well-written letter expressing your interest in a particular position. It should tell how you learned of the opening and why you are interested in the company; it should include highlights of your skills and experiences that demonstrate how you fit the requirements of the position; and it should directly ask for an opportunity to interview for the position.

Cover letter—a short, well-written letter expressing your interest in a particular position.

Prepare a Professional Résumé. The résumé is a summary of your skills and accomplishments; it is your "silent sales representative" (Stewart & Cash, 2000, p. 274). Although there is no universal format for résumé writing, there is

Résumé—a summary of your skills and accomplishments.

2326 Tower Place
Cincinnati, Ohio 45220
April 10, 2006

Mr. Kyle Jones
Acme Marketing Research Associates
P.O. Box 482
Cincinnati, OH 45201

Dear Mr. Jones:

I am applying for the position of research assistant at Acme Marketing Research Associates that I learned about through the Office of Career Counseling at the University of Cincinnati. I am a senior mathematics major at the University of Cincinnati who is interested in pursuing a career in marketing research. I am highly motivated and eager to learn, and I enjoy working with all types of people. I am excited by the prospect of working for a firm like AMRA, where I can apply my leadership and problem-solving skills in a professional setting.

As a mathematics major, I have developed the analytical proficiency that is necessary for working through complex problems. My courses in statistics have especially prepared me for data analysis, while my more theoretical courses have taught me how to construct an effective argument. Through my leadership training and opportunities, I have learned to work effectively in groups and have seen the benefits of both individual and group problem-solving approaches. My work as a student member of the strategic planning committee for a large day school introduced me to the skills associated with strategic planning. Finally, from my theatrical experience, I have gained the poise to make presentations in front of small and large groups alike. I believe that these experiences and others have shaped who I am and have helped me to develop many of the skills necessary to be successful. I am interested in learning more and continuing to grow.

I look forward to having the opportunity to speak with you. I have enclosed my résumé with both my school address and phone number. Thank you for your consideration. I hope to hear from you soon.

Sincerely,

Elisa C. Vardin

Figure 13.1

Sample cover letter

some agreement on what should be included. The following information should appear on your résumé.

1. **Contact information:** your name, mailing address, telephone number, and e-mail address. If any of this information will change after graduation, include additional contact information as well.

2. **Career objective:** a one-line sentence objective focusing on your job search goals.

3. **Employment history:** list of your paid and unpaid experiences beginning with the most recent. List the name and address of the organization, your employment dates, your title, key duties, and noteworthy accomplishments.

4. **Education:** list the names and addresses of the schools you have attended (including specialized military schools), the degrees or certificates earned (or expected), the dates of attendance and graduation, and any academic honors received with degrees or certificates.

5. **Relevant professional affiliations:** list the names of the organizations, dates of membership, and any offices held.

6. **Military background:** list branch and dates of service, last rank held, significant commendations, and discharge status.

7. **Special skills:** list language fluencies, computer expertise, and other specialized qualifications.

8. **Community service:** list significant involvement in community service organizations, clubs, and so on.

9. **References:** list or have available the names, addresses, e-mail addresses, and phone numbers of at least three people who will speak well of your ability, your work product, and your character. Although you may not choose to include your reference list on the résumé, you should at least indicate that "references are available on request."

Notice that the list does not include such personal information as height, weight, age, sex, marital status, health, race, religion, or political affiliation. Nor does it include any reference to salary.

You will want to experiment with the design and layout of your résumé—how wide your margins will be, the fonts and font sizes you will use, how each element will be highlighted, spaced, indented, and so on. The final résumé must be visually attractive and easy to read, neat, error free (proofread carefully), and reproduced on good-quality paper. If you are a traditional college student and have had little work experience, you will be able to format an attractive one-page résumé. If you are a returning student with extensive and substantial work history, you may need one or two additional pages to highlight your accomplishments. Regardless of your experience, however, a résumé should be no more than three pages.

Figure 13.1 displays a sample cover letter and Figure 13.2 a sample résumé for a recent college graduate.

Figure 13.2

Sample résumé

Elisa C. Vardin
2326 Tower Avenue
Cincinnati, Ohio 45220
Phone: (513) 861-2497
E-mail: ElisVardin@UC.edu

PROFESSIONAL OBJECTIVE:
To use my intellectual abilities, quantitative capabilities, communication skills, and proven leadership to further the mission of a high-integrity marketing research organization.

EDUCATIONAL BACKGROUND:
UNIVERSITY OF CINCINNATI, Cincinnati, OH, B.A. in mathematics, June 2006. GPA 3.36. Dean's List.

NATIONAL THEATER INSTITUTE at the Eugene O'Neill Theater Center, Waterford, CT. Fall 2004. Acting, voice, movement, directing, and playwriting.

WORK AND OTHER BUSINESS-RELATED EXPERIENCE:
REYNOLDS & DEWITT, SENA WELLER ROHS WILLIAMS, Cincinnati, OH. Summer 2005.
Intern at brokerage/investment management firm. Provided administrative support. Created new databases, performance comparisons, and fact sheets in Excel and Word files.

MUMMERS THEATRE GUILD, University of Cincinnati, Spring 2003–Spring 2006. Treasurer. Responsible for all financial/accounting functions for this undergraduate theater community.

SUMMERBRIDGE CINCINNATI, Cincinnati Country Day School, Cincinnati, OH. Summer 2004. Teacher in program for "at risk" junior high students. Taught 7th grade mathematics, 6th and 7th grade speech communication, sign language; academic advisor; club leader. Organized five-hour diversity workshop and three-hour tension-reduction workshop for staff.

STRATEGIC PLANNING COMMITTEE, Summit Country Day School, Cincinnati, OH. Fall 2001–2002. One of two student members. Worked with the board of directors developing the first strategic plan for a thousand-student independent school (pre-K through 12).

AYF INTERNATIONAL LEADERSHIP CONFERENCE, Miniwanca Conference Center, Shelby, MI. Summer 2000–2002. Participant in international student conference sponsored by American Youth Foundation.

PERSONAL:
Musical theater: lifetime involvement, including leads and choreography for several shows. A cappella singing group: 2003–2006, director 2004–2006. Swing Club: 2002–2005, president and teacher of student dance club. Junior high youth group leader: 2001. Math tutor: 2003. Aerobics instructor: 2002–2003. University of Cincinnati Choral Society: 2002–2006. American Sign Language instructor: Winter 2003, 2004.

TECHNICAL SKILLS AND TRAINING: SAS, SPSS, Excel, Access, Word. Univariate and multivariate statistics (2 courses), regression analysis (2 courses).

REFERENCES: Available on request.

Many electronic cover letters and résumés are those that are sent to the employer online. Electronic résumés have become quite popular with employers and job seekers. Employers like electronic résumés because they then can use computer programs to sift through large numbers of applicants to look for particular qualifications or characteristics. Candidates like electronic résumés because they save time and money.

Although electronic cover letters and résumés have the same content as traditional paper versions, they may differ in several ways (Schmidt & Conaway, 1999, pp. 98–99). Many of the differences take into account the fact that the documents will be transmitted electronically. Thus, it is wise to avoid using boldface, italics, and bullet points because these design elements "only confuse computerized word searches " (Schmidt & Conaway, 1999, p. 98). The most important thing to remember for an e-mail résumé, or one that is likely to be scanned, is to keep the format simple.

Presenting Yourself During an Interview

An **interview** is a structured conversation with the goal of exchanging information that is needed for decision making. Careful handling of an interview includes getting ready for the interview, conducting yourself during the interview, and performing interview follow-up.

Interview—a structured conversation with the goal of exchanging information that is needed for decision making.

How can you prepare to successfully present yourself in an interview?

Preparing to Be Interviewed

While the résumé and cover letter make you an attractive candidate for an employer, it is your behavior at the interview that will solidify your chances to receive an offer. There are several guidelines that can help you prepare for the interview.

1. **Do your homework.** If you haven't done extensive research on the position and company in preparation for writing your letter, do it before you go to the interview. Be sure you know the company's products and services, its areas of operation, ownership, and financial health. Nothing puts off interviewers more than applicants who arrive at an interview knowing little about the company.

2. **Based on your research, prepare a list of questions about the organization and the job.** The employment interview should be a two-way street where you size up the company as they are sizing you up. So you will probably have a number of specific questions to ask the interviewer. For example, "Can you describe a typical

workday for the person in this position?" or "What is the biggest challenge in this job?" Make a list of your questions and take it with you to the interview.

3. **Rehearse the interview.** Several days before the interview spend time outlining the job requirements and determining how your knowledge, skills, and experiences meet those requirements. Practice answering questions commonly asked in interviews such as those listed in Figure 13.3.

Figure 13.3

Sample interview
questions

School:
How did you select the school you attended?
How did you determine your major?
What extracurricular activities did you engage in at school?
In what ways does your transcript reflect your ability?
How were you able to help with your college expenses?

Personal:
What are your hobbies? How did you become interested in them?
Give an example of how you work under pressure.
At what age did you begin supporting yourself?
What causes you to lose your temper?
What are your major strengths? Weaknesses?
Give an example of when you were a leader and what happened.
What do you do to stay in good physical condition?
What was the last non-school-assigned book that you read? Tell me about it.
Who has had the greatest influence on your life?
What have you done that shows your creativity?

Position:
What kind of position are you looking for?
What do you know about the company?
Under what conditions would you be willing to relocate?
Why do you think you would like to work for us?
What do you hope to accomplish?
What qualifications do you have that would make you beneficial to us?
How do you feel about traveling?
What part of the country would you like to settle in?
With what kinds of people do you enjoy interacting?
What do you regard as an equitable salary for a person with your qualifications?
What new skills would you like to learn?
What are your career goals?
How would you proceed if you were in charge of hiring?
What are your most important criteria for determining whether you will accept a position?

4. **Dress appropriately and conservatively.** You will want to make a good first impression, so it is important to be well groomed and neatly dressed. Although "casual" or "business casual" is common in many workplaces, some organizations still expect employees to be more formally dressed. If you don't know what the dress code is for the organization, call the Human Resources Department and ask. Even when the dress code is casual, you will want to be a little more conservatively attired than the average employee: You are not yet an employee, and you want to make a good impression. So, it is important that you look neat, clean, and appropriate. Men should wear collared shirts (not golf or tee shirts), dress slacks, and a tie. In a business casual setting, a sport coat should be worn or carried. In some situations men will want to wear suits. Men should be recently shaved, with facial hair well groomed. If a man's hair is long, it should be pulled back into a ponytail; if short, it should be recently barbered. Women should wear suits, pant suits, or professional-looking dresses. Skirt length and necklines should be modest, and midriffs should be completely covered. Makeup should be unnoticeable. Hair should be clean and worn away from the face. Very long hair should be worn up or pulled back. When possible, wear clothing that covers body art and piercings to avoid having such personal fashion statements negatively influence an interviewer's perception of your qualifications.

5. **Plan to arrive on time.** The interview is the organization's first exposure to your work behavior. So you don't want to be late. Find out how long it will take you to travel by making a dry run several days before. Plan to arrive ten or fifteen minutes before your appointment.

6. **Bring supplies.** Gather and bring extra copies of your résumé, cover letter, and references, as well as the list of questions you plan to ask. You will also want to have a writing tablet and pen so that you can make notes.

Behavior During the Interview

While interviewing can be stressful, several guidelines can help you put your best foot forward.

1. **Use active listening.** When we are anxious, we sometimes have trouble listening well. So you will need to work on attending, understanding, and retaining what is asked. Remember that the interviewer will be aware of

observe & analyze

Interviewing

Make an appointment to interview a person in the Human Resources Department of a large organization whose job it is to screen candidates for employment. Develop a set of interview questions. Focus your interview on obtaining information about the person's experiences that will help you. For example, you might ask, "What are the characteristics you like to see an interviewee demonstrate?" or "How do you decide who to interview?" Prepare to discuss your findings in class. ■

your nonverbal behavior, so be sure to make and keep eye contact as you listen.

2. **Think before answering.** If you have prepared for the interview, you should be able to tell your story as you answer the questions posed. So take a moment to consider how you can use each answer to portray your skills and experiences. "Tell me about yourself," is not an invitation to give the interviewer your life history. Rather, you can focus your answer on presenting your experiences and qualifications that are related to the job.

3. **Be enthusiastic.** If you come across as bored or disinterested, the interviewer is likely to conclude that you would be an unmotivated employee.

4. **Ask questions.** As the interview is winding down, be sure to ask the questions you prepared that have not already been answered. You may also want to ask how well the interviewer believes your qualifications match the position, and what your strengths are.

5. **Avoid discussing salary and benefits.** The time to discuss salary is when you are offered the job. If the interviewer tries to pin you down, simply say something like "I'm really more interested in talking about how my experiences relate to your needs, and would like to defer talking about salary until we know we have a match." Similarly, discussions of benefits are best held until an offer is made.

Interview Follow-up

When the interview is complete there are several important follow-up steps.

1. **Write a thank-you note.** It is appropriate to write a short note thanking the interviewer for the experience and re-expressing your interest in the job.

2. **Self-assess your performance.** Take time to critique your performance. How well did you do? What can you do to be better next time?

3. **Contact the interviewer for feedback.** If you don't get the job, you might call the interviewer and ask for feedback. Be sure to be polite and to indicate that you are calling simply to get some help on your interviewing skills. Actively listen to the feedback, using questions and paraphrases to clarify what is being said. Be sure to thank the interviewer for helping you.

Managing Relationships at Work

You will use your interpersonal communication skills to develop and maintain healthy relationships with others at work, including your managers and co-workers. Good communication skills are universally recognized as essential for successful interactions with colleagues at work (Whetten & Cameron, 2005, p. 217).

Communicating in Managerial Relationships

Managers are responsible for seeing that their employees perform their job duties. To do this, managers instruct employees, give them feedback on their job performance, and influence them to meet their personal and work goals. Instructing employees requires managers to be adept in describing behavior, using clear and vivid language, and offering constructive criticism. Providing useful feedback to employees requires managers to know how to praise and how to criticize in appropriate ways. Influencing employees to accomplish their tasks well requires managers to understand their employees' needs. Thus, managers must be effective listeners who are skilled at paraphrasing and perception checking. With this information, they can then use influence skills to help employees better accomplish their tasks.

Employees also have a responsibility to communicate effectively with their managers. You can increase the likelihood that your conversations with your managers will be effective by using the skills of listening, questioning, paraphrasing, asking for feedback, and asserting yourself.

When both persons in a manager–employee relationship recognize the importance of communication and jointly assume responsibility for sharing meaning, communication breakdowns are less likely to occur and the needs of both relationship members are likely to be met.

As with any other relationship, the one between a manager and an employee develops over a period of time. Yet, not all individuals who have the same manager establish the same type or level of relationship with that person. In fact, differential treatment from managers is the norm. Workers are aware of such treatment and do talk about it (Sias & Jablin, 1995, p. 5).

Managers look for employees who are willing to perform more than is normally expected (Graen, 1976). As these individuals become more valuable to the manager over time, they establish a greater power base from which to negotiate. In order to maintain a "fair exchange" with these individuals, the manager negotiates special "rewards" for employees performing duties beyond those formally expected of them. Although the rewards may be financial (e.g., bonuses), they are more likely to be in the form of choice task assignments, better office space, public praise for special assignments, access to information not usually shared with employees at that level, and a closer interpersonal relationship with the manager. Employees in these relationships often describe the experience as a mentoring relationship, indicating that what they have gained has helped them to develop skills and expertise beyond the learning that would normally take place on the job. These skills make them more valuable to the organization and will help them to advance in their careers.

Individuals who are performing their role assignments well but without doing anything extra to help out the manager may receive good work evaluations, adequate raises, and fair treatment, but they will find it difficult to be promoted or to develop a close working relationship with their manager. Thus, ambitious employees are likely to ask themselves, "How can I establish a more effective working relationship with my manager?"

To establish a high-quality exchange relationship with your manager, you must begin by assessing the skills and expertise you possess that may be of value in helping your manager accomplish the work that falls outside the formal role prescriptions of your job. These skills may be those that are in short supply in your work unit or those that your manager lacks. If a company is considering a new computer application that is unfamiliar to the manager, an employee might do some research, take a course at the local college, or volunteer for the company training program in order to become a valuable asset.

Once you are aware of what skills you can bring to an exchange relationship, you communicate your willingness to perform extra assignments that require these skills. Thus, if your manager, who might not wish to ask directly for help, says something like "I'm just swamped with work, and now Human Resources says they have to have these affirmative action forms filled out and returned by Monday," a savvy employee sees this as a call for help. Rather than responding "Yeah, HR always needs paperwork. Well, I've got to get back to my desk," the savvy employee, seeking to establish an exchange relationship with the manager, might respond with a supportive statement like: "Gee, Barb, I get the feeling you don't really think you'll have time to do it. How can I help?"

The essential bond in a close manager–employee relationship is mutual trust. These relationships are marked by direct interaction between manager and close employees, which reinforces the level of trust between them (Lee & Jablin, 1995, p. 248). Being willing to take on additional assignments will further your relationship only if you are willing to perform such assignments well and on time. Although doing this often means working more, you may be able to negotiate with your manager to be removed from other, mundane assignments.

As we have seen, communication competence is critical in work-based relationships. By skillful use of listening, perception checking, describing, questioning, and paraphrasing, you can control the manner in which your relationships with your managers develop. Without careful and attentive use of these skills, you are likely to have a distant and ineffective working relationship with your manager and, in time, with your employees.

Communicating in Co-Worker Relationships

Your co-workers are the other members of your work group, team, or department who are at the same job level as you. It has been shown that co-workers influence both the quality of our performance and our satisfaction with our jobs (Jablin & Krone, 1994, p. 647). Like other relationships, your relationships with your co-workers are developed through your communication experiences with them. But just as you will not choose your manager, you will also not be in charge of selecting those with whom you work. Thus, as in manager–employee relationships, how well you get along with your co-workers depends on your communication competence. For example, if you choose to be insensitive to the needs and feelings of your co-workers, either not listening attentively or being unaware of cultural differences, then you are likely to find that your relationships with fellow employees are not satisfying.

What kinds of communication skills are recognized as essential for successful interaction with colleagues at work?

Co-worker cooperation does not mean that co-workers must be close friends or always agree. Indeed, as the workforce becomes more diverse, it is likely that disagreements and misunderstandings between co-workers will become more frequent. Most managers recognize this diversity as a potential strength on which they can draw. They reason that, if well managed, the disagreements and cultural differences may lead to more creative and productive solutions to organizational problems. If this is to happen, co-workers must develop and maintain healthy working relationships. Maintaining them depends on effective interpersonal communication. Skills like turn-taking, listening, use of collaborative problem-solving approaches to conflict management, supportiveness, and effectiveness in group communication will be critical to all workers. As the workforce becomes global, understanding the cultural norms that affect organizations in other countries will become increasingly important.

Communicating on a Work Team

Today, most work that goes on inside organizations uses a team approach (Eisenberg & Goodhall, 2004). A **team** is a formally established group with a clear purpose and a structure in which members know their own and others' roles and are motivated to work together to achieve goals (Conrad & Poole, 2005). Work teams can be short-lived or ongoing. They may comprise people in the same department, or their membership may be drawn from several functional areas of the organization. Teams may be tasked with making recommendations, making decisions, or

Team—formal group with a clear purpose and appropriate structure.

implementing decisions that have been made by others. So a company might form a team to develop a new policy on e-mail archiving or might restructure an entire production department so that it performs its work as a self-managed work team. Regardless of the type of work team, interpersonal communication plays a pivotal role in the overall effectiveness of the team effort.

Characteristics of Effective Work Teams

The hallmarks of effective teams have been studied across a variety of disciplines. In one study of fifty effective teams, Larson and LaFasto (1989) found that the following eight characteristics seemed to characterize effective teams.

1. **A clear group goal that all team members embrace.** It goes without saying that a team that understands and agrees on its goal is likely to be more effective than one that does not. So when managers are considering using a team to accomplish work, it is their job to make sure that each member of the team clearly understands what he or she is expected to accomplish. Likewise, effective managers will also make sure that each member of the team is committed to the goal that has been assigned. Unfortunately, managers sometimes don't do a very good job in defining the group's goal. If you are assigned to a work team, you can use the skills of questioning and paraphrasing to make sure that you and other team members clearly understand what is expected of you. You may find that asking managers for a list the "deliverables" that you are expected to produce is an effective way of making a seemingly abstract goal more concrete. For example, suppose you have been assigned to work on a team whose stated goal is to review the current absentee policy and make recommendations for changes. It will probably help the team to understand the scope of the assignment if the manager states that the recommendation should take the form of a report, complete with the analysis of absence data for the past two years, as well as an analysis of the absentee polices of competing companies, and "best practice" exemplars.

2. **Clear member roles.** It makes no sense for everyone to perform the same role on a team. A major benefit of having many people working together is that different people bring different strengths to the task. Sometimes people are selected for a team because their various skills are complementary. If members are unsure of their roles or are competing to perform the same roles, then team functioning suffers. When people are assigned to a team, or invited to join one, the convener of the group should describe the role envisioned for each individual. For example, if you were asking Jonathan to join a team for enhancing fund-raising among Greek organizations on campus, you might describe his role by saying, "We are hoping that you will share your experience in alumni relations to help this team develop strategies for raising money from former members of fraternities and sororities on campus." You might clarify Ella's anticipated role by saying, "Since you are a public relations major, we hope that you can assist the team in creating a thematic image and some communication strategies for a fund-raising campaign."

3. **Feedback about the performance of group roles.** Even when team members clearly know their roles, they still need regular information about how they are performing in those roles. Such feedback tells us about the quality of our work and gives us information about whether we need to adjust our work performance in any way. Frequent open and honest communication among team members becomes the vehicle for understanding and coordinating team roles and monitoring team performance. Having the group periodically share opinions about the performance of member roles will provide a vehicle for making sure ongoing feedback occurs. To garner feedback, the team leader should say something like "Let's talk about the area of expertise that each person brings to our task and discuss how well we think we are doing in each area. Ella, we value the public relations expertise that you bring to the group. What's the group sentiment about our PR effort so far? Do we have a clear message for our fund-raising campaign, or do we need to develop this area further?" By explicitly communicating team expectations and progress related to each role, leaders allow individual members and the team as a whole to regularly assess performance.

4. **Team members who use their technical and people skills to help the group.** Ideally, team members have among them all of the expertise necessary to accomplish the tasks of the group. But some people who are very proficient at their specialties are unable or unwilling to use these to benefit the group. Sometimes technical experts lack basic interpersonal skills that enable them to express what they know or to politely disagree with someone who is less knowledgeable. Since it is important for the group's success that expertise be shared and divergent viewpoints be aired, it is also important that group members have "people skills" that enable them to understand human psychology, as well as a wide variety of interpersonal skills that will help them facilitate meaningful discussions in the group. As a member of a group, you can help less verbal members to share their expertise by encouraging turn-taking, asking questions of quieter members, and pointing out where members disagree. The interpersonal communication skills presented throughout this textbook can be used to enhance the effectiveness of work teams.

5. **Commitment to the team and its success.** Commitment is a personal decision to work with other team members in order to achieve the group goals. It is not enough for team members to be committed to the goal; it is also impor-

tant that they be committed to achieving the goal by working with each other. Early in the life of a group, it is helpful for the group members to spend time getting to know each other and to dream together about the outcome the group hopes to achieve. Through "team-building" processes like this, groups can help their members make the team and its work a high priority. As a member of the group, you can help to build commitment by taking time to converse with other members and by asking others what excites or intrigues them about the project.

6. **A collaborative climate of open communication.** In effective teams, members cooperate with each other by speaking honestly and directly. For groups to reap the benefits of having several minds thinking or working together, members must be comfortable in sharing their ideas. The interpersonal communication skills of questioning, describing feelings and behavior, asking for and giving criticism, assertiveness, and conflict management aid team members as they interact.

7. **Standards of excellence.** Effective teams expect and receive excellence from each member. There is a uniform pressure for everyone to perform at a very high level. This expectation is communicated from member to member by the way in which each handles work assignments. Other members aid members who are not able to perform to high standards. Members who choose not to perform up to standard are gently but firmly confronted by other members and encouraged to begin to meet the agreed-upon standard.

8. **Strong leadership.** Effective teams have exceptionally good leaders who are focused on the goals and motivate members to perform at the highest levels. Leaders are the people who influence the group's procedures, task accomplishment, and relationships between members by stepping in and assuming a combination of roles needed by the group but not appropriately assumed by other members. Leaders then are adept at listening to the group, and becoming attuned to what the group needs at a particular time. Based on what they have heard, leaders adapt their behavior to the situation, provide what the group needs, and, in so doing, influence the group to attain its goal.

Communicating to Make Team Decisions

Work teams meet regularly to plan their work, troubleshoot problems, and make other decisions. During these meetings, there are a variety of communication roles that members perform to help the group. These roles fall into two general categories: task roles and maintenance roles. **Task roles** comprise communication behaviors that help the group focus on the issues being discussed. **Maintenance roles** are communication behaviors that help the group develop and maintain good member relationships, group cohesiveness, and effective levels of conflict. Task roles include initiator, information/opinion giver, information/opinion seeker, analyzer, and orienter.

1. *Initiator.* You play the initiator role when your comment gets the discussion started or moves it in a new direction. You would be performing the initiat-

Task roles—behaviors that help a group focus on issues.

Maintenance roles—behaviors that improve interaction among people in a group.

ing role by suggesting, "Let's begin by looking at the current problems in our inventory control system," or by saying, "Perhaps we should move on to a discussion of quality concerns we have related to our vendors and suppliers."

2. *Information or opinion giver.* You play this role when you provide content for the discussion. People who perform these roles well are those who have expertise or are well informed on the content of the task and share what they know with the group. Examples of this role performance include statements such as "Well, in the meeting I attended last week with Human Resources, we were told that sales associates could not take vacations between Thanksgiving and New Year's. So I think we want to make sure that our department vacation policy reflects this." Or "In my experience, telling customers that it's against company policy just makes them angrier, so I don't think that is what we want to say in this situation."

3. *Information or opinion seeker.* You play this role when you ask questions that probe others for their ideas and opinions. Typical comments by those performing these roles include remarks such as "Before going further, what information do we have about how raising dues is likely to affect membership?" Or, "How do members of the group feel about this idea?"

4. *Analyzer.* You play this role when you help the group to examine, scrutinize, question, explore, probe, or evaluate an idea or piece of information. In order to make good decisions, team members must critically examine ideas or suggestions provided by members as well as the facts and data gathered by the team. A member would be performing this role by saying such things as "I do think a change to our weekly schedule should be based on our customer needs as well as on our own personal preferences. So let's look at our hourly sales records to see if there is a pattern to when we are busy and when we are slow." Or "The numbers we have here on annual enrollment in our program look very sound to me because they are consistent with monthly totals."

5. *Orienter.* You orient the team when you help it to understand where the team is in its decision or discussion, when you indicate to the team when it is off track, and when you summarize points of agreement and disagreement so that the team understands what issues are unresolved. It's easy for a group to get so involved in a discussion that it loses track of the "big picture" or goes off on many tangents and wastes time with irrelevant issues. Thus, it is important that someone on the team monitor the group process. A member would be performing an orienting role by making comments such as "I think we've agreed that a good solution must be one that fits our budget, but are there other criteria that are important as well?" Or "We had agreed that we would spend this meeting discussing ways to improve record keeping. It seems to me that we are off track right now in our discussion of human resource budgeting." Or "We might want to finish our listing of fund-raising sources before we move to talking about hiring a fund-raising consultant." Or "It seems to me that we are basically in agreement that we need a new website with improved graphics and direct links to each of our product lines.

Is that true? Does everyone agree?" Or "We seem to be coming back again and again to the basic disagreement between having customer support functions at each location or consolidating them centrally. Is that the point we're stuck on right now?"

Maintenance roles include gatekeeper, encourager, and harmonizer.

1. *Gatekeeper.* As the gatekeeper you ensure that everyone has an opportunity to speak and be heard. In some group discussions, certain people may talk more than their fair share while others remain silent, contributing little or nothing. By performing the gatekeeping role, a team member helps to create more balanced participation among members so that the group can benefit from a variety of viewpoints and information sources. Examples of gatekeeping include, "Just a second, Lonnie, I think Dominique has something to say on this topic. Dominique, you have some experience with coaching employees for improved performance, don't you? What has been your experience?" or "Lonnie, your examples of how you have used peer orientation to help new employees are very interesting and I think that we all now understand your process, so I'd like to hear from other folks about alternative ways we might consider handling new-employee orientation."

2. *Encourager.* You are the encourager when your messages provide support for the contributions of other team members. Participants in a group discussion need to have their ideas acknowledged and supported from time to time. Otherwise, they are unsure about whether they are being heard and their ideas are being taken seriously. For examples, you might offer encouragement by saying "That was a really good suggestion that Kent just made because it deals exactly with the problem we have in meeting client specifications." Or "I think we should keep in mind Miranda's point about maintaining requirements until the next quarter. She made some good observations about the dangers of moving too quickly." Notice that in both cases the encourager was able to say something helpful because of first really listening to what had been said.

3. *Harmonizer.* You harmonize when you help the group to relieve tension and manage conflict. It is inevitable that team decision making will become stressful at times, and conflicts may emerge. A team member who acts as a harmonizer may temporarily relieve the tension by saying something witty or may help the group effectively deal with an emerging conflict. Examples of harmonizing behavior include statements like "The task of planning this product launch reminds me of dealing with Godzilla. Anyone see that movie?" or "We seem to be at odds around the issue of partnering with other schools. It seems that Elana and Nils strongly represent alternate perspectives. Before we get too polarized around these two options, maybe we should look at a range of possibilities."

inter-act with

Technology

A Web log, or blog, is a kind of online diary in which a person (called a "blogger") records his or her thoughts about life, including life in the workplace. Recently, some bloggers have found themselves in a conflict between the desire to make comments about their employer versus the needs of their employers to prevent such comments from being broadcast throughout cyberspace. Some bloggers have even lost their jobs as a result of making injudicious comments about their employers online. Have you experienced, or do you know of anyone who has experienced, adverse results from blogging? Discuss this risk with your classmates. ■

Leading Team Meetings

In addition to performing task and maintenance roles in a decision-making meeting, there are duties to be completed before the meeting begins. By performing these jobs before leading a meeting, you can make sure that meeting time is spent productively and little time is wasted. When running a meeting you should complete these five tasks.

1. **Define and communicate the meeting purpose.** It can be frustrating to be expected to attend a meeting for which you do not know the purpose. Participants in a meeting can prepare beforehand if they know the specific purpose of the meeting. They can bring necessary materials to the meeting, as well. For example, if the upcoming meeting of teachers involves curriculum planning, the purpose should be defined even more clearly. The memo announcing the meeting might say, "We will examine our existing curriculum goals and course topics as they relate to state curriculum requirements in the area of science."

2. **List specific outcomes that should be produced from the meeting.** Even with a clearly stated meeting goal, participants may not know what tasks should be accomplished or what decisions should be made during the meeting. Listing specific outcomes keeps the meeting focused on clear goals and serves to keep the group on track. For example, the meeting leader might specify, "By the end of our curriculum planning meeting, we should have a written statement of eleventh and twelfth grade science goals that are consistent with state requirements and we should have a list of state-mandated course topics that are not currently addressed by our eleventh and twelfth grade science courses."

3. **Communicate and stick to starting and ending times for the meeting.** To use time efficiently and to be fair to those members who arrive on time, meetings should begin promptly. By waiting for latecomers, meeting leaders enable members to be late in the future because they know that the meeting will be delayed until everyone arrives. Likewise, in the workplace, people have very busy schedules and need to know when a meeting will end. The meeting leader should closely monitor time as the meeting proceeds to make sure of ending on time.

4. **Send out a detailed agenda, which includes the date, time, and location of the meeting as well as the topics to be discussed, with an approximate amount of time allocated to each agenda item.** This schedule of topics and times will allow the discussion to proceed efficiently and will keep the group discussion focused on concrete items. An agenda like the one shown in Figure 13.4 is useful also for participants who cannot attend the entire meeting or guests who need not be present for the whole meeting. By knowing, ahead of time, which items will be discussed when, those not concerned with the entire agenda can schedule their attendance accordingly.

5. **Make physical arrangements.** This may include reserving a meeting room, arranging for a particular seating format, and ordering meeting supplies or

Figure 13.4

Agenda for Discussion
Group Meeting

March 1, 2006
To: Interns at Metrotek
From: Janelle Smith
Re: Agenda for discussion group meeting, March 8, 2006, 3:00–5:00 P.M.,
          Conference Room A

Agenda for Group Discussion
Please come prepared to discuss questions 1 through 5. We will consider question 6 on the basis of our resolution of the other questions.

Meeting topic: What should be done to integrate interns into planning, decision-making, and social functions at Metrotek?

1. What is the number of interns per department?   (3:00–3:10)
2. Why aren't interns involved in planning, decision-making,
   and social activities?   (3:10–3:30)
3. What specific factors hinder their involvement?   (3:30–3:50)
                                     BREAK   (3:50–4:00)
4. What criteria should be used to test possible solutions
   to the problem?   (4:00–4:15)
5. What are some of the possible solutions to the problem?   (4:15–4:45)
6. What one solution or combination of solutions will work
   best to solve the problem?   (4:45–5:00)

food. The physical space for a meeting can have a large impact on the productivity of a meeting. A space that is too crowded or impedes members' ability to see each other or information presented visually can hinder team effectiveness.

Member Responsibilities in Team Meetings

Although members specialize in particular roles during team meetings, members of effective groups also assume common responsibilities for making their meetings successful. Here are some guidelines to help team members prepare for, participate in, and follow up on a meeting in order to increase its effectiveness.

Preparing. Too often people think of a team meeting as a "happening" that requires attendance but no particular preparation. People often arrive at a meeting unprepared even though they are carrying packets of material that they received in advance of the meeting. The reality is that meetings should not be treated as impromptu events but as carefully planned interactions that pool information from well-prepared individuals. Here are some important steps to take prior to attending a meeting.

The Group: A Japanese Context
By Delores Cathcart and Robert Cathcart

Team roles and decision-making styles are greatly influenced by culture. In this excerpt, the authors describe how interdependence leads to a climate of agreement and decision making based on consensus in Japanese groups.

One of Japan's most prominent national characteristics is the individual's sense of the group. Loyalty to the group and a willingness to submit to its demands are key virtues in Japanese society. This dependency and the interdependency of all members of a group is reinforced by the concept of *on*. A Japanese is expected to feel indebtedness to those others in the group who provide security, care, and support. This indebtedness creates obligation and when combined with dependency is called *on*. *On* functions as a means of linking all persons in the group in an unending chain because obligation is never satisfied, but continues throughout life. *On* is fostered by a system known as the *oyabun–kobun* relationship. Traditionally the *oyabun* is a father, boss, or patron who protects and provides for a son, employee, or student in return for his or her service and loyalty. This is not a one-way dependency. Each boss or group leader recognizes his own dependency on those below. Without their undivided loyalty he or she could not function. *Oyabun* are also acutely aware of this double dimension because of having had to serve a long period of kobun on the way up the hierarchy to the position at the top. All had *oyabun* who protected and assisted them, much like a father, and now each must do the same for their *kobun*. *Oyabun* have one or more *kobun* whom they look after much as if they were children. The more loyal and devoted the "children," the more successful the "father."

This relationship is useful in modern life where large companies assume the role of superfamily and become involved in every aspect of their workers' lives. Bosses are *oyabun* and employees are *kobun*....

This uniquely Japanese way of viewing relationships creates a distinctive style of decision-making known as *consensus decision*. The Japanese devotion to consensus building seems difficult for most Westerners to grasp but loses some of its mystery when looked at as a solution to representing every member of the group. In a system that operates on *oyabun–kobun* relationships nothing is decided without concern for how the outcome will affect all. Ideas and plans are circulated up and down the company hierarchy until everyone has had a chance to react. This reactive process is not to exert pressure but to make certain that all matters affecting the particular groups and the company are taken into consideration. Much time is spent assessing the mood of everyone involved and only after all the ramifications of how the decision will affect each group can there be a quiet assent. A group within the company may approve a decision that is not directly in its interest (or even causes it difficulties) because its members know they are not ignored, their feelings have been expressed and they can be assured that what is good for the company will ultimately be good for them. For this reason consensus decisions cannot be hurried along without chancing a slight or oversight that will cause future problems.

The process of consensus building in order to make decisions is a time-consuming one, not only because everyone must be considered, but also because the Japanese avoid verbalizing objections or doubts in order to preserve group harmony. The advice, often found in American group literature, that group communication should be characterized by open and candid statements expressing individual personal feelings, wishes, and dislikes, is the antithesis of the Japanese consensus process. No opposing speeches are made to argue alternate ideas; no conferences are held to debate issues. Instead, the process of assessing the feelings and mood of each work group proceeds slowly until there exists a climate of agreement. This process is possible because of the tight relationships that allow bosses and workers to know each other intimately and to know the group so well that needs and desires are easy to assess. ■

Excerpted from Cathcart D., and Cathcart R. (1997). The group: A Japanese context. In L. A. Samovar and R. E. Porter (Eds.), *Intercultural Communication: A Reader* (8th ed., pp. 329-339). Belmont, Calif.: Wadsworth. Reprinted by permission of the authors.

1. **Study the agenda.** Consider the purpose of the meeting and determine what you need to do to be prepared. The agenda is an outline for your preparation.

2. **Study the minutes.** If this is one in a series of meetings, study the minutes and your own notes from the previous meetings. Since such meetings are not unrelated events, what happened at one meeting should provide the basis for preparation for the next meeting.

3. **Prepare for your contributions.** Read the material distributed prior to the meeting and do your own research to become better informed about items on the agenda. If no material is provided, you identify the issues and learn what you need to know to be a productive member of the group. Bring any materials that you have uncovered that will help the group accomplish the agenda. If appropriate, discuss the agenda with others who will not be attending the meeting and solicit their ideas concerning issues to be discussed in the meeting.

4. **Prepare to play a major role.** Consider which roles you are assigned or which you are interested in playing. What do you need to do to play those roles to the best of your ability?

5. **List questions.** Make a list of questions related to agenda items that you would like to have answered during the meeting.

Participating. Go into the meeting with the expectation that you will be a full participant. If there are five people in the group, all five should be participating.

1. **Listen attentively.** Concentrate on what others are saying so that you can use your material to complement, supplement, or counter what has been presented.

2. **Stay focused.** In a group setting, it is easy to get the discussion going in nonproductive directions. Keep your comments focused on the specific agenda item under discussion. If others have gotten off the subject, do what you can to get people back on track.

3. **Ask questions.** "Honest" questions whose answers you do not already know help to stimulate discussion and build ideas.

4. **Take notes.** Even if someone else is responsible for providing the official minutes, you will need notes that help you follow the line of development. Also, these notes will help you remember what has been said and any responsibilities you have agreed to take.

5. **Play devil's advocate.** When you think an idea has not been fully discussed or tested, be willing to voice disagreement or encourage further discussion.

6. **Monitor your contributions.** People who are well prepared have a tendency to dominate discussions. Make sure that you are neither dominating the discussion nor abdicating your responsibility to share insights and opinions.

Following Up. When meetings end, too often people leave and forget about what took place until the next meeting. But what happens in one meeting provides a basis for what happens in the next; be prepared to move forward at the next meeting.

1. **Review and summarize your notes.** Try to do this shortly after you have left the meeting, while ideas are still fresh in your mind. Make notes of what needs to be discussed next time.

2. **Evaluate your effectiveness.** How effective were you in helping the group move toward achieving its goals? Where were you strong? Where were you weak? What should you do next time that you did not do in this meeting?

3. **Review decisions.** Make note of what your role was in making decisions. Did you do all that you could have done?

4. **Communicate progress.** Inform others who need to know about information conveyed and decisions that were made in the meeting.

5. **Follow up.** Make sure you complete all assignments you received in the meeting.

6. **Review minutes.** Compare the official minutes of the meeting to your own notes, and report any significant discrepancies that you find.

Communicating in a Diverse Workplace

Today's workplace reflects the increasing diversity of our culture as women and men, and people of various races, ethnicities, ages, socioeconomic status, and political and religious perspectives come together to work side by side. In the United States increasing workplace diversity stems from two sources: increased immigration and global business activity (Potoker, 2005). This means that for you to be successful in the workplace, it is increasingly important to be able to understand and communicate with people who are different from you. It also means that you may face different challenges at work stemming from diversity such as organizational romances, sexual harassment, differing culture-based work styles, and intergenerational conflicts.

Organizational Romance

Organizational romance is the term for sexual or romantic involvement between people who work for the same organization. Since co-workers have much in common and are in frequent contact, it is no surprise that some become attracted to each other. And employees who spend long hours at work may have little free time in which to meet partners elsewhere.

> **Organizational romance**—Sexual or romantic involvement between people who work for the same organization.

The issue of organizational romance is a controversial one, however. Some people believe in separating workplace from personal relationships, while others see the workplace as a good source of social relationships. Most organizations allow co-workers to date but forbid romantic relationships between supervisors and their subordinates because of the inherent conflict of interest in such a relationship (Berryman-Fink, 1997). The factors to consider in a decision about dating a work colleague include company policies on romantic relationships, reactions from co-workers and managers, effects on your careers, and the possibility that the relationship could end badly and continuing to work together would be a challenge for both former partners. Workplace employees who agree that they would like to be romantically involved should review and follow the workplace policy about organizational romance. If the policy allows co-workers to date, then the partners should agree upon standards for appropriate verbal and nonverbal communication with each other at work. Finally, each person should practice self-monitoring of communications to make sure that professional behavior is exhibited in the workplace at all times.

Sexual Harassment

Sexual harassment—unwanted verbal or physical sexual behavior that interferes with work performance.

According to the Federal Equal Economic Opportunity Commission (EEOC), "**sexual harassment** is a form of sex discrimination that violates Title VII of the Civil Rights Act of 1964." It includes "unwelcome sexual advances, requests for sexual favors, and other verbal or physical conduct of a sexual nature when this conduct explicitly or implicitly affects an individual's employment, unreasonably interferes with an individual's work performance, or creates an intimidating, hostile, or offensive work environment." The EEOC recognizes that sexual harassment can occur in a variety of circumstances, "including but not limited to the following:

- The victim as well as the harasser may be a woman or a man. The victim does not have to be of the opposite sex.
- The harasser can be the victim's supervisor, an agent of the employer, a supervisor in another area, a co-worker, or a non-employee.
- The victim does not have to be the person harassed but could be anyone affected by the offensive conduct.
- Unlawful sexual harassment may occur without economic injury to or discharge of the victim.
- The harasser's conduct must be unwelcome."

Prevention is the best tool to eliminate sexual harassment in the workplace. Employers are encouraged to take steps necessary to prevent sexual harassment from occurring. They should clearly communicate to employees that sexual harassment will not be tolerated. They can do so by disseminating a policy statement that defines and gives examples of sexual harassment, providing training to their employees, so that they can both avoid and identify sexual harassment, establishing an effective complaint or grievance process, and taking immediate and appropriate action when an employee complains.

If you perceive that you are the target of sexual harassment in the workplace, there are two main communication strategies to use. You may choose to begin by informing the harasser directly that the conduct is unwelcome and must stop. At the first instance of harassment, you should privately create a writtten document of the communication exchange, which you date and sign and keep for possible future use. Then you must decide whether to use any employer complaint mechanism or grievance system available. People who perceive the first instance of harassment to be extremely offensive or serious usually make a formal complaint. On the other hand, if you consider the first instance of sexual harassment to be only mildy offensive, you may refrain from making a formal complaint. If the offensive behavior continues after you have communicated to the harasser that the conduct is unwelcome, you should inform the harasser of your intentions to file a formal complaint and then follow through with the appropriate authorities. Again, it is important to keep an objective written record of all communication with the harasser and with workplace authorities handling the complaint. This written record of communication will prove invaluable in the event of a formal investigation, which may take place long after the harassing episodes have occurred and memories of specific remarks have faded. Once a formal complaint has been made at work, it is the responsibility of the organization to investigate and provide appropriate remedies.

Culture-Based Differences in Work Styles

People from different cultures approach work differently, and communication challenges can arise in a multicultural workplace when participants in conversations, interviews, and meetings come from different cultural backgrounds. There tends to be a link between results-oriented cultures doing tasks in a linear, sequential fashion and relationship-oriented cultures doing tasks in a wholistic or simultaneous style (Varner & Beamer, 1995).

In results-oriented cultures, like the United States, emphasis is on the results or outcomes of work, while in **relationship-oriented cultures,** like Japan, Spain, and Mexico, building relationships takes priority over achieving work results (Varner & Beamer, 1995). Employees who come from cultures that are oriented toward achieving results spend little time establishing or maintaining relationships and want to get right down to business. Time is precious, and the ultimate goal is to get the work done. Getting to know others or catching up with customers or business associates before doing business with them is not necessary. In fact, anything that deters from the business objective would be seen as annoying or counterproductive. Those who come from relationship-oriented cultures, on the other hand, see the quality of their personal relationships with business associates as a primary business concern. People from these cultures prefer not to conduct business until they have established or refreshed a personal relationship.

Business associates who come from such different cultures may experience problems. Imagine that Geoffrey, a "typical results-oriented American," is making a first sales call on Rosa, a "typical relationship-oriented Mexican," who is the new purchasing manager of one of the sales rep's largest clients. After being escorted into Rosa's office, and quickly introducing himself, Geoffrey immediately begins his sales pitch by describing the new product line that he thinks Rosa's company will be interested in purchasing. Unless Rosa has worked with typical Americans before, she may think Geoffrey rude because he introduced business topics before they had an opportunity to get to know each other. Rosa may find it odd that they haven't talked about each other's families or that they haven't dined together. For Rosa, getting to know Geoffrey personally is part of doing business. She needs to learn about his personality and his family background so she can decide whether to

Results-oriented culture—a culture that emphasizes the outcomes of work.

Relationship-oriented culture—a culture that emphasizes building relationships at work.

trust him. Meanwhile, Geoffrey may find Rosa's questions about his family to be violation of his privacy and unrelated to their business relationship. In fact, he may even misperceive Rosa's questions as flirting.

Another culturally based work style difference relates to how a person approaches a task. People in some cultures tend to approach a task in a linear or sequential manner. In the United States and other **sequential task completion** cultures, people break tasks down into separate parts or steps and do each part, one at a time, in turn. Step A is done before step B is begun, and so on. Another cultural pattern is to complete tasks wholistically or simultaneously. In **wholistic task completion** cultures, people do not work breaking tasks into component parts. Rather, someone may work on different parts at once or tackle the task in an iterative fashion, going from one part to another and then back to the first part again. Suppose that assistant managers Greg (who is a "typical American sequential task completer") and Carmella (a "typical Mexican wholistic task completer") have been asked by their boss to work together to develop a plan for displaying the store's new fall merchandise. Carmella would be inclined to look at the whole problem at once, talking for a few minutes about what to put where, then bouncing to her ideas about how to physically handle the moves, then describing how possibly to involve the sales associates in the plan, and finally returning to discussing new ideas about what to put where. While another wholistic task completer would be comfortable with this approach, Greg is likely to become confused and frustrated, and wishing Carmella would focus on one issue, work through it, and make decisions before moving on to the next topic. Likewise, if Greg initiates the discussion and tries to hold Carmella to his step-by-step process, she is likely to become frustrated and bored.

Effective business communication depends on awareness of and sensitivity to cultural differences in work styles. It is also important to realize that a person from a particular culture may or may not communicate in a style typical of that culture. A strategy for dealing with cultural differences is to acknowledge and communicate about respective cultural styles. Parties working across global lines may benefit from talking about preferred ways of doing business and negotiating an agreement between the business partners. Indeed, as workplaces become more diverse culturally, employees may need to be flexible in using various styles, including their natural work style and learned alternate styles.

Intergenerational Differences

In the United States, misunderstandings between older and younger people at work seem to be more prevalent today than in the past. Because there is no mandatory retirement age in the United States and because larger numbers of young people are entering the workplace at younger ages, there is a greater age range at work than there used to be. Today co-workers can range in age from fourteen years old to over ninety.

Authors Ron Zempke, Claire Raines, and Bob Filipczak (2000) have described how different generations working side by side bring different work values to the

---

Sequential task completion—a process of breaking a task into separate parts in order to complete one part at a time.

Wholistic task completion—a process of working on an entire task at once.

How can you communicate effectively across generational differences at work?

job that result in more misunderstandings and conflict than ever before. Five common areas in which older and younger employees tend to differ include views of authority, approaches to rules, opinions on the importance of work versus leisure, technology competence, and career development.

In general, people aged 60 or older tend to have greater respect for authority and for peers. They grew up in a time when questioning authority figures like parents, teachers, religious leaders, or bosses was unacceptable. They demonstrate their respect by using formal terms of address such as referring to people by Mr., Ms, Dr., Sir, and so on. People under the age of thirty tend to be more skeptical of authority and less formal in dealing with authorities. They grew up in an era of more permissiveness, where questioning parents, teachers, and religious leaders was tolerated, and so they are more likely to question their managers and to openly disagree with decisions are made by those in authority. Likewise younger people are more likely to call authority figures and co-workers by their first names. This communication difference may lead to misunderstandings and resentments among employees.

Similar to views of authority, co-workers may display age-related differences in how they view company rules. Older individuals are more likely to strictly adhere to company rules and expect others to do so as well. They are likely to perceive that employers have the right to make rules and employees have the responsibility to follow those rules as a condition of employment. Older people may view company rules as comforting and providing predictability. For many younger co-workers, rules may be seen as suggestions to be followed or not, depending on one's own analysis of a situation. Having been raised with situational ethics, younger people may believe that extenuating circumstances call for flexibility, thus allowing them to ignore rules. Such differences in perspective may cause us to judge one another, thereby impeding team cohesiveness at work.

For many older individuals, work takes priority over family and leisure. In fact, there is a strong separation of work and leisure time pursuits in the minds of many older folks. Family responsibilities may have led many folks over the age of sixty to sacrifice leisure in order to work hard and provide for their families. Many individuals under thirty may have had their needs provided for and may not have experienced the challenges of providing for a family, so they may place a higher priority on leisure. Other younger workers, having seen the toll that work has taken on their parents and other older workers, are more aware of the need to balance work and leisure. The presence of these generational tendencies at work may cause us to wrongly attribute motives of work professionalism and commitment to our colleagues or to become defensive with each other.

There may also be generational differences regarding the use of and competence with technology. For those over sixty years of age, technological expertise is an acquired skill, developed as an adult. They did not grow up with the vast amount of information, communication, and entertainment technology that exists today. For many older employees, learning to use technology is challenging and creates anxiety. It may not be regarded as an asset, but as a burden. For younger people, especially very young employees, technology is a given part of life, and the need to learn and relearn to adapt and readapt to the evolving tools is a natural and ever-present aspect of life. Some employees may be expected to use technology for which they have no expertise, while other employees may resent the added burden of assisting colleagues with technological tasks.

The approach to one's career can vary between generations. Many older employees began work in the era when loyalty to an employer was expected and rewarded. Many older workers began their careers expecting to work in the same profession, and perhaps for the same organization, for their entire work lives. Staying with one company for a long time was the means to advancement and a definition of success. Frequent job changes were viewed by employers and co-workers to be problematic. With the massive layoffs that have been the hallmark of business during the last twenty-five years, however, both older and younger employees have seen the concept of employer loyalty severely compromised. Because of layoffs, mergers, and downsizing in many organizations, employers have not been able to be loyal to workers. Today some older and most younger employees understand that career success depends on personal expertise regardless of how often one changes organizations. In fact, for many younger employees, frequent job change is seen as the means of career advancement. Unless we understand these varying perspectives on career trajectories, we may mistakenly hold others to our own standards of how a career should be managed.

These differences in values can conflict when older and younger employees work together. There is not one right set or values and one wrong set of values. But generational differences in values and behaviors can create enormous challenges in workplace communication. The more we understand and are sensitive to age-related differences in workplace behavior, the more we can be flexible in communicating across the age span at work. Communicating directly about one's values and asking for the behavior you would like to receive can go a long way in manag-

what would you do?

A Question of Ethics

After three years of working at Everyday Products as a clerk, Mark had decided to look for another job. As he thought about preparing a résumé, he was struck by how little experience he had for the kind of job he wanted. When he talked with Ken about this, Ken said, "Exactly what have you been doing at Everyday?"

"Well, for the most part I've been helping others look for information—I've also done some editing of reports."

"Hm," Ken thought for a while. "Why not retitle your job as editorial assistant? It's more descriptive."

"But my official title is clerk."

"Sure, but it doesn't really describe what you do. This way you show major editorial experience. Don't worry, everybody makes these kinds of changes—you're not really lying."

"Yeah, I see what you mean. Good idea!"

1. Is it interpersonally ethical for Mark to follow Ken's advice? Why?

2. How should we deal with statements like "Everybody does it"?

ing generational differences in behavior. Using interpersonal skills of assertiveness, questioning, perception checking, describing behavior, and owning feelings may prove useful in preventing or managing intergenerational communication conflicts at work. For example, an older employee may say to a younger colleague, "Being quite a bit older than you, I was raised to see formal terms of address like Mr. and Mrs. as a sign of respect. I realize that you do not mean any disrespect when you call me by my first name, but I would prefer that you address me as Mrs. Sofranko rather than Edna. How would you like me to refer to you?" Or a younger colleague may say to his older counterpart, "I can understand that you have not had a great deal of experience with database management. But this project requires all of us to maintain and manipulate sales data. Would you consider taking the database management course that Human Resources offers? I understand that it is quite good, and employees with little technology experience have praised the instructors for their patience and thoroughness with all participants."

Such open and direct communication can allow us to understand our colleagues and to appreciate different workplace values rather than harboring resentments that may lead to conflict episodes at work.

Summary

At work we use our interpersonal skills to get a job, to relate to managers and co-workers, to participate in and lead teams, and to interact with a diverse workforce.

Before you are interviewed for a job, you need to take the time to learn about the company and prepare an appropriate cover letter and résumé designed to motivate an employer to schedule an interview with you. If you choose to send these materials electronically, make sure you edit and format them appropriately. For the interview itself, you should be prompt, be alert and look directly at the interviewer, give yourself time to think before answering difficult questions, ask intelligent questions about the company and job, and show enthusiasm for the position.

The majority of work relationships occur between managers and employees and among co-workers. As a manager, you are likely to establish exchange relationships with employees that call for them to do extra work in order to receive intangible rewards for successfully completing additional assignments. In order to engage in exchange relationships, employees must communicate their willingness to take on extra work and perform both it and regular assignments well.

To function well on a work team, you should know and be able to practice the characteristics of an effective work team, perform task and maintenance roles in team decision making, and have skills for leading team meetings as well as participating in team meetings. To communicate effectively at work, it is important to understand the complex issues of organizational romance, sexual harassment, culuture-based work styles, and intergenerational differences. We need to know our company's policy about organizational romance and follow standards of professional behavior at the workplace. Organizations need to implement strategies to prevent sexual harassment, and individuals who are the targets of sexual harassment should follow guidelines for communicating with the harasser and with workplace authorities. Culture-based work style differences and generational differences among employees require understanding, sensitivity, and discussion to arrive at flexible behaviors that respect individual needs.

Chapter Resources

Communication Improvement Plan: Workplace Communication

FIND MORE
on the web
Additional plans @
www.oup.com/us/interact

Would you like to improve your use of the following skills discussed in this chapter?

Task roles in decision making

Maintenance roles in decision making

Pick a skill and write a communication improvement plan. You can find a communication improvement plan worksheet on our website at www.oup.com/us/interact

Key Words

Cover letter, *p. 349*	**Organizational romance,** *p. 369*
Résumé, *p. 349*	**Sexual harassment,** *p. 370*
Interview, *p. 353*	**Results-oriented culture,** *p. 371*
Team, *p. 359*	**Relationship-oriented culture,** *p. 371*
Task roles, *p. 362*	**Sequential task completion,** *p. 372*
Maintenance roles, *p. 362*	**Wholistic task completion,** *p. 372*

Skill Practice

Skill Practice exercises challenge you to master the material you have read in this chapter.

For additional Skill Practice activities, visit our website at www.oup.com/us/interact

PREPARING A COVER LETTER AND A RÉSUMÉ

Prepare a cover letter and a résumé that reflect your current experience and expertise. What is missing on your résumé? Are there some experiences, skills, or accomplishments that would make you more competitive? Develop a plan to gain these experiences, skills, or accomplishments.

Inter-Act with Media

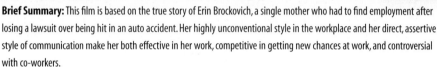

CINEMA

Steven Soderbergh (Director). (2000). *Erin Brockovich*. Julia Roberts, Albert Finney.

Brief Summary: This film is based on the true story of Erin Brockovich, a single mother who had to find employment after losing a lawsuit over being hit in an auto accident. Her highly unconventional style in the workplace and her direct, assertive style of communication make her both effective in her work, competitive in getting new chances at work, and controversial with co-workers.

IPC Concepts: Interviewing, relationships at work, diversity in the workplace, communicating with managers and co-workers, leadership.

Lasse Hallstrom (Director). (2001). *The Shipping News*. Kevin Spacey, Judi Dench, Julianne Moore, Cate Blanchett, Pete Postlethwaite, Rhys Ifans, Scott Glenn.

Brief Summary: This is a story about a shy man's efforts to achieve meaningful levels of self-respect and respect from others. His relational efforts are a disaster until he returns to his childhood roots in Newfoundland, where he obtains employment at the local newspaper covering the shipping news. His efforts include dealing with an eccentric owner, clashes with the daily manager, forming bonds with his co-workers, and balancing his work with caring for his daughter.

IPC Concepts: Interviews, communicating with supervisors, co-workers, customers, coaching, leadership, and ethical issues.

WHAT'S ON THE WEB

Have a Blog, Lose Your Job, by Krysten Crawford http://money.cnn.com/2005/02/14/news/economy/blogging/

Brief Summary: This article at CNN/Money discusses the growing danger of engaging in online Web logs, or blogs, as a risk to one's job. Comments made in such blogs that may be critical of the employer can result in a lose of employment.

IPC Concepts: Manager–subordinate communication.

Virtual Resume Interview Information Resources

http://www.virtualresume.com/interviewing.html

Brief Summary: The site provides links to practical articles on job interviewing and links to other sites with information about interviewing. It offers articles on interviewing, as well as tips on how to act in a traditional employment interview and in behavioral interviews. The latter category focuses on the applicant's behavior in order to establish the applicant's competency for the job in question. A sample question is "Give me a specific example of a time when you had to address an angry customer. What was the problem, and what was the outcome?" Traditional interview aids include suggestions for résumés, using recruiters, Internet site searches, common mistakes made during interviews, a guide to successful interviewing, elements of a successful interview, preparing for interviews, guerrilla interviewing, a headhunter's interview secrets, the telephone interview, and favorite interviewing questions. This is an excellent site for supplementary material on employment interviewing.

IPC Concepts: Employment interviewing, getting the interview, and preparing for and taking part in the interview.

references

Chapter 1

Andersen, P. (2000). Cues of culture: The basis of intercultural differences in nonverbal communication. In L. A. Samovar & R. E. Porter (Eds.), *Intercultural Communication: A Reader* (9th ed., pp. 258–266). Belmont, Calif.: Wadsworth.

Berger, C. R. (2002). Goals and knowledge structure in social interaction. In M. L. Knapp & J. A. Daly (Eds.), *Handbook of Interpersonal Communication* (pp. 181–212). Thousand Oaks, Calif.: Sage.

Johannesen, R. L. (2002). *Ethics in Human Communication* (5th ed.). Prospect Heights, Ill.: Waveland Press.

Pritchard, M. (1991). *On Becoming Responsible*. Lawrence: University of Kansas Press.

Samovar, L. A., & Porter, R. E. (2000). Understanding intercultural communication: An introduction and overview. In L. A. Samovar & R. E. Porter (Eds.), *Intercultural Communication: A Reader* (9th ed., pp. 5–16). Belmont, Calif.: Wadsworth.

Spitzberg, B. H. (2000). A model of intercultural communication competence. In L. A. Samovar & R. E. Porter (Eds.), *Intercultural Communication: A Reader* (9th ed., pp. 375–387). Belmont, Calif.: Wadsworth.

Spitzberg, B. H., & Duran, R. L. (1995). Toward the development and validation of a measure of cognitive communication competence. *Communication Quarterly, 43*, 259–274.

Terkel, S. N., & Duval, R. S. (Eds.). (1999). *Encyclopedia of Ethics*. New York: Facts on File.

U.S. Department of Commerce. Census Bureau (March 18, 2004). www.usinfo.state.gov.

Watzlawick, P., Beavin, J. H., & Jackson, D. D. (1967). *Pragmatics of Human Communication*. New York: Norton.

Wright, J. W. (2002). *New York Times Almanac*. New York: New York Times.

Chapter 2

Baron, R. A., & Byrne, D. (2000). *Social Psychology* (9th ed.). Boston: Allyn & Bacon.

Berger, C. R., & Bradac, J. J. (1982). *Language and Social Knowledge: Uncertainty in Interpersonal Relations.* London: Arnold.

Campbell, J. D. (1990). Self-esteem and clarity of the self-concept. *Journal of Personality and Social Psychology, 59*, 538.

Centi, P. J. (1981). *Up with the Positive: Out with the Negative.* Englewood Cliffs, N.J.: Prentice-Hall.

Chen, G. M., & Starosta, W. J. (1998). *Foundations of Intercultural Communication.* Boston: Allyn & Bacon.

Demo, D. H. (1987). Family relations and the self-esteem of adolescents and their parents. *Journal of Marriage and the Family, 49*, 705–715.

Downey, G., Freitas, A. L., Michaelis, B., & Khouri, H. (2004). The self-fulfilling prophecy in close relationships: Rejection sensitivity and rejection by romantic partners. In H. T. Reis & C. E. Rusbult (Eds.), *Close Relationships* (pp. 435–455). New York: Psychology Press.

Hattie, J. (1992). *Self-Concept.* Hillsdale, N.J.: Erlbaum.

Hazen, C., & Shaver, P. R. (2004). Attachment as an organizational framework for research on close relationships. In H. T. Reis & C. E. Rusbult (Eds.), *Close Relationships* (pp. 153–174). New York: Psychology Press.

Hendrick, S. S. (2004). *Understanding Close Relationships.* New York: Pearson Education.

Hollman, T. D. (1972). Employment interviewer's errors in processing positive and negative information. *Journal of Psychology, 56*, 130–134.

Jones, M. (2002). *Social Psychology of Prejudice.* Upper Saddle River, N.J.: Prentice Hall.

Kenny, D. A. (1994). *Interpersonal Perception: A Social Relations Analysis.* New York: Guilford Press.

Leary, M. R. (2002). When selves collide: The nature of the self and the dynamics of interpersonal relationships. In A. Tesser, D. A. Stapel, & J. V. Wood (Eds.), *Self and Motivation: Emerging Psychological Perspectives* (pp. 119–145). Washington, D.C.: American Psychological Association.

Littlejohn, S. W. (2002). *Theories of Human Communication* (7th ed.). Belmont, Calif.: Wadsworth.

Michener, H. A., & DeLamater, J. D. (1999). *Social Psychology* (4th ed.). Orlando, Fla.: Harcourt Brace.

Mruk, C. (1999). *Self-Esteem: Research, Theory, and Practice* (2nd ed.). New York: Springer.

Neuliep, J. W., & McCroskey, J. C. (1997). The development of a U.S. and generalized ethnocentrism scale. *Communication Research Reports, 14*, 385–398.

Rayner, S. G. (2001). Aspects of the self as learner: Perception, concept, and esteem. In R. J. Riding & S. G. Rayner (Eds.), *Self Perception: International Perspectives on Individual Differences* (Vol. 2, p. 42). Westport, Conn.: Ablex Publishing.

Sampson, E. E. (1999). *Dealing with Differences: An Introduction to the Social Psychology of Prejudice.* Fort Worth, Tex.: Harcourt Brace.

Sunnafrank, M., & Ramirez, A. (2004). At first sight: Persistent relational effects of get-acquainted conversations. *Journal of Social and Personal Relationships, 21*, 361–379.

Thurlow, C., Lengel, L., & Tomic, A. (2004). *Computer Mediated Communication: Social Interaction and the Internet.* Thousand Oaks, Calif: Sage.

Weiten, W. (1998). *Psychology: Themes and Variations* (4th ed.). Pacific Grove, Calif.: Brooks/Cole.

Chapter 3

Aron, A., Aron, E. N., Tudor, M., & Nelson, G. (2004). Close relationships as including other in the self. In H. T. Reis & C. E. Rusbult (Eds.), *Close Relationships* (pp. 365–379). New York: Psychology Press.

Baxter, L. (1982). Strategies for ending relationships: Two studies. *Western Journal of Speech Communication, 46*, 223–241.

Baxter, L. A., & Bullis, C. (1993). Turning points in developing romantic relationships. In S. Petronio, J. K. Alberts, M. L. Hecht, & J. Buley (Eds.), *Contemporary Perspectives on Interpersonal Communication* (pp. 358–374). Chicago: Brown and Benchmark.

Baxter, L. A., & Erbert, L. A. (1999). Perceptions of dialectical contradictions in turning points of development in heterosexual romantic relationships. *Journal of Social and Personal Relationships, 16,* 547–569.

Baxter, L. A., & Montgomery, B. M. (1996). *Relating: Dialogues & Dialectics.* New York: Guilford Press.

Baxter, L. A., & West, l. (2003). Couple perceptions of their similarities and differences: A dialectical perspective. *Journal of Social and Personal Relationships, 20,* 491–514.

Berger, C. R., & Bradac, J. J. (1982). *Language and Social Knowledge: Uncertainty in Interpersonal Relations.* London: Arnold.

Canary, J. C., & Dainton, M. (2002). Preface. In J. C. Canary & M. Dainton, (Eds.), *Maintaining Relationships Through Communication: Relational, Contextual and Cultural Variations* (pp. xiii–xv.). Mahwah, N.J.: Erlbaum.

Cupach, C. R., & Metts, S. (1986). Accounts of relational dissolution: A comparison of marital and non-marital relationships. *Communication Monographs, 53,* 319–321.

Duck, S. (1987). How to lose friends without influencing people. In M. E. Roloff & G. R. Miller (Eds.), *Interpersonal Processes: New Directions in Communication Research* (pp. 278–298). Beverly Hills, Calif.: Sage.

Duck, S. (1998). *Human Relationships* (3rd ed.). Thousand Oaks, Calif.: Sage.

Duck, S. (1999). *Relating to Others.* Philadelphia: Open University Press.

Duck, S., & Gilmour, R. (Eds.). (1981). *Personal Relationships.* London: Academic Press.

Katz, J. E., & Aspden, P. (2004). Social and public policy Internet research: Goals and achievements. www.communitytechnology.org/aspden.

Knapp, M. L. & Vangelisti, A. L. (2000). *Interpersonal Communication and Human Relationships* (4th ed.). Boston: Allyn & Bacon.

LaFollette, H. (1996). *Personal Relationships: Love, Identity, and Morality.* Cambridge, Mass.: Blackwell.

Littlejohn, S. W. (2002). *Theories of Human Communication* (7th ed.). Belmont, Calif.: Wadsworth.

Luft, J. (1970). *Group Processes: An Introduction to Group Dynamics.* Palo Alto, Calif.: Mayfield.

McDowell, S. W. (2001). The Development of Online and Offline Romantic Relationships: A Turning Point Study. Unpublished Master's Thesis. University of Washington.

Patterson, B. R., Bettini, L., & Nussbaum, J. F. (1993). The meaning of friendship across the life-span: Two studies. *Communication Quarterly, 41,* 145.

Rabby, M., & Walther, J. B. (2003). Computer mediated communication effects in relationship formation and maintenance. In D. J. Canary & M. Dainton (Eds.), *Maintaining Relationships Through Communication* (pp. 141–162). Mahwah, NJ: Erlbaum.

Rusbult, C. E., Olsen, N., Davis, J. L., & Hannon, P. A. (2004). In H. T. Reis & C. E. Rusbult (Eds.), *Close Relationships* (pp. 287–304). New York: Psychology Press.

Samter, W. (2003). Friendship interaction skills across the lifespan. In J. O. Greene & B. R. Burleson (Eds.). *Handbook of Communication and Social Interaction Skills* (pp. 637–684). Mahwah, N. J.: Erlbaum.

Schutz, W. (1966). *The Interpersonal Underworld.* Palo Alto, Calif.: Science & Behavior Books.

Taylor, D. A., & Altman, I. (1987). Communication in interpersonal relationships: Social penetration theory. In M. E. Roloff & G. R. Miller (Eds.), *Interpersonal Processes: New Directions in Communication Research* (pp. 257–277). Beverly Hills, Calif.: Sage.

Thibaut, J. W., & Kelley, H. H. (1986). *The Social Psychology of Groups* (2nd ed.). New Brunswick, N.J.: Transaction Books.

Trenholm, S. (1991). *Human Communication Theory* (2nd ed.). Englewood Cliffs, NJ: Prentice-Hall.

Ward, C. C., & Tracey, T. J. G. (2004). Relation of shyness with aspects of online relationship involvement. *Journal of Social and Personal Relationships, 21,* 611–623.

Walther, J. B. (1996). Computer mediated communication: Impersonal, interpersonal, and hyperpersonal interaction. *Western Journal of Communication, 57,* 381–398.

Wood, J. T. (2000). Dialectical theory. In K. M. Galvin & P. J. Cooper (Eds.), *Making Connections: Readings in Relational Communication* (pp. 132–138). Los Angeles: Roxbury Publishing Company.

Wood, J. T., & Inman, C. C. (1993). In a different mode: Masculine styles of communicating closeness. *Journal of Applied Communication Research, 21,* 279–295.

Chapter 4

Burke, K. (1968). *Language as Symbolic Action.* Berkeley: University of California Press.

Chen, G. M., & Starosta, W. J. (1998). *Foundations of Intercultural Communication.* Boston: Allyn & Bacon.

Foot, H. C. (1997). Humor and laughter. In O. D. W. Hargie (Ed.), *The Handbook of Communication Skills* (pp. 259–285). New York: Routledge.

Giles, H. & Coupland, N. (1991). *Language: Contexts and Consequences.* Pacific Grove, Calif: Wadsworth.

Gmelch, S. B. (1998). *Gender on Campus: Issues for College Women.* New Brunswick, N.J.: Rutgers University Press.

Griffin, E. A. (1997). Muted groups theory of Cheris Kramarae. In Griffin, E. A., *A First Look at Communication Theory* (pp. 459–473). New York: McGraw-Hill.

Holtgraves, T. (2002). *Language as Social Action: Social Psychology and Language Use.* Mahwah, N.J.: Erlbaum.

Larkey, L. K. (1996). Toward a theory of communicative interactions in culturally diverse work groups. *Academy of Management Review, 21,* 463–491.

Leeds-Hurwitz, W. (Ed.). (1995). *Social Approaches to Communication.* New York: Guilford Press.

Littlejohn, S. (2002). *Theories of Human Communication* (7th ed.). Belmont, Calif.: Wadsworth.

Merriam-Webster's Collegiate Dictionary (11th ed.). (2004). Springfield, Mass.: Merriam-Webster.

Ogden, C. K., & Richards, I. A. (1923). *The Meaning of Meaning.* London: Kegan, Paul, Trench, Trubner.

Philipsen, G. (1995). The coordinated management of meaning theory of Pearce, Cronen and associates. In D. P. Cushman & B. Kovacic (Eds.), *Watershed Research Traditions in Human Communication Theory* (pp. 13–43). Albany: State University of New York Press.

Sillars, A. L. (1998). (Mis)Understanding. In B. H. Spitzberg & W. R. Cupach (Eds.), *The Dark Side of Close Relationships* (pp. 73–102). Mahwah, N.J.: Erlbaum.

Stewart, L. P., Cooper, P. J., Stewart, A. D., & Friedley, S. A. (1998). *Communication and Gender* (3rd ed.). Boston: Allyn & Bacon.

Thurlow, C., Lengel, L., & Tomic, A. (2004). *Computer-Mediated Communication: Social Interaction and the Internet.* Thousand Oaks, Calif.: Sage.

Chapter 5

Axtell, R. E. (1998). *Gestures: The Do's and Taboos of Body Language Around the World* (rev. ed.). New York: Wiley.

Burgoon, J. K. (1994). Nonverbal signals. In M. L. Knapp & G. R. Miller (Eds.), *Handbook of Interpersonal Communication* (2nd ed., pp. 229–285). Thousand Oaks, Calif.: Sage.

Burgoon, J. K., Buller, D. B., & Woodall, W. G. (1989). *Nonverbal Communication: The Unspoken Dialogue.* New York: Harper & Row.

Cegala, D. J., & Sillars, A. L. (1989). Further examination of nonverbal manifestations of interaction involvement. *Communication Reports, 2,* 45.

Chen, G. M, & Starosta, W. J. (1998). *Foundations of Intercultural Communication.* Boston: Allyn & Bacon.

Furlow, F. B. (1996). The smell of love. *Psychology Today, 29* (Mar/Apr), 38–45.

Gudykunst, W. B., & Kim, Y. Y. (1997). *Communicating with Strangers: An Approach to Intercultural Communication* (3rd ed.). Boston: Allyn & Bacon.

Hall, E. T. (1969). *The Hidden Dimension.* Garden City, N.Y.: Doubleday.

Henley, N. M. (1977). *Body Politics: Power, Sex and Nonverbal Communication.* Englewood Cliffs,N.J.: Prentice-Hall.

Johnson, K. R. (2004). Black kinesics: Some non-verbal communication patterns in the black culture, In R. L. Jackson (Ed.), *African-American Communication and Identities* (pp. 39–46). Thousand Oaks, Calif: Sage.

Knapp, M. L., & Hall, J. A. (2002). *Nonverbal Communication in Human Interaction* (5th ed.). Belmont, Calif.: Wadsworth/Thomson Learning.

Martin, J. N., & Nakayama, T. K. (2000). *Intercultural Communication in Contexts* (2nd ed.). Mountain View, Calif: Mayfield.

Mehrabian, A. (1972). *Nonverbal Communication.* Chicago: Aldine.

Patterson, M. L. (1994). Strategic functions of nonverbal exchange. In J. A. Daly (Ed.), *Strategic Interpersonal Communication* (pp. 273–293). Hillsdale, N.J.: Erlbaum.

Pearson, J. C., West, R. L., & Turner, L. H. (1995). *Gender and Communication* (3rd ed.). Dubuque, Iowa: Brown & Benchmark.

Samovar, L. A., & Porter, R. E. (2001). *Communication Between Cultures* (4th ed.). Belmont, Calif.: Wadsworth.

Walther, J. B., & Parks, M. R. (2002). Cues filtered out, cues filtered in: Computer-mediated communication and relationships. In M. C. Knapp & J. A. Daly (Eds.), *Handbook of Interpersonal Communication* (pp. 529–563). Thousand Oaks, Calif: Sage.

Wood, J. T. (2003). *Gendered Lives: Communication, Gender, and Culture* (5th ed.). Belmont, Calif.: Wadsworth.

Chapter 6

Bach, K., and Harnish, R. M. (1979). *Linguistic Communication and Speech Acts.* Cambridge, Mass.: MIT Press.

Berger, C. R. (2002). Goals and knowledge structures in social interaction. In M. L. Knapp & J. A. Daly (Eds.), *Handbook of Interpersonal Communication* (pp. 181–212). Thousand Oaks, Calif: Sage.

Brown, P., & Levinson, S. (1987). *Politeness: Some Universals in Language Usage.* Cambridge, U.K.: Cambridge University Press.

Duck, S. (1998). *Human Relationships* (3rd ed.). Thousand Oaks, Calif.: Sage.

Eggins, S., & Slade, D. (1997). *Analyzing Casual Conversation.* Washington, D.C.: Cassell.

Ford, C. E., Fox, B. A., & Thompson, S. A. (2002). Introduction. In C. E. Ford, B. A. Fox, & S. A. Thomson (Eds.), *The Language of Turn and Sequence* (pp. 3–13). New York: Oxford University Press.

Fraley, B., and Aron, A. (2004). The effect of a shared humorous experience on closeness in initial encounters. *Personal Relationships, 11,* 61–78.

Grice, H. P. (1975). *Logic and conversation.* In P. Cole & J. L. Morgan (Eds.), *Syntax and Semantics* (Vol. 3, *Speech Acts*, pp. 41–58). New York: Academic Press.

Gudykunst, W. B., & Matsumoto, Y. (1996). Cross-cultural variability of

communication in personal relationships. In W. B. Gudykunst, S. Ting-Toomey, & T. Nishida (Eds.), *Communication in Personal Relationships Across Cultures* (pp. 19–56). Thousand Oaks, Calif.: Sage.

Holtgraves, T. (2002). *Language as Social Action: Social Psychology and Language Use.* Mahwah, N.J.: Erlbaum.

Johannesen, R. L. (2000). *Ethics in Human Communication* (5th ed.). Prospect Heights, Ill.: Waveland Press.

Kellerman, K., & Park, H. S. (2001). Situational urgency and conversational retreat: When politeness and efficiency matter. *Communication Research, 28,* 3–47.

Kennedy, C. W., & Camden, C. T. (1983). A new look at interruptions. *Western Journal of Speech Communication, 47,* 55.

Littlejohn, S. W. (2003). *Theories of Human Communication* (7th ed.). Belmont, Calif.: Wadsworth.

McLaughlin, M. L. (1984). *Conversation: How Talk Is Organized.* Newbury Park, Calif.: Sage.

Sakamoto, N. M. (1995). Conversational ballgames. In R. Holton (Ed.), *Encountering Cultures.* Englewood Cliffs, N.J.: Prentice-Hall, pp. 60–63.

Sawyer, R. K. (2001). *Creating Conversations: Improvisation in Everyday Discourse.* Creskill, N.J.: Hampton Press.

Shimanoff, S. B. (1980). *Communication Rules: Theory and Research.* Beverly Hills, Calif.: Sage.

Svennevig, J. (1999). *Getting Acquainted in Conversation: A Study of Initial Interactions.* Philadelphia: John Benjamins.

Chapter 7

Anderson, R. (1997). The new digital presence: Listening, access and computer-mediated life. In M. Purdy & D. Borisoff (Eds.), *Listening in Everyday Life: A Personal and Professional Approach* (2nd ed., pp. 139–161). New York: University Press of America.

Bostrom, R. N. (1990). *Listening Behavior: Measurement and Applications.* New York: Guilford Press.

Bostrom, R. N. (1996). Memory, cognitive processing, and the process of "listening": A reply to Thomas and Levine. *Human Communicaiton Research, 23,* 298–305.

Bostrom, R. N. (1997). The process of listening. In O. Hargie (Ed.), *Handbook of Communicaiton Skills* (2nd ed., pp. 236–258). New York: Routledge.

Brownell, J. (2002). *Listening: Attitudes, Principles, and Skills* (2nd ed.). Boston, Mass.: Allyn & Bacon.

Carbaugh, D. (2002). American Indian students and the study of public "communication." In J. N. Martin, T. K. Nakayama, & L. A. Flores (Eds.), *Readings in Intercultural Communication* (pp. 138–148). New York: McGraw-Hill.

Ellinor, L., & Gerard, G. (1998). *Dialogue: Rediscover the Transforming Power of Conversation.* New York: Wiley.

Estes, W. K. (1989). Learning theory. In A. Lesgold & R. Glaser (Eds.), *Foundations for a Psychology of Education* (pp. 1–49). Hillsdale, N.J.: Erlbaum.

Halone, K. K. & Pecchioni, L. L. (2001). Relational listening: A grounded theoretical model. *Communication Reports, 14,* 59–72.

Pew Internet & American Life Project (2001). Teenage life on line: The rise of the instant message generation and the Internet's impact on friendships and family relationships. www.pewinternet. org/reports/toc.asp?report=36.

Purdy, M. (1996). What is listening? In M. Purdy & D. Borisoff (Eds.), *Listening in Everyday Life: A Personal and Professional Approach* (2nd ed., pp. 1–20). New York: University Press of America.

Steil, L. K., Barker, L. L., & Watson, K. W. (1983). *Effective Listening.* Reading, Mass.: Addison-Wesley.

Ward, C. C., & Tracey, T. J. G. (2004). Relation of shyness with aspects of online relational involvement. *Journal of Social and Personal Relationships, 21,* 611–623.

Wolvin, A., & Coakley, C. G. (1996). *Listening* (5th ed.). Dubuque, Iowa: Brown & Benchmark.

Chapter 8

Barbee, A. P., & Cunningham, M. R. (1995). An experimental approach to social support communication: Interactive coping in close relationships. In B. R. Burleson (Ed.), *Communication Yearbook 18* (pp. 381–413). Thousand Oaks, Calif.: Sage.

Burleson, B. R. (1994). Comforting messages: Significance, approaches, and effects. In B. R. Burleson, T. L. Albrecht, & I. G. Sarason (Eds.), *Communication of Social Support: Messages, Interactions, Relationships, and Community* (pp. 3–28). Thousand Oaks, Calif.: Sage.

Burleson, B. R. (2003). Emotional support skills. In J. O. Green & B. R. Burleson (Eds.), *Handbook of Communication and Social Interaction Skills* (pp. 551–594). Mahwah, N.J.: Erlbaum.

Burleson, B. R., & Goldsmith, D. J. (1998). How the comforting process works: Alleviating emotional distress through conversationally induced reappraisals. In P. A. Andersen & L. K. Guerrero (Eds.), *Handbook of Communication and Emotion: Research, Theory, Applications, and Contexts* (pp. 248–280). San Diego, Calif.: Academic Press.

Burleson, B. R., & MacGeorge, E. L. (2002). Supportive communication. In M. L. Knapp, J. A. Daly, & G. R. Miller (Eds.), *Handbook of Interpersonal Communication* (3rd ed., pp. 374–424). Thousand Oaks, Calif.: Sage.

Burleson, B. R., & Samter, W. (1990). Effects of cognitive complexity on the perceived importance of communication skills in friends. *Communication Research, 17,* 165–182.

Cunningham, M. R., & Barbee, A. P. (2000). Social support. In C. Hendrick & S. S. Hendrick (Eds.), *Close Relationships: A Sourcebook* (pp. 272–285). Thousand Oaks, Calif.: Sage.

Eisenberg, N., & Fabes, R. A. (1990). Empathy: Conceptualization, measurement, and relation to prosocial behavior. *Motivation and Emotion, 14,* 131–149.

Holtgraves, T. (2002). *Language as Social Action: Social Psychology and Language Use.* Mahwah, N.J.: Erlbaum.

Kunkel, A. W., & Burleson, B. R. (1999). Assessing explanations for sex differences in emotional support: A test of the different cultures and skill specialization accounts. *Human Communication Research, 25* (March), 307–340.

Leathers, D. G. (1997). *Successful Nonverbal Communication: Principles and Applications* (3rd ed.). Boston: Allyn & Bacon.

Omdahl, B. L. (1995). *Cognitive Appraisal, Emotion, and Empathy.* Mahwah, N.J.: Erlbaum.

Samter, W., Burleson, B. R., & Murphy, L. B. (1987). Comforting conversations: The effects of strategy type of evaluations on messages and message producers. *Southern Speech Communication Journal, 52,* 263–284.

Segrin, C. (1998). Disrupted interpersonal relationships and mental health problems. In B. H. Spitzberg & W. H. Cupach (Eds.), *The Dark Side of Close Relationships* (pp. 327–365). Mahwah, N.J.: Erlbaum.

Stiff, J. B., Dillard, J. P., Somera, L., Kim, H., & Sleight, C. (1988). Empathy, communication, and prosocial behavior. *Communication Monographs, 55,* 198–213.

Walther, J. B., & Parks, M. R. (2002). Cues filtered out, cues filtered in: Computer-mediated communication and close relationships. In M. L. Knapp & J. A. Daly (Eds.), *Handbook of Interpersonal Communication* (3rd ed., pp. 529–563). Thousand Oaks, Calif.: Sage.

Weaver III, J. B., & Kirtley, M. B. (1995). Listening styles and empathy. *Southern Communication Journal 60,* 131–140.

Zillman, D., (1991). Empathy: Affect from bearing witness in the emotions of others. In J. Bryant & D. Zillmann (Eds.), *Responding to the Screen: Reception and Reaction Processes* (pp. 135–167). Hillsdale, N.J.: Erlbaum.

Chapter 9

Altman, I. (1993). Dialectics, physical environments, and personal relationships. *Communication Monographs, 60,* 26–34.

Berg, J. H., & Derlega, V. J. (1987). Themes in the study of self-disclosure. In J. H. Berg & V. J. Derlega (Eds.), *Self-Disclosure: Theory, Research, and Therapy* (pp. 1–8). New York: Plenum Press.

Derlega, V. J., Metts, S., Petronio, S., & Margulis, S. T. (1993). *Self-Disclosure.* Newbury Park, Calif.: Sage.

Dindia, K., Fitzpatrick, M. A., & Kenny, D. A. (1997). Self-disclosure in spouse and stranger interaction: A social relations analysis. *Human Communication Research, 23* (March), 388–412.

Gudykunst, W. B., & Kim, Y. Y. (1997). *Communicating with Strangers: An Approach to Intercultural Communication* (3rd ed.). Boston: Allyn & Bacon.

Knobloch, L. K., & Carpenter-Theune, K. E. (2004). Topic avoidance in developing romantic relationships: Association with intimacy and relational uncertainty. *Communication Research, 31,* 173–205.

Pearson, J. C., West, R. L., & Turner, L. H. (1995). *Gender and Communication* (3rd ed.). Dubuque, Iowa: Wm. C. Brown.

Petronio, S. (2002). *Boundaries of Privacy: Dialectics of Disclosure.* Albany: State University of New York Press.

Rabby, M., & Walther, J. B. (2003). Computer mediated communication effects in relationship formation and maintenance. In D.J. Canary & M. Dainton (Eds.), *Maintaining Relationships through Communication* (pp. 141–162). Mahwah, N.J.: Erlbaum.

Reis, H. T. (1998). Gender differences in intimacy and related behaviors: Context and process. In D. J. Canary & K. Dindia (Eds.), *Sex Differences and Similarities in Communication: Critical Essays and Empirical Investigations of Sex and Gender in Interaction* (pp. 203–232). Mahwah, N.J.: Erlbaum.

Samovar, L. A., & Porter, R. E. (2001). *Communication Between Cultures* (4th ed.). Belmont, Calif.: Wadsworth.

Stewart, L. P., Cooper, P. J., Stewart, A. D., & Friedley, S. A. (1998). *Communication and Gender* (3rd ed.). Boston: Allyn & Bacon.

Tannen, D. (1990). *You Just Don't Understand.* New York: Morrow.

Tracy, K., Dusen, D. V., & Robinson, S. (1987). "Good" and "bad" criticism. *Journal of Communication, 37,* 46–59.

Chapter 10

Alberti, R. E., & Emmons, M. L. (1995). *Your Perfect Right: A Guide to Assertive Living* (7th ed.). San Luis Obispo, Calif.: Impact Publishers.

Chebat, J. C., Filiatrault, P., & Perrien, J. (1990). Limits of credibility: The case of political persuasion. *Journal of Social Psychology 130,* 157–167.

Dillard, J. P., Anderson, J. W., & Knobloch, L. K. (2002). Interpersonal Influence. In M. L. Knapp & J. A. Daly, (Eds.), *Handbook of Interpersonal Communication* (3rd ed., pp. 425–474). Thousand Oaks, Calif.: Sage.

Dillard, J. P., & Marshall, L. J. (2003). Persuasion as a social skill. In J. O. Greene & B. R. Burleson (Eds.), *Handbook of Communication and Social Interaction Skills* (pp. 479–513). Mahwah, N.J.: Erlbaum.

French, Jr., J. R. P., & Raven, B. (1968). The bases of social power. In D. Cartwright & A. Zander (Eds.), *Group Dynamics* (3rd ed., pp. 259–269). New York: Harper & Row.

Hample, D., & Dallinger, J. M. (1998). On the etiology of the rebuff phenomenon: Why are persuasive messages less polite after rebuffs? *Communication Studies, 49,* 305–321.

Hample, D., & Dallinger, J. M. (2002). The effects of situation on the use or suppression of possible compliance-gaining appeals. In M. Allen, R. W. Preiss, B. M. Gayle, & N. Burrell, (Eds.), *Interpersonal Communication Research: Advances through Meta-Analysis* (pp. 187–209). Mahwah, N.J.: Erlbaum.

Hinken, T. R., & Schriesheim, C. A. (1980). Development and application of new scales to measure the French and Raven (1959) Bases of Social Power. *Journal of Applied Psychology, 74,* 561–567.

Jandt, F. E. (2001). *Intercultural Communication: An Introduction* (3rd ed.). Thousand Oaks, Calif.: Sage.

Jorgensen, P. E. (1998). Affect, persuasion, and communication process. In P. A. Anderson & L. K. Guerrero (Eds.), *Handbook of Communication and Emotion: Research, Theory, Applications, and Contexts* (pp. 403–422). San Diego, Calif.: Academic Press.

Kellerman, K., & Cole, T. D. (1994). Classifying compliance gaining messages: Taxonomic disorder in strategic confusion. *Communication Theory, 4,* 3–60.

Kellermann, K., & Shea, B. C. (1996). Threats, suggestions, hints, and promises: Gaining compliance efficiently and politely. *Communication Quarterly, 44*(2), 145–165.

Knowles, E. R., Butler, S., & Linn, J. A. (2001). Increasing compliance by reducing resistance. In J. P. Forgas & K. D. Williams (Eds.), *Social Influence: Direct and Indirect Processes* (pp. 41–60). Philadelphia: Psychology Press.

Martin, M. M., Anderson, C. M., & Horvath, C. L. (1996). Feelings about verbal aggression: Justifications for sending and hurt from receiving verbally aggressive messages. *Communication Research Reports, 13*(1), 19–26.

Miller, L. C., Cody, M. J., & McLaughlin, M. L. (1994). Situations and goals as fundamental constructs in interpersonal communication research. In M. L. Knapp & G. R. Miller (Eds.), *Handbook of Interpersonal Communication* (2nd ed., pp. 263–313). Beverly Hills, Calif.: Sage.

O'Hair, D., & Cody, M. J. (1987). Machiavellian beliefs and social influence. *Western Journal of Speech Communication, 51,* 286–287.

Petty, R. E., & Cacioppo, T. T. (1996). Attitudes and persuasion: Classic and contemporary approaches. Boulder, CO: Westview Press.

Petty, R. E. DeSteno, D., & Rucker, D. (2001). The role of affect in persuasion and attitude change. In J. Forgas (Ed.), *Handbook of Affect and Social Cognition* (pp. 212–233). Mahwah, N.J.: Erlbaum.

Petty, R. E., Wheeler, S. C., & Bitzer, G. Y. (2000). Attitude functions and persuasion: An elaboration likelihood approach to matched versus mismatched messages. In G. R. Maio & J. M. Olson (Eds.), *Why We Evaluate: Functions of Attitudes* (pp. 133–162). Mahwah, N.J.: Erlbaum.

Samovar, L. A., & Porter, R. E. (2001). *Communication Between Cultures* (4th ed.). Belmont, Calif.: Wadsworth.

Tedeschi, J. T. (2001). Social power, influence, and aggression. In J. P. Forgas & K. D. Williams (Eds.), *Social Influence: Direct and Indirect Processes* (pp. 109–126). Philadelphia: Psychology Press.

Trenholm, S. (1989). *Persuasion and Social Influence.* Englewood Cliffs, N.J.: Prentice-Hall.

Chapter 11

Adler, R. B. (1977). *Confidence in Communication: A Guide to Assertive and Social Skills.* New York: Holt, Rinehart, & Winston.

Canary, D. J. (2003). *Maintaining Relationships through Communication: Relational, Contextual, and Cultural Variations.* Mahwah, N.J.: Erlbaum.

Canary, D. J., Cupach, W. R., & Messman, S. J. (1995). *Relationship Conflict: Conflict in Parent–Child, Friendship, and Romantic Relationships.* Thousand Oaks, Calif.: Sage.

Caughlin, J. P., & Huston, T. L. (2002). A contextual analysis of the association between demand/withdraw and marital satisfaction. *Personal Relationships, 9,* 95–119.

Cloven, D. H., & Roloff, M. E. (1991). Sense-making activities and interpersonal conflict: Communicative cures for the mulling blues. *Western Journal of Speech Communication, 55,* 134–158.

Cupach, W. R., & Canary, D. J. (1997). *Competence in Interpersonal Conflict.* New York: McGraw-Hill.

Gordon, T. (1970). *Parent Effectiveness Training.* New York: Peter H. Wyden.

Gordon, T. (1971). *The Basic Modules of the Instructor Outline for Effectiveness Training Courses.* Pasadena, Calif.: Effectiveness Training Associates.

Lulofs, R. S., & Cahn, D. D. (2000). *Conflict: From Theory to Action* (2nd ed.). Boston: Allyn & Bacon.

Martin, J. N., & Nakayama, T. K. (1997). *Intercultural Communication in Contexts.* Mountain View, Calif.: Mayfield.

Roloff, M. E., & Cloven, D. H. (1990). The chilling effect in interpersonal relationships: The reluctance to speak one's mind. In D. D. Cahn (Ed.), *Intimates in Conflict: A Communication Perspective* (pp. 49–76). Hillsdale, N.J.: Erlbaum.

Sillars, A. L., & Weisberg, J. (1987). Conflict as a social skill. In M. E. Roloff & G. R. Miller (Eds.), *Interpersonal Processes: New Directions in Communication Research* (pp. 140–171). Beverly Hills, Calif.: Sage.

Ting-Toomey, S. (2006). Managing intercultural conflicts effectively. In L. A. Samovar & R. E. Porter (Eds.), *Intercultural Communication: A Reader* (11th ed., pp. 366–377). Belmont, Calif.: Wadsworth.

Whetten, D. A., & Cameron, K. S. (2005). *Developing Management Skills* (6th ed.). Upper Saddle River, N.J.: Prentice Hall.

Chapter 12

Argyle, M., & Furnham, A. (1983). Sources of satisfaction and conflict in long-term relationships. *Journal of Marriage and the Family, 45,* 481–493.

Bloch, J. D. (1980). *Friendship.* New York: Macmillan.

Boon, S. D. (1994). Dispelling doubt and uncertainty: Trust in romantic relationships. In S. Duck (Ed.), *Dynamics of Relationships* (pp. 86–111). Thousand Oaks, Calif.: Sage.

Demo, D. H. (1987). Family relations and the self-esteem of adolescents and their parents. *Journal of Marriage and the Family, 49,* 705–715.

Dickson, F. C. (1995). The best is yet to be: Research on long-lasting marriages. In J. T. Wood & S. Duck (Eds.), *Under-Studied Relationships: Off the Beaten Track* (pp. 22–50). Thousand Oaks, Calif.: Sage.

Duck, S., & Wright, P. H. (1993). Reexamining gender differences in same-gender friendships: A close look at two kinds of data. *Sex Roles, 28,* 709–727.

Family time: An interview with Bill Doherty. (2002).The Early Show. CBSWorldwide.: New York. http://www.cbsnews.com/stories/2002/09/20/earlyshow/living/ parenting/main522830.shtml.

Fehr, B. (1996). *Friendship Processes.* Thousand Oaks, Calif.: Sage.

Fischer, J. L., & Narus, Jr., L. R., (1981). Sex roles and intimacy in same-sex and other-sex relationships. *Psychology of Women Quarterly, 5,* 444–455.

Fitzpatrick, M. A. (1988). *Between Husbands and Wives: Communication in Marriage.* Beverly Hills, Calif.: Sage.

Fitzpatrick, M. A., & Badzinski, D. M. (1994). All in the family: Interpersonal communication in kin relationships. In M. L. Knapp & G. R. Miller (Eds.), *Handbook of Interpersonal Communication* (2nd ed., pp. 726–771). Thousand Oaks, Calif.: Sage.

Fitzpatrick, M. A., & Bochner, A. (1981). Perspectives on self and other: Male-female differences in perceptions of communication behavior. *Sex Roles, 7,* 523–535.

Fitzpatrick, M. A., & Caughlin, J. (2003). Interpersonal communication in family relationships. In M. Knapp & J. Daly (Eds.), *Handbook of Interpersonal Communication* (pp. 726–778). Thousand Oaks, Calif.: Sage.

Fitzpatrick, M. A., & Koerner, A. (2002). A theory of family communication. *Communication Theory, 12*(1), 70–91.

Fitzpatrick, M. A., & Ritchie, L. D. (1994). Communication schemata within the family: Multiple perspectives on family interaction. *Human Communication Research, 20,* 275–301.

Frei, J. R., and Shaver, P. R. (2002). Respect in close relationships: prototype definition, self-report assessment, and initial correlates. *Personal Relationships, 9,* 121–139.

Galvin, K. M., & Brommel, B. J. (1996). *Family Communication: Cohesion and Change* (4th ed.). New York: HarperCollins.

Gould, O. (2004). Telling stories and getting acquainted: How age matters. In M. W. Pratt & B. H. Fiese (Eds.), *Family Stories and the Lifecourse* (pp. 327–351). Mahwah, N.J.: Erlbaum.

Knobloch, L. K., & Solomon (2002). Information seeking beyond initial interaction: Negotiating relational uncertainty within close relationships. *Human Communication Research, 28,* 243–257.

LaFollette, H. (1996). *Personal Relationships: Love, Identity, and Morality.* Cambridge, Mass.: Blackwell.

Marsh, P. (Ed.). (1988). *Eye to Eye: How People Interact.* Topsfield, Mass.: Salem House.

Mills, J., & Clark, M. S. (2001). Viewing close romantic relationships as communal relationships: Implications for maintenance and enhancement. In J. Harvey & A. Wenzel (Eds.), *Close Romantic Relationships: Maintenance and Enhancement* (pp. 13–25). Mahwah, N.J.: Erlbaum.

O'Meara, J. D. (1989). Cross-sex friendship: Four basic challenges of an ignored relationship. *Sex Roles, 21,* 525–543.

Perlman, D., & Fehr, B. (1987). The development of intimate relationships. In D. Perlman & S. Duck (Eds.), *Intimate Relationships: Development, Dynamics, and Deterioration* (pp. 13–42). Beverly Hills, Calif.: Sage.

Pleck, J. H. (1975). Man to man: Is brotherhood possible? In N. Glazer-Malbin (Ed.), *Old Family/New Family: Interpersonal Relationships* (pp. 229–244). New York: Van Nostrand.

Prisbell, M., & Andersen, J. F. (1980). The importance of perceived homophily, level of uncertainty, feeling good, safety, and self-disclosure in interpersonal relationships. *Communication Quarterly, 28,* 22–33.

Reis, H. T. (1998). Gender differences in intimacy and related behaviors: Context and process. In D. J. Canary & K. Dindia (Eds.), *Sex Differences and Similarities in Communication: Critical Essays and Empirical Investigations of Sex and Gender in Interaction* (pp. 203–231). Mahwah, N.J.: Erlbaum.

Rusbult, C. E., Olsen, N., Davis, J. L., & Hannon, P. A. (2001). Commitment and relationship maintenance mechanisms. In J. Harvey & A. Wenzel (Eds.), *Close Romantic Relationships: Maintenance and Enhancement* (pp. 87–113). Mahwah, N.J.: Erlbaum.

Ryan, E. B., Pearce, K. A., Anas, A. P., & Norris, J. E. (2004). Writing a connection: Intergenerational communication through stories. In M. W. Pratt & B. H. Fiese (Eds.), *Family Stories and the Lifecourse* (pp. 375–398). Mahwah, N.J.: Erlbaum.

Sabourin, T. C. (1996). The role of communication in verbal abuse between spouses. In D. D. Cahn & S. A. Lloyd (Eds.), *Family Violence from a Communication Perspective* (pp. 199–217). Thousand Oaks, Calif.: Sage.

Sabourin, T. C., & Stamp, G. H. (1995). Communication and the experience of dialectical tensions in family life: An examination of abusive and nonabusive families. *Communication Monographs, 62*(3), 213–242.

Segrin, C. (1998). Disrupted interpersonal relationships and mental health problems. In B. H. Spitzberg & W. R. Cupach (Eds.), *The Dark Side of Close Relationships* (pp. 327–365). Mahwah, N.J.: Erlbaum.

Sillars, A. L. (1998). (Mis)Understanding. In B. H. Spitzberg & W. R. Cupach (Eds.), *The Dark Side of Close Relationships* (pp. 73–102). Mahwah, NJ: Erlbaum

Werking, K. J. (1997). Cross-sex friendship research as ideological practice.

In S. Duck (Ed.), *Handbook of Personal Relationships: Theory, Research, and Interventions* (2nd ed., pp. 391–410). New York: Wiley.

Werner, C. M., Altman, I., Brown, B. B., & Ginat, J. (1993). Celebrations in personal relationships: A transactional/dialectical perspective. In S. Duck (Ed.), *Social Context and Relationships* (pp. 109–138). Newbury Park, Calif.: Sage.

Williams, A., & Nussbaum, J. F. (2001). *Intergenerational Communication Across the Lifespan.* Mahwah, N.J.: Erlbaum.

Winstead, B. A., Derlega, V. J., & Rose, S. (1997). *Gender and Close Relationships.* Thousand Oaks, Calif.: Sage.

Wood, J. T., & Inman, C. C. (1993). In a different mode: Masculine styles of communicating closeness. *Journal of Applied Communication Research, 21,* 279–295.

Wood, J. T. (2003). *Gendered Lives: Communication, Gender and Culture* (5th ed.). Belmont, Calif.: Wadsworth.

Yerby, J., Buerkel-Rothfuss, N., & Bochner, A. P. (1995). *Understanding Family Communication* (2nd ed.). Scottsdale, Ariz.: Gorsuch Scarisbrick.

Chapter 13

Berryman-Fink, C. (1997). Gender issues, management style, mobility and harassment. In P. Y. Byers (Ed.), *Organizational Communication: Theory and Behavior.* (pp. 259–283). Boston: Allyn & Bacon.

Conrad, C., & Poole, M. S. (2005). *Strategic Organizational Communication in a Global Economy.* Belmont, Calif.: Thompson Wadsworth.

Eisenberg, E. M., & Goodall, H. L. (2004). *Organizational Communication: Balancing Creativity and Constraint.* New York: Bedford St. Martin's.

Graen, G. (1976). Role making processes within complex organizations. In M. D.

Dunette (Ed.), *Handbook of Industrial and Organizational Psychology* (pp. 1201-1245). Chicago: Rand McNally.

Jablin, F. M., & Krone, K. J. (1994). Task/work relationships: A life-span perspective. In M. L. Knapp & G. R. Miller (Eds.), *Handbook of Interpersonal Communication* (2nd ed., pp. 621-675). Thousand Oaks, Calif.: Sage.

Larson, C. E., & LaFasto, F. M. J. (1989). *Team Work: What Must Go Right / What Can Go Wrong.* Newbury Park, Calif.: Sage.

Lee, J., & Jablin, F. M. (1995). Maintenance communication in superior-subordinate work relationships. *Human Communication Research, 22,* 220-257.

Potoker, E. S. (2005). *Managing Diverse Working Styles: The Leadership Competitive Advantage.* Mason, Ohio: South Western Publishing.

Schmidt, W. V., & Conaway, R. N. (1999). *Results-Oriented Interviewing: Principles, Practices, and Procedures.* Boston: Allyn & Bacon.

Sias, P. M., & Jablin, F. M. (1995). Differential superior–subordinate relations, perceptions of fairness, and coworker communication. *Human Communication Research, 22,* 5-38.

Stewart, C. J., & Cash, W. B. (2000). *Interviewing: Principles and Practices* (9th ed.). Dubuque, Iowa: William C. Brown.

Varner, I., & Beamer, L. (1995). *Intercultural Communication in the Global Workplace.* Chicago: Irwin.

Whetten, D. A., & Cameron, K. S. (2005). *Developing Management Skills* (6th ed.). Upper Saddle River, N.J.: Prentice Hall.

Zemke, R., Raines, C., & Filipczak, B. (2000). *Generations at Work.* New York: AMACOM.

glossary

Accommodating—*resolving conflict by satisfying others' needs or accepting others' ideas while neglecting our own.*

Acquaintances—*people we know by name and talk with when the opportunity arises, but with whom our interactions are limited.*

Adaptors—*gestures that respond to a physical need.*

Advice giving—*presenting relevant suggestions and proposals that a person could use to satisfactorily resolve a situation.*

Affection need—*a desire to express and to receive love.*

Aggressive behavior—*the lashing out at the source of one's discontent with little regard for the situation or for the feelings, needs, or rights of those who are attacked.*

Appreciative listening—*focusing on a message in order to enjoy what is said.*

Appropriateness—*being polite and following situational rules of conversation.*

Artifacts—*objects we own and decorations of our territory and body.*

Assertiveness—*the art of declaring our personal preferences and defending our personal rights while respecting the preferences and rights of others.*

Attending—*the perceptual process of selecting to concentrate on specific stimuli from the countless stimuli reaching the senses.*

Attributions—*reasons we give for others' behavior.*

Authenticity—*direct, honest, straightforward communication of all information and feelings that are relevant and legitimate to the subject at hand.*

Badgering—*light teasing, taunting, and mocking behavior.*

Behavioral flexibility—*analyzing a communication situation and adapting your use of skills to fit the situation.*

Body orientation—*posture in relation to another person.*

Casual social conversations—*interactions between people whose purpose is to enhance or maintain a relationship through spontaneous interactions about general topics.*

Channels—*both the route traveled by the message and the means of transportation.*

Chronemics—*the use of time.*

Claims—*statements of belief or requests for action.*

Clarify supportive intentions—*openly state that our goal in the conversation is to support and help our partner.*

Clarifying question—*a response designed to get further information, to clarify information already received, or to encourage another to continue speaking.*

Close friends or intimates—*those with whom we share our deepest feelings.*

Coercive power—*derives from the perception that people can harm their partners physically and/or psychologically, should the partners resist an influence attempt.*

Collaborating—*resolving conflict by trying to fully address the needs and issues of each party and arrive at a solution that is mutually satisfying.*

Comfortable level of closeness—*spending an appropriate amount of time with a relational partner.*

Comforting—*helping people feel better about themselves and their behavior.*

Communal relationship—*relationships where we allow the costs to exceed the rewards.*

Communication accommodation theory—*describes the practice of changing language patterns to adjust to a speaker.*

Communication competence—*the impression that communicative behavior is both appropriate and effective in a given relationship.*

Comparison-level of alternatives—*other choices a person perceives as being available that affect the decision of whether to continue in a relationship.*

Competence—*the impression made by people who seem to know what they're talking about, who have good information and are perceived as clear thinkers.*

Complementary exchanges—*difference in power between people in an interaction.*

Compliance-gaining strategies—*strategies influencing others to do what you want them to do.*

Comprehensive listening—*focusing on verbal and nonverbal messages in order to learn, remember, and recall information.*

Compromising—*a form of conflict management in which people attempt to resolve their conflict by providing at least some satisfaction for both parties.*

Co-narration—*two people finishing each other's sentences in a conversation.*

Concrete words—*words that appeal to our senses.*

Confirmation—*nonpossessive expressions of warmth that affirm others as unique persons without necessarily approving of their behaviors or views.*

Connotation—*the feelings or evaluations we personally associate with a word.*

Constructive criticism—*describing the specific negative behaviors or actions of another and the effects that these behaviors have on others.*

Content paraphrase—*A response that conveys your understanding of the denotative meaning of a verbal message.*

Context—*the setting in which communication occurs, including what precedes and follows what is said.*

Control need—*a desire to influence the events and people around us.*

Convergence—*making language similar to another's language.*

Conversational coherence—*the extent to which the comments made by one person relate to those made by others earlier in the conversation.*

Conversations—*locally managed, sequential interchanges of thoughts and feelings between two or more people.*

Cooperative principle—*states that conversation will be satisfying when the contributions made by conversationalists are in line with the purpose of the conversation.*

Coordinated management of meaning—*a theory explaining how people come to agree on the meaning of language and behavior.*

Costs—*outcomes that a person does not wish to incur.*

Cover letter—*a short, well-written letter expressing your interest in a particular position.*

Covert intimacy—*messages showing closeness, trust, and equality by mild insults, competition and put-downs of a partner.*

Credibility—*the extent to which the target believes in the speaker's expertise, trustworthiness, and likability.*

Critical–evaluative listening—*focusing on verbal and nonverbal messages in order to judge or evaluate information.*

Critically evaluating—*the process of evaluating what you have understood and interpreted in order to determine how truthful, authentic, or believable you judge the meaning to be.*

Cultural context—*the set of beliefs, values, attitudes, meanings, social hierarchies, religion, notions of time, and roles of the participants.*

Culture—*systems of knowledge shared by a relatively large group of people.*

Cyberspace—*the electronic system of interlinked networks of computers, bulletin boards, and chat rooms.*

Dating information—*specifying the time period that a statement was true or known to be true.*

Decoding—*the process of interpreting another's message.*

Denotation—*the direct, explicit meaning a speech community formally gives a word.*

Dependable partner—*one who can be relied upon at all times, under all circumstances.*

Describing behavior—*accurately recounting the specific actions of another without commenting on their appropriateness.*

Describing feelings—*naming emotions you are feeling without judging them.*

Direct-request strategies—*strategies in which a person seeks compliance by asking another to behave in a particular way.*

Discrimination—*a negative action toward a social group or its members on account of group membership.*

Discriminative listening—*focusing on verbal and nonverbal messages in order to notice details.*

Displaying feelings—*expressing feelings through facial reactions, body responses, or paralinguistic reactions.*

Dispositional attributions—*causes related to the person.*

Distributive strategies—*strategies in which a person seeks compliance by threatening or making the other person feel guilty.*

Divergence—*making language different from another's language.*

Diversity—*variations between and among people.*

Ectomorph—*tall and thin body type.*

Effective conflict-resolving partner—*one who can help manage conflicts in a collaborative way.*

Efficiency—*being direct in the interest of achieving conversational goals in a short amount of time.*

Ego conflicts—*conflicts that occur when the people involved view "winning" the conflict as central to maintaining their positive self-image.*

Emblems—*gestures that can substitute for words.*

Emoticons—*typed symbols that convey emotional aspects of online messages.*

Empathic listening—*focusing on verbal and nonverbal messages in order to understand another's feelings.*

Empathic responsiveness—*experiencing an emotional response parallel to another person's actual or anticipated display of emotion.*

Empathy-based strategies—*strategies in which a person seeks compliance by appealing to another's love, affection, or sympathy.*

Empathy—*demonstrated by comments that show you understand another's point of view without giving up your own position or sense of self; the cognitive process of identifying with or vicariously experiencing the feelings, thoughts, or attitudes of another.*

Encoding—*the process of putting our thoughts and feelings into words and nonverbal cues.*

Endomorph—*round and heavy body type.*

Equality—*achieved by treating conversational partners on the same level, regardless of the status differences that separate them from other participants.*

Ethics—*a set of moral principles that may be held by a society, a group, or an individual.*

Exchange strategies—*strategies in which a person seeks compliance by offering trade-offs.*

Exchange theory—*says that relationships can be understood in terms of the exchange of rewards and costs that takes place during the individuals' interaction.*

Expert power—*derives from people having knowledge that their relational partners don't have.*

External noises—*the sights, sounds, and other stimuli that draw people's attention away from intended meaning.*

Eye contact or gaze—*how and how much we look at people with whom we are communicating.*

Face-maintenance strategies—*strategies in which a person seeks compliance while using indirect messages and emotion-eliciting statements.*

Face-saving—*helping others preserve self-image or self-respect*

Facial expression—*the arrangement of facial muscles to communicate emotional states or reactions to messages.*

Fact conflict or simple conflict—*conflict that occurs when the information one person presents is disputed by the other.*

Factual statements—*statements whose accuracy can be verified or proven.*

Fairness—*achieving the right balance of interests without regard to one's own feelings and without showing favor to any side in a conflict.*

Faithful partner—*one who is secure in the belief that the other person is trustworthy and that the relationship will endure.*

Family—*a group of intimates who generate a sense of home and group identity, complete with strong ties of loyalty and emotion, and experience a history and a future.*

Feedback—*responses to messages; verbal and physical responses to people and/or their messages.*

Feelings paraphrase—*A response that conveys your understanding of a speaker's state of mind—the emotions behind the words.*

Forcing—*resolving conflict by attempting to satisfy your own needs or advance your own ideas with no concern for the needs or ideas of others and no concern for the harm done to the relationship.*

Formality—*the degree to which a conversation must follow rules and procedures.*

Framing—*the skill of providing comfort by offering information, observations, and opinions that enable the receiver to better understand or reinterpret an event or circumstance.*

Friends—*people with whom we have negotiated more personal relationships voluntarily.*

Generic language—*words that may apply only to one sex, race, or other group used as though they represent everyone.*

Gestures—*movements of hands, arms, and fingers that we use to describe or to emphasize.*

Good relationship—*one in which the interactions are satisfying to and healthy for those involved.*

Gossip—*talking about other people who are not present.*

Halo effect—*perceiving that a person has a whole set of characteristics when you have actually observed only one characteristic, trait, or behavior.*

Haptics—*putting part of the body in contact with something; touch.*

High power-distance culture—*a culture in which power is distributed unequally.*

High-context culture—*a culture in which messages are indirect, general, and ambiguous.*

Historical context—*the background provided by the previous communication episodes between the participants that influences understandings in the current encounter.*

Idea exchange messages—*speech that conveys facts, opinions, and beliefs in a conversation.*

Impersonal relationship—*one in which a person relates to the other merely because the other fills a role or satisfies an immediate need.*

Impression management—*the process of trying to influence others' impressions of you.*

Inclusion need—*a desire to be in the company of other people.*

Incongruence—*the gap between our inaccurate self-perceptions and reality.*

Independent couples—*those who share an ideology that embraces change and uncertainty in the marriage relationship but, like traditional couples, are interdependent and apt to engage in rather than avoid conflict to resolve differences.*

Indexing generalizations—*the mental and verbal practice of acknowledging the presence of individual differences when voicing generalizations.*

Inferences—*claims or assertions based on observation or fact.*

Integrity—*having a consistency of belief and action (keeping promises).*

Internal noises—*the thoughts and feelings that interfere with meaning.*

Interpersonal communication—*the process through which people create and manage their relationships, exercising mutual responsibility in creating meaning.*

Interpersonal conflict—*a situation in which the needs or ideas of one person are perceived to be at odds with or in opposition to the needs or ideas of another.*

Interpersonal influence—*symbolic efforts to preserve or change the attitudes or behavior of others.*

Interpersonal needs theory—*whether or not a relationship is started, built, or maintained depends on how well each person meets the interpersonal needs of the other.*

Interpersonal power—*a potential for changing attitudes, beliefs, and behaviors of a relational partner.*

Interpersonal relationship—*a series of interactions between two individuals known to each other.*

Interview—*a structured conversation with the goal of exchanging information that is needed for decision making.*

Intimate relationships—*relationships that are marked by high degrees of warmth and affection, trust, self-disclosure, and commitment, and are formalized through symbols and rituals.*

Intimates—*people who share a close, caring, and trusting relationship characterized by mutual self-disclosure and commitment.*

Intonation—*variety, melody, or inflection of voice.*

Jargon—*technical terminology whose meaning is idiosyncratic to a special activity or interest group.*

Jealousy—*the suspicion of rivalry or unfaithfulness.*

Johari window—*a tool for examining the relationship between disclosure and feedback.*

Kinesics—*the technical name for the study of body motions used in communication.*

Language—*the body of words and the systems for their use in messages that are common to a group of people.*

Legitimate power—*derives from using the status that comes from being elected, being selected, or holding a position to influence a partner.*

Likability—*the combination of congeniality, attractiveness, warmth, and friendliness.*

Listening—*the process of receiving, constructing meaning from, and responding to spoken and/or nonverbal messages.*

Loneliness—*the condition of a person whose desired level of social interaction is lower than the level achieved.*

Low power-distance culture—*a culture in which power is distributed equally.*

Low-context culture—*a culture in which messages are direct, specific, and detailed.*

Maintenance of relationships—*keeping a relationship at a particular level of closeness or intimacy.*

Maintenance roles—*behaviors that improve interaction among people in a group.*

Managing privacy—*making a conscious decision to withhold information or feelings from a relational partner.*

Manner maxim—*requirement to be specific and organized when communicating your thoughts.*

Marking—*the unnecessary use of sex, race, age, or other designations in addition to a general word.*

Masking feelings—*concealing verbal or nonverbal cues that would enable others to understand the emotions that a person is actually feeling.*

Maxims—*rules of conduct that cooperative conversational partners follow.*

Meaning—*thoughts in our minds and interpretations of other's messages.*

Mediator—*an uninvolved third party who serves as a neutral and impartial guide, structuring an interaction that enables the conflicting parties to find a mutually acceptable solution to their problems.*

Mesomorph—*muscular and athletic body type.*

Messages—*a person's verbal utterances and nonverbal behaviors to which meaning is attributed during communication.*

Mnemonic device—*any artificial technique used as a memory aid.*

Monochronic—*doing one thing at a time.*

Moral dilemma—*a choice involving unsatisfactory alternatives.*

Morality maxim—*the requirement to meet moral/ethical guidelines.*

Mutual respect—*treating each other with dignity.*

Negative facework—*messages that support the partner's need for independence and autonomy by verbally using indirect methods when offering information, opinions, or advice.*

Neutralization—*compromising in order to partially satisfy needs related to relationship contradictions.*

Noise—*any stimulus that interferes with the process of making sense of messages.*

Nonparallel language—*language in which terms are changed because of the sex, race, or other characteristic of the individual.*

Nonverbal communication behaviors—*bodily actions and vocal qualities that typically accompany a verbal message.*

Olfactory communication—*meanings attached to smells and scents.*

Organizational romance—*sexual or romantic involvement between people who work for the same organization.*

Other-benefit strategies—*strategies in which a person seeks compliance by identifying behaviors that benefit the other person.*

Other-centered messages—*utilize active listening, express compassion and understanding, encourage partners to talk about what has happened, elaborate on it, and explore their feelings about the situation.*

Owning feelings or opinions (crediting yourself)—*making "I" statements to identify yourself as the source of a particular idea or feeling.*

Paralanguage or vocalics—*the nonverbal "sound" of what we hear—how something is said.*

Paraphrasing question—*an attempt to verify your understanding of a message by putting it into your own words.*

Participants—*the people who communicate by assuming the roles of senders and receivers during the communication.*

Passive behavior—*the reluctance or failure to state opinions, share feelings, or assume responsibility for one's actions.*

Patterns—*sets of characteristics that differentiate some things from others used to group those items having the same characteristics.*

Perception check—*a message that reflects your understanding of the meaning of another person's s behavior.*

Perception—*the process of selectively attending to information and assigning meaning to it.*

Personal relationship—*one in which people share large amounts of information with each other and meet each other's interpersonal needs.*

Perspective taking—*imagining yourself in the place of another.*

Persuasion—*the intentional use of verbal messages to influence the attitudes or behaviors of others using ethical means.*

Physical context—*where communication takes place, the environmental conditions (temperature, lighting, noise level), the distance between communicators, seating arrangements, and time of day.*

Pitch—*the highness or lowness of vocal tone.*

Platonic relationship—*a relationship in which the partners are not sexually attracted to each other or do not choose to act on the sexual attraction they feel.*

Polarized language—*words based on opposites or extremes.*

Policy conflicts—*conflicts that occur when two people in a relationship disagree about what should be the appropriate plan, course of action, or behavior in dealing with a perceived problem.*

Politeness—*relating to others in ways that meet their need to be appreciated and protected.*

Politeness maxim—*the requirement to show respect for others by acting with courtesy.*

Polychronic—*doing several things at once.*

Positive facework—*messages that protect the partner's need to be respected, liked, and valued by verbally affirming the person or the person's actions in the present difficulty.*

Posture—*the position and movement of the body.*

Power distance—*the amount of difference in power between people, institutions, and organizations.*

Praise—*describing the specific behaviors or accomplishments of another and the positive effects that this behavior has on others.*

Precise words—*words that narrow a larger category to a smaller group within that category.*

Prejudice—*positive or negative attitudes or judgments directed toward people simply because they happen to be members of a specific group.*

Presence of a plan or life vision—*agreeing on long-term goals.*

Presentness—*a willingness to become fully involved with another person, demonstrated by taking time, avoiding distraction, being responsive, and risking attachment.*

Probing questions—*questions that search for more information or try to resolve perceived inconsistencies in a message.*

Problem-consideration conversations—*interactions between people in which the goal of at least one of the participants is to solicit cooperation in meeting a specific goal.*

Proxemics—*the study of informal space.*

Pseudoconflict—*conflict that is apparent, not real.*

Psychological context—*the moods and feelings each person brings to an interpersonal encounter.*

Quality—*the sound of voice.*

Quality maxim—*the requirement to provide information that is truthful.*

Quantity maxim—*the requirement to provide a sufficient or necessary amount of information—not too much and not too little.*

Racism, ethnocentrism, sexism, ageism, able-ism—*beliefs that the behaviors or characteristics of one group are inherently superior to those of another group and that this gives the "superior" group the right to dominate or discriminate against the "inferior" group.*

Rapport-talk—*sharing experiences and stories to establish bonds with others.*

Rate—*the speed at which a person speaks.*

Reasons—*statements that provide the basis or cause for some behavior or action.*

Referent power—*derives from people being attracted to others because of their physical appearance, image, charisma, or personality.*

Reframing—*putting less emphasis on a dialectical contradiction in a relationship.*

Relational uncertainty—*being unclear about the nature of a relationship.*

Relationship dialectic—*contradictory pulls in relationships.*

Relationship—*a set of expectations two people have for their behavior based on the pattern of interaction between them.*

Relationship-oriented culture—*a culture that emphasizes building relationships at work.*

Relevancy maxim—*requirement to provide information that is related to the topic being discussed.*

Repetition—*saying something two, three, or even four times.*

Report-talk—*sharing information, displaying knowledge, negotiating, and preserving independence.*

Respect—*showing regard or consideration for a person and for that person's rights.*

Responsibility—*accountability for one's actions.*

Responsive partner—*one whose actions are geared toward the other person's particular needs. At times this may require one person to sacrifice his or her needs for the good of the other.*

Results-oriented culture—*a culture that emphasizes the outcomes of work.*

Résumé—*a summary of your skills and accomplishments.*

Reward power—*derives from providing partners with monetary, physical, or psychological benefits that the partners desire.*

Rewards—*outcomes that are valued by a person.*

Ritualized touch—*touch that is scripted rather than spontaneous.*

Role—*a pattern of learned behaviors that people use to meet the perceived demands of a particular context.*

Romantic relationship—*a relationship in which the partners act on their sexual attraction to each other.*

Rules—*unwritten prescriptions that indicate what behavior is required, preferred, or prohibited in certain contexts.*

Sapir–Whorf hypothesis—*a theory stating that a culture's language shapes how people think and perceive.*

Selective perception—*the tendency to pay attention only to what we expect to see or hear.*

Self-concept—*self-identity-the idea or mental image that we have about our skills, our abilities, our knowledge, our competencies, and our personality.*

Self-disclosure—*sharing biographical data, personal ideas, and feelings that are unknown to the other person; divulging biographical data, personal ideas, and feelings.*

Self-esteem—*our overall evaluation of our competence and personal worthiness.*

Self-fulfilling prophecies—*events that happen as the result of being foretold, expected, or talked about.*

Self-monitoring—*an internal process of observing and regulating your own behavior based on others' responses.*

Semantic noise—*unintended meanings aroused by a speaker's symbols.*

Separate couples—*those who share traditional ideology but differ from traditional and independent couples in that they engage in less emotional sharing.*

Sequential task completion—*a process of breaking a task into separate parts in order to complete one part at a time.*

Sexual harassment—*unwanted verbal or physical sexual behavior that interferes with work performance.*

Situational attributions—*causes based on aspects of the situation.*

Skills—*goal-oriented actions or action sequences we can master and repeat in appropriate situations.*

Slang—*informal nonstandard use of vocabulary.*

Small talk—*conversations that meet social needs with low amounts of risk.*

Social context—*the nature of the relationship that exists between the participants.*

Social perception—*a set of processes by which people perceive themselves and others (also known as social cognition).*

Specific words—*words that clear up ambiguity caused by general words.*

Strategic ambiguity—*purposeful vagueness in interactions.*

Supporting response—*a statement whose goal is to show approval, bolster, encourage, soothe, console, or cheer up.*

Supporting-evidence strategies—*strategies that draw primarily on reasoning and include all those strategies in which a person seeks compliance by presenting reasons and/or evidence.*

Supportive messages—*create a conversational environment that encourages the person needing support to talk about and make sense of the situation that is causing distress.*

Supportiveness—*encouraging other participants to communicate by praising their worthwhile efforts.*

Symbolic interactionism—*a theory stating that the meaning of words results from social interaction.*

Symbols—*words, sounds, and actions that are generally understood to represent meaning.*

Symmetrical exchanges—*similarity in power between people in an interaction.*

Sympathetic responsiveness—*a feeling of concern, compassion, or sorrow for another because of a distressing situation.*

Task roles—*behaviors that help a group focus on issues.*

Task-related touch—*touch used to perform a certain function.*

Team—*formal group with a clear purpose and appropriate structure.*

Temporal selection—*selecting one side of a dialectical contradiction for a period of time.*

Territory—*space over which we may claim ownership.*

Theory of muted groups—*a theory stating that by controlling language, those in power silence the voices of others.*

Topical segmentation—*separating situations or spheres of life as a way to manage dialectical tension in a relationship.*

Traditional couples—*those who have a traditional ideology but maintain some independence in the marriages.*

Trust—*confidence placed in another in a way that almost always involves some risk.*

Trustworthiness—*the impression made by people who seem to be dependable and honest, who keep the promises they have made and are perceived to be acting for the good of others more than for self.*

Truthfulness and honesty—*refraining from lying, cheating, stealing, or deception.*

Turning point—*an event or occurrence associated with relationship change.*

Turn-taking—*the process by which people alternate between speaking and listening in a conversation.*

Uncertainty reduction theory—*explains the ways individuals monitor their social environments and come to know more about themselves and others.*

Understanding—*accurately decoding a message so that you share its meaning with the speaker (or writer or actor).*

Unnecessary association—*emphasizing one person's association with another when you are not talking about the second person.*

Value conflicts—*conflicts over the deep-seated beliefs people hold about what is good or bad, worthwhile or worthless, desirable or undesirable, moral or immoral.*

Vocal interferences—*extraneous sounds or words that interrupt fluent speech.*

Volume—*the loudness or softness of tone.*

Wholistic task completion—*a process of working on an entire task at once.*

Withdrawal—*resolving conflict by physically or psychologically removing oneself from the conflict.*

photo credits

index